Using Excel for Business and Financial Modelling

Founded in 1807, John Wiley & Sons is the oldest independent publishing company in the United States. With offices in North America, Europe, Australia and Asia, Wiley is globally committed to developing and marketing print and electronic products and services for our customers' professional and personal knowledge and understanding.

The Wiley Finance series contains books written specifically for finance and investment professionals as well as sophisticated individual investors and their financial advisors. Book topics range from portfolio management to e-commerce, risk management, financial engineering, valuation and financial instrument analysis, as well as much more.

For a list of available titles, visit our Web site at www.WileyFinance.com.

Using Excel for Business and Financial Modelling

A practical guide

Third Edition

DANIELLE STEIN FAIRHURST

WILEY

This third edition first published 2019
© 2019 John Wiley & Sons Ltd

Edition History
John Wiley & Sons Ltd (1e, 2012 and 2e, 2015)

Registered office
John Wiley & Sons Ltd, The Atrium, Southern Gate, Chichester, West Sussex, PO19 8SQ,
United Kingdom

For details of our global editorial offices, for customer services and for information about how
to apply for permission to reuse the copyright material in this book please see our website at
www.wiley.com.

Wiley publishes in a variety of print and electronic formats and by print-on-demand. Some material
included with standard print versions of this book may not be included in e-books or in print-on-
demand. If this book refers to media such as a CD or DVD that is not included in the version you
purchased, you may download this material at http://booksupport.wiley.com. For more information
about Wiley products, visit www.wiley.com.

Designations used by companies to distinguish their products are often claimed as trademarks.
All brand names and product names used in this book are trade names, service marks, trademarks or
registered trademarks of their respective owners. The publisher is not associated with any product or
vendor mentioned in this book.

Library of Congress Cataloging-in-Publication Data is Available

ISBN 978-1-119-52038-2 (paperback) ISBN 978-1-119-52037-5 (ePDF)
ISBN 978-1-119-52035-1 (epub) ISBN 978-1-119-52034-4 (Obook)

Cover Design: Wiley
Cover Image: © Mike Fairhurst

Set in 10/12pt TimesLTStd by SPi Global, Chennai, India

Printed in Great Britain by TJ International Ltd, Padstow, Cornwall, UK

10 9 8 7 6 5 4 3 2 1

For Mike

Contents

Preface

This book was written from course materials compiled over many years of training in analytical courses in Australia and globally—most frequently courses such as Financial Modelling in Excel, Data Analysis & Reporting in Excel, and Budgeting & Forecasting in Excel, both as face-to-face workshops and online courses. The common theme is the use of Microsoft Excel, and I've refined the content to suit the hundreds of participants and their questions over the years. This content has been honed and refined by the many participants in these courses, who are my intended readers. This book is aimed at you, the many people who seek financial analysis training (either by attending a seminar or self-paced by reading this book), because you are seeking to improve your skills to perform better in your current role, or to get a new and better job. When I started financial modelling in the early 1990s, it was not called *financial modelling*—it was just "using Excel for business analysis", which is what I called the first two editions of this book. The title was edited in the third edition to "Using Excel for Business and Financial Modelling". It was only just after the new millennium that the term *financial modelling* gained popularity in its own right and became a required skill often listed on analytical job descriptions. This book spends quite a bit of time in Chapter 1 defining the meaning of a financial model, as it's often thought to be something that is far more complicated than it actually is. Many analysts and financial professionals I've met are building financial models already without realising it, but they do themselves a disservice by not calling their models, "models"!

However, those who are already building financial models are not necessarily following good modelling practice as they do so. Chapter 3 is dedicated to the principles of best modelling practice, which will save you a lot of time, effort, and anguish in the long run. Many of the principles of best practice are for the purpose of reducing the possibility of error in your model, and there is a whole section on strategies for reducing error in Chapter 4.

The majority of Excel users are self-taught, and therefore many users will often know highly advanced Excel tools, yet fail to understand how to use them in the context of building a financial model. This book is very detailed, so feel free to skip sections you already know. Because of the comprehensive nature of the book, much of the detailed but less commonly used content, such as instructions for the older versions of Excel, has been moved to the companion website at www.wiley.com/go/steinfairhurstrevised. There you will also find templates, checklists, and other useful materials. References to the content on the website, and many cross-references to other sections of the book, can be found throughout the book.

I'm passionate about supporting the financial modelling community, and especially about encouraging more women into what I believe is a highly rewarding and in-demand profession. There is a whole world of financial modelling awards, championships, standards, certifications, and meetup groups all over the world you can tap into to learn, network, and progress your career. If this book has piqued your interest, then I invite you to connect with me directly on LinkedIn and other social media platforms to find out more about how to get more involved in the wonderful world of financial modelling.

BOOK OVERVIEW

This book has 12 chapters, which can be grouped into three sections. Whilst they do follow on from each other with the most basic concepts at the beginning, feel free to jump directly to any of the chapters. The first section—Chapters 1 to 3—addresses the least technical topics about financial modelling in general, such as tool selection, model design, and best practice.

The second section—Chapters 4 to 8—is extremely practical and hands on. Here I have outlined all of the tools, techniques, and functions in Excel that are commonly used in financial modelling. Of course, it does not cover everything Excel can do, but it covers the "must know" tools.

The third section—Chapters 9 to 12—is the most important in my view. This covers the *use* of Excel in financial modelling and analysis. This is really where the book differs from other "how to" Excel books. Chapter 9 covers some commonly used techniques in modelling, such as escalation, tiering tables, and depreciation—how to actually use Excel tools for something useful! Chapter 11 covers the several different methods of performing scenarios and sensitivity analysis (basically the whole *point* of financial modelling to my mind). Lastly, Chapter 12 covers the often-neglected task of presenting model output. Many modellers spend days or weeks on the calculations and functionality, but fail to spend just a few minutes or hours on charts, formatting, and layout at the end of the process, even though this is what the user will see, interact with, and eventually use to judge the usefulness of the model.

ACKNOWLEDGEMENTS

This book would not have been written had it not been for the many people who have attended my training sessions, participated in online courses, and contributed to the forums. Your continual feedback and enthusiasm for the subject inspired me to write this book and it was because of you that I realised how much a book like this was needed.

The continued support of my family and network made this project possible. In particular, Mike, my husband, for his unconditional commitment and to whom this book is dedicated; my children who give me so much joy; as well as my remarkable parents and siblings, who have always inspired and encouraged me without question. I would like to give special thanks to my ever-patient assistant Susan Wilkin for her continuing dedication and diligence, as always. I could not do it without you all.

I hope you find the book both useful and enjoyable. Happy modelling!

Using Excel
for Business
and Financial
Modelling

CHAPTER 1

What is Financial Modelling?

There are all sorts of complicated definitions of financial modelling, and in my experience there is quite a bit of confusion around what a financial model is exactly. A few years ago, we put together a Plum Solutions survey about the attitudes, trends, and uses of financial modelling, asking respondents "What do you think a financial model is?" Participants were asked to put down the first thing that came to mind, without any research or too much thinking about it.

I found the responses interesting, amusing, and sometimes rather disturbing. Some answers were overly complicated and highly technical:

- "Representation of behaviour/real-world observations through mathematical approach designed to anticipate range of outcomes."
- "A set of structured calculations, written in a spreadsheet, used to analyse the operational and financial characteristics of a business and/or its activities."
- "Tool(s) used to set and manage a suite of variable assumptions in order to predict the financial outcomes of an opportunity."
- "A construct that encodes business rules, assumptions, and calculations enabling information, analysis, and insight to be drawn out and supported by quantitative facts."
- "A system of spreadsheets and formulas to achieve the level of record keeping and reporting required to be informed, up-to-date, and able to track finances accurately and plan for the future."

Some philosophical:

- "A numerical story."

Some incorrect:

- "Forecasting wealth by putting money away now/investing."
- "It is all about putting data into a nice format."

- "It is just a mega huge spreadsheet with fancy formulas that are streamlined to make your life easier."

Some ridiculous:

- "Something to do with money and fashion?"

Some honest:

- "I really have no idea."

And some downright profound:

- "A complex spreadsheet."

There are many (often very complicated and long-winded) definitions available from different sources, but I actually prefer the last, very broad, but accurate description: "a complex spreadsheet". Whilst it does need some definition, my definition of a financial model is pretty broad.

As long as a spreadsheet has financial inputs and outputs, and is dynamic and flexible, I'm happy to call it a financial model! Pretty much the whole *point* of financial modelling is that you change the inputs and the outputs. This is the major premise behind scenario and sensitivity analysis; this is what Excel, with its algebraic logic, was *made* for. Most of the time, a model will contain financial information and serve the purpose of making a financial decision, but not always. Quite often it will contain a full set of financial statements: profit and loss, cash flow, and balance sheet; but not always.

According to the more staid or traditional definitions of financial modelling, the following items would all most certainly be classified as financial models:

- A business case that determines whether to go ahead with a project.
- A five-year forecast showing profit and loss, cash flow, and balance sheet.
- Pricing calculations to determine how much to bid for a new tender.
- Investment analysis for a joint venture.

But what about other pieces of analysis that we perform as part of our roles? Can these also be called financial models? What if something does not contain financial information at all? Consider if you were to produce a spreadsheet for the following purposes:

- **An actual versus budget monthly variance analysis** that does not contain scenarios and for which there are no real assumptions listed.
- **A risk assessment**, where you enter the risk, assign a likelihood to that risk, and calculate the overall risk of the project using probability calculations. This does not contain any financial outputs at all.

■ **A dashboard report** showing a balanced scorecard type of metrics reporting like headcount, quality, customer numbers, call volume, and so on. Again, there are few or no financial outputs.

See the section "Types and Purposes of Financial Models" later in this chapter for greater detail on business models that don't actually contain financial information.

Don't get hung up on whether you're building something that meets the definition of a financial model or not. As long as you've got inputs and outputs that change flexibly and dynamically, you can call it a financial model. If you're using Excel to any extent whereby you are linking cells together, chances are you're already building a financial model whether you realise it or not. The most important thing is that you are building the model (or whatever it's called) in a robust way, following the principles of best practice, which this book will teach you.

Generally, a model consists of one or more input variables along with data and formulas that are used to perform calculations, make predictions, or perform any number of solutions to business (or non-business) requirements. By changing the values of the input variables, you can do sensitivity testing and build scenarios to see what happens when the inputs change.

Sometimes managers treat models as though they are able to produce the answer to all business decisions and solve all business problems. Whilst a good model can be of significant aid, it's important to remember that models are only as good as the data they contain, and the answers they produce should not necessarily be taken at face value.

"The reliability of a spreadsheet is essentially the accuracy of the data that it produces, and is compromised by the errors found in approximately 94 percent of spreadsheets."[1] When presented with a model, the savvy manager will query all the assumptions and the way it has been built. Someone who has had some experience in building models will realise that they must be treated with caution. Models should be used as one tool in the decision-making process, rather than the definitive solution.

WHAT'S THE DIFFERENCE BETWEEN A SPREADSHEET AND A FINANCIAL MODEL?

Before we continue, let me make one thing clear: I am not partial to the use of the word *spreadsheet*; in fact, you'll hardly find it used at all in this book.

---

[1] Ruth McKeever, Kevin McDaid, and Brian Bishop, "An Exploratory Analysis of the Impact of Named Ranges on the Debugging Performance of Novice Users" (presented at the Annual Conference of the European Spreadsheet Risks Interest Group, Paris, France, July 2–3, 2009). Available at arxiv.org/abs/0908.0935.

I've often been asked the difference between the two, and there is a fine line of definition between them. In a nutshell, an Excel spreadsheet is simply the medium that we can use to create a financial model.

At the most basic level, a financial model that has been built in Excel is simply a complex spreadsheet. By definition, a financial model is a structure that contains input data and supplies outputs. By changing the input data, we can test the results of these changes on the output results, and this sort of sensitivity analysis is most easily done in an Excel spreadsheet.

One could argue, then, that they are in fact the same thing; there is really no difference between a spreadsheet and a financial model. Others question if it really matters what we call them as long as they do the job. After all, both involve putting data into Excel, organising it, formatting, adding some formulas, and creating some usable output. There are, however, some subtle differences to note:

1. **"Spreadsheet" is a catch-all term for any type of information stored in Excel, including a financial model.** Therefore, a spreadsheet could really be anything: a checklist, raw data output from an accounting system, a beautifully laid out management report, or a financial model used to evaluate a new investment.

2. **A financial model is more structured.** A model contains a set of variable assumptions, inputs, outputs, calculations, scenarios, and often includes a set of standard financial forecasts such as profit and loss, balance sheet, and cash flow, which are based on those assumptions.

3. **A financial model is dynamic.** A model contains variable inputs, which, when changed, impact the output results. A spreadsheet might be simply a report that aggregates information from other sources and assembles it into a useful presentation. It may contain a few formulas, such as a total at the bottom of a list of expenses or average cash spent over 12 months, but the results will depend on direct inputs into those columns and rows. A financial model will always have built-in flexibility to explore different outcomes in all financial reports based on changing a few key inputs.

4. **A spreadsheet is usually static.** Once a spreadsheet is complete, it often becomes a stand-alone report, and no further changes are made. A financial model, on the other hand, will always allow a user to change input variables and see the impact of these assumptions on the output.

5. **A financial model will use relationships between several variables to create the financial report, and changing any or all of them will affect the output.** For example, Revenue in Month 4 could be a result of Sales Price × Quantity Sold Prior Month × Monthly Growth in Quantities Sold. In this example, three factors come into play, and the end user can explore different mixes of all three to see the results and decide which reflects their business model best.

6. **A spreadsheet shows actual historical data, whereas a financial model contains hypothetical outcomes.** A by-product of a well-built financial model is that we can easily use it to perform scenario and sensitivity analysis. This is an important outcome of a financial model. What would happen if interest rates increase by half a basis point? How much can we discount before we start making a loss?

In conclusion, a financial model is a complex type of spreadsheet, whilst a spreadsheet is a tool that can fulfil a variety of purposes, financial models being one. The list of attributes above can identify the spreadsheet as a financial model, but in some cases we really are talking about the same thing. Take a look at the Excel files you are using. Are they dynamic, structured, and flexible, or have you simply created a static, direct input spreadsheet?

TYPES AND PURPOSES OF FINANCIAL MODELS

Models in Excel can be built for virtually any purpose—financial and non-financial, business-related or non-business-related—although the majority of models will be financial and business-related. The following are some examples of models that do not capture financial information:

- **Risk management.** A model that captures, tracks, and reports on project risks, status, likelihood, impact, and mitigation. Conditional formatting is often integrated to make a colourful, interactive report.
- **Project planning.** Models may be built to monitor progress on projects, including critical path schedules and even Gantt charts. (See the next section in this chapter, "Tool Selection", for an analysis of whether Microsoft Project or Excel should be used for building this type of project plan.)
- **Key performance indicators (KPIs) and benchmarking.** Excel is the best tool for pulling together KPI and metrics reporting. These sorts of statistics are often pulled from many different systems and sources, and Excel is often the common denominator between different systems.
- **Dashboards.** The popularity of dashboards has increased in recent years. The dashboard is a conglomeration of different measures (sometimes financial, but often not), which are also often conveniently collated and displayed as charts and tables using Excel.
- **Balanced scorecards.** These help provide a more comprehensive view of a business by focusing on the operational, marketing, and developmental performance of the organisation as well as financial measures. A scorecard will display measures such as process performance, market share, or penetration, and learning and skills development, all of which are easily collated and displayed in Excel.

As with many Excel models, most of these could be more accurately created and maintained in a purpose-built piece of software, but quite often the data for these kinds of reports is stored in different systems, and the most practical tool for pulling the data together and displaying it in a dynamic monthly report is Excel.

Although purists would not classify these as financial models, the way that they have been built should still follow the fundamentals of financial modelling best practices, such as linking and assumptions documentation. How we classify these models is therefore simply a matter of semantics, and not particularly important. Going back to our original definition of financial modelling, it is a structure (usually in Excel) that contains inputs and outputs and is flexible and dynamic.

TOOL SELECTION

In this book, we will use Excel exclusively, as that is most appropriate for the kind of financial analysis we are performing when creating financial models. We often hear it said that Excel is the "second-best solution" to a problem. There is usually a better, more efficient piece of software that will also provide a solution, but we often default to the "Swiss army knife" of software, Excel, to get the job done. Why do many financial modelling analysts use Excel almost exclusively, when they know that better solutions exist? At Plum Solutions, our philosophy is also one of using only "plain vanilla" Excel, without relying on any other third-party software, for several reasons:

- No extra licences, costly implementation, or software download is required.
- The software can be installed on almost any computer.
- Little training is needed, as most users have some familiarity with the product, which means other people will be able to drive and understand your model.
- It is a very flexible tool. If you can imagine it, you can probably do it in Excel (within reason, of course).
- Excel can report, model, and contrast virtually any data, from any source, all in one report.
- But most importantly, Excel is commonly used across all industries, countries, and organisations, meaning that the Excel skills you have are highly transferrable.

What this last point means to you is that if you have good financial modelling skills in Excel, these skills are going to make you more in demand, especially if you are considering changing industries or roles or getting a job in another country. In fact, **one of the best things you can do for your career is to improve your Excel skills**. Becoming an expert developer on a proprietary piece of software is useful, but becoming a highly skilled Excel expert will stand you in good stead throughout your career.

Excel has its limitations, of course, and Excel's main downfall is the ease with which users can make errors in their models. Therefore, a large part of financial modelling best practice relates to reducing the possibility of errors. See Chapter 3, "Best Practice Principles of Modelling", and "Error Avoidance Strategies" in Chapter 4 for details on errors and how to avoid them.

The other issue with using Excel is capacity; we simply run out of rows, especially in this age of "Big Data". Microsoft worked hard to keep Excel relevant by introducing Power Pivot, which was a free add-in when it was first introduced in Excel 2010 and is now native to later versions. Power Pivot can handle much bigger data than plain Excel, which gets around Excel's capacity limitations.

For more information on the different capabilities of Excel, see the section on "Excel Versions" in Chapter 5.

Is Excel Really the Best Option?

Before jumping straight in and creating your solution in Excel, it is worth considering that some solutions may be better built in other software, so take a moment to contemplate your choice of software before designing a solution. There are many other forms of modelling software on the market, and it might be worth considering other options besides Excel. There are also a number of Excel add-ins provided by third parties that can be used to create financial models and perform financial analysis. The best choice depends on the solution you require.

The overall objective of a financial model determines the output as well as the calculations or processing of input required by the model. Financial models are built for the purpose of providing timely, accurate, and meaningful information to assist in the financial decision-making process. As a result, the overall objective of the model depends on the specific decisions that are to be made based on the model's output.

As different modelling tools lend themselves to different solutions or output, before selecting a modelling tool it is important to determine precisely what solution is required based on the identified model objective.

Evaluating Modelling Tools

Once the overall objective of the model has been established, a financial modelling tool that will best suit the business requirements can be chosen.

To determine which financial modelling tool would best meet the identified objective, the following must be considered:

- The output required from the model, based on who will use it and the particular decisions to be made.
- The volume, complexity, type, and source of input data, particularly relating to the number of interdependent variables and the relationships between them.

- The complexity of calculations or processing of input to be performed by the model.
- The level of computer literacy of the users, as they should ideally be able to manipulate the model without the assistance of a specialist.
- The cost versus benefit set off for each modelling tool.

As with all software, financial modelling programs can either be purchased as a package or developed in-house. Whilst purchasing software as a package is a cheaper option, in a very complex industry, in-house development of specific modelling software may be necessary in order to provide adequate solutions. In this instance, one would need to engage a qualified specialist to plan and develop appropriate modelling software.

Which package you choose depends on the solution you require. Customer relationship management (CRM) data lends itself very well to a database, whereas something that requires complex calculations, such as those in many financial models, is more appropriately dealt with in Excel.

Excel is often described as a "band-aid solution", because it is such a flexible tool that we can use to perform almost any process—albeit not as fast or as well as fully customised software, but it will get the job done until a long-term solution is found: "Spreadsheets will always fill the void between what a business needs today and the formal installed systems.".[2]

Budgeting and Forecasting   Many budgets and forecasts are built using Excel, but most major general ledger systems have additional modules available that are built specifically for budgeting and forecasting. These tools provide a much easier, quicker method of creating budgets and forecasts that is less error-prone than using templates. However, there are surprisingly few companies that have a properly integrated, fully functioning budgeting and forecasting system, and the fallback solution is almost always Excel.

There are several reasons why many companies use Excel templates over a full budgeting and forecasting solution, whether they are integrated with their general ledger system or not:

- A full solution can be expensive and time-consuming to implement properly.
- Integration with the general ledger system means a large investment in a particular modelling system, which is difficult to change later.
- Even if a system is not in place, invariably some analysis will need to be undertaken in Excel, necessitating that at least part of the process is built using Excel templates.

---

[2]Mel Glass, David Ford, and Sebastian Dewhurst, "Reducing the Risk of Spreadsheet Usage—A Case Study" (presented at the Annual Conference of the European Spreadsheet Risks Interest Group, Paris, France, July 2–3, 2009). Available at arxiv.org/abs/0908.1584.

Microsoft Office Tools: Power Excel and Access "Plain vanilla" Excel (and by this, I mean no add-ins) is the most commonly used tool and the one we are focusing on in this book. There are also other Microsoft tools, both outside and within Excel, that could also serve to create the solution, depending on the requirements. Any version of Excel released from Excel 2010 onwards contains access to the tools we sometimes refer to as "Power Excel". The introduction of these tools was the most exciting thing to happen in the Excel world in a long time, and it has truly changed the landscape for Excel users. Note, however, that at the time of writing, none of these tools are yet available for a Mac.

The Power Excel suite consists of:

- Power Query (also called Get & Transform)
- Power Pivot
- Power BI

Power BI is technically a Power Excel tool, but it is a separate desktop tool primarily used for building dashboards and visualisations, so we won't be going into detail on it here.

Power Excel: Microsoft Power Query (Get & Transform) First introduced as a free add-in in Excel 2010, Power Query is now an inbuilt feature which, if you're using Excel 2016 or later, can be accessed via the Get & Transform section of the Data Tab. It extracts data from various sources, such as websites or other systems, and allows you to cleanse and format the data. When you perform a series of actions, this procedure can be saved, which can be repeatedly performed each time the data is refreshed. Whilst not a modelling tool, Power Query is useful for cleansing and preparing the data, ready to use in your financial model.

Power Excel: Microsoft Power Pivot Power Pivot extends the capabilities of the PivotTable data summarisation and cross-tabulation feature by introducing the ability to import data from multiple sources. It will allow you to do things you couldn't do before in plain Excel, like matching data from multiple sources and pulling them together into a single report. Because it is a relational database, Power Pivot makes it easy to link together data from various sources, employing a simple "drag and drop" graphical user interface.

Marvellous as it is, we know that plain vanilla Excel stops being quite so wonderful when your data is more than 1,048,576 records long, or if the data needs to be consolidated from multiple sources. When faced with this problem, Excel users find themselves migrating to a data warehouse or other, more powerful software. Microsoft has tried to retain these users by introducing Power Pivot, which addresses these problems with added capacity and speed, yet retains the familiar Excel interface that we all know and love.

As a self-service business intelligence (BI) product, Power Pivot is intended to allow users with no specialised BI or analytics training to develop data models and calculations, sharing them either directly or through SharePoint document libraries. For more sophisticated users, Power Pivot can:

- Create your own BI solutions without purchasing expensive software.
- Manipulate large data sets quickly, even if they consist of millions of rows (Excel can't do that).
- Construct complex what-if reporting systems with data modelling and data analysis expressions (DAX).
- Link data from various sources quickly and easily.

Although more appropriate for data analysis than pure dynamic financial models, Power Pivot is certainly worth some consideration when you are building an Excel solution with large quantities of data. If you find that your model has the following attributes, then you should consider using Power Pivot:

- Your data contains many thousands of rows and your model is starting to slow down.
- PivotTables or Tables are used extensively.
- Data needs to be sourced from multiple locations.

One of the great things about Power Pivot is that it is already part of your existing Microsoft licence, so there are no extra licensing costs. There are a number of differences between versions, and as this is an area of rapid change, I have no doubt that the availability of versions and features may have changed by the time this book goes to print.

The disadvantage of using Power Pivot is that although you don't need to be a BI specialist to use it, learning how to use Power Pivot is not particularly straightforward even for advanced users. We offer a number of Power Pivot and Power BI training courses at Plum Solutions through our partners, and there are many videos and online resources that can help you to get started if you decide that Power Pivot is the solution that you need.

If you are trying to decide whether your Excel skills are advanced enough to consider tackling Power Pivot, here are some questions that will help you to determine whether you are ready to take on Power Pivot. You should:

- Understand and have used Excel's SUMIF function.
- Have a working knowledge of filtering data in Excel (e.g., Auto or Advanced Filters).
- Know how to deal with multiple criteria (e.g., SUMIFS, SUMPRODUCT, or DBASE functions).
- Be able to import data from third-party databases and/or files (e.g., Access, SQL, MIS systems).
- Regularly use, adapt, and modify PivotTables (see Chapter 8 for more on PivotTables).

- Have created calculated fields in PivotTables.
- Have created and/or modified an Excel Table (a structured reference table, not a data table—see Chapter 8 for more on Excel Tables).

It took a while to catch on, but Power Pivot has certainly gained in popularity to the point where it has now become almost mainstream amongst Excel users. Microsoft has devoted a lot of resources to developing the Power Pivot product, so its use can only continue to spread in the near future. It's worth investing some time in learning it: being skilful in Power Pivot may become similar to having advanced Excel skills and will be a valuable addition to your résumé, and benefit your career as an analyst.

Bear in mind, however, that *Power Pivot is not primarily a financial modelling tool*. It was designed for the purpose of data analysis, not financial modelling. Remember that—as we talked about at the beginning of the chapter—a financial model, by definition, has inputs and outputs, is dynamic and flexible, but a model built in Power Pivot summarises a large quantity of data into PivotTables, so, whilst not impossible, adjusting assumptions and toggling between scenarios is difficult to do in Power Pivot.

MS Access   Since the introduction of Power Pivot to the Microsoft suite of products, Access is less often used, but it's still worth a mention. There is often some resistance to using Access, and it is certainly less popular than it used to be. Prior to the release of Excel 2007, Excel users were restricted to only 65,000 rows, and many analysts and finance staff used Access as a way to get around this limit. With now over 1.1 million rows (and purportedly up to a billion rows with Power Pivot), Excel is able to handle a lot more data, so there is less need for the additional row capacity of Access. If you've been using Access over the years, you might have noticed that not very much has changed in Access between versions. It seems that Microsoft is investing more of its efforts into the new Power Excel rather than Access.

Advantages of Excel
- Excel is included in most basic Microsoft Office packages (unlike Access, which often needs to be purchased separately), and therefore comes as standard on most PCs. Excel is much more flexible than Access, and calculations are much easier to perform.
- It is generally faster to build a solution in Excel than in Access.
- Excel has a wider knowledge base among users, and many people find it to be more intuitive. This means it is quicker and easier to train staff in Excel.
- It is very easy to create flexible reports and charts in Excel.
- Excel can report, model, and contrast virtually any data, from any source, all in one file.

- Excel easily performs calculations on more than one row of data at a time, which Access has difficulty with.

Advantages of Access

- Access can handle much larger amounts of data: Excel 2003 was limited to 65,536 rows and 256 columns, and later versions of Excel are limited to around 1.1 million rows (1,048,576 rows, to be precise) and 16,384 columns. Access's capability is much larger, and it also has a greater memory storage capacity.
- Data is stored only once in Access, making it work more efficiently.
- Data can be entered into Access by more than one user at a time.
- Access is good at crunching and manipulating large volumes of data.
- Due to Access's lack of flexibility, it is more difficult for users to make errors.

In summary, Access is probably most commonly used for legacy software; databases that have been around for a long time. If it's a brand spanking new solution that you need, consider Power Pivot instead.

Excel Add-Ins   Add-ins are programs that add optional commands and features to Excel. There are many add-ins on the market that have been developed specifically for the purpose of financial modelling. For more complex calculations or processing of input, it may be useful to activate or install one or more add-ins, especially tools such as Solver, which are included in your MS Excel licence. Bear in mind that other users will probably not have add-ins enabled, so they will not be able to see how your model has been created or calculated.

Excel add-ins from all sources can be used to perform a variety of tasks that assist in the financial modelling process. These add-ins can be broadly defined as:

- Standard Excel add-ins such as the Analysis ToolPak and Solver.
- Audit tools.
- Integration links between Excel and the general ledger system.

The most commonly used add-ins are the Analysis ToolPak and Solver, which are standard add-in programs that are available when you install Microsoft Office or Excel. They are included in the program but are disabled by default, so if you want to use them, you need to enable them.

Prior to the release of Excel 2007, the only way to access certain functions (e.g., EOMONTH and SUMIFS) in Excel 2003 was to download the Analysis ToolPak. However, these functions are now standard in Excel, so the Analysis ToolPak is now less commonly used. Other features in the Analysis ToolPak are tools like the Data Analysis ToolPak, which has some powerful statistical and engineering functions not commonly used in financial modelling. Solver, however, is an extremely useful but quite advanced tool for calculating optimal values in financial modelling.

Audit add-ins for Excel are used to ensure the accuracy of data and calculations within a spreadsheet or workbook. They can very quickly identify formula errors by looking at inconsistent formulas, comparing versions, and getting to the bottom of complex named ranges. There are several custom add-ins available both from Microsoft and other parties that will facilitate accuracy by performing formula investigations, precedent/dependent analysis, worksheet analysis, and sensitivity reporting.

Whilst they can assist with checking for formula errors, there are many other types of errors that can easily be overlooked and using these add-ins can provide a false sense of security. See the section "Error Avoidance Strategies" in Chapter 4 for greater detail.

Integration add-ins allow information from the financial reporting system to be transferred into Excel for further analysis, or data stored in Excel to be transferred into the financial reporting system. These are often used for the purpose of:

- Transferring information from the general ledger system into Excel for the purposes of reporting and analysis. Many management reports are built in Excel and extract up-to-date data directly from the general ledger system into the reports.
- Loading information in the form of journal entries back into the general ledger system. Data is often manipulated in Excel and then loaded into the general ledger as a journal. For example, if an invoice needs to be split among different departments based on headcount allocation, this calculation might be done in Excel, split to departments in the journal, and loaded into the general ledger system.

The Final Decision The more sophisticated a financial model is, the more expensive it is to maintain. It is, therefore, best to use a model with the lowest possible level of sophistication needed to provide a specific solution. For this reason, purchasing a software package, provided it can deliver the desired solution, might be advisable.

Once the decision has been made to purchase a software package, it must be determined which package will provide the best solution as certain solutions may be better provided by particular software packages.

There are many forms of software and Excel add-ins on the market that can be used to create financial models. However, provided that it can deliver an adequate solution, we recommend using plain Excel, as it is easy to use, and no extra licences, training, or software downloads are required. If additional functionality is needed, Excel add-ins may be considered.

For the purposes of this book, we are going to assume that you don't use any other software besides "plain vanilla" Excel.

32-Bit versus 64-Bit Microsoft Excel

Since the introduction of Microsoft Excel 2010 several versions ago, Excel has been available in 64-bit; this has been a topic of discussion and interest for many Excel users. With all the buzz around the 64-bit version, many of us wonder: Is 64-bit Excel better than 32-bit Excel? Should I make the switch? Is 64-bit MS Excel the solution to poor Excel performance?

First, let's explore exactly what 32-bit and 64-bit really means. A 32-bit system can process the data in 32-bit pieces whereas 64-bit can process double that. Because more data is being processed at once, the system will operate more quickly and will use the physical memory more efficiently. Installing the 64-bit version of Excel will certainly make your Excel models run faster and more efficiently, but consider whether it's really necessary before you take the plunge.

You need to consider three components: the software, the operating system, and the hardware. Just because you have 64-bit-capable hardware does not mean you have a 64-bit operating system or software, but if you want to run the 64-bit, your machine and operating system need to be 64-bit. See below to check which hardware, operating system, or software you are running.

Increasing to the 64-bit version of Excel will increase the speed, capacity, and efficiency of working in Excel significantly. For those working in Office, what this means is that you are no longer limited to 2GB file sizes. Anything over around 50MB does not work very efficiently on 32-bit hardware. Most Excel files rarely exceed 20MB, unless you are working in Power Pivot. So, if you're a heavy-duty file size Excel user, you'll notice a big difference, but otherwise, consider whether you are really going to gain much advantage with the upgrade. If you're having trouble with your memory, see the section on "Improving Model Performance" in Chapter 10.

The file size supported by 64-bit Excel is limited only by the system capacity (hard drive) and memory (RAM) available for storage and computation, respectively. Also, the 64-bit solutions offer much better security features than the 32-bit versions.

What are You Using at the Moment?   To figure out what is on your machine, there are three different things that you need to consider here: first, is your machine 64-bit-capable, is the operating system 64-bit, and is the version of Office you've installed 32-bit or 64-bit? Whilst you can't install 64-bit Office on a 32-bit machine, it is entirely possible (and very common) to have 32-bit Office installed on a 64-bit-capable machine. In fact, this is often the default option when you install Office, even if you are running the 64-bit edition of Windows. It is also important to note that 64-bit computers can still use 32-bit-based software programs, even when the Windows operating system is a 64-bit version.

To check whether your computer is 32-bit or 64-bit-capable:

Windows Version	Steps
Windows 10	1. In the Windows search bar, type **About your PC**. 2. Select **About your PC** in the list of results. The **Version** and **System type** are shown on the **About** screen.

Windows 8	1. Swipe in from the right edge of the screen, and then tap **Search**. Or, if you are using a mouse, point to the lower-right corner of the screen, and then click **Search**.
	2. Type **system** in the **Search** box, and then tap or click **Settings**.
	3. Tap or click **System**.
	  ▪ If "32-bit Operating System" is displayed in the **System type** field, the computer is running a 32-bit version of Windows.
	  ▪ If "64-bit Operating System" is displayed in the **System type** field, the computer is running a 64-bit version of Windows.

Windows 7/Vista	1. Click **Start**, and type **system** in the **Start Search** box.
	2. Click **System Information** in the **Programs** list.
	3. Select **System Summary** in the navigation pane, locate **System Type** under **Item** in the details pane.
	  ▪ If the value starts with x86, the computer is running a 32-bit version of Windows.
	  ▪ If the value starts with x64, the computer is running a 64-bit version of Windows.

Lastly, to check if your version of Excel is 32-bit or 64-bit, do the following:

Excel Version	Steps
2013, 2016, or 2019	Select the **File** tab from the Excel ribbon, select **Account** and then **About Excel**. The version and bit-level of Excel will be displayed in the top line of the window.

(continued)

Excel Version	Steps
2010	Select the **File** tab from the Excel ribbon, and then select **Help**. The version and bit-level of Excel will appear under **About Microsoft Excel**.
2007	This version is 32-bit.

What to be Wary of Before Installing the 64-Bit Version Once you have established that you have a 64-bit-capable computer, this doesn't mean you necessarily should instantly install the 64-bit operating system and Office software. Bigger is better, right? Hold on a minute. While 64-bit does improve the capacity of the file size, there are some limitations with the 64-bit. Despite the fact that it has been around for several versions, there are still a few features, add-ins, and other pieces of software that don't work well with the 64-bit version of Office.

The 64-bit Excel is a little more stable, but if you are sticking to fairly standard Excel functionality, the switch from 32-bit to 64-bit will probably not impact you; in fact, you probably won't even notice the increased capacity. For Power Pivot users though, the additional amount of RAM that 64-bit can access might well come in handy, especially if you are regularly working with data models that contain over a million rows.

However, if you need to use advanced features with add-ins like ActiveX, VBA codes from an older Excel version, or other third-party add-ins, you could encounter all sorts of problems. This is because many Excel add-ins are 32-bit versions that are not fully compatible with the 64-bit Excel. Of course, if you upgrade to 64-bit Excel, then you'll need to upgrade for the rest of Office, and you may encounter similar problems with add-ins for these products as well. Users have particularly complained about add-ins for Outlook, such as not syncing with mobile phones or other devices.

Microsoft's latest version of VBA is Visual Basic 15.5, which comes in 32-bit and 64-bit formats. For ActiveX controls and other third-party add-ins, you need to either edit the source code (if you can access it) for 64-bit compatibility or look for an alternative or upgrade.

Lastly, if you are planning to build a solution or a tool using 64-bit Excel, you need to ensure that your solution will work on both 32-bit and 64-bit Excel. Given that 64-bit Excel is still not as prevalent as 32-bit, building a 64-bit-compatible solution could be detrimental to its popular adoption or usage.

In summary, if you are looking at moving to 64-bit Excel, you need to evaluate how you use Excel today. Unless you are a data-hungry Power Pivot user with the need to generate Excel files bigger than 2GB, there is no real value in making the switch, as 32-bit Excel is perfectly adequate for everyday financial model building.

WHAT SKILLS DO YOU NEED TO BE A GOOD FINANCIAL MODELLER?

When you decide your financial models are not as good as they should be, should you immediately take an advanced Excel course? Whilst this is helpful, there's a great deal more to financial modelling than being good at Excel!

When considering the skills that make up a good financial modeller, we need to differentiate between conceptual modelling, which is to have an understanding of the transaction, business, or product being modelled, and spreadsheet engineering, which is the representation of that conceptual model in a spreadsheet. Spreadsheet skills are reasonably easy to find, but a modeller who can understand the concept of the purpose of the model and translate it into a clear, concise, and well-structured model is much rarer.

People who need to build a financial model sometimes think they need to become either an Excel super-user or an accounting pro who knows every in and out of accounting rules. I'd argue you need a blend of both, as well as a number of other skills, including some business common sense!

Spreadsheet and Technical Excel Skills

It's very easy for financial modellers to get bogged down in the technical Excel aspects of their model, get carried away with complex formulas, and not focus on key high-level, best-practice procedures, such as error-checking strategies and model stress testing.

Excel is an incredibly powerful tool, and almost no single Excel user will have the need or desire to utilise most of the functionality this program offers. As with most software, the 80/20 rule applies: 80 percent of users use only 20 percent of the features, although some would argue that 95 percent of Excel users use only 5 percent of the features! Still, there are those select few who understand every in and out of Excel, every single function, and work out how to do practically anything in Excel. Do you need to have this level of Excel skill to become a good financial modeller? Unfortunately, having great software skills doesn't always help when it comes to applying them to a specific area of business. Realise that Excel is used in several capacities, so being an Excel super-user doesn't automatically mean you'll be a super financial modeller. The best financial models are clear, well structured, flexible, and dynamic; they are not always the biggest and most complicated models that use the most advanced tools and functions. Many of the best financial models use only Excel's core functionality.

Having said that, to be a good financial modeller, you do need to know Excel exceptionally well. Those people who maintain that you don't need good Excel skills to be a financial modeller are usually those with weak Excel skills. You should be building a superb model using simple and straightforward tools because you've chosen to make your model clear and easy to follow, not because that's all you know how to do. You don't have to be a super-user—the 99th percentile in Excel knowledge—but you must certainly be above average. A complex financial model might use features in Excel that the everyday user doesn't know. The best financial model will always use the solution that is the simplest tool to complete the task (as simple as possible and as complex as necessary, right?), so the more familiar you are with the tools available in Excel, the easier it will be. An array formula or a macro might be the only way to achieve what you need to achieve, but a simpler solution may well be—and often is—superior. You might also need to take apart someone else's model, which uses complex tools, and it's very difficult to manipulate an array formula or a macro if you've never seen one before. So, if you are considering a career as a financial modeller (as I assume you are), improving your Excel knowledge is an excellent place to start.

EXAMPLES OF TECHNICAL EXCEL SKILLS QUESTIONS

- How do I use the appropriate formula? For example, should I use a VLOOKUP or a SUMIF?
- How do I hide a sheet and then protect it so that the user can't access it?
- How do I construct a complex but concise formula?

Industry Knowledge

One of the fantastic things about financial modelling is that it is applicable across so many different industries. Good financial modelling skills will always stand you in good stead, no matter which industry or country you are working in. Financial modelling consultants or generalists will probably work in many different industries during their careers and be able to build models for different products and services. They will probably not be experts in the intricacies of each industry, however, and that's why it's important for a financial modelling generalist to consult carefully with the subject matter expert for the inputs, assumptions, and logic of the financial model. Don't be afraid to ask lots and lots of questions if the details are not absolutely clear. It's quite likely that the person who has commissioned the model hasn't actually thought through the steps, inputs, assumptions, and even what the outputs should look like until you ask the right question.

Financial modelling consultants are very careful to transfer responsibility for the assumptions to the end user, which is a very sensible course of action. The person building the model is often not the one who has commissioned it or the person who is actually using it. Model builders are often not overly familiar with the product or even the organisation, and they cannot (and should not) take responsibility for the inputs. (See the section "Document Your Assumptions" in Chapter 3 for greater detail on the importance of documentation of assumptions.)

For example, when building a pricing model, the modeller needs to understand the product and how the costs and revenue work. Experience with regulatory constraints will help the modeller to understand the basis of regulation and its components (e.g., cost building blocks, cost index, revenue cap, weighted average price cap, maximum prices, etc.). Understanding of economic concepts, such as efficient cost calculation, return on and of a regulatory asset base, operating costs and working capital, long-run versus short-run marginal costs, and average costs, are other examples of industry knowledge that is useful for the financial modeller.

EXAMPLES OF INDUSTRY KNOWLEDGE

- Regulatory constraints.
- Industry standards.
- Maximum price that can be charged for a certain item.

Accounting Knowledge

Elements such as financial statements, cash flow, and tax calculations can be an important aspect of many financial models. Professional accountants know every single accounting rule and law there is, but this certainly does not by definition make them good financial modellers. If a highly skilled accountant built a financial model, you would guess that the calculations, layout, and structure of the financial statements will be 100 percent correct, but will they be linked properly? If you change some of the inputs, does the balance sheet still balance? Sometimes not! A good accountant, or even someone qualified who has a Master's degree in applied finance, for example, might not be familiar with all the modelling technical tools, even if he or she is a competent Excel user. As with the other modelling skills, you don't need a top level of accounting knowledge to build a financial model. In fact, financial models are often relatively straightforward from an accounting standpoint. You certainly do not need to be a qualified accountant to become a financial modeller, although a good understanding of accounting and knowledge of finance certainly helps.

There are some situations where industry knowledge and accounting are required for financial modelling. For example, in manufacturing or, particularly, in the oil and gas industry, the modeller needs to know whether FIFO (first in, first out) or LIFO (last in, first out) accounting is being used, as this has a big impact on the way that inventory is being modelled. A financial modeller who has never worked in these industries may not have ever heard of FIFO and LIFO, and would probably have no idea how to model them.

EXAMPLES OF ACCOUNTING KNOWLEDGE

- How is a profit and loss statement structured?
- How do I construct a cash flow forecast from my model?
- How do I turn capital expenditure into a depreciation expense?

Business Knowledge

A modeller with wide-ranging business experience is well equipped to probe for the facts and assumptions that are critical for building a financial model. This is probably the most difficult skill to teach, as it's most easily picked up by working in a management role.

Business acumen is particularly important when commissioning, designing, and interpreting a financial model. When creating the model, the modeller needs to consider the purpose of the model. What does the model need to tell us? Knowing the desired outcome will assist with the model's build, design, and inputs. If, for example, we are building a pricing model, we need to consider the desired outcome—normally, the price we need to charge in order to achieve a certain profit margin. What is an acceptable margin? What costs should we include? What cost will the market bear? Modellers should also have an understanding of economic concepts, such as efficient costs and how these are calculated, an expected return on an asset base, operating costs and working capital, or long-run versus short-run marginal costs.

Of course, the answers to these questions can be obtained from other people, but a modeller with good business sense will have an innate sense of how a model should be built, and what is the most logical design and layout to achieve the necessary results.

EXAMPLES OF BUSINESS KNOWLEDGE

- What is the cost of capital and how does that affect a business case?
- Which numbers are important?
- What does the internal rate of return mean, and what is an acceptable rate?

Aesthetic Design Skills

This is an area that many modellers and analysts struggle with, as aesthetics simply do not come naturally to left-brain thinkers like us. We are mostly so concerned with accuracy and functionality that we fail to realise that the model looks—and I'm not going to mince words here—ugly! Although it's just a simple matter of taking our time when formatting, most of us could not be bothered with such trivial details as making models pretty, and consequently most models I see use the standard gridlines, font, and black and white colouring that are Excel defaults. I'm certainly not suggesting that you embellish your models with garish colours, but you should take some pride in your model. See the section "Bulletproofing Your Model" in Chapter 7 for some ideas on how to remove gridlines and change some of the standard settings so that your model looks less like a clunky spreadsheet and more like a reliable, well-crafted model you've taken your time over. Research shows that users place greater faith on models with aesthetic formatting than those without, so one of the fastest and easiest ways to give your model credibility is to simply spend a few minutes on the colours, font, layout, and design.

Some aesthetic formatting is critical for the functionality and to avoid error (see the section "Error Avoidance Strategies" in Chapter 4), but mostly it adds credibility and makes your model easier to work with.

Models can become complex very quickly and without a well-planned design, they can be unintelligible. Some basic components of a model should be a cover sheet, instructions, and clearly labelled inputs, outputs, workings, and results. For extremely long and complex models with many sheets, a hyperlinked table of contents is also a valuable addition to help the user navigate the model.

Communication and Language Skills

This is also an area that we analytical, financially orientated people are not always good at. Some analysts like to lock themselves away, working on spreadsheets without communicating with other people. If this is your tendency, then you might need to consider whether financial modelling is a good career choice for you, because there is a surprising amount of human interaction required for most financial modellers.

- **Assumptions validation.** In order to gain buy-in from stakeholders, the key assumptions and inputs often need to be communicated verbally or in writing. People in various parts of the business should be involved in order to check the accuracy and appropriateness of inputs for inclusion in a model. Stakeholders will often query the assumptions or the way they have been used and provide extremely valuable insight for modellers (particularly for a consultant or modeller with little industry or product knowledge). Performing this task well is a critical step in the modelling process.

■ **Data gathering.** There are some modelling projects where more time is spent gathering and collating data than actually building the model. Holders of information can be guarded about giving access to data, sometimes irrationally, but often it's because they've had bad experiences in the past. This can occur when someone provides estimates off the record and later discovers that those numbers have been used in budgets or other documents to which they are held accountable. So, people can be understandably reticent about providing data when requested for an ad hoc project such as a financial model. A modeller with good communication skills will be able to dig, delve, and coax the information out of them!

■ **Presentation skills.** Senior management, when approving a project, often want to hear about the financial implications of the project from the person who actually built the model, and so modellers are sometimes required to present the key outcomes to a board or executive committee. Being able to distil a 30MB, extremely complex financial model that contains 20 tabs and took you six weeks to build, into three PowerPoint slides and a six-minute summary presentation, can be quite a challenge!

■ **Client skills.** Whether you are a consultant or an in-house employee, working well with clients is a useful skill. Even in-house modellers have clients; every person you work with or for should be considered a client and treated with the same respect and consideration as though they were paying your bill.

In all of these interactions with other people, financial modellers must show confidence in their model. Build the model to the best of your ability. Use best practices, check for errors, and follow a good and logical thought process, so that when you present or discuss your model, you can do so in a way that exudes absolute confidence. Doing so reduces questions about the accuracy, usefulness, and validity of your model. Be honest about the fallibility of your model and its known shortcomings (let's face it, no model is perfect), but be confident that you have built it to best-practice standards within the limitations of time, data, or scope. This will serve to increase your model's credibility, building your reputation within your company, and, of course, enhancing your career!

Numeracy Skills

Financial models, of course, have a significant mathematical component, and people with good numeracy skills are best suited to them. Solid mathematical skills can be particularly useful in error-checking and sense-checking. The ability to make rough estimates quickly means they will be able to spot errors more easily. If we sell 450 units at $800 each, will our sales revenue be $3.6 million, or $360,000? If we've made a calculation error, the numerate modeller will pick up the mistake much more quickly.

The modeller with numerical aptitude will also have a gut feel for differentiating between critical assumptions that need further verification, and input that is insignificant or immaterial to the model. The less numerate modeller will have to test it manually, and will probably end up with the same result, but it will simply take longer.

General numeracy is a skill that is difficult to teach, and one that can easily be tested for in the recruitment process. Experience working with models over time can drastically improve these skills, as the modeller who is less numerate will learn ways to compensate through error-testing, and these techniques will become acquired, innate habits.

Ability to Think Logically

Modelling is often like programming, and complex logic needs to be interpreted into the language of Excel so that the program can understand and create the modeller's expected results. For example, if we want to show a value, but only if the cell being tested is in the future, we would vocalise it by saying: "Show me the value, but only if the test cell is greater than or equal to today's date". The way that we need to translate this into Excel's language is to use the formula

$$IF(test\_cell>=today,value,0)$$

Logic is also critical for model layout, design, and the use of assumptions in calculations. The issue of timing in annual models is one that I use often when demonstrating logic in my training workshops. If we are estimating the revenue for a new insurance product, and the assumption is that we acquire 30,000 customers every year, we can't assume revenue for the full 30,000 customers, as not all of them will begin on the very first day of Year 1. Customers will be acquired gradually throughout the year, so we need to take an average in order to calculate revenue. This is an example of how it is very easy to get logic wrong and overestimate revenue by a substantial amount.

Logic is one of those analytical skills that is very difficult to teach, but modellers who have made a logic error (like the one illustrated above) learn quickly from their mistakes and are quite careful to use clear, well-documented logic for others to follow and check.

THE "IDEAL" FINANCIAL MODELLER

In general, most modellers have at least some of the aforementioned skills, and at times it is necessary to consult specialists in order to create a successful financial model. Having read the section on the skills that you need to be a good financial modeller, you should have a fairly good idea about which areas you are lacking in. Once you have identified these areas, you can work to improve them and liaise with other specialists to ensure that your model is not lacking as a result of your weaknesses.

What financial modellers bring to the table is a combination of skills. First, they know Excel well enough to be able to choose the simplest and most functional tool to build a model. They can create a PivotTable, array formula, or macro (but only when necessary, of course), use a simple or complex nested formula, and choose the best technical tool to perform a scenario analysis. They also understand all the relevant business and accounting principles. At the end of the day, the balance sheet has to balance, and the ending cash on your cash flow statement needs to tie to the balance sheet, for example.

The ideal financial modeller brings a unique combination of skills that neither an Excel guru nor an accounting whiz possesses. He or she understands sensitivity and relationships between variables, how fluctuations in inputs will impact the outcomes, and how this needs to be modelled in Excel. A financial modeller can also take a step back and realise what the ultimate goal of the model should be. Are we building a model for in-house use, or to present to investors? Do we need a valuation, a variance analysis, a nice summary, or a detailed month-by-month profit and loss report? The financial modeller can take information, build an Excel model that is technically correct from an accounting standpoint, set up the model, and ultimately reflect what the business is looking to achieve.

What's the Typical Background for a Financial Modeller?

A key problem in the financial modelling industry is that modelling is often incorrectly considered a junior task and is often given to inexperienced graduate analysts who undoubtedly have good Excel skills but simply do not have the depth of business experience to create good financial models. If a modeller is able to check off all of the above boxes (i.e., good financial skills, good communicator, able to resolve ambiguity), he or she is likely to quickly move into a more senior position to execute more management responsibilities and spend less time building financial models.

Most financial modellers come from a finance background and have gradually been exposed to industry knowledge. They often become specialists in a field, picking up business acumen, communication skills, and logic along the way. Quite often engineers, project managers, construction specialists, or even scientists who are required to build their own financial models end up pursuing a career in financial modelling. They have the industry and product knowledge and are able to learn the Excel skills but may struggle with the finance side of things. Some would argue that it is easier to teach an engineer or scientist financial skills than it is to teach a financial accountant about the industry, but I think both have a tough job. Every modeller will have strengths and weaknesses, but a good financial modeller will span different skill sets and will have a little bit of everything.

Training Courses

As a specialist financial modelling consultant and trainer, I spend a lot of my time running training courses and, consequently, many people expect me to be a firm advocate of the face-to-face training workshop, right? Not necessarily. I've come under fire from my training partners in the past for publicising this opinion, but I'm not entirely convinced that going on a training course is always the best option for someone keen to improve their financial modelling skills.

Excel is the backbone of any custom-built financial model, and as discussed in the previous section, one of the core attributes of a financial modeller is to have good technical Excel skills. When struggling with financial models, some managers' first reaction is to send their staff on an advanced Excel course to improve their modelling skills. However, with training budgets under constant scrutiny, you really need to make sure that you get the best value out of your training options. Is a training course really what you need?

When considering an advanced Excel course, there are a few points you should consider:

- As financial modellers, our use of Excel is quite narrow. I know it's hard for us to conceive, but there *is* a whole world of Excel outside the finance industry. Statisticians, database programmers, and engineers, to name a few, are able to use Excel's advanced functions to create non-financial spreadsheets. Most advanced Excel courses are very broad and will cover functions and capabilities that do not apply to your needs as a financial modeller. You may learn a few tricks, but the time and money spent could be invested elsewhere.
- Research shows that a large percentage of the skills learned in training courses are not retained. Will you really remember everything that you learn? A program of continuous, applied learning is often more effective than an intensive training course.
- Are your Excel skills really the problem? Following best practices and mastering the logic behind a financial model is more important than building complex formulas and, for the most part, you will want to keep formulas as simple as possible.

Alternatives to Attending a Training Course   Other options to improve your financial modelling skills without going on an advanced Excel course include:

- Read a book. Buying this book is a great start. You'll still have it to refer to when the excitement and enthusiasm you felt after completing a training course are long gone, and you're back to struggling with building your financial models.
- Take an interest in what work your colleagues have done and how they did it—you can always learn from the techniques of others.

- Read, use, and dissect other people's models. Sometimes the best way to learn is to see what someone else has done. Try taking someone else's model apart and see how he or she built it. It's probably best to use your company's models, but if you don't have access to those, take a look at some of the sample models provided on this book's companion website, which can be found at www.wiley.com/go/steinfairhurst.
- Read specialist financial modelling publications or subscribe to e-mail newsletters about using Excel. They often contain useful articles about specific techniques and tips that can enhance your skills. Getting a short e-mail tip every day is much more effective than reading many all at once. You'll retain the information better in bite-size pieces.
- Search online. If you're struggling with a formula or layout problem and are convinced that there must be an easier way to do something, there usually is. Chances are that others have had the same problem in the past and, if you're lucky, they've documented it as a blog post. There are some fantastic, publicly available online resources including tutorials, articles, blogs, forums, and videos specialising in Excel and financial modelling that can be used at your convenience rather than taking an entire day or two to attend a course. You will find links to some of my favourite websites and online resources listed on the companion website at www.wiley.com/go/steinfairhurst.

Select the Right Training Option for You The strategies outlined here are great for continually improving your Excel and financial modelling skill set, and they certainly won't break the budget, but what if you really need to give your skills a quick boost to get you ready for an upcoming project? There are a number of options available:

- Try to find a course specifically aimed at Excel for financial modellers, and even better find one dedicated to your industry. Although good financial modelling skills are relevant across many different industries, there is nothing like specialised training dedicated to the modelling issues inherent in your own industry. In recent years, many more specialist financial modelling courses have become available, especially in major cities.
- If your company is able to arrange a group in-house training course, this will be even better, as you may be able to learn with the templates and models actually used within your organisation. You also have the added advantage of choosing a time and location that suit you.
- If you can afford a private session, this is the most convenient and time-efficient method, as you can ask questions and cover only topics that are useful to you. Many specialist training companies provide one-on-one mentoring sessions with Excel.

Do You Really Need an Advanced Excel Course? It's true that "you don't know what you don't know", and so some people go on training courses because they want to make sure there isn't something about the subject that they are missing. Having heard or seen something in a training course gives you exposure to something that you might never have heard about, but if it's simply inspiration you're after, a good newsletter might well suffice (and be a lot cheaper).

You might learn a few tricks on a course, but most people have got to think really hard before spending the money and taking a day or two out of their schedules to commit to training workshops. There is no question that face-to-face workshops are very effective; for many people, they are the best way to learn. However, I would recommend that potential attendees exhaust the available blogs, forums, and newsletters first.

In summary, an advanced Excel course would certainly benefit those who plan on extensively using Excel in their role for multiple purposes. However, if your main objective is to become an expert financial modeller, focus instead on mastering the few tools you need—such as logic and methodology—either in a course or via another medium, rather than expending time and money to learn things you may not use.

SUMMARY

In this chapter, we have discussed the definition of a financial model and determined that, at a basic level, a financial model is really just a complex spreadsheet that contains inputs and outputs in a dynamic way. However, not every spreadsheet could be called a financial model. Models in Excel can be built for virtually any purpose, both financial and non-financial, business or non-business, although the majority of models will be financial and business-related and these are the kinds of examples we will mainly focus on.

Although this book is about how to use Excel in the context of business analysis and financial modelling, consider that there are many other available modelling tools besides Excel, including Microsoft products, add-ins, and third-party software. Excel is the most commonly used software for this type of analysis, and in terms of building your skill set, improving your Excel skills will always stand you in good stead for a career in finance.

Having good technical Excel skills is not the only attribute of a good financial modeller: industry knowledge, accounting, business acumen, design skills, communication, logic, and numeracy are also important. Modellers will have all these skills in varying degrees, so think about which skills you need to work on the most. Going on a training course, using and taking apart others' models, reading specialist publications and blogs, and using other online resources are all great ways to improve your financial modelling skills.

CHAPTER 2

Building a Model

Before launching in to build a model, it's important to think about model design, structure, layout, and planning. A well-thought-out design and clear project plan can make a huge difference to the quality and success of the modelling project.

MODEL DESIGN

Design can sometimes be the most difficult part of building a financial model and, in my experience, one of the most difficult to teach and learn. The best way to develop design skills is to critically assess other people's models, taking note of what works and doesn't, and then applying it to your own models.

Even the simplest models can become complex if poorly designed, and a well-designed model will be so straightforwardly logical that it will simply speak for itself. It's pretty easy to just dive in and start building a model without thinking about the implications of the design. It's not a bad idea to spend some time thinking about the layout before you get started. The layout and structure of the model relate to the look and feel of the model, and how users navigate through the model.

The following examples outline a couple of different challenges you might come across when designing the layout of a model.

Practical Example 1: Assumptions Layout

Let's say you are creating a high-level 5-year forecast. We've got 15,065 customers in 2020, and we are expecting that number to increase by 5 percent every year. If you set up your model as shown in Layout Option 1 in Figure 2.1, with only one growth assumption, you're very much restricted to a single input for the growth number.

If we change the design of the calculations by adding multiple input assumption cells, and change the formula just a little, we are making our model a lot more

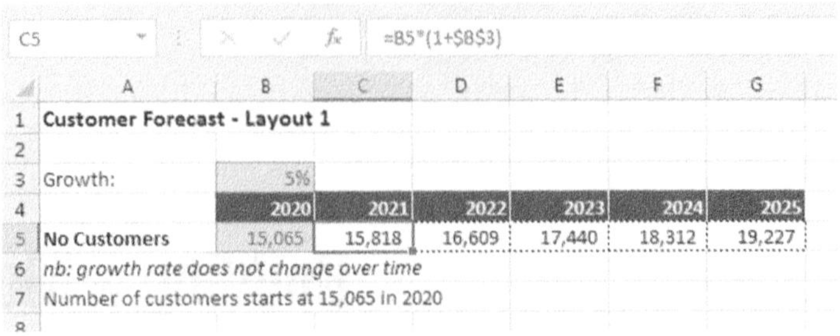

FIGURE 2.1　Model Layout Option 1

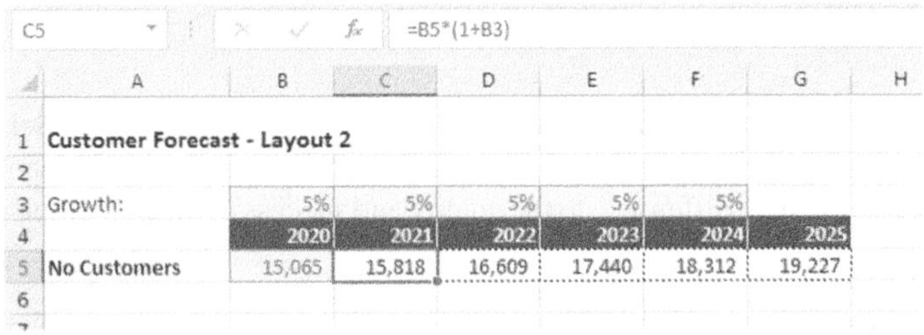

FIGURE 2.2　Model Layout Option 2

flexible and useful in the long term. This way, if we decide to change the growth number for each year, as shown in Figure 2.2, we won't need to change any of our formulas in the future, and our model is much more robust and less prone to error.

Of course, Layout Option 2 is slightly more complex but is more functional for the user. This example demonstrates the constant balance that a modeller needs to maintain between functionality and simplicity when building a financial model.

Practical Example 2: Summary Categorisation

Arranging products to display into categories in a model is another potentially difficult model layout problem. Let's say you're creating a pricing model for some advertising products. You've got print ads and digital ads, and these are both split into Display and Text Only. The question is, should you display the output of the model as shown in Figure 2.3 or Figure 2.4?

The example in Figure 2.4 is more concise but shows less detail, so it really depends on how much detail you want to show your user. This comparison demonstrates the constant balance that a modeller needs to maintain between detail and conciseness when building a financial model.

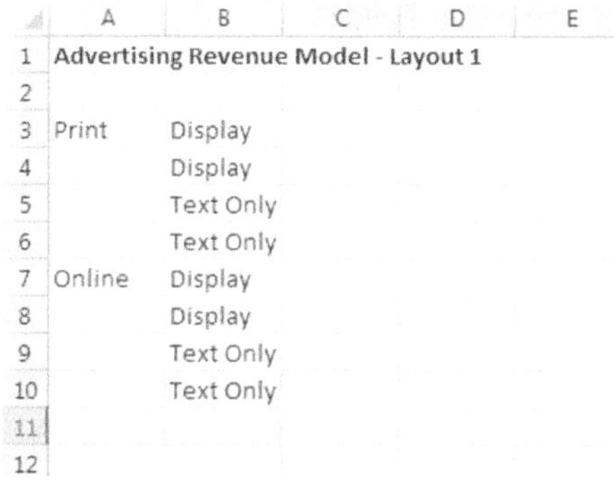

◢	A	B	C	D	E
1	Advertising Revenue Model - Layout 1				
2					
3	Print	Display			
4		Display			
5		Text Only			
6		Text Only			
7	Online	Display			
8		Display			
9		Text Only			
10		Text Only			
11					
12					

FIGURE 2.3 Model Categorisation Option 1

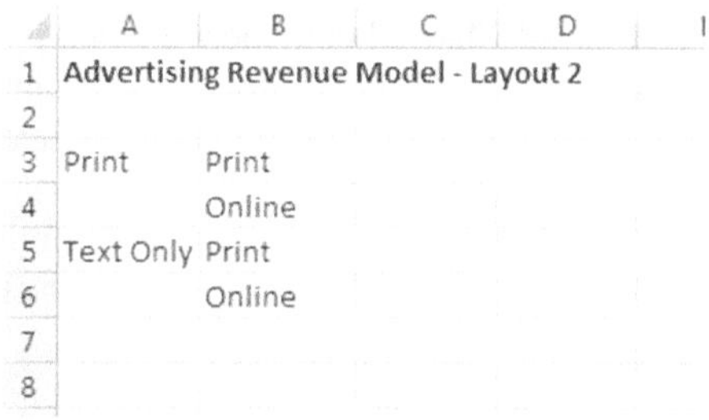

◢	A	B	C	D	I
1	Advertising Revenue Model - Layout 2				
2					
3	Print	Print			
4		Online			
5	Text Only	Print			
6		Online			
7					
8					

FIGURE 2.4 Model Categorisation Option 2

THE GOLDEN RULES FOR MODEL DESIGN

There are a few rules for model design that should be followed when designing the layout of a model. Most experienced modellers will follow these instinctively, as they are generally common sense.

Separate Inputs, Calculations, and Results, where Possible

Clearly label which sections of the model contain inputs, calculations, and results. They can be on separate worksheets or separate places on a given worksheet, but make sure that the user knows exactly what each section is for. Colour coding can help with ensuring that each section is clearly defined.

See the forthcoming section entitled "The Workbook Anatomy of a Model" for more discussion on whether it is always practical to separate these sections.

Use Each Column for the Same Purpose

This is particularly important for models involving time series. For example, in a time-series model, knowing that labels are in Column B, unit data in Column C, constant values in Column D, and calculations in Column E makes it much easier when editing a formula manually.

Use One Formula per Row or Column

This forms the basis of the best-practice principle whereby formulas are kept consistent using absolute, relative, and mixed referencing, as described in greater detail in Chapter 3, "Best Practice Principles of Modelling". Keep formulas consistent when in a block of data, and never change a formula halfway through.

Refer to the Left and Above

The model should read logically, like a book, meaning that it should be read from left to right and top to bottom. Calculations, inputs, and outputs should flow logically to avoid circular referencing. Be aware that there are times when left-to-right or top-to-bottom data flow can conflict somewhat with ease of use and presentation, so use common sense when designing the layout. By following this practice, we can avoid having calculations link all over the sheet, which makes it harder to check and update.

Excel will also calculate more quickly if you build formulas in this way because it calculates left to right, and top to bottom, so not only does it make your model easier to follow, it will calculate more efficiently.

Use Multiple Worksheets

Avoid the temptation to put everything on one sheet. Especially when blocks of calculations are the same, use separate sheets for those that must be repeated to avoid the need to scroll across the screen.

Include Documentation Sheets

A documentation sheet—where assumptions and source data are clearly laid out—is a critical part of any financial model. A cover sheet should not be confused with an assumptions sheet. A model can never have too much documentation!

DESIGN ISSUES

Here are four key issues you need to think about before you start a model:

1. **Time series.** Most financial models include a time-series element, and the majority of these will be monthly, quarterly, or annual. It's important to get

this right from the start, as it's much easier to summarise a monthly model up to an annual basis than it is to split an annual model down to a monthly basis!

2. **Data collection.** Often, the majority of time is spent not in building a model, but rather collecting, interpreting, analysing, and manipulating data to put into the model. For example, you could be building an annual model for your company's fiscal year, which goes from July 1 to June 30, but the survey data you've collected and want to include is for the period January 1 to December 31. If you've got access to the raw data on a monthly basis, you'll be able to manipulate the data so that it's accurate—or else you'll need to extrapolate.

3. **Model purpose.** Think about what it is that you want the model to do. What outputs do you expect the model to show? See "Types and Purposes of Financial Models" in Chapter 1 for greater detail on different types of financial models. The outcome that you want the model to show will greatly influence the design of the model. For example, in a business case or project evaluation model, the outcome that we are working towards is the net present value (NPV), and in order to get that, we need cash flow, for which we need a profit and loss statement, and this then determines how we build the model.

4. **Model audience.** Who will be using your model in the future? If it's only for your use, no need to make it very fancy, but most models are built for others to use. If so, you will need to make your model as user-friendly as possible, and clearly define which cells are input variables and which cannot be changed. If you expect users to have limited knowledge of Excel, the model needs to be as simple to use as possible.

THE WORKBOOK ANATOMY OF A MODEL

Typically, modellers will work from back to front when building their model. The output, or the part they want the viewer or user to see, will be at the front, calculations will go in the middle, and source data and assumptions should go at the back. Figure 2.5 shows an example of what your tabs in a well-structured model might look like.

Like the executive summary, a board paper, or other report, the first few pages should contain what casual viewers need to see at a glance. If they need further information, they can dig deeper into the model.

FIGURE 2.5 Model Structure

Unless a model is very small, there should be a dedicated tab worksheet for each major component of the model. Whilst by no means a prescriptive list, the following is an example of what might be included on each tab.

- **Cover sheet.** The cover sheet contains many details about the model. Whether or not a cover sheet is necessary is an issue for debate; one can include (but is not limited to) details such as:
  - A log of changes and updates to the model with date, author, change details, and their impact on the output of the model. This is important for version control.
  - Flowchart of the model structure.
  - Table of contents.
  - Instructions on how to use the model.
  - The purpose of the model for which it should be used.
  - Disclaimers as to the limitations of the model, legal liability, and caveats.
  - Global or key assumptions integral to the use of the model.
- **Input sheet.** This is the only place where hardcoded data is permissible. There may be one or more input sheets if there are copious amounts of data, but the input data should be laid out in logical blocks, for example: consumption data, WACC data, assets and depreciation data, inflation and indices, pricing and tariffs, assumptions and constants (such as tax rate, discount rates, concession rates).
- **Output, summary, and scenario sheets.** These present the final outcomes. They may also contain scenario drop-down boxes, spin buttons, or checkboxes that allow the users of the model to generate their own outputs. Tables and charts summarising the outputs should be set up in such a way that they can easily be printed or used to generate reports. Ensure that these can easily be printed directly from the model, or copied or linked to other programs such as Word or PowerPoint.
- **Calculation or workings sheets.** Split the calculation sheets logically and then, within each sheet, set them up consistently. If calculation sheets are split, ensure that the layout and formatting are as consistent as possible across all sheets.
- **Error check sheet.** This sheet contains links to all error checks in the model. Error checks should be performed in the calculation section, but a summary of all error checks in one location means that once the model is in use, the modellers can quickly check to see if any of the error checks have been triggered.

Workbook Anatomy Issues

Matters to consider when designing the layout and structure of the model include:

- **A cover sheet.** Is a cover sheet necessary? It's not absolutely critical, but it is generally good practice to put one in. In my experience, cover sheets and instruction pages are rarely used. If you decide not to include a cover sheet, make sure that the model contains explicit instructions regarding operation, purpose, assumptions, source data, and disclaimers.

- **Input and output locations.** Should there be a dedicated input sheet, or should the inputs and outputs be contained in one sheet? Many modelling specialists maintain that inputs, outputs, and calculations must be clearly separated, but this is not always practical. Generally, larger models should have a dedicated input sheet, whilst smaller models may show inputs and outputs on the same sheet. However, if you've created a large model with inputs and outputs on different sheets, and then want to perform a scenario analysis using a data table, you'll need to move the inputs and outputs to the same sheet. For example, in a small model that takes inputs and generates simple tables of output data and charts in reports, the modeller may set up the sheet to have a block of input at the top of the worksheet with the calculations and charts directly underneath. You may consider splitting the charts and ratio calculations into separate worksheets to avoid the worksheet becoming too long and unwieldy.
- **Calculation organisation.** Should calculations be on one or multiple sheets? Depending on the size of the model, all calculations could be contained within one worksheet, spread over several worksheets, or even spread over several workbook files. If the calculations become long and confusing, it makes sense to split them into logical sections. For example, they can be split by type of service, customers, financial tables, geographical location, or business segments.
- **Colour coding.** If you decide to use colour (and I recommend that you do, or else your model will look pretty boring), make sure that the colours you use are consistent. For example, if African regions are yellow, Europe is blue, and Asia is pink, make sure that you use those same colours every time numbers for Africa, Europe, and Asia are displayed.

    These colours should be consistent in calculations in your model, display tables, and charts. Some companies have standard colour coding, but if your company does not, you might consider developing a standard. You could consider including a colour code key on the cover page. The use of predefined styles (found on the Home tab) can make colour coding very quick and easy. Below are some commonly used colour codes that are supported by the inbuilt styles in Excel that you may consider adopting in your company:
    - Blue font and beige background for input cells.
    - Pink or grey for error checks.
    - Green or orange for external links.

Formatting can be quite time-consuming and using styles is a much faster way of creating consistent formatting. Figure 2.6 shows where to find the Styles menu on the Home tab.

FIGURE 2.6   Using the Styles Menu to Format Input Cells

	A	B	C	D
1				
2		2021	2022	2023
3	Existing HoneyCorp Customers	2,200,000	2,219,864	2,239,479
4	HoneyCorp Pet Owners	1,188,000	1,198,726	1,209,319
5	Expected Customer Acquisition	29,700	29,968	30,233
6	Gross Cumulative Customers at YE	29,700	59,668	89,901
7	Average no cumulative customers	14,850	44,684	74,785
8	Churn		(2,234)	(3,739)
9	**Net Average Cumulative Customers**	14,850	42,450	71,045
10	Gross Premiums	$5,940,000	$17,489,348	$30,148,830
11	**Premium Revenue**	$594,000	$1,748,935	$3,014,883
12				

FIGURE 2.7   Commonly Used Formatting for Inconsistent Formulas

Use a double border to indicate that the calculations change. In Figure 2.7, the double line shows that the formula is not consistent across the row.

Many companies have their predefined colour coding loaded as style templates, which ensures consistency in colour coding in financial models.

PROJECT PLANNING YOUR MODEL

Whilst planning ahead is very important for successful modelling, it is unrealistic to expect that a detailed project plan can be created prior to starting to build it. Quite often the modellers do not have much idea of the size and scope of a model until they get in and start working on it.

How Long Does it Take to Build a Financial Model?

Whether you are a consultant building a model for a client, or an internal modeller, you or the person who has commissioned the model build will, understandably, want to know how long it will take. The answer is never straightforward. As with many other tasks, it really depends on how much time you have (and there's never enough time), and how much detail the users need. The more time you have, the better the model will be! Some models could take months and months of dedicated work, but it is also possible to throw together a very high-level model in a day or two.

In a high-level model, the assumptions would probably be only estimates, as you won't have had time to validate them with stakeholders, and the calculations will be pretty rough. You also might not have much in the way of fancy colours, formatting, drop-down boxes, or checkboxes, but the numbers should still be reasonably accurate.

Building a Model Under Pressure

It's a critical point to remember that even when under immense time pressure, the modeller should never compromise on good work practices. Even in a high-level model, best practices should be adhered to, and correct labelling and documentation of assumptions should be maintained. For this reason, there should be surprisingly little difference in the base numerical outcome between a high-level model that takes a few days, and a detailed model that could take months. If pressed for time, cosmetic features such as those shown below can be omitted.

Time permitting, the detailed model may show:

- Detailed assumptions documentation, validated by key project stakeholders.
- Scenarios and sensitivity analysis, using drop-down boxes, checkboxes, or data tables.
- Table of contents or navigation tools.
- Colours and formatting, conditional formatting, and insertion of company logos.
- Output summary and detailed analysis of output.

Time should be spent on quick wins. Use your judgement to spend your time on calculations that are material to the model. Don't waste time on validating minor assumptions that are not material to the outcome of the model.

MODEL LAYOUT FLOWCHARTING

Based on an initial concept discussion of the problem, modellers can map out the structure of the model and how it will arrive at the required outputs. For models that will be viewed by external parties and large or more complex models, a flowchart diagram that maps the model's structure and how it solves the problem is essential. Not only does this help in building the model, it also helps users of the model to better understand the model's logic, design, and purpose, and can be used as a presentation tool when explaining the model. Taking the time to design the layout and structure of the model is particularly helpful if there is uncertainty about what the model needs to cover, in terms of both breadth and depth.

Such flowcharts, if created, should become part of the model's final documentation. There are some pieces of software that will automatically create model flowcharts, but most modellers will create them manually using PowerPoint, Visio, or Excel. Of course, it is highly likely that your model will be amended during the build or as the result of a review. Therefore, if you create the flowchart manually, remember to update it as the design of your model changes.

Practical Exercise: Model Design Customer Support Pricing Model

Let's say for example that you are offering a customer support option for an existing product. Your financial model needs to answer the question: "How much should we charge per customer per month for support?"

You have the following pieces of information:

- You have 500 customers who you think will take up the support offer.
- We expect that each customer will make 10 calls per month.
- It is expected to take 5 minutes to answer each call and resolve their problem.
- Staff normally answer calls for 6 hours a day on average, for 20 days per month.
- We are currently paying support centre staff $70k per annum.
- There are around $10k in fixed costs per annum.
- We expect to make a 20 percent markup.

Follow these steps to calculate the pricing per customer:

1. Open up a blank Excel file and add a title such as "Customer Support Pricing Model" in cell B1.
2. Start entering inputs as shown in Figure 2.8. Enter 500 customers in cell B3 and 10 service calls in cell B4 and add the descriptions in column C.
3. Format cells B3 and B4, and all subsequent assumption input cells as inputs using the input style from the Home tab, or your preferred input format. For where to find input styles, see Figure 2.6.
4. Calculate the total service calls per month in cell B5 using the formula =B3*B4.
5. In cell B6 enter the average call length of 5 minutes and the description in column C.
6. In cell B7 calculate the total number of minutes needed for all 5,000 service calls using the formula =B5*B6. This now needs to be converted to hours,

and this could be done all in one cell, but it's better to lay it out separately so that it's easier to follow.

7. In cell B8 we'll convert the number of minutes to hours using the formula =B7/60. Normally, entering hardcoded numbers into formulas is not considered good practice in financial modelling, however, in this case, we consider that the 60 minutes in an hour is not a variable likely to change and therefore hardcoding is acceptable.

8. In cell B9, we will also hardcode as the number of available hours is an assumption, but also a formula. Enter the formula =6*20 as we will assume six hours a day, 20 days a month. You could simply enter 120 as a value, but it's better to show how you came up with the number.

9. In cell B10, we then need to figure out how many staff will be required to run the service centre. If we need 416 hours per month, and each member of staff has 120 hours available, we can calculate this with the formula =B8/B9. We want to hire full-time staff, so use a ROUNDUP formula to round it up to the nearest decimal place. Your formula should be =ROUNDUP(B8/B9,0).

10. In cell B11, enter the monthly staff costs with the formula =70000/12, bearing in mind that this is also an input cell that might change.

11. The total staff costs can be calculated in cell B12 using the formula =B11*B10.

12. Enter the fixed costs in cell B13 using the formula =10000/12.

13. Add up the total in cell B14 using the formula =B12+B13.

14. Enter the 20 percent markup input in cell B15.

15. Calculate the total revenue in cell B16 using the formula =B14*(1+B15).

16. We can find the unit support price in cell B17 by dividing the total revenue by the number of customers with the formula =B16/B3.

The completed model will look something like the image shown in Figure 2.8. The completed version of this model can be found, along with the accompanying models to the rest of the screenshots in this book, at www.plumsolutions.com.au/book.

This is a very simple example with limited complexity, and it's easy enough for a user to follow, so it would not be necessary to document it using a flowchart. If you did decide to create a flowchart, it would look as shown in Figure 2.9.

STEPS TO BUILDING A MODEL

Once the aforementioned factors have been determined, you can begin to create your model. Most modellers will just dive in and start building, and whilst it's good to encourage innovation and creativity in creating financial models, it's still important to follow some ordered steps to achieve the best outcome.

If you're working as the sole financial modeller in a company or as a consultant, you might be able to follow a less formal process, and so I've provided a

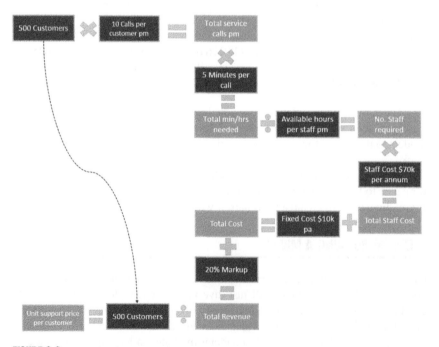

B18		✕ ✓ f_x	=(B16-B14)/B16	
◢	A	B	C	D
1		**Customer Support Pricing Model**		
2				
3		500	No Customers	
4		10	Service calls per customer per month	
5		5,000	Total service calls per month	
6		5.00	Average call length (min)	
7		25,000	Total minutes needed	
8		416.67	Total hours needed	
9		120	Available hours per staff per month	
10		4.00	Staff required	
11		$5,833	Staff cost per head per month	
12		$23,333	Total staff costs pm	
13		$833	Fixed costs pm	
14		$24,167	Total costs pm	
15		20%	Markup	
16		$29,000	Total revenue	
17		$58	Unit support price per customer	
18		17%	Profit Margin	
19				

FIGURE 2.8   Completed Customer Support Pricing Model

FIGURE 2.9   Sample Flowchart of Model Calculations

more streamlined version of the steps to follow (see "The Streamlined Version", below). If you are working as part of a team of financial modellers, the steps are more detailed, as it's more important to follow a documented and structured process, particularly if there are many modellers and stakeholders providing input (see "The Team Version", further on).

The Streamlined Version

This version of the model-building process is for less formal projects, especially those models designed to be used exclusively by their creator. The seven steps to the streamlined version are as follows:

1. **Design the high-level structure.** You're not going to know exactly what the layout of the model will be until you dig into it, but you should have some idea of the tabs. Start by assembling the data you have so far into the tabs as shown in Figure 2.5.
2. **Design outputs: summaries, charts, and reports.** Begin with the end in mind. By thinking about the output of your model early on in the process, you'll be more focused and will ensure that all your calculations work towards the desired end result.
3. **Design inputs.** Thinking about the input design issues, get your input data into the right format or layout so that you can link your calculations to it.
4. **Plan calculations by breaking larger problems into smaller ones.** Now begin your calculations. You might begin by thinking that all expenses can go on one tab, but if staff costs, for example, begin getting rather complicated, you might decide that the staff costs calculation needs a tab of its own.
5. **Finalise outputs.** Link through your calculations to the outputs page. Test at every stage to make sure that the model makes sense and adjust as necessary.
6. **Design sensitivities and scenario analysis.** Once the model is working correctly, you can add sensitivities and scenario analysis. See "Overview of Scenario Analysis Tools and Methods" in Chapter 11 for greater detail to help you choose which methods of scenario analysis to use.
7. **Document as you go.** Assumptions documentation should not be left to the end. Do it *as you go*!

The Team Version

If you are working in a large organisation and the modelling project is large, involving several financial modellers and stakeholders, you'll need to follow a more formal process. The larger the size of the model and the scale of the project, the more upfront project planning will be required. This detailed process is simply to provide a framework in the absence of one; it should by no means make the process more complex or constrict it, and how closely you stick to the process will depend on the size and scale of the project.

The 12 steps have been split into two stages: planning and building.

Planning Stage

1. **Scope out the project.** Assess what needs to be done in order to complete the model.
   - What is the purpose of the model? Clarify the scope and parameters of the model. Be clear about what the model will be designed to do and its limitations.
   - What is the problem we are trying to solve? Is a model really required and is Excel necessarily the best solution? See "Tool Selection" in Chapter 1 for greater detail on alternative tools. (The rest of this book assumes that the model will continue to be built in Excel.)
   - What's the time frame? Create a project plan by separating the work that needs to be done into sections and assign the tasks and milestones.
2. **Assign project tasks.** Once the project has been defined and scoped, you'll be able to determine the skills and resources required to complete the project.
   - What kind of skills will be needed for this project? Make sure you have a balance of industry, finance, and business skills in the team. (See "What Skills Do You Need to Be a Good Financial Modeller?" in Chapter 1 for greater detail.) Consider hiring external consultants if the skills are not available in-house.
   - Who will be involved? Identify the stakeholders who need to provide input and validations on the model. Communicate with them about their project requirements and time frame expectations.
3. **Determine the users of the model.** The modeller must know who will be using the model, as this will affect the technical development. Creating a model for others to use will require designing an interface that is suitable for their needs and, in particular, their level of familiarity with Excel. This requires consideration of several issues that impact the model build:
   - **Excel version.** The modeller needs to consider whether the user may be opening the model in an earlier version of Excel. There are several considerations the modellers need to make if the model must be compatible with the older versions of Excel. For example, the file must be saved as an .xls version, not .xlsx, and the modeller must avoid some of the newer functions. See "Excel Versions" in Chapter 5 for more information on this issue, and "Reducing File Size" in Chapter 10 for how to change the file type.
   - **User friendliness.** The weaker that users' skills are with spreadsheets and modelling, the more user-friendly the model will need to be, for example, by incorporating more instructions, control tools (such as drop-down boxes, option boxes), and simple macros. In some cases, a model may be supplied to a third party or made publicly available, through a website, for example.

In such cases, the modeller should assume the user has an extremely low level of Excel skill, and the model should be highly protected to make sure that users do not damage the model. See "Bulletproofing Your Model" in Chapter 7 for more information on how to protect models.

- **Data validation.** The model can be constructed so as to minimise the risk of users entering incorrect data. For example, when entering staff names, they may enter "William Jones" as "Will Jones", "W. Jones", "Jones, W.", or any other number of variations, which can cause errors in a model. The modeller must consider how much validation of inputs should be included, and if error messages should be provided, as this functionality can be quite time-consuming to build and test.

- **Frequency of use.** The modeller needs to consider how outputs can be located and generated and how often the model will be used. If the model is to be used often, the design of the outputs and the time it takes to run should take this into account. Most models will calculate automatically, but more complex models may include a procedure that needs to be manually updated or macros that may take time. If the model is only to be used occasionally, it may be of less importance if it takes longer to create the outputs each time the model is used.

- **Testing and adapting.** Creating a model for your own use may not require as much work as creating a model for others. However, it is important to keep in mind that someone else will need to test and validate the model, and others may need to use or adapt the model in the future. Modellers should always ensure that the model is generally logical and user-friendly.

4. **Design the high-level structure.** Create a flowchart as discussed in "Model Layout Flowcharting" earlier in this chapter.
   - The flowchart will include a place for the input, outputs, summaries, and charts. Create a list of all the outputs needed and how they may be presented (e.g., in a table, chart, diagram, or another method). The outputs and their presentation format should be taken into account when designing the layout of the model.
   - Translate the flowchart into the model. You should have an idea of the number of tabs and how they will be arranged within the model. Try to ensure that the data will flow logically in one direction (right to left) throughout the model, so that links do not jump around, making it confusing to the user.
   - Remember to update the flowchart if the design of the model changes during the building process.

5. **Create a data collection plan.** Data collection can be the most time-consuming part of a financial modelling project, so this needs to be carefully incorporated into the project plan to ensure that the data used in the model is as accurate as possible and received on time.
   - Create a list of inputs that will be required and where they will be sourced. These will feed into the project plan as tasks.

- At this stage, you may be able to identify data-related issues that need attention and consider solutions to anticipated problems. If you are creating a risk register as part of the project planning process, this is a key risk. For example, some inputs may be critical to the model but rely on the data being available. You will need to consider risk mitigation strategies to ensure the availability and reliability of data to be provided by your sources.
- The model should be designed to accommodate the format in which the necessary data is available and the output is required. For example, if the data is provided in a weekly format, but the output is required as monthly, you need to consider whether you want to preserve the original data as weekly and consolidate it as part of the model, or consolidate it prior to entering the data into the model.
- You may even consider designing an information request form for sources to fill in so that the data can easily be extracted and entered into the model.

    With the plan in place and layout, structure, and logic determined, you can now begin to build the model.

Building Stage

6. **Build inputs.** Enter the data into the input pages. Make sure that you follow best practices by documenting all assumptions and source referencing. It is critical that this is done as you enter the data, or when you record from where you got the data. If there is any possible misinterpretation or lack of clarity about how a calculation works, make sure that it is explicitly documented, either in the calculations page or as part of the assumptions. See "Methods and Tools of Assumptions Documentation" in Chapter 3 for greater detail on tools and techniques that can be used for documenting assumptions.

    As inputs become available and the model is populated with actual data, it is critical that the source of that data is kept up-to-date. Source referencing of inputs should be sufficiently detailed to allow a third party to track it back to the source easily. Information should include title, date, author, page number, web page, and so on to allow for easy tracing and validation of the model's input data.

    Documentation should include:

- A description of the model's functionality so users will be able to see the general purpose of the model and its limitations, often graphically displayed by a flow diagram of the model's structure.
- Instructions on how to use the model, including a colour code key explaining the colours and styles used in the model.
- If a calculation or data point in one section is treated differently from the rest of the model, an explanation of the reason for the difference.
- Changes to the structure of a model in the version log on the cover page, detailing what structural or major changes were done, when, and by whom.

7. **Build calculations and workings.** Building accurate and clearly auditable calculations is a critical step in building a financial model. A logical calculation should allow users to follow and trace the calculation easily—from the inputs to the outputs, and back again.

   - Follow best practices by linking to input cells, only enter data once, and always refer to the original source's cell where possible, rather than linking to another link.
   - Don't mix hardcoded data with formulas. If you need to hardcode a number into a cell, it should be included in the assumptions or source data sheet and linked from there.
   - Try to work from left to right and top to bottom where possible.
   - Use name ranges in Excel to name single cell constants or tables of inputs. This can make it easier to build and validate formulas in a financial model. (See "Named Ranges" in Chapter 5 for details on that topic.)
   - Use the superior method and the most efficient functions. This method will be the simplest, most efficient, and easiest to follow.
   - Link logically throughout the model. Try to make sure links go in one direction (from left to right) instead of jumping backwards and forwards between different tabs.
   - Build error checks wherever possible, and sense check and test for errors as you go.
   - Double-check calculations using alternative calculation methods or by manually calculating from first principles.
   - Document the calculations and their logic as you go; don't leave it all to the end. Your process may seem obvious to you at the time, but it is probably not clear to someone else reviewing your model. There is a fairly high likelihood that later on, you won't remember why you've calculated something a certain way.
   - Long calculations should be broken up into logical components of simpler calculations. This will avoid one long formula in Excel, making it easier to understand, test, and update, and greatly reduce the possibility of error. (See "How Long Should a Formula Be?" in Chapter 4 for an example of how trying to do too much in one cell can make a calculation extremely difficult to follow.)
   - A more detailed flowchart expanding out the calculations into subcomponents may be the clearest way to present the model's logic if a calculation is particularly complex. This can be done in Excel by taking an example piece of input data and documenting its flow throughout the calculations.

8. **Build outputs: summaries, charts, and reports.** Begin to summarise the calculation on the output page.
   - Continue to test and check for formula and logic errors at every stage of building.
   - Follow best practices as outlined above for outputs as well as calculations.

9. **Peer and client review of the draft model.** Now that the model's design, logic, and calculations have been determined, it is important to go through it with the rest of the team to ensure that the model meets its purpose. Get the team together, take a key input, and follow it through from beginning to end. The timing of this review is important, as it needs to occur after some of the model has been built, to allow the reviewers to check the expected outputs and how the model operates in practice; however, the model should not be finalised yet in case there are significant structural changes required as a result of the review.

   Not only must a model solve the problem for which it is designed; user acceptance of the model is also important. Clients (end users) must accept and understand the model. A walkthrough at this stage may assist to identify areas where corrections or modifications are needed and will also allow the user to become familiar with how the model is intended to work.

   Factors to be considered in the peer draft review are:
   - Walk through the calculations: Are they accurate at a high level?
   - Are the assumptions and source data clearly driving the output?
   - Does the model solve the problem it is being designed to solve?
   - Are the flow and structure easy to follow?
      Note that this peer review is your last chance to ensure that there are no formula or logic errors in the model prior to the formal quality assurance (QA) of the model. Modellers should be confident that their models submitted for formal QA are free from mistakes.

10. **Design sensitivities and scenario analysis.** Once the base model is completed and working correctly, you can add sensitivities and scenario analysis. The inputs for scenario analysis may not have been determined as part of the planning process, and now that the base model is complete, you will be able to test the inputs to see their impact. This may influence your decision as to what to show in the scenario analysis.

11. **Formal model QA check.** This final QA check of the model is a formal process and should not be confused with the continual testing and debugging that should have taken place during the model build. (See "Error Avoidance Strategies" in Chapter 4 for greater detail on the tests and checks that should be done by the modeller during the build process.) It is the modeller's responsibility to ensure that the model is accurate, robust, and operational. The QA process should not uncover formula or logic errors at this late stage, and discovery of such will raise questions about the competency of the modeller. The model's final QA testing process includes:
   - Stress testing the inputs with a wide range of values to check the inner workings of the model. This includes testing values at the extremes to ensure that the model processes the input as expected, especially where validation and protection are used. Also, test a wide range and combination of input variables, as some hidden bugs may exist in the calculations. Using 0 or 1

can help to highlight obvious errors, as the outputs should be simple. For example, a unit price of zero should generate a revenue of zero and if it does not, you'll need to investigate why not.

- Check that Excel errors such as "#DIV/0!" have not been triggered by entering zeros or other invalid data as inputs.
- Make sure that all inputs can still be entered properly. By applying protection to a model, a modeller can inadvertently cause switches and drop-downs to stop working. If protection is applied, additional testing and checking will need to be carried out.
- Check the sensitivity of outputs (dependent variables) to changes in the inputs (independent variables). Part of the QA process should be to check that the direction and magnitude of the change are in accordance with how you logically expect the outputs to behave.
- Check all documentation for spelling, grammar, colour coding consistency, and presentation.
- As the model goes through several iterations, it's common to find that redundant calculations are included even though they are no longer useful or applicable to the model. Tracing dependents is useful for identifying input data that is not being used.

12. **Maintain the model.** Once a model is completed and provided to the users, it is fairly likely that at some point—weeks, months, or years after the model has been completed—maintenance or updating of the model will need to be undertaken. If it's simply to change inputs, this can be done by the user, but if the change is major or structural, a model developer should be the one to make the changes.

Depending on the availability of resources, it is preferable that a member of the original model-building team undertake the update, but if best practices have been followed throughout the build process, if it has been well documented and built in a robust fashion, and if the modeller doing the update is well versed in financial modelling procedure, updating the model should not pose any problem.

When the model is updated or amended, especially if the change is structural, version control processes need to be followed to ensure that the correct version of the model is used. Below is some more information on how to document versions correctly.

INFORMATION REQUESTS

The collection of data is a critical part of financial modelling, as a model is only as good as its inputs and, in many cases, the inputs of the model rely solely on information from other parties, whether internal or external to the organisation. Therefore, the receipt of timely and accurate information from these parties is important. Sometimes as much time can be spent collecting data as actually building the model, and if this is an issue, you may consider creating a formalised information request procedure.

Larger organisations, particularly government agencies, often already have information templates in place for purposes such as compliance and monitoring, and will not encounter much resistance internally to their introduction. However, advice on how to go about implementing information requests is outlined in the following:

- Incorporate tables for key data and make provisions for executive sign off.
- Liaise at an early stage with the other parties about the information requested and its purpose. Different departments and other companies have different information systems, and so the form in which data is available may differ. Work closely with the other parties to communicate the purpose of the information, and to devise templates that facilitate easy collection of input data.
- Design the information request so that the data is provided in the correct format by using import and export sheets. This is useful for large data sets and, if used frequently, macros speed up the insertion of data into the model.
- Design the data collection sheets such that once completed, they can be fed directly into the model by copying and pasting or using links. No manual data entry should be required, to save time and reduce the possibility of error.
- Make clear what is expected in terms of data quality. It is possible that the information provided by other parties is not entirely accurate, so you may consider subjecting that information to internal QA processes. Normally, model input data is simply taken at face value, and the source documented in the assumptions, but a QA of the data will provide a greater degree of assurance that the data being input to the model is complete, accurate, and consistent. Make sure that the party providing the information is aware of this procedure in advance.
- Provide a timeline that is sufficient for the parties to respond to information requests. This will feed into the project plan as outlined above. The modellers will also need to allow time to check the quality and reliability of the information that has been submitted.
- Ensure consistency of information request templates with previous templates that have been issued and try to ensure consistency with previous requests that may have been distributed in the past.
- Pre-fill information request documents with existing information where available, as this will expedite the process.
- Even if the modeller sets up an information request in the correct format that is required to input directly into the model, there is always the risk that the person entering the data will insert or delete rows, columns, or formulas. It is advisable to protect the worksheets to prevent this from happening, as an extra row when copying, pasting, or linking data can be disastrous!

VERSION-CONTROL DOCUMENTATION

A new version of the model means structural changes to the design or new calculations. It should not be confused with changes to input variables such as those in blue font on the source data page. Changes to input variables are simply changes to scenarios or sensitivity, not a new version.

A version control log is usually located on the cover sheet of a model, although in particularly long or complex models it may warrant having its own worksheet tab.

It's important to remember that any new versions of a model subsequent to its being completed still need to go through the QA process. There is no point in creating a model that has been through the sign-off process only to make changes that do not meet the same standards.

Below are a few generally accepted guidelines to follow when creating a new model version.

- File names should end with a version number. For example:
  - [description of model] [date] [Version number].xlsx
  - HoneyCorp Repricing Model 16 July 2016 V1.xlsx
- If this is a sizable project and it's going through multiple versions, which need to be tracked, each model should contain a log (usually located on the cover sheet) that lists the original version of the model and details the calculation changes made to that version since inception. Information that needs to be included on the version control log is:
  - Version number and date.
  - Description of changes clearly detailing each change that was made for that version.
  - Where in the model the changes were made.
  - Who made the changes.
  - A mark to show that the changes have been through QA.
  - Any necessary comments explaining the changes (e.g., a change in cost structure or a new scenario needed to be built).

File Structure

Over the course of a complex modelling project with multiple versions, you need to put some thought into the file structure to ensure ease of finding the correct version. A modeller who picks up and works on the incorrect file can experience disastrous results and also waste a lot of time.

Your file directory might look something like Figure 2.10.

Keep a separate folder for each project. In this case, the HoneyCorp Repricing project has its own folder. Underneath you find:

- **Models.** A list of the model with version control nomenclature applied. If there are several models pertaining to the project, create subfolders in this

Organize ▼	Include in library ▼	Share with ▼	Burn	New folder		
▲ 📁 Financial Modelling			▲	Name		Date mod
📁 Business Cases				📄 HoneyCorp Repricing Model - 16 July 2020 - V1		17/08/20:
📁 Dashboards				📄 HoneyCorp Repricing Model - 19 July 2020 - V2		17/08/20:
▲ 📁 HoneyCorp Repricing				📄 HoneyCorp Repricing Model - 21 July 2020 - V3		17/08/20:
📁 Models				📄 HoneyCorp Repricing Model - 22 July 2020 - Exec Review		17/08/20:
📁 Project Planning						
📁 Source Data						
📁 Management Reporting						

FIGURE 2.10 Sample File Structure

section. You might delete older versions of the model (if you are sure that they are completely redundant) once the project is complete to save on file space.

■ **Project planning.** Documents relating to the project plan, resource allocation, and timelines.
■ **Source data.** All the details about where the data for the model came from. The models should be linked to this folder for auditability. Be extremely careful with linking if there are several versions of the source data files. Use the "edit links" function to manage the links between the files.

This sample folder directory is only a guideline and assumes a medium-sized financial modelling project in terms of size and complexity. Add as many folders as you need, but make sure they're well organised and easy to navigate so you can find the required information.

SUMMARY

In conclusion, considering the layout and design of a financial model is an important part of the model build. It takes a unique mixture of logic, clarity of thought, and graphic layout skills by the financial modeller to build a well-designed model, and this often proves to be difficult to implement in practice. Model design can sometimes be the most difficult part of building a financial model and it is, in my experience, one of the most difficult aspects to teach and learn. When building your model, pay close attention to the design layout and ensure that it is clear, coherent, and logically structured.

CHAPTER 3

Best-Practice Principles
of Modelling

The principles of best practice outlined here are for the purpose of reducing errors and making a model easier to read, audit, update, and use for its intended purpose. This chapter is by no means exhaustive, but outlines the most important principles in using Excel for business analysis and financial modelling. By following these key principles, your model is easier to navigate and check, and much more likely to be robust, accurate, reliable, and error-free.

DOCUMENT YOUR ASSUMPTIONS

Good assumptions documentation is one of the most important principles of best practice. It is impossible to check, validate, or use a model if you are unable to verify the integrity of the data sources or methods of calculation in the model. Your model design, layout, and structure can be perfect, but its validity is heavily reliant on the assumptions that go into it (i.e., garbage in, garbage out). The most beautifully structured model in the world is pretty useless if the assumptions that go into it are garbage.

Documentation of assumptions helps with validation and avoids misinterpretation. If there is any possible misunderstanding about why, how, or what the assumptions are in the model, make sure it's recorded in black and white on the assumptions page.

List assumptions on a separate page, clearly labelled. For a smaller model, you might decide to mix source data and assumptions together, or they could be separated in a large model.

The more detail, the better. If your assumptions are extremely detailed, you could have a section for key assumptions, where you summarise the important assumptions but leave all the detail in case it is needed.

Document source data and unique calculations as you go. Don't leave it all to the end and don't rely on your memory. Months later you or another modeller will have no idea why you calculated something a certain way. Make sure it's well documented.

LINKING, NOT HARDCODING

Financial models are, by definition, dynamic and changing, depending on the input variables, and they need to include links in order to facilitate this. This becomes particularly important when performing scenario and sensitivity analysis. Always link as much as possible in your model so that when the inputs change, the outputs also change. As discussed in Chapter 1, this is pretty much the whole *point* of financial modelling because, by definition, a financial model must contain links which change as the input variables change. Also, by linking, you can trace source data back through the links, which makes your model auditable, traceable, and easy to validate.

- When you link to external files, make sure that you use named ranges. (See "Linking to External Files" in Chapter 4 for greater detail on this.)
- There should be no hardcoding except for input variables unless referenced, or source data is listed, or it is otherwise *blindingly obvious* where you got the number from.
- Never use a value within a formula. The only exceptions are those things that are considered standard or commonly accepted and will not change, such as:
  - 24 hours in a day
  - 7 days in a week
  - 60 minutes in an hour

You may notice that many modellers put input variables in blue font. Whilst this is a bit old-fashioned, it's still quite standard practice and it acts as a signal to your user or another modeller that this is a hardcoded input variable that can change (i.e., *you are allowed to change this value*). The problem with blue font, though, is that you can't see it when there is no value in the cell, so many modellers use a beige or yellow background with blue font. The use of styles makes it much easier to format, and Microsoft has helpfully created a style called "input" in Excel that has become a fairly commonly used standard nowadays in financial modelling and seems to be used more frequently than the old blue-font standard. Styles can be found on the Home tab in the Styles group, and you can see how to find the input style in Figure 2.6 of Chapter 2. Also, see "The Workbook Anatomy of a Model" in Chapter 2 for greater detail on colour coding.

ENTER DATA ONLY ONCE

Source data should always be entered only once. For example, list inflation assumptions on the source data or assumption documentation page and, *every* time you use inflation in the model, reference back to that cell or row of cells. This will make the model easier and faster to update and less prone to error.

Never use a value within a formula. For example, **=IF(G$6=$E7,136800,0)** should have a link, not 136800 typed in. This means that you don't have to edit each cell when the value changes and makes the model much easier to audit. However, make sure that you do not link source data to a cell that itself has been linked to the original source. Always go directly to the source data. The result of this malpractice has been aptly termed "daisy chaining" in financial modelling best-practice circles.[1] It is an inefficient and error-prone (yet tempting!) practice and should be avoided when building financial models. It causes the link flow throughout the model to be a lot longer and more complex than it needs to be, and will cause errors if a section of the model is deleted.

AVOID BAD HABITS

Here are a few bad habits financial modellers can get into:

- **Not hitting the Enter key or the checkbox after editing a formula.** Don't just click elsewhere. It's a bad habit many people have, and one that can cause unintentional errors. See "Avoiding Simple Formula Errors" in Chapter 4 for more explanation on how this common habit can cause errors.
- **Highlighting the entire row or column instead of a range only.** Using the entire row or column is tempting, but it takes up too much memory and can really slow down the calculation speed. This is often done because the modeller wants to be able to add extra rows to the data; consider using Tables instead to avoid this problem. See "Structured Reference Tables" in Chapter 8 for how to create Tables.
- **Daisy chaining links throughout the entire model instead of linking to the source**, as described above.

USE CONSISTENT FORMULAS

In a table or block of data, the same formula should exist all the way across and down the entire block. Use mixed cell referencing to achieve this. (See the section "Cell Referencing Best Practices" in Chapter 5 for a practical exercise on how to

---

[1]FAST Modelling Standard, www.fast standard.org.

do this.) It saves time and avoids errors—and this practice is a keystone to good financial modelling technique. If you only pick up one modelling technique from this book, let this be it!

If you really need to change formulas so that they differ across adjacent cells, you can indicate this with a double border to show that the formula has been broken. This will help with auditing. See the section "Model Design" in Chapter 2 on colour coding for an example of how this looks.

- Avoid blank rows or columns in data blocks where possible, as this can cause problems with sorting, filters, and PivotTables.
- If sheets are similar, use a template where possible and copy the same sheet. Then when you need to update it, group the sheets to make global changes.
- Try not to use macros to perform lengthy calculations or manipulations, because this reduces transparency. Only in limited areas, such as goal seek on the scenario generation page, should macros be used, and these instances should be clearly documented.

FORMAT AND LABEL CLEARLY

Formatting and labelling in a model will reduce error and make your model easier to understand. It sounds simple, but, like mixing apples and oranges, mixing units is a common source of error in financial modelling. Clear formatting and labelling will avoid this.

- Format cells appropriately. Use symbols for currency (e.g., $, €, £, ¥), the percent symbol (%) for percentages, and commas for thousands. This makes your model easier to read and avoids mistakes and misinterpretations.
- Include a dedicated units column (e.g., column C) and make sure the units are entered into that column (e.g., $, 1,000s, MWh, litres, headcount, etc.).
- If you decide to round figures into thousands, show this clearly at the top of the row with a descriptive heading such as "Revenue ($1,000s)" to avoid confusion and misinterpretation.
- Column and row headings should have unit or currency headings and only contain one type of unit or currency.
- When building multi-sheet models, columns should be used consistently. For example, if building a model for the period 2021–2030, use column F on each worksheet for 2021, column G for 2022, and so on.
- It is often a good idea to reserve a column (e.g., column D) for constants that apply to all years, months, or days. For example, if the growth rate is 5 percent, have that in column D and then link all calculations to column D.

In general, these best-practice guidelines are really just common sense. Whilst some of them may seem tedious and overly prescriptive to the beginner, most of these points are for the purpose of reducing error and bringing increased robustness and clarity to the model. These practices are probably second nature to the experienced financial modeller, who will most likely already follow these guidelines by instinct.

METHODS AND TOOLS OF ASSUMPTIONS DOCUMENTATION

Many senior managers put a lot of faith in a business case, new venture, or decision supported by a financial model. I've seen many cases where managers will blindly decide to go ahead with a project because the financial model seems to indicate that they should. Unless the assumptions are clearly understood and listed beside the outputs of the model, the financial model should not be considered a definitive decision-making tool. Important decisions are made based on the outputs of the model, and it is critical to list the assumptions that have gone into the model. A model is only as good as the accuracy of the assumptions. It is important to mitigate your liability by documenting your assumptions thoroughly and adding caveats where necessary.

As documentation of assumptions is one of the key points of best practice in financial modelling, let's take a look at some commonly used methods and Excel tools for including this documentation in a model. All assumptions should be listed somewhere in the model, but key assumptions should be visible and easily accessible (e.g., via footnotes or statements). The definition of what is classified as a key assumption is somewhat subjective. As the modeller, you need to assess and identify the assumptions that are critical to the model. This could be something to which the model is very sensitive, and in this case, sensitivities should be performed. You may also choose to include the assumptions on which, in your opinion, there has been little research available and you are perhaps not entirely comfortable with the data. In such cases, this should be stated, and a recommendation to perform more research proposed.

General notes and instructions about the model should be entered on the cover page of the model, but notes relating to a certain worksheet should be placed in the top area of that particular worksheet. Most assumptions will simply be documented on the assumptions page using straightforward pasted text, but there are a few other sections of the model that may contain assumptions documentation as well, and there are several different methods and techniques for doing this. Greater detail on each tool is outlined in the following list:

- In-cell comments
  - Red triangle comment
  - Input message
- Footnotes
- Hyperlinks

- Hardcoded text
- Linked, dynamic text

In-Cell Comments

There are two different methods of creating in-cell comments: the ordinary comment with the red triangle or purple shape in the corner (which I will continue to call red triangle comments, as Excel rather unhelpfully simply calls them "comments"), and the less commonly used data validation input message.

Documentation of assumptions using in-cell comments is most appropriate for specific matters relating to only one cell or set of calculations, as they can be viewed only in a single cell. These are useful for communicating details to another modeller about specific calculation details, as they will be shown only on the soft copy of the model. More wide-ranging, generic assumptions should be documented using other methods.

Useful comment entries would be sources or assumptions relating to the data in the commented cell. For example, the casual observer of a model may wonder why volume is so low at that time of the year. This can be documented with a comment as shown in Figure 3.1.

"Red Triangle" Comments

The most commonly used method is to simply insert a comment within the cell, as shown in Figure 3.1. If you are using Excel 2019/365 or later, you'll be able to

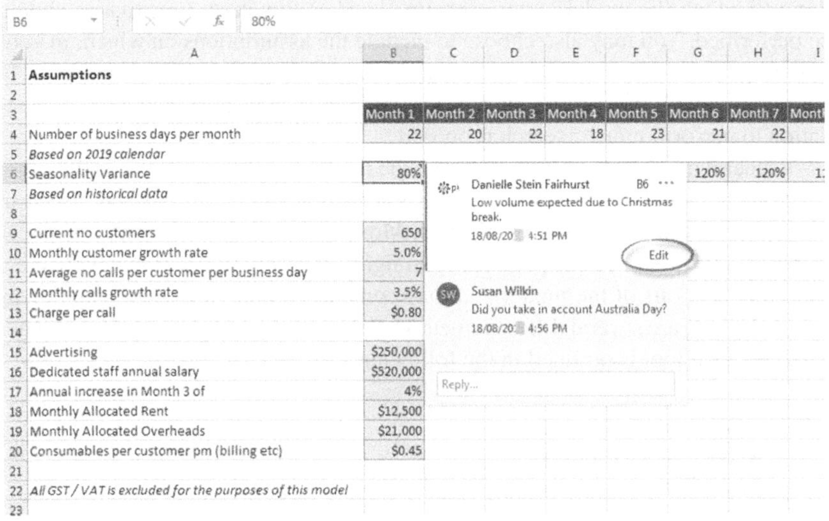

FIGURE 3.1 Assumptions Documentation Using In-Cell Comment

use threaded comments where a reply to the first comment can be made. For users of prior versions, only one comment per cell can be added.

HOW TO INSERT A COMMENT

Go to the Review tab and select the New Comment icon from the Comments section. Alternatively, you can right-click on the cell and select Insert Comment.

   To make a change, click on the cell so that the comment shows, and then hover the mouse over the comment until the Edit option appears as shown in Figure 3.1. In previous versions of Excel, right-click on the cell with the comment and select Edit Comment to edit. Similarly, right-click and select Delete Comment to delete.

When you open a model which includes these kinds of comments, you see the red triangle, but the comment doesn't appear until you hover your mouse over the cell.

   In-cell comments are a good way of documenting models, but they are not usually printed, so they are only helpful on a soft copy of the model. It is possible to print comments, but this isn't a great option, as they look messy and can cover other numbers or text in the model.

HOW TO VIEW ALL IN-CELL COMMENTS IN THE WORKSHEET

Go to the Review tab and select the Show Comments button on the Comments section. Unselect it to hide the comments.

Data Validation Input Messages   The less commonly used type of in-cell comment is to use data validations. These types of comments are more discreet, as they do not have the red triangle in the corner, and you don't see the comment until you actually click on the cell. See Figure 3.2.

   This sort of in-cell comment is especially useful for creating little instructions and warnings regarding input data to users, as they won't see it until they actually click on the cell to enter the data.

   The dialog box will look like Figure 3.3.

   Data validations are incredibly useful in financial modelling. For other uses, see the section "Bulletproofing Your Model" in Chapter 7. Table 3.1 is an overview comparison of the different types of in-cell comment methods.

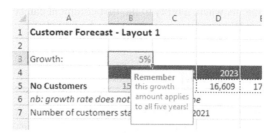

FIGURE 3.2 Assumptions Documentation Using Data Validation Input Messages

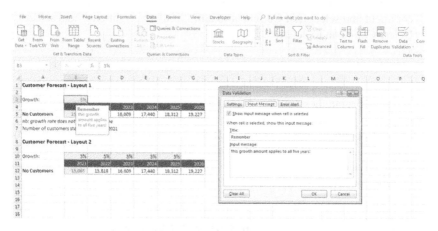

FIGURE 3.3 Data Validation Input Message Dialog Box

TABLE 3.1 Comparison of In-Cell Comment Methods

Red Triangle Comments	Input Message Comments
Can detract from the model, making it look messy.	More discreet; don't distract the eye of the user.
Can be viewed all at once.	Can only be viewed one at a time.
More obvious to the user.	Easily overlooked.
Most appropriate for details about a cell-specific calculation for another modeller's information.	Most appropriate for instructions relating to inputs for the user, as opposed to the modeller.

HOW TO INSERT AN INPUT MESSAGE

Go to the Data tab and select the Data Validation icon from the Data Tools section. Select the second tab entitled Input Message and type the message you wish to see. This message will appear only when the cell is selected.

My personal preference is to use input message comments wherever possible, as they are neater and cleaner looking. Remember, though, that if the cell isn't selected, the comment won't be viewed, so make sure that the comment is only cell-specific. More important, general assumptions and comments should use plain text or another method of documentation.

Footnoting

Unfortunately, the footnote tool in Excel is almost completely useless for assumptions documentation in financial modelling because:

- It cannot be linked to sections of the model, which greatly limits its usefulness.
- The modeller cannot see the footnote in the ordinary softcopy working view whilst building the model.

For these reasons, the footnote tool in Excel is really only useful for information such as file names, page numbers, print dates, and times. However, linked footnotes can be done manually by formatting the cell font to superscript.

Footnotes are highly recommended for noting sources of data, assumptions, and other important information. For an example, see Figure 3.4.

We can go further with this by making the assumptions documentation linked so that the numbers update automatically. How to do this is detailed later in this chapter, in the section "Linked Dynamic Text Assumptions Documentation".

⊿	A	B	C	D	E	F	G
1							
2	Staff Costs[1]	$53,230					
3							
4							
5	1. Staff costs include oncosts such as taxes, leave, training & recruitment.						
6							
7							

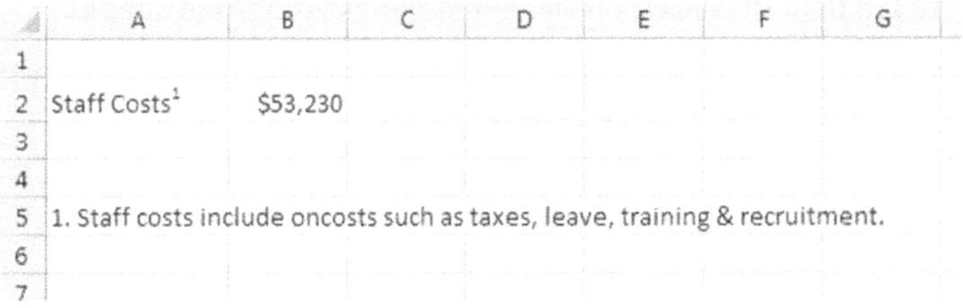

FIGURE 3.4 Example of Manual Footnoting in Excel

Hyperlinks

There are two different types of hyperlinks that are useful in financial modelling: URL web links and links to other files or locations within the model.

Cell and File Hyperlinks You can also create hyperlinks to source or other reference files and other sections of a model. They can aid in navigation of a long and complex model and are especially helpful for new users to find their way around the model.

HOW TO FORMAT TO SUPERSCRIPT

If you select the cell, the entire cell's format will change. Alternatively, you can highlight part of the cell's text, which will change only the highlighted section.

Right-click, go to the Format Cells option and choose the Superscript box on the Font tab.

HOW TO INSERT A HYPERLINK

1. On the Insert tab, select Insert Link from the Links section.

2. On the left-hand side of the dialog box, select Place in This Document (note that in Excel for Mac, you must instead select the This Document menu). Type the name or select the range you wish to link to in the Anchor text box.

3. Select the sheet and cell reference or named range of the hyperlink source.

4. You can change the Text to Display field at the top to display something like Go to Staff Salaries instead of Salaries!A45, for example.

Similarly, you can insert a hyperlink to another file in your source referencing as shown below.

Test this out on one of your models. This is useful if you obtained data from another file and want to document it as a source reference without retaining links in the model.

> **WARNING**
>
> Bear in mind that unlike formula links, hyperlinks do not move if the source cell moves. If you create a hyperlink to a cell on another tab (e.g., A1), and then insert a row above row 1, the hyperlink will not automatically update to A2 as a linked formula would.

For this reason, it is a good idea to hyperlink to a named range rather than a cell reference, as hyperlinks do not follow insertion or deletion of rows and columns, and this will make your model more robust. To learn how to create a named range, see the box on "How to Create a Named Range" in Chapter 5.

> **HOW TO INSERT A HYPERLINK TO ANOTHER FILE**
>
> 1. On the Insert tab, select Insert Link from the Links section.
> 2. Click on the Browse for File icon, which is located at the top right-hand corner. Select the file that you want to insert (note that in Excel for Mac, you will select the This Document menu, then select the file you want to insert. It can be any file type).
> 3. Hit OK, and this will create your hyperlink.
> 4. You can also create a hyperlink to another file or web page that does not show the full web or file address of the file. Follow the instructions above but change the Text to Display field at the top of the Edit Hyperlink dialog box such that it shows your desired text rather than the full file path or web address.

Web URL Hyperlinks Hyperlinks can also be used to refer to relevant Internet or intranet sites directly from your spreadsheet. For example, if an input assumption we have used in our model was obtained from the World Health Organization (WHO), we should put a reference to the WHO next to the assumption as shown in the "How to Insert a Website Hyperlink" box.

HOW TO INSERT A WEBSITE HYPERLINK

1. In the cell next to or beneath your assumption, type www.who.int/topics/research or copy it from the URL.
2. Make sure you hit Enter after you finish typing, and it will turn into a hyperlink.
3. Test it out by clicking on the link.
4. If you would prefer to show text such as Health Research rather than the web address, open the hyperlink dialog box as shown in the box above, and change the text to display to Health Research. This will display the text, but retain the website link.

Hardcoded Text

This method of assumptions documentation is not very sophisticated, but like with many things in financial modelling, a simple solution is often best.

It's fairly obvious in the calculations in row 5 of Figure 3.5 that the growth rate does not change over time, but the modeller is making it absolutely, explicitly clear by typing the hardcoded text below the table. There is no danger here that a modeller or user can overlook this assumption, whether it is being viewed in softcopy or has been printed out.

LINKED DYNAMIC TEXT ASSUMPTIONS DOCUMENTATION

Documenting assumptions liberally within your model is very important—however, it is very difficult to keep the documentation up-to-date when your model is dynamic and inputs are continually changing.

For example, in a business case, it would be useful to put the cost of capital next to the net present value (NPV), as this is a very important assumption. If we

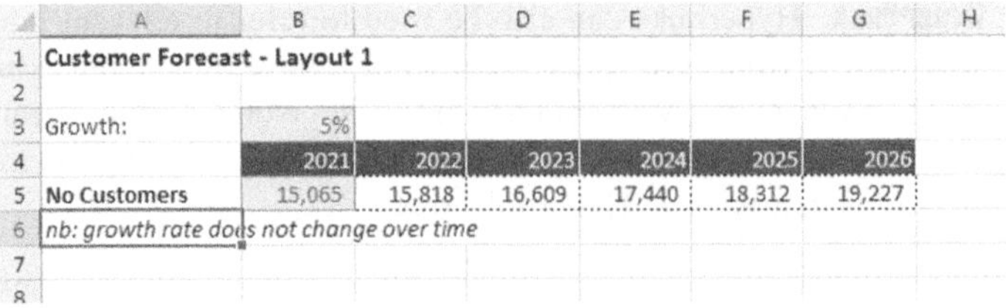

	A	B	C	D	E	F	G	H
1	Customer Forecast - Layout 1							
2								
3	Growth:	5%						
4		2021	2022	2023	2024	2025	2026	
5	No Customers	15,065	15,818	16,609	17,440	18,312	19,227	
6	nb: growth rate does not change over time							
7								
8								

FIGURE 3.5   Hardcoded Assumptions Documentation

type "Cost of capital is 12 per cent", however, it will be out-of-date as soon as we change the assumption, and there is a very high risk that we could distribute the model with incorrect assumption documentation. The answer to this is to use an ampersand (the "&" symbol). The CONCATENATE function will do a similar thing, but using the ampersand is quicker to build (and easier to spell!). You can join any cells together by using this symbol.

Practical Exercise 1

Let's try a basic exercise of seven steps to get the hang of how the ampersand works. This is demonstrated in Figure 3.6.

1. Practice this in a blank worksheet: Type **Hello** in cell A1 and **Robert** in cell B1.
2. In another cell, type the formula **A1&B1**, which will give you the result **HelloRobert**.
3. Now try adding some text. For example, =**A1&B1&"how are you?"** will give you the result **HelloRobert how are you?**
4. Next add a space between **Hello** and **Robert** like this: =**A1&" "&B1&" how are you?"**
5. Now add a comma after **Robert** like this: =**A1&" "&B1&", how are you?"**
6. Your sheet should look like the sample in Figure 3.6.
7. Now change the word **Robert** to **Mary** and see how your text changes.

Practical Exercise 2

1. Go to a model and practice creating a sentence using linked text to document an assumption.
2. For example, number of customers starts at 15,065 in 2021, as shown in Figure 3.7.
3. Practice changing either the date or the beginning number of customers and watch the text change.

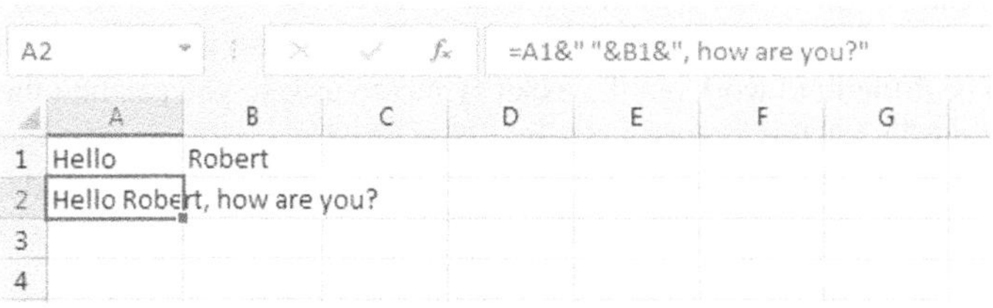

FIGURE 3.6 Linking Text Using Ampersand

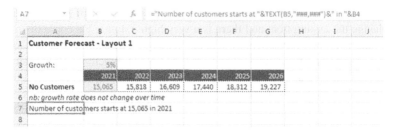

FIGURE 3.7 Linked Dynamic Assumptions Documentation

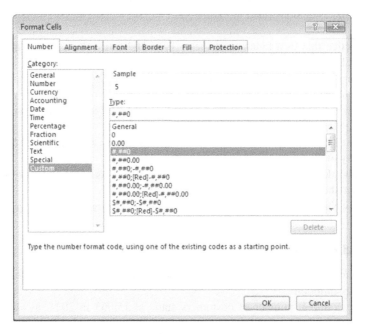

FIGURE 3.8 Format Cells Dialog Box

4. If you want to format the number so that it shows as 15,065 instead of 15065, you can use the TEXT function like this: TEXT(B5,###,###). Remember that this function turns the data to text, so it is no longer a number. Sometimes it can be difficult to work out the exact syntax to use, so you can find the format that the TEXT function requires by going into Custom Formatting, as shown in Figure 3.8, by right-clicking on a cell, selecting Format Cells, and Custom.

5. The total formula would be: **="Number of customers starts at "&TEXT(B5,"###,###")&" in "&B4**.

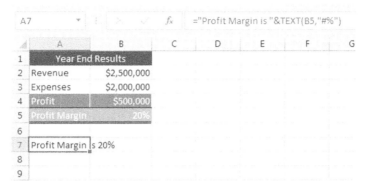

The completed version of this exercise can be found, along with the accompanying models to the rest of the screenshots in this book, at www.plumsolutions.com.au/book.

Practical Exercise 3

This seven-step method of documentation can also be used in reporting to create commentary on outputs. This commentary can then easily be copied to Word or PowerPoint.

1. Create a simple calculation on a new worksheet as shown in Figure 3.9.
2. The formula in cell B4 should be **B2-B3** and the formula in cell B5 should be **B4/B2**.
3. Now in cell A7 create a comment that says **Profit margin is 20%**. Remember to use the TEXT function to format it as a percentage.
4. Your formula should be **"Profit Margin is "&TEXT(B5,"#%")**.
5. Now try changing the revenue amount to $3 million. Your profit margin changes to 33 percent, and your text commentary still remains accurate.
6. If you would like the text to say **Profit margin is 33.33%** instead of **33%**, add some decimal places to your formula after the # symbol: **"Profit Margin is "&TEXT(B5,"#.##%")**.
7. Your sheet should look like Figure 3.10.

WHAT MAKES A GOOD MODEL?

A well-built model will have the following user-friendly features and structural attributes.

A7				f_x	="Profit Margin is "&TEXT(B5,"#.##%")		
	A	B	C	D	E	F	G
1	Year End Results						
2	Revenue	$3,000,000					
3	Expenses	$2,000,000					
4	Profit	$1,000,000					
5	Profit Margin	33%					
6							
7	Profit Margin is 33.33%						
8							

FIGURE 3.10 Practical Commentary Exercise (Completed)

User-Friendly Features
- Well-documented assumptions, so there is no possibility of misunderstanding or misinterpretation of the model.
- Explanation of the functionality. Many models lack this. What is the model for? How do I use it and where do I input data?
- Logical flow (left to right and top to bottom).
- Inputs and outputs, workings, and results are clear and easy to find.
- Built-in error checks and input validation such that the user is aware as soon as there is an invalid entry or calculations are not correct.
- Easy navigation to help users find desired information. Use a hyperlinked table of contents to help users find their way around if there are a large number of tabs.
- Instructions on how to use it if the functionality is not self-explanatory or obvious. These instructions could be dispersed throughout the document in the form of comments (my preference) or as a separate instructions page.
- Printability so outputs are summarised and fit onto printable pages, which are easy to read. Reports are legible and colours are not too dark.
- Formatting that is easy on the eye and consistent. The whole model should have the same look and feel, even if different modellers have built different parts of it.
- The user should be able to access summarised information as well as the detail. Each page should form the backup data and source information. Users should be able to print or distribute this page if further information is required.

Structural Features
- The only hardcoding should be the inputs and source data. The sources or assumptions for these must be documented. All other information is linked.
- Duplication is minimised.
- Names, formulas, and formats should follow a consistent convention.
- The model should be built in a modular form so that pieces can be removed and reused if required.

- The build is logical such that each topic is handled on a different section, and similar inputs or calculations are grouped together.
- The most efficient function is used.
- The model should be scalable so that greater detail or a large number of units, for example, can be added with minimal rework.

At www.plumsolutions.com.au/book, under the supplementary content for Chapter 3, you will be able to download a model assessment checklist, which will help you to assess how a model stacks up against financial modelling best practices.

Standards in Financial Modelling

There have been some good attempts in recent years to standardise financial modelling practice, with good reason. Excel is such a flexible tool that anyone can jump in and start creating the most frighteningly poorly designed and error-prone models—and they do! The FAST Modelling Standard is a philosophy that promotes FAST (Flexible, Accurate, Structured, and Transparent) design, and another methodology called SMART focuses on transparency, flexibility, and presentation. To download these standards, refer to the list of online resources that can be found at www.plumsolutions.com.au/book.

Whichever methodology you follow, using the key principles outlined in this chapter or in the above methodologies, your model will be easier to navigate and check, and much more likely to be robust, accurate, reliable, and error-free.

SUMMARY

By following the points of modelling best practice—such as assumptions documentation, linking, only entering data once, ensuring formulas are consistent, and avoiding bad modelling habits—financial modellers can be sure that their models are more robust, have fewer errors, and are easier to audit. One of the most important principles of best practice is to document assumptions, and this chapter lists different technical methods of assumptions documentation, such as comments, footnoting, hyperlinks, and linked text. We also explored the features and structural attributes of a well-built financial model.

CHAPTER 4

Financial Modelling Techniques

In this chapter, we'll take a look at some of the more frequently used techniques, as well as some of the common errors (and avoidance strategies), issues, and decisions a financial modeller encounters when building models in Excel.

As discussed in Chapter 1, in "Tool Selection", Excel is by far the most commonly used tool for financial modelling due to its wide acceptance and ubiquity in the market. However, it most certainly has its flaws, mostly to do with the prevalence of undetected mistakes in Excel-built models. Astute financial modellers need to understand the dangers of a poorly built financial model and the ease with which mistakes can be made.

THE PROBLEM WITH EXCEL

A well-built financial model or piece of analysis is an invaluable tool in decision-making and financial management, but all too often a wrong calculation can have disastrous consequences. Many executives and decision-makers rely far too heavily on Excel models—probably because they don't fully understand the risks involved.

There are many well-documented cases of high-profile Excel model blunders. Some of those documented by EuSpRiG, the European Spreadsheet Risks Interest Group,[1] include:

- The auditor's office that divided the growth from one year to the next by the second year, rather than the first year, specifically, calculated it using (Year 2− Year 1)/Year 2 instead of (Year 2−Year 1)/Year 1.

---

[1]European Spreadsheet Risks Interest Group (EuSpRiG), "EuSpRIG Original Horror Stories", available at www.eusprig.org/stories.htm.

■ Aspiring police officers who were told they had passed an exam only to discover that the administrators had incorrectly sorted the results to the names and the scores were mismatched.
■ A gas company submitted the wrong week's gas storage figures, leading to artificial inflation of natural gas prices and a lawsuit.
■ Shares of a self-storage company dropped when it was disclosed that it had overpaid its chief executive and another investor $700,000 each. It took more than six months to find and correct the error, which was due to using the wrong spreadsheet.

The list of Excel horror stories continues to grow, reminding us that simple mistakes in spreadsheets and financial models can cause companies to lose significant amounts of money—not to mention the resulting embarrassment.

Figure 4.1 is an example of one of many very simple and yet common formula mistakes often found in Excel models. In the figure, row 13 has been entered, but it has not been picked up in the summary total below it.

To avoid this error, when creating summary totals, leave an extra gap row between the last row of values and the sum formula. Therefore, when new rows are inserted, the summation formula will automatically include the newly inserted rows. This will minimise the chance of error when the model needs to be expanded. The use of error checks can also help to alert the user or modeller when this happens.

Excel is just such an amazingly flexible program that you can do anything with it; however, it is for this very reason that it is so prone to user error. So, what's the solution to Excel's error problem? It is extremely difficult to ensure an error-free

◢	A	B	C	D	E
1	**Stock Report**				
2	Make	Transmission	Stock		
3	BMW	Automatic	3		
4	BMW	Manual	2		
5	Chevrolet	Automatic	4		
6	Chevrolet	Manual	5		
7	Citroen	Automatic	1		
8	Citroen	Manual	1		
9	Daewoo	Automatic	8		
10	Daewoo	Manual	3		
11	Daihatsu	Automatic	4		
12	Daihatsu	Manual	5		
13	Holden	Automatic	6		
14		Total	=SUM( )		
15					

FIGURE 4.1 Common Excel Error in Modelling

model, but by employing certain strategies, you can most definitely reduce their number and impact. When building a model in Excel, it's recommended to proceed carefully and build and use it with caution.

ERROR AVOIDANCE STRATEGIES

There are certain strategies the modeller can employ *during the build process* that will help identify errors as they occur. Even extremely skilled modellers make mistakes all the time. A good, experienced modeller, however, will pick up these errors *as they are made* and avoid situations where mistakes are likely to happen.

Avoiding Simple Formula Errors

Silly formula mistakes are the easiest to avoid and the most embarrassing when they are not picked up. Commonly, it's the wrong cell being picked up or a dollar sign in the wrong place.

Use the Enter Key   Many Excel users get into the bad habit of clicking elsewhere in the page when they have finished typing a formula. This is a dangerous practice. Instead, always hit the Enter key when you've finished with a formula. Most of the time you'll get away with neglecting this, but every now and then it can cause problems, so you must get out of the habit.

In Figure 4.2 you can see that the modeller had his or her cursor in the middle of the formula, and by clicking on another cell has inadvertently changed the formula entirely.

As you can see in Figure 4.2, it's easy to accidentally pick up the wrong formula if your cursor happens to be in the wrong place. More importantly, however, the modeller is moving on to another cell without thinking about the formula that has just been written. You need to be deliberate about entering the formula and checking it before moving on to the next cell. When modelling quickly, it's easy to mentally move on to the next task before completely finishing the last one.

Once you've finished the formula, hit the Enter key and look at the formula. Does it look right? Does it look sensible? Is this what you intended to show?

	A	B	C	D	E
1	Borrowing	7.5%	8.0%	8.5%	
2	$250,000	=A2*C3B1			
3	$500,000				
4	$1,000,000				
5					
6					

FIGURE 4.2   Clicking Elsewhere Instead of Using the Enter Key Can Cause Errors

Check Your Work and Use the F2 Shortcut Key The worst kind of error is one that you are not aware of. Constantly performing rough checks on the results of the formulas as you build will minimise the chance of an error. Every time you hit the Enter key (and you *must* use the Enter key), check the result. Is the number what you expected? Before you add anything else to the formula, make sure the first part is right.

A lot of modelling is trial and error, and it's okay to make mistakes—just make sure you pick up mistakes before someone else does. **The only thing worse than finding a mistake in your model is *not* finding the mistake in your model, and your model being wrong.** Worse than that is having your boss find the error! There's no faster way to lose credibility as a modeller or analyst than having your mistakes pointed out in public.

Clicking in the cell or hitting the F2 key (as demonstrated in Figure 4.3) will also show the source cells or precedents of a formula. This is most useful if the source cells are nearby and on the same sheet. When you've copied down all the cells in a block of data, do a spot check with the F2 key to make sure it's picking up the correct cells. Note that this shortcut now works in Excel for Mac, or you can also use the Control+U shortcut on a Mac as well.

Have Someone Else Check Your Work Once you've checked and checked again, it's good to have your model reviewed or audited by someone else, as that person will bring a fresh perspective. Sometimes you've looked at your model for so

| CELL | ▾ | : | ✕ | ✓ | ƒx | =B13+B8 |

◢	A	B	C	D
1		April		
2	Admin			
3	Printing	$8,250		
4	Stationery	$5,280		
5	Staff Amenities	$2,530		
6	Bank Charges	$880		
7	Taxis	$17,160		
8	Total Admin	$34,100		
9	Property			
10	Rent	$123,600		
11	Electricity	$8,925		
12	Cleaners	$7,560		
13	Total Property	$140,085		
14	Grand Total	=B13+B8		
15				

FIGURE 4.3 Showing Formula Source Cells

long you just can't see the glaring error in front of you. Working in pairs can be very effective.

If the model is high-profile or critical to the business, it might be worth getting it audited by a model audit firm. There are many organisations that specialise in conducting professional model audits. This is really the best way to be confident that there are no errors and your model is working correctly.

> *Now that the reality of spreadsheet error has been established, the next step is to ask what we can do to reduce spreadsheet errors. Unfortunately, only one approach to error reduction has been demonstrated to be effective. This is code inspection, in which a group of spreadsheet developers checks a spreadsheet cell-by-cell to discover errors. Even this exhausting and expensive process will catch only about 80 percent of all errors.*[2]

Stress Testing   Test the technical workings of the model by stress testing it (i.e., varying the inputs to see how much the outputs change). Insert some ridiculous numbers into the inputs and see if the results are what you expect. The following are some stress tests you can perform:

- Set inputs to zero and check that the outputs respond as you would expect. For example, by setting price to zero, you would expect revenue to also be zero.
- If you add one unit, is the output increased by the value of one unit?
- Double your headcount. Do your staff costs roughly double?
- If you are indexing costs, try setting the indexation percentage to zero and see if the costs remain flat.
- If you double the pricing, does gross revenue double as well? If not, why not? The answer could be due to the effect of discounting or a complex pricing structure. Make sure that you get to the bottom of any anomalies and discrepancies.
- Chart metrics on a line graph such as cost per head, price per unit, cost to serve a customer, or other metrics relevant to your business. Look at the curve and make sure that you can explain each and every trend, spike, and downturn.

Thorough stress testing, along with scenario and sensitivity analysis, will provide your business case with the rigour and robustness to cope with various fluctuations in economic inputs. Greater detail on how to perform scenarios and sensitivity analysis is provided in Chapter 11.

---

[2]Raymond R. Panko, "Spreadsheet Errors: What We Know. What We Think We Can Do", European Spreadsheet Risks Interest Group.

Avoiding Logic Errors Compared to formula mistakes, logic errors can be more difficult to spot. They include things like incorrect timing, inserting the wrong inputs and source data assumptions, and using pre-tax instead of post-tax inputs, to name a few. Sometimes the mistakes can be a combination of both formula and logic errors, and we need to diligently guard against both types of errors.

Validate Your Assumptions A model is only as good as the accuracy of the assumptions. The phrase "garbage in, garbage out" has never been more relevant than in the context of financial modelling. Even the most beautifully built, best-designed model will be completely worthless if the assumptions that go into it are not validated. This is one of the most important points of financial modelling best practice, and different technical assumptions documentation methods are detailed in Chapter 3, under "Methods and Tools of Assumptions Documentation".

Important decisions are made based on the outputs of the model, and it is absolutely critical to list clearly (and often painstakingly) the assumptions that have gone into the model. While a good model can aid your business or decision-making process significantly, it's important to remember that models are only as good as the data they contain, and the answer they produce should most certainly not be taken at face value. When presented with a model, a smart manager or decision-maker will query all the assumptions, and the way it's built.

As a financial modeller, ensure that all the assumptions have been validated to the best of your ability. Document clearly where the numbers came from so that there can be *no possible misinterpretation* of the assumptions you have used; the assumptions can then be revisited and possibly revised at a later date.

Document Your Methodology Using a flowchart format, document the inflows and outflows of your data within the model. This helps to check your logic but is also useful in explaining the methodology of your model to other people.

For example, you can calculate the customer acquisition of a business case using the following methodology. If you start with the total population, apply the number of pet owners and then a take-up rate, you get the number of acquired customers. This methodology can be documented as in Figure 4.4.

Use Models in the Right Context Some managers treat models as though they are able to produce the answer to all their business decisions and solve all their business problems. It's absolutely terrifying to see the blind faith that many managers have in their financial models. Anyone with any real experience in model building will appreciate how *incredibly easy* it is to get a dollar sign in the wrong place and end up with the wrong result. Models should be used as one tool in the decision-making process, rather than the definitive solution.

All too often, back-of-the-envelope models turn into something more permanent. They'll then perhaps be used to determine pricing. Then used as a cash flow forecast. Then later, when it's budget time, the same model gets used for that

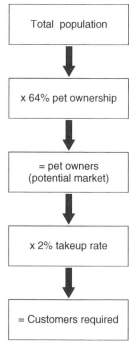

FIGURE 4.4 Methodology Documentation

too, and you end up with an important model based on hastily gathered assumptions and a flaky design structure. Models should always be built for a specific purpose. If you do pick up a model to use for another purpose, make sure you understand the model fully before making any changes. See "Rebuilding an Inherited Model" in Chapter 10 for more information on how to take someone else's model apart.

Sensitivities and Scenario Analysis Do lots and lots of sensitivities and scenario analysis. If the absolute worst happens, what happens to my bottom line? How sensitive is my model to changes in key assumptions? This will help to test the logic and robustness of your model, as well as the soundness of the business, product, or project the model is representing. At the minimum, you should do at least a best case, a base case, and a worst case.

This can often flush out anomalies in the model. Look carefully at the results of your scenario analysis. Is it what you would expect to see? Compare the sensitivity results side by side. If you increase the escalation factor from 2 percent to 3 percent, do costs increase by the same margin as if you increase escalation from 3 percent to 4 percent?

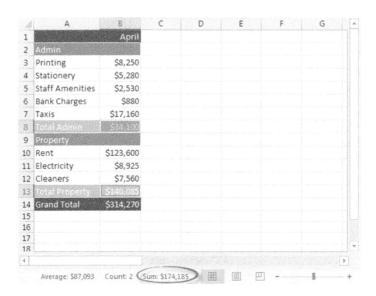

FIGURE 4.5   Sense-Checking Methodology Using the Sum Total

See Chapter 11 for more information on stress testing, scenarios, and sensitivity analysis in financial modelling.

Sense-Checking Methodology   Let's look at an example of using sense-checking methodology.

Figure 4.5 shows a pretty common one. Let's say you are adding up these totals and accidentally double-count by including the subtotals in your grand total. If you look at the subtotals you can see that the grand total should be around $170,000. Instead of doing this in your head, you could highlight the two subtotals using the Control key, and the total will appear at the bottom right-hand side of the screen, as shown by the highlighted section at the bottom of Figure 4.5.

Highlighting cells and checking totals using this method is a good way of sense checking for errors, and by employing a sense-checking methodology, you are less likely to let errors slip through the cracks.

HOW LONG SHOULD A FORMULA BE?

If you've been modelling for a while, you'll know that it's very easy to end up with a really long formula. Excel will handle them—as long as they are constructed correctly—but they can be pretty tricky to follow, especially for other people. Even if you've written a lengthy formula yourself, you'll struggle to follow it at a later date.

As with most concepts in financial modelling, a formula should be as simple as possible and as complex as necessary.

The way to make a formula shorter, of course, is to break it down into several steps, by adding additional working cells. Too much of this can make your model cumbersome; therefore, the good modeller needs to strike a balance between the following two extremes:

1. Making the formula too long and complex.
2. Having a model with additional working rows and columns.

If you do have a very long formula, one way to make it a bit easier to understand is to put the cursor in the middle of the formula and then press Alt+Enter to force the next section of the formula onto another line (note that this shortcut is Control+Option+Enter in Excel for Mac).

For an example of what this looks like, see Figure 4.6.

Of course, a formula of this length is not recommended. One of the new features in later versions of Excel is the expandable formula bar, but it is generally accepted best practice that a formula should not exceed about half of the width of the formula bar. This does not include file paths if the formula is linking to an external file that is currently closed, and therefore the full file path is included in the formula (as shown in Figure 4.7). Keep formulas particularly short when linked to external files for this reason.

FIGURE 4.6 Very Long Formula Broken into Several Lines

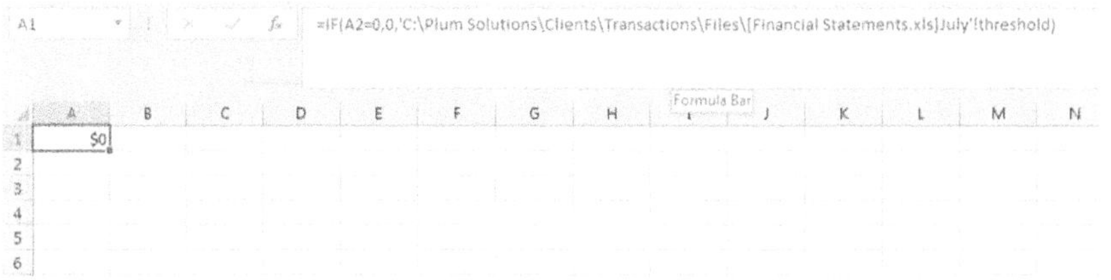

FIGURE 4.7 Formula Linking to a Closed External File

B9			f_x	=Assumptions!$B$9*(1+cust_growth)^(B2-$B$2)*B4*Assumptions!B6*Assumptions!B4*price				

	A	B	C	D	E	F	G	H	I
1	Telecommunications Product Projected Profitability								
2	Month:	1	2	3	4	5	6	7	8
3	Forecast no Customers	650	683	717	752	790	830	871	915
4	Forecast no Calls per customer per day	7.0	7.2	7.5	7.8	8.0	8.3	8.6	8.9
5	Forecast no calls with seasonality	5.6	6.5	7.5	7.8	8.8	10.0	10.3	9.8
6	Total no Calls per day	3,640	4,450	5,374	5,840	6,981	8,276	8,994	8,960
7	Total no Calls per month	80,080	89,005	118,221	105,117	160,565	173,804	197,876	197,122
8	Forecast Revenue (calculated in detail)	$64,064	$71,204	$94,577	$84,094	$128,452	$139,043	$158,301	$157,697
9	Forecast Revenue (calculated in one row)	$64,064	$71,204	$94,577	$84,094	$128,452	$139,043	$158,301	$157,697
10									

FIGURE 4.8   Revenue Calculated Two Different Ways

Figure 4.8 reveals two different ways of achieving the same result. The first example shows that revenue has been calculated by:

Row 3: Forecasting the number of customers.

Row 4: Forecasting how many calls per day each will make.

Row 5: Applying seasonality to these calls.

Row 6: Multiplying row 3 by row 5 to get the total number of calls per day.

Row 7: Multiplying row 6 by the number of days in the month to get the number of calls per month.

Row 8: Multiplying row 7 by the price to get the total revenue.

Alternatively, the whole calculation could be done in row 9 using the complex formula

=Assumptions!$B$9*(1+cust_growth)^(B2−$B$2)*B4*Assumptions! B6*Assumptions!B4*price

You could argue that this is a more succinct, sparse way of modelling. However, it makes it very difficult to take apart this formula for checking or debugging. Calculating the revenue step by step, as shown in the first example, is a much better way of modelling.

LINKING TO EXTERNAL FILES

One of the important principles in Excel modelling best practice is to link to the source data. Wherever possible, hardcoding should be avoided, and you should always try to link your cells so that as variables change, the results remain accurate.

However, if your source data exists in an external file, this can cause many problems, such as broken links, incorrect data, and error messages. In fact, some analysts avoid linking to external files at all costs. However, if done properly, external links add value to your models.

The following is a list of reasons you should link to external files:

- It's best practice to never hardcode when you could link.
- Your numbers are auditable. There's nothing more frustrating than trying to audit a model and finding hardcoded numbers with no annotation.
- The numbers will automatically update, so the model is less prone to error.
- It saves time because you'll spend less time entering and checking your data and more time analysing.

Table 4.1 shows the problems and solutions as to why many analysts don't link to external files.

Why You Should Use Named Ranges in External Links

One of the main issues with linking to external files is that if users insert or delete rows or columns in the source file, this can easily mess up the files that are linking to it.

Imagine you want to use a pricing threshold in your financial model, which is being generated in another model. Using best practices, you decide to create a link, rather than hardcoding the number. This will make your model more auditable, so that we can see exactly how that threshold amount was calculated. You create a link from your financial model to another source file, using the link

='C:\Plum Solutions\Clients\Transactions\Files\[Financial Statements.xlsx]July'!$C$46

TABLE 4.1 Why External Links are Not Used

Problem	Solution
The links break	Avoid moving files. Use Edit Links to fix. Use named ranges to minimise the number of formulas to fix when this does happen (and it will).
People move the data and my formulas are wrong	Use named ranges to refer to external files, which will minimise this. Use more robust formulas such as INDEX & MATCH.
The numbers keep changing	Yes, they should. Consider saving in one location to maximise version control.

If you are using Excel for Mac, your file name might look more like this, as it does not show the entire file path:

='[Financial Statements.xls]July'!$C$46

If both files are open at the same time, and you insert a row in the Financial Statements file, the link will automatically update from **$C$46** to **$C$47**. However, if your file is closed, your model will not update. This means that next time you open it, your model will be picking up the wrong cell!

The way around this issue is to create a named range in the source file (e.g., **threshold**) and then if that cell moves in the source file, the cell will still retain its name, and the formula in your model will still be correct.

See "Named Ranges" in Chapter 5 for how to do this.

='C:\Plum Solutions\Clients\Transactions\Files\[Financial

Statements.xlsx]July'!threshold)

The next time your model tries to update the link, it will look for the name **threshold**, rather than **$C$46**, and the integrity of the link will be maintained. This is why using named ranges when dealing with external links is considered best practice; it is a much more robust way of linking files together.

Dealing with Links and the Potential Errors They Can Cause

If you have linked two files together, you should not start moving either of the files around into other drives or directories. If you do, Excel will not be able to find the file that has been moved, and the link will be broken. If a file *has* been moved or had a name change, you can try to amend this by using Edit Links as described in the following text.

How to Edit Links   Click on Edit Links on the Data tab, in the Connections group. Use the Change Source button to tell your model the new location of the file it has been linked to.

TIP
_____

Another handy use for Edit Links is to break all links in a file. If you are emailing a file, it is not recommended that you leave links in it. You could paste the cell values one by one, but breaking links will convert every single formula in the entire file to their hardcoded values. Click on Edit Links, and then you will be able to select the external files and click on the Break Link button. See Figure 4.9.

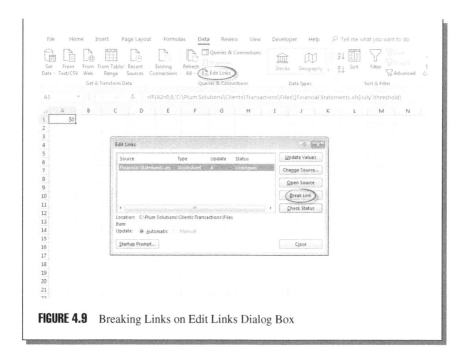

FIGURE 4.9 Breaking Links on Edit Links Dialog Box

Before you start linking workbooks together you need to think about what will happen to the workbooks in the long term. Will other people be using them? Will they be making copies? Will they be mailing copies to other people? If so, then perhaps, in that case, you should avoid creating a link to an external spreadsheet.

Linking Dos and Don'ts Here are some common dos and don'ts to keep in mind when linking:

- Do use named ranges when linking to external files.
- Don't email files that contain links. Save another version and use Break Links in such cases.
- Don't change file names and sheet names unless you really need to.

BUILDING ERROR CHECKS

Basic reconciliations can be built within a model, and a well-built financial model should have error checks included where possible so that the user or modeller can see at a glance if the formulas are calculating correctly. For example, when creating management reports, check that the sum of each individual department's report adds to the company-wide total. This can be done by inserting a simple IF function, or several other methods, as shown in the next section.

Note that error checks are **not a substitute for good practices** such as checking and auditing your formulas. Error checks are most appropriate for capturing errors a subsequent user has made; they are less likely to highlight a model-building error. See "Error Avoidance Strategies" in this chapter for greater detail on how to reduce errors when building models.

Error-Check Exercise

Let's say, for example, that you have the following cars in stock in a showroom. You want to know how many of each type of transmission you have in stock, so you have created a SUMIF formula to summarise how many of each type are in stock (see Figure 4.10). "Aggregation Functions" in Chapter 6 discusses how to create a SUMIF formula.

If someone is updating this model and accidentally types **Autmatic** in cell B3 instead of **Automatic**, your totals at the bottom will be wrong.

In cell C18, we can create an error checking formula that will alert us if something like this happens. There are two different formulas we could put in cell C18 that will alert us if the model is not balancing properly:

1. **=C17=C13** will return the value TRUE if they are the same, or FALSE if not. However, this is also subject to a false error, as shown in the following section.

C15   fx   =SUMIF($B$3:$B$12,B15,$C$3:$C$12)

	A	B	C	D	E	F	G
1	Stock Report						
2	Make	Transmission	Stock				
3	BMW	Automatic	3				
4	BMW	Manual	2				
5	Chevrolet	Automatic	4				
6	Chevrolet	Manual	5				
7	Citroen	Automatic	1				
8	Citroen	Manual	1				
9	Daewoo	Automatic	8				
10	Daewoo	Manual	3				
11	Daihatsu	Automatic	4				
12	Daihatsu	Manual	5				
13		Total	36				
14							
15		Manual	16				
16		Automatic	20				
17		Total	36				
18							

FIGURE 4.10 Summary Report

2. **=C17 − C13** is the easiest formula to build that would serve as an error check, as it would return a value in the case of an error. Although this would not necessarily alert the user immediately that an error had been made, it is certainly quick and easy to follow and for this reason, a fairly common error check favoured by many modellers. It's a good idea to format it using the Comma Style (found on the Home tab in the Numbers group) and then remove the decimal place and format it to red font. This will mean that the zero will not show if there is no error, and a red number will show if there *is* an error.

Allowing Tolerance for Error

=IF(C17<>C13,"error",0) is a superior error check, but on a small number of occasions, there can be an issue with this.

This formula usually works, but it can occasionally return a false error result, even though the values are the same. This is a bug caused by the fact that Excel carries calculations to 14 decimal places. After that, it truncates the value and can cause a minute discrepancy, which will report an error when it's only 0.00000000000001 off.

Therefore, to avoid this potential issue, you could use an absolute value formula, which would allow a tolerance for error. **=IF(ABS(C17-C13)> 0.1, "error", 0)** will allow the values to be off by 0.1 before it reports an error. If you use the ABS function in Excel, this will take the absolute value of the result, such that it does not matter if it is a positive or a negative number.

In Figure 4.11, if the sum of each individual item does not equal the grand total, the cell will return the word **error**; otherwise, it will show a zero. There are

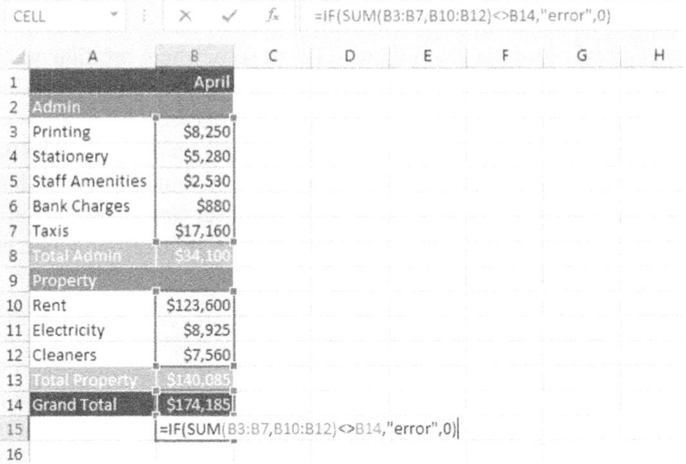

FIGURE 4.11 Error-Check Example

many variations of this formula, and I'm sure you can come up with various of them. Many modellers prefer to show the word **OK** if the numbers are right, and **Check** if they are not.

To make the error check even more prominent to the user, use conditional formatting to add a rule that makes the entire cell turn red if the error check has been triggered. See "Conditional Formatting" in Chapter 7 for how to do this.

Error-Check Alerts

Consider adding in an error checking page at the very back of your model that links through to all the error checks in the entire model. This page can be hidden, as the user does not need to see it, and the modeller can unhide it if necessary.

Create a summary cell that will identify, in a single cell, whether or not there are any errors in the entire model. This can be achieved with a COUNTIF formula like this:

$$=COUNTIF(\$A\$3:\$A\$21,"error")$$

See "Aggregation Functions" in Chapter 6 for greater detail on how to use a COUNTIF function. The completed version of this exercise can be found, along with the accompanying models to the rest of the screenshots in this book, at www .plumsolutions.com.au/book.

The COUNTIF function returns a one if there are errors. Now nest this with an IF statement, which will show the text **Errors exist within this model** if any of the error checks have been triggered:

$$=IF(COUNTIF(\$A\$3:\$A\$21,"error")>0,"Errors\ exist\ within\ this$$
model",0)

Now copy this formula (see Figure 4.12) to somewhere prominent at the top of each page (such as within the header) to create a global error check indicator, which will alert users to any error as soon as it is triggered.

Global error-check alerts are particularly useful for a modeller who has users working with the model regularly. The error check will alert the user that something has gone wrong in the model—usually the user has simply entered some incorrect data—and hopefully, the user will be able to correct the input, ensuring the continuing integrity of the model.

Avoid Error Displays in Formulas

Sometimes a formula may return an error message. Usually, you will want to know when a formula error occurs. But now and then, you may prefer to avoid the messages. For example, if you are calculating a percentage in a column and one of the entry fields contains a zero, you will get a #DIV/0! error. Or, if using a VLOOKUP

| A1 | ▾ | ⋮ | | fx | =IF(COUNTIF($A$3:$A$21,"error")>0,"Errors exist within this model",0) | | | | | | |

	A	B	C	D	E	F	G	H	I	J	K
1	Errors exist within this model										
2											
3		0									
4		0									
5		0									
6		0									
7	error										
8		0									
9		0									
10		0									
11		0									
12		0									

FIGURE 4.12   Error-Check Alert Formula

function, the criteria you have entered does not exist in the data, a #N/A error will appear. You can stop these errors from appearing by using an IFERROR function to check for an error:

=IFERROR(VLOOKUP("payback",Payback!B1: C109,2,0),0)

Note that many modellers do not agree with avoiding error displays and recommend that you always show errors. The reason for this is that using error suppression can mask other—genuine—errors, so use this function with caution.

CIRCULAR REFERENCES

If you have been using Excel for any length of time, you've probably come across a circular reference. If your formula is trying to refer to itself, you'll end up with a circular reference. A common (and easily fixed) cause of this is when a sum range includes the sum itself. For example, in the formula in Figure 4.13, cell B11 refers to cell B11, and this means that the formula cannot calculate properly and is returning a zero value. You can see in the status bar at the bottom where the circular reference resides.

You cannot rely on a model that contains circular references. The calculations may not work, and you can't be sure the other formulas are calculating properly.

How to Fix Circular References

In certain rare situations, you can have intentional circular formulas that you have deliberately allowed in your model (in which case you'll have to enable iterative calculations, as shown in the box below) but it's more likely that your circular reference is unintentional, so you'll have to get rid of it as soon as possible. If you

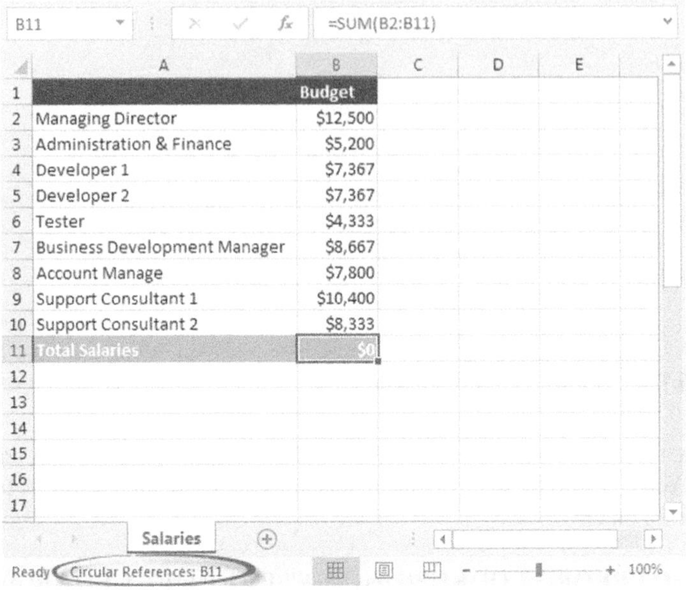
B11
=SUM(B2:B11)
A
B
C
D
E
Budget
1
2 Managing Director $12,500
3 Administration & Finance $5,200
4 Developer 1 $7,367
5 Developer 2 $7,367
6 Tester $4,333
7 Business Development Manager $8,667
8 Account Manage $7,800
9 Support Consultant 1 $10,400
10 Support Consultant 2 $8,333
11 Total Salaries $0
12
13
14
15
16
17
Salaries
Ready Circular References: B11
100%

FIGURE 4.13 Formula Creating a Circular Reference

leave it and try to find it later, or worse still, leave it for someone else to fix, the formulas can become more complicated, meaning that the circular reference can become further embedded in the model, making it more difficult to track down and fix.

You'll get a warning message as soon as the circular reference happens, so the simplest way to fix this is to stop and simply undo the last thing you did. You really just need to find the offending cell and remove the link. Sounds simple, but sometimes it's not that easy. The notification in the status bar in the bottom left-hand corner of Figure 4.14 may help find the cell causing the problem.

However, you need to be on the correct tab in order for this message to show. If you aren't sure which tab the circular reference is on, you need to hunt it down by going to each tab to see if it shows on the status bar. Alternatively, you can use the auditing tool to locate the circular reference, as shown in the box below.

17
Salaries
Ready Circular References: B11

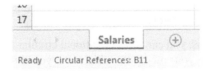

FIGURE 4.14 Circular Reference Notification in the Status Bar

LOCATING A CIRCULAR REFERENCE WITH THE AUDITING TOOL

On the Formulas tab, in the Formula Auditing group, click the arrow on the Error Checking button. Select Circular References, and this will show the circular reference in the model. Click on the reference to go to the circular reference. See Figure 4.15.

FIGURE 4.15 Finding the Circular Reference Auditing Tool in the Ribbon

In Excel for Mac, there was no circular reference tool in Excel for Mac 2011, but one has been introduced in Excel for Mac 2016, as shown in Figure 4.16. It now works in the same way as the Windows version.

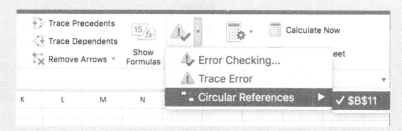

FIGURE 4.16 Finding the Circular Reference Auditing Tool in the Ribbon in Excel for Mac

You can move between cells in a circular reference by double-clicking the tracer arrows. Keep reviewing and correcting the circular reference until the status bar no longer shows the words **Circular References**.

Circular References in Interest Calculations

There are a few instances where you might wish to keep a circular reference within the model. A common reason for this is when you are calculating interest payments on a profit and loss statement, as shown in Figure 4.17.

When modelling financial statements, this circular reference can be avoided in a few different ways:

- Hardcode one of the inputs, such as the interest amount. This is not recommended, as it will impede the flow of numbers throughout the model.

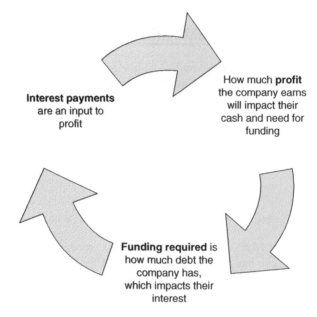

FIGURE 4.17   Circular Reference in Interest Calculations

- Use a macro to update the numbers, keep the links flowing, but paste the number to avoid the circular reference. This will work, but it needs some good testing to make sure it works properly. See "Macros" in Chapter 8 for points to consider before including macros in a financial model.
- Calculate the interest based on the closing balance of the debt amount in the previous period. This is most appropriate for statements modelled on a monthly basis, as the variance between debt balances from year to year can mean that the interest amount calculated using this method is less accurate. Although not perfect, this is still my preferred method for getting around the problem of circular references in interest calculations.
- Last, another commonly used method in financial statements is to allow the circular reference by enabling iterative calculations. The problem with this method is that it might allow other circular references to be enabled, which means that other parts of the model might not calculate properly.

Enabling Iterative Calculations

If you decide to enable iterative calculations, you must determine how many times the formula should recalculate. When you turn on iterative calculations without changing any of the defaults, Excel stops calculating after 100 iterations or after all values in the circular reference change by less than 0.001 between iterations, whichever comes first. However, you can control the maximum number of iterations and the amount of acceptable change.

HOW TO ENABLE ITERATIVE CALCULATIONS

Go to Excel Options by clicking the File tab and then select Options and click on the Formulas category. In the Calculation Options section, select the Enable Iterative Calculation checkbox. See Figure 4.18.

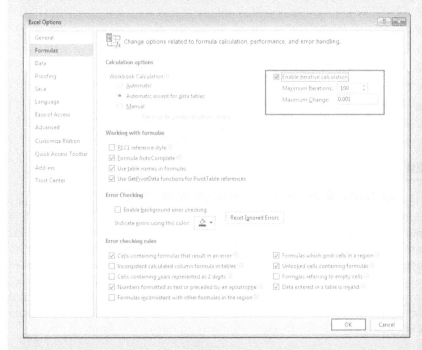

FIGURE 4.18   Enabling Iterative Calculations

Excel for Mac. Select Preferences from the Excel menu at the top (or hit Command+comma). In the Formulas and Lists section, select Calculation, then select the Use Iterative Calculation checkbox. See Figure 4.19.

(continued)

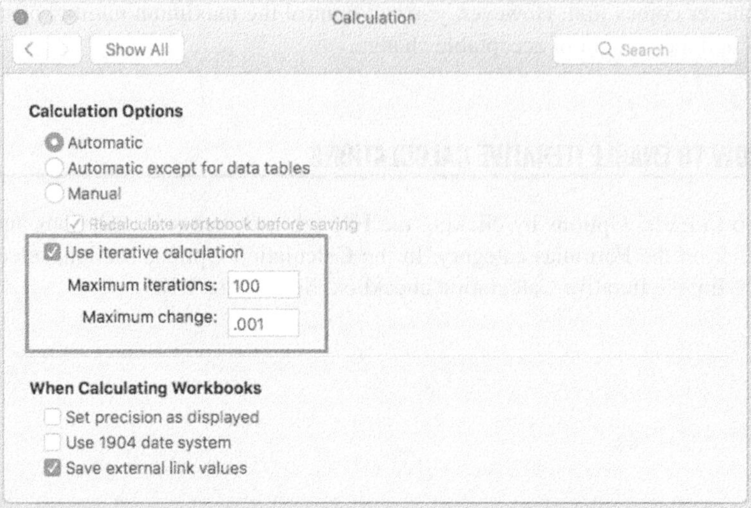

FIGURE 4.19 Enabling Iterative Calculations in Excel for Mac

SUMMARY

This chapter has discussed a collection of techniques and strategies commonly used in financial modelling. Those who have been using Excel for any length of time will know how easy it is to make a mistake, and what a huge effect this can have on their business models. Therefore, knowing and using strategies for reducing errors is an important skill for the Excel modeller to have. We also looked at how to avoid overly long and complex formulas, and how to dissect them if we are unfortunate enough to have inherited a model that includes overly complicated formulas. Linking to external files, building error checks, and dealing with circular references are also issues that are commonly encountered in financial models.

CHAPTER **5**

Using Excel in Financial Modelling

In this chapter, we take a look at some of the practical tools, functions, and formulas commonly used in financial modelling in Excel.

FORMULAS AND FUNCTIONS IN EXCEL

Excel now contains close to 500 different formula codes, called functions. The most commonly used function is SUM, which totals a range of cells. Most Excel users only use a very small percentage of the available functions, and many of them are irrelevant for use in finance and financial modelling. It is impossible to go over all of them here, but we will cover the ones that are going to be the most useful in using Excel for business analysis and financial modelling.

In most cases, you will find it easiest to use the Insert Function dialog box, accessible via the Insert Function button on the Formulas tab as shown in Figures 5.1 (for Windows) and 5.2 (for Mac). Alternatively, you can hit the little *fx* icon located to the left of the formula bar.

Note that the Insert Function dialog box (which used to be called the Function Wizard in previous versions of Excel) is called the Formula Builder in Excel for Mac; however, we will refer to it as the Insert Function dialog box in this book for consistency.

It's fair to say that some Excel users simply use the tool as a fancy calculator. If so, you'd be just using a formula in Excel, such as =**A1+A2** or =**452*12**. This is fine, but in order to build financial models, you'll need to do a lot more than that! There are many predefined formulas in Excel, such as IF, SUM, VLOOKUP, INDEX (and several hundred more). These are referred to as **functions**.

So, you could write a formula containing a function, like =**MAX(A1:B20)**, or you could just write a simple formula that does not contain a function, like =**A1/A2**. Many of us use the words *formula* and *function* interchangeably, but they do have slightly different meanings.

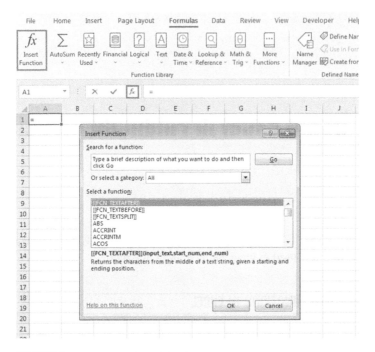

FIGURE 5.1   Insert Function Dialog Box

Because there are so many hundreds of functions in Excel, you should famil-iarise yourself with as many as possible, so that you know what is available.

For use in business and financial modelling, the most useful functions fall into the categories of logical, aggregation, lookup, and financial. The most commonly used functions in financial modelling are listed here:

- **Logical** functions (IF, AND, etc.) are used when you need to evaluate a condition. For example: "Shall we include tax in our calculation?" If the user enters **yes**, the calculation will include the tax; if **no**, it is excluded. **Aggregation** functions (SUMIF, COUNTIF, etc.) are helpful when there is a lot of data arranged either vertically or horizontally that must be added together.

- **Lookup** functions (HLOOKUP, VLOOKUP, etc.) are used when you need to look up a value to return a single amount.

- **Financial** functions (NPV, IRR, PMT, etc.) can usually be created manu-ally using a long and complicated formula, but the predefined function in Excel saves time and makes it much easier to calculate commonly used finan-cial calculations such as net present value, interest payments, or depreciation amounts.

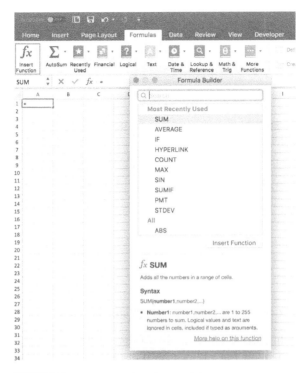

FIGURE 5.2 Formula Builder in Excel for Mac

Choose the Simplest Solution

There is a lot more to becoming a skilled modeller, however, than simply knowing lots and lots of functions in Excel. Often there are several functions which will achieve the same or similar results, so choosing the right function in the correct context takes practice. Use the simplest formula to perform the task you need it to do. Choose one that is not overly complicated and don't try to do too much in one cell. If it starts getting difficult to decipher, consider breaking the formula into several parts. See "How Long Should a Formula Be?" in Chapter 4 for an example of this.

As with most tools in financial modelling, you should choose the simplest option—not because you don't know how to do a more sophisticated function, but because you want to make the model as clear, simple, and transparent as possible. However, you still need to arm yourself with as many different functions as possible. Thus, the more you know, the more options you have available to you, and the more likely you are to find the best solution.

For example, Figure 5.3 shows the calculation of a compound growth rate when escalating the starting sales number by 5 percent to the power of the year.

FIGURE 5.3 Compounding Growth Rate Calculation Using a Helper Row

C5					f_x	=$B$5*((1+$B$2)^(C4-$B$4))		
	A	B	C	D	E	F	G	H
1								
2	Growth:	5%						
3		Actual			Forecast			
4			2020	2021	2022	2023	2024	2025
5	Sales	$5,015	$5,266	$5,529	$5,805	$6,096	$6,401

FIGURE 5.4 Compounding Growth Rate Calculation Without a Helper Row

In order to do this, we've had to insert a helper row to link to. This makes the formula easier to follow, but a helper row is distracting and makes the model look messy, so it needs to be hidden. The entire row cannot be hidden in this instance, so we'd probably change the font to a pale grey to make it less distracting.

Alternatively, we can achieve the same result without the helper row, as shown in Figure 5.4, by calculating it all in one cell. Instead of inserting 1, 2, 3, and so on across the top, we can do the entire calculation in one cell by looking at the difference between the years; in this case, 2020 minus 2020 equals zero, and 2021 minus 2020 equals one, and so on.

Using the second method, the value 1 in the helper row has been replaced by the formula **(C9-$B$9)**. This makes the second formula more difficult to follow, but the model is less cluttered.

This is an example of how a modeller needs to strike the balance between having a streamlined model, yet with formulas that are easy to follow.

Either of these methods would be perfectly acceptable, but as this is not a terribly long or complicated formula, the second option is preferable in my opinion because it avoids the addition of a potentially confusing helper row. For more detail on using different escalation methods in financial models, see the section on "Escalation Methods for Modelling" in Chapter 9.

EXCEL VERSIONS

There are currently still several different versions of Excel available in Microsoft Windows that modellers are likely to be using. Each time an updated version of Excel is launched, new features are introduced and subtle changes in the look and feel take place. The biggest change was way back when the big jump from Excel 2003 to 2007 occurred. The introduction of the ribbon and change of file types caused all sort of difficulties for heavy-duty Excel users, financial modellers included. In the versions since then, the changes have been somewhat less traumatic for users and in recent years Microsoft has been moving towards a subscription-based model, making the changes incrementally rather than all at once.

What is the Difference Between a Perpetual and a Subscription-Based Licence?

Historically, Microsoft has always sold a "perpetual" licence that is purchased outright and owned forever. With this type of licence, the user does not receive any updates to their software until the next version is released and installed. Large organisations with many users that have purchased perpetual licences often wait several years before upgrading—due to the cost—and are usually at least one or two versions behind. This means that at any one time there has always been a wide range of versions in use in the general community. It is not unusual for me to run a public training course and have three or four different versions of Excel being used by different participants in the class. As a consultant, I have always had to take care to find out the oldest version of Excel the client is likely to be using and make sure that I don't use any features or functions in the model that won't work in their version of Excel.

Users with perpetual licences understandably become impatient because they don't have access to new features they have seen or heard about, or because they cannot view or use the new features those with later versions have included in a model. When the upgrade finally does happen, the updates so eagerly anticipated by some can cause confusion and frustration for others, either because they dislike the sudden new look or can't find what they are looking for.

With subscription-based Office 365, updates are regularly released and any changes are gradual, which makes it easier for users to become accustomed to the differences. Organisations on the subscription model can choose their "update channel", which will determine how often updates are made, either monthly or semi-annually. In theory, all versions should be the same, but these differences in the frequency of updates mean that not all users receive the updates at the same time.

Whilst it is possible to purchase an Excel 2019 licence, Microsoft is *strongly* encouraging users and organisations to take up the subscription option, presumably because they prefer the recurring revenue and stable cash flow it generates. As more organisations move to this model, the compatibility problem of users being on different versions will become less of an issue and should make my life as a trainer and consultant a lot easier! To seal the deal, Microsoft announced in 2017 than those running Office 2016 on a perpetual licence will be unable to connect to Microsoft's cloud-based services after 2020, and I expect 2019 will have similar limitations. It seems likely that Office 2019 will be the last version that Microsoft offers as a perpetual licence.

Excel Version Compatibility

If you are building financial models or spreadsheets in Excel that other people with prior versions need to use, then you need to find out which version of Excel they are using and consider their version capabilities when building your models. For example, a model containing a TreeMap chart will simply not show at all in a version of Excel prior to 2016—in fact, all they will see is a white, blank square where the chart should be. Some of the biggest culprits are often new functions—it's very frustrating to build a model with a TEXTJOIN function, only to discover that the model user sees a #N/A error instead of the function result. For this reason, you'll save yourself some trouble when building a model if you don't include features in the first place that are not supported in the version of Excel in which it might be used. The problem is that we don't often know which features are included in which version.

To help you with this, here are some of the features that were introduced in various versions over the past decade or so.

Excel 2019/365   The following features were introduced in Excel 2019 or for those with an Office 365 subscription:

- **Custom visuals**, such as word clouds, bullet charts, and speedometers, which were previously only available in Power BI. (Note, as with many features of Excel, just because you *can* doesn't necessarily mean that you *should*.)
- Microsoft Office now has full **SVG graphics** support plus the Excel application has 500 built-in icons. These are now supported, which look great on dashboards and infographics.
- The **Insights** feature has been expanded upon. Click on a table of data and by selecting Insights from the Insert tab, several charts will appear on the right-hand side of the page to give you "insights" into your data. This is probably more of a data analysis tool than one for financial modelling, but still rather handy.
- **3D Models**, which are fun, but I struggle to find a use-case for them in financial modelling.
- You can create your own **custom functions** using JavaScript. It's always been possible to create user-defined functions using VBA, but JavaScript allows for greater interconnection. Again, this is probably not necessary for the garden-variety financial model.
- Excel connects to **Flow**, which you can use to create automated workflows to automatically collect data or synchronise data sources. This is particularly useful for automating data refreshes for models that need to be constantly updating, such as stock prices or currency exchange rates.

- Excel also connects to **Forms**, so you can have a nice form user interface, with a very easy-to-use tool, that can be shared through a link.
- Lots of **new functions**; most notably, IFS, SWITCH, TEXTJOIN, MAXIFS, and MINIFS.
- **Map & funnel charts**; the latter is just a centred bar chart, but map charts allow you to display data on a map using countries, states, provinces, and even zip codes/postcodes. You can either display numbers as a heat map or colour coded.
- Lots of new features in Excel's ground-breaking **Power Query data cleansing feature**, including parameters, conditional columns, and new transformations. Note also the name "Power Query" was changed to Get & Transform for Excel 2016 but has now **reverted to Power Query**, presumably to fit with the rest of the "Power suite": Power Pivot, Power BI, etc.
- Multiple users can edit at the same time with **co-authoring** if a file is stored on SharePoint or OneDrive.
- Multiple comments can be made in a cell with **threaded comments**. See the section "In-Cell Comments" in Chapter 3 for more information.
- If you regularly change your preferences for PivotTables, you can now assign a **default behaviour for PivotTables**.
- Previously, cells only contained a single, flat piece of text upon which formatting can be applied. With new AI-powered **online data types**, a cell could have a region or country value from which more information—such as the population, capital city, area, and many more details—can be extracted. The first two data types supported are Geography and Stocks, with more promised.

Note that you must have either Excel 2019 or Excel 365 to use the tools listed above. If a model containing any of these new features is opened in a previous version of Excel, in most cases you'll be able to view the feature, just not make any changes to it. With new functions, however, the formula will simply stop working if opened in a non-compatible version of Excel, which will undermine the functionality of the model—unless viewed using Excel Online. So, if you are building models in Excel that other people with prior versions need to use, then you need to consider the version capabilities as you build.

Excel 2016 Lots of new features were introduced in Excel 2016 and here are some of the most useful:

- **Forecast Sheet.** The ordinary FORECAST or TREND functions are very useful for forecasting along a linear trend in previous versions of Excel, but if you want to create a forecast based on seasonality, then it's quite a detailed process. The new Forecast Sheet feature makes it very easy to forecast based on historicals, including seasonality, and you can even apply confidence intervals to your forecast. See Chapter 6 for more detail on how to use this tool.

- **Additional chart types**—such as Waterfall Charts, Histograms, Pareto, Box Plots (Box & Whisker), TreeMap, and Sunburst.
- Better analysis in **PivotTables** and **PivotCharts**. PivotTables handle dates and times even better than they did before with automatic grouping, and you can drill down directly into PivotCharts with new plus and minus buttons.
- **Power Query (Get & Transform)** is now on the Data tab so no need to install it.

Excel 2013   Similarly, here are some of the most useful features that were added in Excel 2013:

- **Flash Fill** to learn the pattern of the data you're entering and complete it for you.
- **Quick Analysis** makes it easy to analyse your data with formatting and charts after highlighting with the mouse.
- **Chart Recommendations and Customisations**; data labelling using "value from cells" and the way that the chart is built changed. The only notable new chart type was the Combo Chart (a chart combining both a line and a column chart on two separate axes), which doesn't cause compatibility issues.
- **PDURATION()** returns the number of investment periods required for the invested amount to get to the specific value.
- **IFNA()** allows you to suppress a #N/A error only.
- **ISFORMULA()** will return the value TRUE if the cell contains a formula.
- **FORMULATEXT()**; when linked to a cell with a formula, it displays that formula. This can be a useful auditing tool.
- Single window per worksheet allows the same session of Excel to **show different files on multiple monitors** (my personal favourite).
- **New web-based functions** help in building links to web services, reading XML content, and connecting with online content.
- You can **create relationships between tables** for enhanced data analysis without having to consolidate all the information into a single table and create PivotCharts.
- **Slicers**, previously only available for PivotTables, became available in Excel tables as well.
- **A timeline** also became available for PivotTable. Similar to a slicer, the timeline allows filtering by dates.
- **Power Pivot** became a built-in feature of Excel 2013.

Excel 2010   The following features were introduced in Excel 2010:

- **Power Pivot** was first available as an add-in (see Chapter 1).
- **Sparklines** (see Chapter 7).

- **Slicers** in PivotTables (see Chapter 8).
- The **AGGREGATE** function.
- An overhaul of **statistical functions**.

Which Features Cause Compatibility Problems? Below is a summary of commonly used new features which were first introduced in different versions and should be avoided, depending on which version your user has. Of course, you don't need to worry about avoiding any of these if everyone who might possibly ever open the model is using the same version of Excel. If it's a financial model only used internally, and your entire company is on Office 365, then go ahead and use IFS or SWITCH to your heart's content. But if you have cause for concern regarding compatibility, then you should avoid new features which were first introduced in a version more recent than the one your model users are on.

Version	Feature

Excel 2019/365	- Custom visuals
	- New functions, such as:
	  - IFS
	  - SWITCH
	  - TEXTJOIN
	  - MAXIFS
	  - MINIFS

Excel 2016	- Forecast Sheet (because of the functions used, such as FORECAST.ETS)
	- New chart types, such as:
	  - Waterfall Charts
	  - Histograms
	  - Pareto
	  - Box & Whisker
	  - TreeMap
	  - Sunburst

Excel 2013	- Slicers were introduced to tables as well as PivotTables
	- New functions, such as:
	  - PDURATION()
	  - IFNA()
	  - ISFORMULA()

Excel 2010	- Slicers for PivotTables - Sparklines

As more users move towards Excel 365 subscriptions, compatibility issues will become less of a problem. For more detailed explanations of the changes between versions and how they impact model building, please see www .plumsolutions.com.au/book to download supplementary material in PDF format. This section also discusses the difference between using Windows and Mac for financial modelling.

This book assumes readers are using Windows Excel 2019, but in most cases, instructions for previous versions and Excel for Mac have also been provided.

HANDY EXCEL SHORTCUTS

Working in Excel—particularly for the purpose of financial modelling—can be very time-consuming; increasing your speed and accuracy will increase productivity significantly. Excel users just starting out with Excel would be very comfortable with using the mouse for navigation and editing purposes. However, with growing familiarity, the mouse is not the fastest or most efficient way of modelling. Excel offers a lot of shortcuts to tackle this problem, and as you become faster, you will find them very handy.

There are many advantages to using Excel shortcuts:

- **Ease of use.** Whilst intuitively it may seem that a mouse is a more comfortable option, it is a lot more comfortable for your wrist, arm, and shoulders to punch the keys on the keyboard than to align the cursor on the screen.
- **Easier on the body.** Given the natural placement of keyboard and mouse on any desktop, using the keyboard more often is less stressful on the body. Using the mouse constantly can cause stress on the wrists and shoulders. With the mouse, most users typically end up using just the wrists and index finger, which can cause fatigue and long-term problems.
- **Speed of execution.** Keystrokes are much faster than the mouse. To put this to the test, try creating a new worksheet in Excel using the mouse by clicking on File (or the Microsoft button in Excel 2007), then New—Blank Workbook. Alternatively, try the shortcut CTRL + N. There is a distinct improvement in speed with keystrokes over the mouse click.
- **Standard shortcuts.** Within the Windows environment, you will find that similar functions have the same shortcuts, so the expertise you develop can be applied to programs other than Excel. The shortcuts in Excel are generally common across all other Office suites and even other applications like browsers, Notepad, Paintbrush, and more.
- **No other choice.** There are some functions for which shortcuts are necessary to get the desired results, unless you want to insert manual edits. For example, when creating an array formula in Excel 2016 or earlier, the Control + Shift + Enter shortcut is the only way to get your array formula to insert correctly.

Windows Shortcuts

Table 5.1 is a small selection of some of the most common and particularly useful shortcuts that are invaluable when using Excel for financial modelling. Note that a printable list of these shortcuts is also available at www.plumsolutions.com .au/book.

TIP

Any command that is shown on the ribbon can be activated by clicking on the icon using the mouse, but can also be activated using shortcut keys. These are displayed when the ALT key is pressed, as can be seen in Figure 5.5. For example, Wrap Text can be selected by using the shortcut ALT, pressing H (not case-sensitive), and then W.

Also, note that the Quick Access toolbar (highlighted in Figure 5.5) can be customised to contain commands that are frequently used. In Figure 5.5, Paste Values and Print Preview have been added to the Quick Access toolbar, so that the user can simply press ALT, then 5 to Print Preview, hence saving three mouse clicks. The Quick Access toolbar options need to be manually customised, and this can be done by clicking on the drop-down menu to the right of the Quick Access toolbar, and then selecting More Commands.

FIGURE 5.5   Shortcut Keys Shown After Pressing the ALT Key

Note that if you are using a laptop, you will often need to hold down the Function (Fn) key for the function keys across the top of the keyboard to work correctly. For example, in Table 5.1, where it says to use F2 to edit and show formulas, on many Mac as well as Windows laptops, you'll need to hold down Fn + F2 for this shortcut to work. You can change the settings on your laptop to change this if you prefer your function keys to behave as standard.

TABLE 5.1   Useful Windows Keyboard Shortcuts for Financial Modellers

Editing	
CTRL+S	Save workbook
CTRL+C	Copy
CTRL+V	Paste
CTRL+X	Cut
CTRL+Z	Undo
CTRL+Y	Redo
CTRL+A	Select all
CTRL+R	Copies the far left cell across the range
CTRL+D	Copies the top cell down the range
CTRL+B	Bold
ALT+TAB	Switch program
ALT+F4	Close program
CTRL+N	New workbook
SHIFT+F11	New worksheet
CTRL+W	Close workbook
ALT+E+L	Delete a sheet
CTRL+TAB	Switch workbooks
Navigating	
CTRL+9	Hide row
SHIFT+CTRL+9	Unhide row
SHIFT+Spacebar	Highlight row
CTRL+Spacebar	Highlight column
CTRL+Minus sign	Delete selected cells
Arrow keys	Move to new cells
CTRL+Pg Up/Down	Switch worksheets
CTRL+Arrow keys	Go to end of continuous range and select a cell
SHIFT+Arrow keys	Select range
SHIFT+CTRL+Arrow	Select continuous range
Home	Move to beginning of line
CTRL+Home	Move to cell "A1"
SHIFT+ENTER	Move to cell above
TAB	Move to cell to the right
SHIFT+TAB	Move to cell to the left
ALT+Down arrow	Display a drop-down list

TABLE 5.1 (*Continued*)

Formatting	
CTRL+1	Format box
ALT+H+0	Increase decimal
ALT+H+9	Decrease decimal
SHIFT+CTRL+B	General format
SHIFT+CTRL+!	Number format
SHIFT+CTRL+#	Date format
SHIFT+CTRL+$	Currency format
SHIFT+CTRL+%	Percentage format
In formulas	
F2	Edit formula, showing precedent cells
ALT+ENTER	Start new line in same cell
SHIFT+Arrow	Highlight within cells
F4	Change absolute referencing ("$")
ESC	Cancel a cell entry
= (equal sign)	Start a formula
ALT+=	Sum selected cells
CTRL+'	Copy formula from above cell
F9	Recalculate all workbooks
SHIFT+CTRL+Enter	Enter array formula
ALT+M+P	Trace immediate precedents
ALT+M+D	Trace immediate dependents
ALT+M+A+A	Remove tracing arrows
CTRL+[	Highlight precedent cells
CTRL+]	Highlight dependent cells
F5+Enter	Go back to original cell
SHIFT+CTRL+{	Trace all precedents (indirect)
SHIFT+CTRL+}	Trace all dependents (indirect)

Mac Shortcuts

Almost all of the keyboard shortcuts that are available for Windows are available on the Mac version as well. If you are new to Mac, remember that in most cases, Command replaces Control, and Option replaces Alt.

Note that additional shortcuts in Excel for Mac may be created manually through System Preferences.

CELL REFERENCING BEST PRACTICES

Formula consistency is critical for fundamental best practice, both in financial modelling and any other sort of analysis using Excel, for that matter. In order to have consistent formulas across and down the block of data, you need to understand how cell referencing works. Whilst this is a very basic feature of Excel that is taught in introductory Excel courses, it is surprising how many modellers don't understand its importance.

The "$" sign in a cell referencing tells Excel how to treat your references when you copy the cell. If there is a dollar sign in front of a row number or column letter, the row or column does not change when you copy it. Otherwise, it does change.

Relative and Absolute Referencing

Cell references are relative, by default. This means that when you copy the cell, it will change. In Figure 5.6, we have created a calculation in cell B3 which refers to the price in cell B2. When cell B2 is copied down, the reference **=B2** will change to **=B3** and so on, down the row, which is not accurate.

However, if you want the formula to anchor itself to cell B2, you'd need to use absolute referencing. So, if you wanted to calculate the price below of $450 at various numbers of units, you'd need to anchor the cell reference to the price as shown in Figure 5.7.

This means that when you copy the formula down, as shown in Figure 5.8, the reference to cell A3 is relative, and changes to A4, A5, or wherever you paste it, but $B$2 remains anchored to cell B2 because it is an absolute reference.

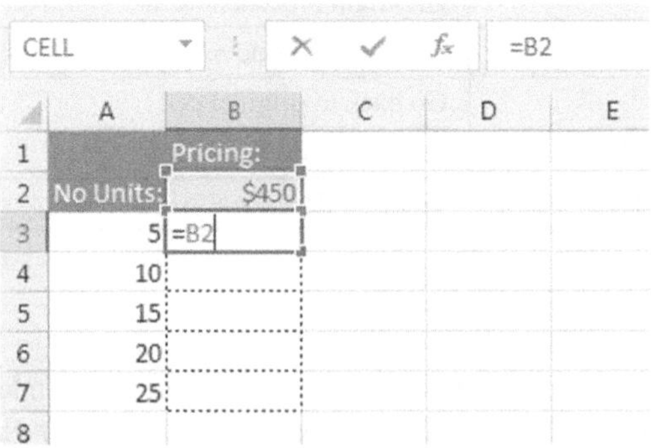

FIGURE 5.6   Relative Cell Referencing

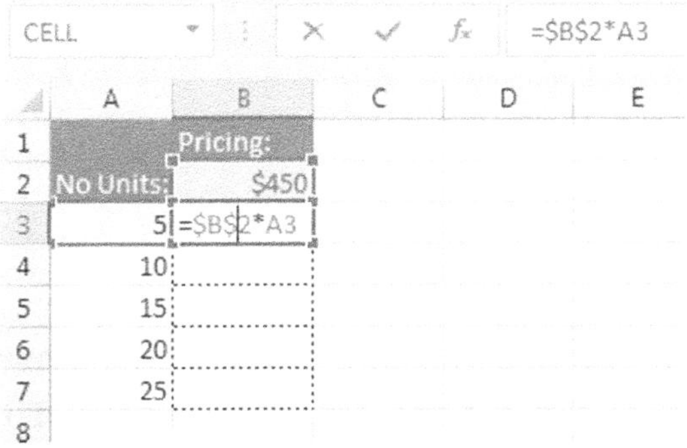

FIGURE 5.7 Absolute Cell Referencing

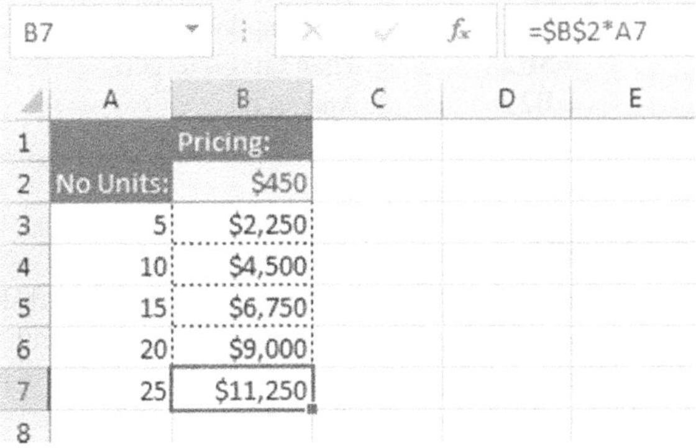

FIGURE 5.8 Copied Absolute Cell Referencing

Mixed Referencing

To illustrate further, suppose the following formulas are in cell B3 and you copy them to cell B4. Here are the results in each case:

=B2	copies as:	**=B3**
=$B$2	copies as:	**=$B$2**
=B$2	copies as:	**=B$2**
=$B2	copies as:	**=$B3**

The "$" sign anchors a row number or column letter when you copy it. You can anchor both the column and the row (this is absolute referencing), or you can anchor one or the other (called mixed referencing).

In summary:

=B2 is relative referencing

=$B2 or **= B$2** is mixed referencing

=$B$2 is absolute referencing

TIP

A quick way to fix a reference is to enter a reference like **=B3** and then tap the F4 key. Each time you hit F4, Excel cycles to another option. To illustrate:

=B2	Then tap F4 to get:
=$B$2	Then tap F4 to get:
=B$2	Then tap F4 to get:
=$B2	Then tap F4 to get:
=B2	And so on ...

Mixed Referencing Exercise

1. Type the table shown in Figure 5.9 into a blank Excel worksheet. You can create this sheet yourself or a template can be found, along with the accompanying models to the rest of the screenshots in this book, at www.plumsolutions .com.au/book.
2. In cell B2, create a formula, using absolute referencing, that can be dragged across and down the entire block to cell D4 in one action (without editing), hence showing the interest payable for different borrowing amounts at different interest rates.
3. Remember that if you want to anchor the row, the dollar sign goes in front of the row, and to anchor the column, the dollar sign should be in front of the

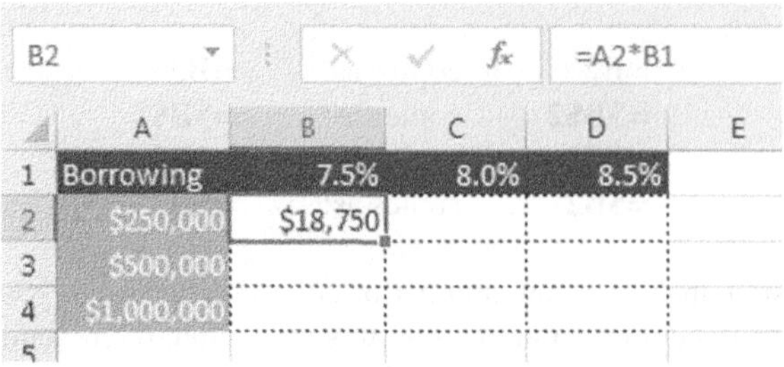

FIGURE 5.9   Mixed Referencing Exercise

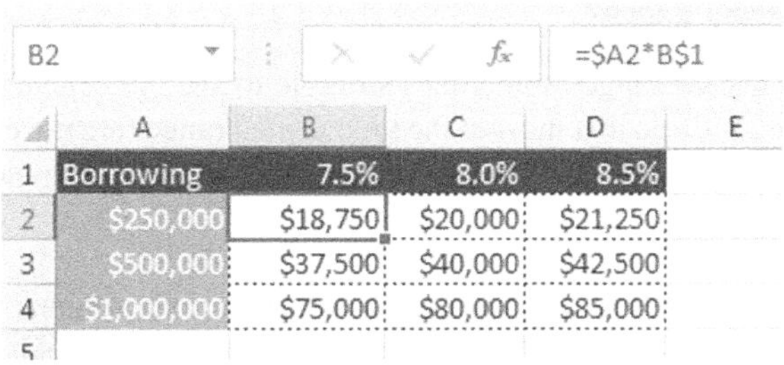

FIGURE 5.10 Answer to Mixed Referencing Exercise

column. Spend a few minutes on this before looking at the answer in the next step, and in Figure 5.10.

4. Your formula in cell B2 should look like this: **=$A2*B$1**. Copy your formula across and down the block of data so that it looks like Figure 5.10.

NOTE

Note that understanding mixed cell referencing is critical for good financial modelling practice and so it's important for a financial modeller to understand it. The fewer unique formulas in your model, the better. Formula consistency is fundamental to best practice for a number of reasons. Consistent formulas using mixed references are:

- Faster to build and more efficient
- Less prone to error
- Cheaper to audit

For more information about financial modelling best practice, see Chapter 3.

NAMED RANGES

Excel allows you to select a single cell or a range of cells, and give it a name. You can then use the name to move to the cells and select them, or include them in a formula.

In the last section in Figure 5.7, we used an absolute reference to anchor our formula to the consistent price of $450.

This cell is called B2, and this won't change; however, we can also change the name of it to something else.

Why Use a Named Range?

Those new to named ranges sometimes struggle to see the benefits of including them in models. It's true that most of the time named ranges are not entirely necessary, but there are some good reasons to use named ranges when building a model:

- **It makes your formulas easier to follow.** A formula containing lots of cell references can be confusing to look at and difficult to edit, but if the cell references are replaced by a range name, it becomes much easier to understand. For example, the formula **=SUM(B3:B24)-SUM(F3:F13)** could be expressed as **=TotalIncome–TotalExpenditure**.
- **It doesn't need absolute referencing.** By default, a named range is an absolute reference, so you don't need to add in any.
- **Drop-down lists with off-sheet sources.** You won't be able to create drop-down boxes with dynamic sources unless you use a named range. (See the section "Using Validations to Create a Drop-Down List" in Chapter 7 for a practical example of this.)
- **Linking to external files.** It's best practice to use named ranges when linking to external files. This means that when the source file changes, the data linking to it will automatically update.

HOW TO CREATE A NAMED RANGE

1. Select the cell, in this example B2.
2. Go to the Name box in the top left-hand corner. See Figure 5.11.
3. Type over the name and call it something else, like Price, and press Enter. Alternatively, you can select Define Name from the Defined Names group on the Formulas tab, but typing over the cell reference in the name box is faster.

Note that the name must not contain any spaces or special characters. For instance, if you want to call it Year 1 Price, you'd need to call it Year1Price or Year1_Price.

Named ranges don't necessarily need to be confined to only a single cell; you can also create named ranges for an entire range of cells, and these can be used in formulas. Simply highlight the range instead of a single cell and type over the name as shown above.

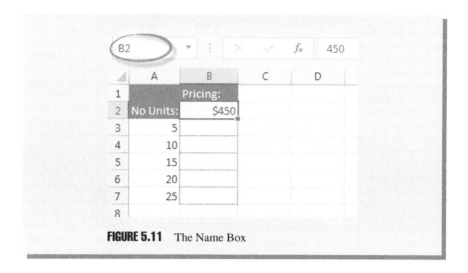

FIGURE 5.11   The Name Box

Finding, Using, Editing, and Deleting Named Ranges Clicking on the drop-down arrow next to the name will show all the defined names in the workbook (as shown in Figure 5.12). Clicking on the name will take you directly to the cell(s).

Excel will then move to and select the range. It doesn't matter what sheet you are in when you select the name. This can make finding your way around the named ranges in a model much faster.

Having created a range name, you can now use that name in a formula instead of cell references. For example, if you have created the range name called **TotalIncome** for the cell containing the total income result, and a range named **TotalExpenditure** for the cell containing the total expenditure result, you can create a formula =**TotalIncome** – **TotalExpenditure** (just by typing this text into a cell).

Another example. If you have created the range name **Costs** for all the cells in a column containing your numerical costs data, you can calculate the total costs using the formula =**Sum(Costs)**.

A cell does not need to be an input field in order to assign a name to it, although it often is in financial models. The cell can also contain a formula as well as a hardcoded input value.

Named ranges can be useful, but it's not good practice to have too many. They can be confusing, especially if you have not used a consistent naming methodology. It's also quite easy to accidentally name the same cell twice. So, in order to keep the names neat and tidy, you might need to edit or delete them.

FIGURE 5.12 Finding a Named Range Using the Name Box

Also, if you have added more data to a spreadsheet, and a range name no longer expresses the correct range of cells, you can redefine the named range.

HOW TO EDIT OR DELETE A NAMED RANGE

On the Formulas tab, in the Defined Names group, click on the Name Manager. Here you can add, edit, or delete existing named ranges.

In Excel for Mac, it is not called the Name Manager but you can edit names in a similar way by clicking on Define Name in the Formulas tab. You can also add comments to named ranges in Windows, which you cannot do for Mac, but otherwise changing a name works in the same way in Excel for Mac.

BASIC EXCEL FUNCTIONS

Now that we understand the basics of formulas and functions in Excel, it is time to start looking at some of the basic Excel functions. With financial modelling—or any other use of Excel for that matter—it is highly unlikely that the entire range of Excel functions will get used. However, the more functions we know, the better equipped we are to translate our business logic into a highly functional, dynamic, and robust financial model.

There are some common basic functions that are used frequently, and understanding them is important for any modeller. Some of the basic mathematical functions included in the Excel suite are: SUM(), MAX(), MIN(), COUNT(), and AVERAGE(). The function names are indicative of the functions they perform.

SUM()

This function is used to sum up a series of numbers. You can add individual cells, by separating them with commas, and you can also specify a range of cells. Figure 5.13 is an example of using a comma in the SUM function.

NOTE

You can use ranges as well as numbers in the SUM() function; just separate each entry by a comma.

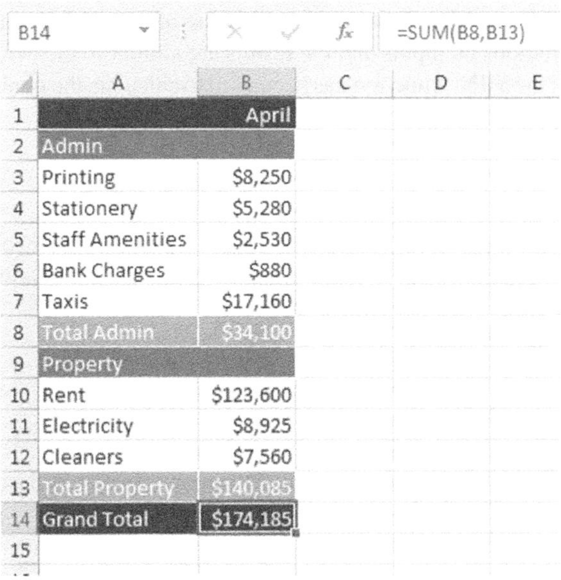

| B14 | ▼ : | × ✓ *fx* | =SUM(B8,B13) |

◢	A	B	C	D	E
1		April			
2	Admin				
3	Printing	$8,250			
4	Stationery	$5,280			
5	Staff Amenities	$2,530			
6	Bank Charges	$880			
7	Taxis	$17,160			
8	Total Admin	$34,100			
9	Property				
10	Rent	$123,600			
11	Electricity	$8,925			
12	Cleaners	$7,560			
13	Total Property	$140,085			
14	Grand Total	$174,185			
15					

FIGURE 5.13 Using the SUM Function

> **TIP**
>
> Select the cell at the end of the series of numbers you want to sum and click on the AutoSum button under the Editing section of the Home tab. The AutoSum button is found in the Function section of the Formulas tab in Excel for Mac. Also, try using the ALT+= shortcut instead of clicking the mouse. Note that this shortcut is Command+Shift+T in Excel for Mac.

MAX()

This function helps to identify the maximum value. The syntax for this function is very similar to SUM(); you can enter a range of cells, individual cells separated by commas, or a combination of both. This function will return an error if the cells you need to analyse have some text that cannot be converted appropriately. Similarly, if the cells do not contain any numbers, the function returns 0. See Figure 5.14 in which the maximum average monthly temperatures have been calculated for various cities around the world.

MIN()

This function is the inverse of the MAX() function, giving the least value in the list. The MIN() function can also use any combination of ranged series and individual cells. The limitations on inputs and the results are similar to the MAX() function. In Figure 5.15, the MIN() function has been used to calculate the minimum average monthly temperatures.

AVERAGE()

As the name suggests, this function calculates the average, or mean, of the numbers in the list. AVERAGE() is a very useful function in certain situations, as can be seen in Figure 5.16.

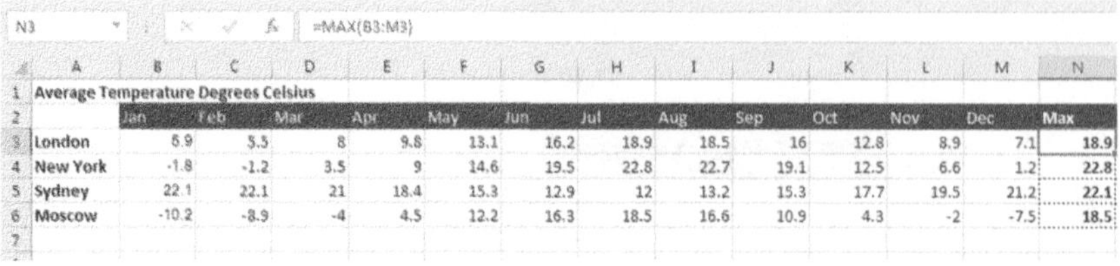

	A	B	C	D	E	F	G	H	I	J	K	L	M	N
1	Average Temperature Degrees Celsius													
2		Jan	Feb	Mar	Apr	May	Jun	Jul	Aug	Sep	Oct	Nov	Dec	Max
3	London	6.9	5.5	8	9.8	13.1	16.2	18.9	18.5	16	12.8	8.9	7.1	18.9
4	New York	-1.8	-1.2	3.5	9	14.6	19.5	22.8	22.7	19.1	12.5	6.6	1.2	22.8
5	Sydney	22.1	22.1	21	18.4	15.3	12.9	12	13.2	15.3	17.7	19.5	21.2	22.1
6	Moscow	-10.2	-8.9	-4	4.5	12.2	16.3	18.5	16.6	10.9	4.3	-2	-7.5	18.5

FIGURE 5.14   Using the MAX Function

FIGURE 5.15 Using the MIN Function

FIGURE 5.16 Using the AVERAGE Function

TIP

It is important to note that the AVERAGE() function only counts the cells with values. Make sure that your model recognises the difference between no value and zero. The AVERAGE() function will count the cells with value 0 but it will ignore the empty cells. In most cases, there is not a lot of difference between a blank cell and a cell containing a zero value, as most functions, such as SUM() for example, will treat them the same way, but when using the AVERAGE() function, it's important to distinguish the difference.

Combining Basic Functions

These basic functions can be used individually to calculate the respective results, but they can also be used in combination for various calculations. For example, if you want to find the maximum deviation (or range of values) in the values, you could subtract the maximum and minimum value. So you would have a formula such as **=MAX(B2:B8)-MIN(B2:B8)**, as shown in Figure 5.17.

Nesting: Combining Simple Functions to Create Complex Formulas

Excel allows you to include more than one function in a formula. For example, you can add two totals using the formula

$$=SUM(A1:A2)+SUM(B1:B2)$$

but this does not make it a nested formula.

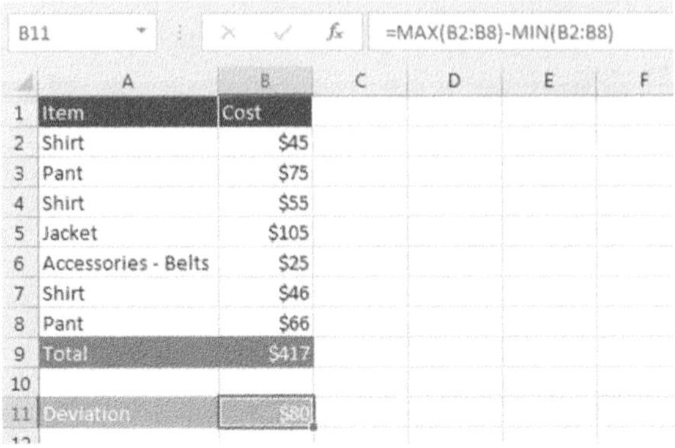

FIGURE 5.17 Combining Functions to Calculate the Deviation

A nested formula is one in which a function is included in the field of another function. This technique allows you to build more complex formulas. Fields appear in parentheses after the function. Some functions require several fields; some require only one. A field can be a number, a reference, or text (usually in inverted commas). If a formula has more than one field, they will be separated by commas.

Some examples follow. This formula has one field range:

$$=SUM(A3:A23)$$

This formula has three fields; a reference, text, and another reference:

$$=SUMIF(A1:A10,"ProductA",B1:B10)$$

Finally, we have an example of a nested function, containing another function in a field. This one calculates the average of two totals:

$$=AVERAGE(SUM(A3:A23),SUM(D3:D23))$$

See the section "Nested IF Statement" later in this chapter for more examples on how to build nested formulas.

LOGICAL FUNCTIONS

Logical functions, particularly IF statements, are very commonly used in financial models because they allow the user to turn on and off certain calculations, and to create scenarios and certain conditions or thresholds for calculations to maintain. Because of their common usage in financial models, we'll be focusing on logical functions for the rest of this chapter.

IF Statement

The IF statement takes three fields (Excel calls them arguments, but I'm going to stick with the term "field"):

Field 1 = the logical expression that is evaluated

Field 2 = the result if Field 1 is true

Field 3 = the result if Field 1 is false

The syntax, therefore, looks like this:

=IF(statement being tested, value if true, value if false)

The first field consists of a logical expression (i.e., something that, when evaluated, is either TRUE or FALSE). The expression in the first field is evaluated. If it is TRUE, then the IF statement returns the value of the second field. If it is FALSE, then the IF statement returns the value of the third field.

Consider the following example:

=IF(6>5 ,"greater","less than")

The statement being tested is TRUE, so the "greater" value is returned. Try this out, using the Insert Function dialog box, if you're new to IF statements.

NOTE

Using the Insert Function dialog box is highly recommended as it will help you figure out which inputs go into which field. To open the Insert Function dialog box, select the *fx* symbol to the left of the formula bar, or go to the Formulas tab and select Insert Function from the Function Library group. The easiest way to get to an IF statement, for example, is to type **=IF(** and then hit the *fx* symbol, or Control+A.

Consider another example:

=IF(4>5,"greater","less than")

The first expression is false, so the "less than" value is returned.

Practical Example 1 Let's look at a practical example of an IF statement in a financial model. In the valuation model shown in Figure 5.18, we have decided that if the value of the deal is greater than the cost of the deal, then we should accept

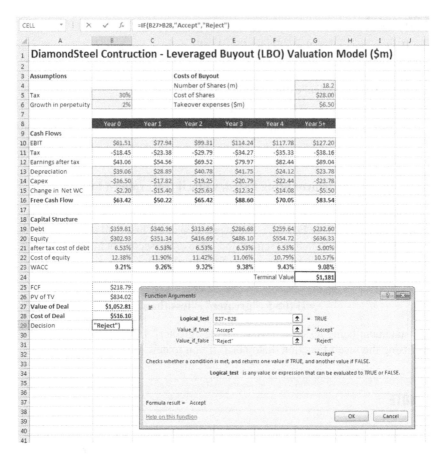

FIGURE 5.18 Using an IF Statement for Decision Analysis

it, otherwise, we should reject it. The syntax is =**IF**(**value of deal>cost of deal,** **"Accept"** , **"Reject"**), and because the value is greater than the cost, it will return the decision "Accept". If any of the inputs in this model change, such that the value becomes lower than the cost, then the formula will automatically show "Reject" instead.

Practical Example 2 Here's another practical example of using an IF statement in a financial model, but this time in a consistent block of data. If you had a list of projects as shown in Figure 5.19, and wanted to show these in a spend schedule, you could use the IF function in cell D3 to do this:

$$=IF(D\$2=\$B3, \$C3, 0)$$

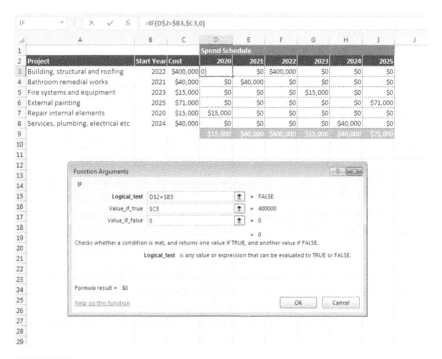

FIGURE 5.19 Using an IF Statement to Create a Spend Schedule

Because mixed referencing has been used, you'll be able to copy the formula in cell D3 all the way across the block of data. You can try this out for yourself by recreating this sheet or a template can be found, along with the accompanying models to the rest of the screenshots in this book, at www.plumsolutions.com.au/book.

NESTING LOGICAL FUNCTIONS

IF statements can also be nested, meaning that it is possible to have an IF statement inside another IF statement. The IF function is normally used to test a cell and perform two different actions, depending on the outcome of the test. But by nesting another IF function inside an IF function, you can test a cell and perform three different actions depending on the outcome of the tests.

For example:

$$=IF(6>5, IF(11>10, "both","second"), "first")$$

The first field is TRUE so the second field is then evaluated. Because the second field is also true, it returns its second field. Hence, the result for this formula is **both**.

Test this formula in Excel and enter criteria in the first field such that it returns **second** and **first**.

Whilst you'll still see this type of function used in financial models, note that nesting an IF using this method has now been superseded by the IFS function. See the "IFS Function" section in this chapter for further information.

AND Statement

The AND statement tests statements you enter and returns TRUE only if all the logical expressions are TRUE.

For example:

$$=AND(2<3,4<5)$$

Both of these fields are true, so the result of the formula will be TRUE.

For example:

$$=AND(2<3,4<3)$$

Only one of these fields is true, so the result of the formula will be FALSE.

The AND statement is most commonly used in conjunction with IF as a nested function. For example:

$$=IF(AND(2<3,4<5),"A","B")$$

Only if both of the fields are true will the second field be returned. If one or both is false, then the third will be returned.

The result of this formula is A, because both AND fields are TRUE.

OR Statement

The OR statement is very similar to the AND statement except that either field can be true, rather than both.

For example:

AND(2<3,4<3) is FALSE, because only one of these fields is true

However:

OR(2<3,4<3) is TRUE, because any one of these fields is true.

Nested IF Functions

In basic terms, a nested function is a function within a function, and the IF statement is probably most commonly used as a nested function. Prior to the introduction of the IFS function, modellers would often need to nest many IF statements together—in fact, it is possible to actually nest up to 64 functions within a formula model, however, this is not recommended, and *certainly* not good modelling practice.

Nesting IF and AND Functions A common nested formula is to nest an IF and an AND function together to test whether or not a certain date or value falls within certain parameters. Let's take a look at a practical example of a useful nested IF formula. You can create this sheet yourself or a template can be found, along with the accompanying models to the rest of the screenshots in this book, at www .plumsolutions.com.au/book.

In the example shown in Figure 5.20, we need to forecast the staff costs over the 10-year period, based on start date and end date. There is no BETWEEN function in existence (yet), but we can calculate this with a nested formula www .plumsolutions.com.au/book

Start by evaluating the start date only, ignoring the end date for now. By following these seven steps, let's build an IF statement that will show the cost only if the date in the schedule is greater than, or equal to, the start date of the employee.

1. In cell G7, add the IF function **=IF(G6>=E7,D7,0)** and the result will be $136,800.
2. Add in some cell referencing, so that you'll be able to copy it across and down. Your formula in cell G7 should be **=IF(G$6>=$E7,$D7,0)**.
3. Copy it all the way across and down the range G7:P26.
4. Select a cell and do a spot check by selecting a cell within the block such as cell I10 and using the F2 function key to make sure it's picking up the correct cells, as shown in Figure 5.20.

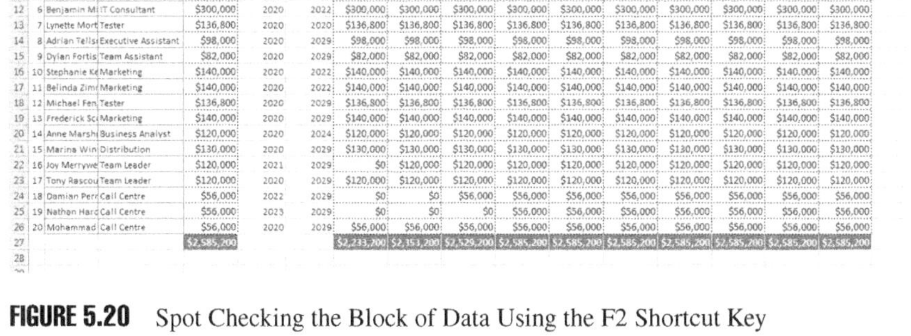

SUMIF =IF(I$6>=$E10,$D10,0)

HoneyCorp Business Case - Staff Costs

Projected Staff Costs

	Name	Position	Cost	Start Date	End Date	2020	2021	2022	2023	2024	2025	2026	2027	2028	2029
1	Jo Brown	Tester	$136,800	2020	2029	$136,800	$136,800	$136,800	$136,800	$136,800	$136,800	$136,800	$136,800	$136,800	$136,800
2	Henrietta Ste	Project Manager	$240,000	2020	2020	$240,000	$240,000	$240,000	$240,000	$240,000	$240,000	$240,000	$240,000	$240,000	$240,000
3	Susan Tyler	Business Analyst	$120,000	2020	2029	$120,000	$120,000	$120,000	$120,000	$120,000	$120,000	$120,000	$120,000	$120,000	$120,000
4	Mark Smith	Tester	$136,800	2020	2022	$136,800	$136,800	=IF(I$6>=$E10,$D10,0)	$136,800	$136,800	$136,800	$136,800	$136,800	$136,800	$136,800
5	Claire Doble	Business Analyst	$120,000	2022	2029	$0	$0	$120,000	$120,000	$120,000	$120,000	$120,000	$120,000	$120,000	$120,000
6	Benjamin Mi	IT Consultant	$300,000	2020	2022	$300,000	$300,000	$300,000	$300,000	$300,000	$300,000	$300,000	$300,000	$300,000	$300,000
7	Lynette Mort	Tester	$136,800	2020	2020	$136,800	$136,800	$136,800	$136,800	$136,800	$136,800	$136,800	$136,800	$136,800	$136,800
8	Adrian Tellsi	Executive Assistant	$98,000	2020	2029	$98,000	$98,000	$98,000	$98,000	$98,000	$98,000	$98,000	$98,000	$98,000	$98,000
9	Dylan Fortis	Team Assistant	$82,000	2020	2029	$82,000	$82,000	$82,000	$82,000	$82,000	$82,000	$82,000	$82,000	$82,000	$82,000
10	Stephanie Ke	Marketing	$140,000	2020	2022	$140,000	$140,000	$140,000	$140,000	$140,000	$140,000	$140,000	$140,000	$140,000	$140,000
11	Belinda Zimi	Marketing	$140,000	2020	2022	$140,000	$140,000	$140,000	$140,000	$140,000	$140,000	$140,000	$140,000	$140,000	$140,000
12	Michael Fen	Tester	$136,800	2020	2029	$136,800	$136,800	$136,800	$136,800	$136,800	$136,800	$136,800	$136,800	$136,800	$136,800
13	Frederick Sc	Marketing	$140,000	2020	2029	$140,000	$140,000	$140,000	$140,000	$140,000	$140,000	$140,000	$140,000	$140,000	$140,000
14	Anne Marsh	Business Analyst	$120,000	2020	2024	$120,000	$120,000	$120,000	$120,000	$120,000	$120,000	$120,000	$120,000	$120,000	$120,000
15	Marina Win	Distribution	$130,000	2020	2029	$130,000	$130,000	$130,000	$130,000	$130,000	$130,000	$130,000	$130,000	$130,000	$130,000
16	Joy Merrywe	Team Leader	$120,000	2021	2029	$0	$120,000	$120,000	$120,000	$120,000	$120,000	$120,000	$120,000	$120,000	$120,000
17	Tony Rascou	Team Leader	$120,000	2020	2029	$120,000	$120,000	$120,000	$120,000	$120,000	$120,000	$120,000	$120,000	$120,000	$120,000
18	Damian Perr	Call Centre	$56,000	2022	2029	$0	$0	$56,000	$56,000	$56,000	$56,000	$56,000	$56,000	$56,000	$56,000
19	Nathan Hard	Call Centre	$56,000	2023	2029	$0	$0	$0	$56,000	$56,000	$56,000	$56,000	$56,000	$56,000	$56,000
20	Mohammad	Call Centre	$56,000	2020	2029	$56,000	$56,000	$56,000	$56,000	$56,000	$56,000	$56,000	$56,000	$56,000	$56,000
			$2,585,200			$2,233,200	$2,353,200	$2,529,200	$2,585,200	$2,585,200	$2,585,200	$2,585,200	$2,585,200	$2,585,200	$2,585,200

FIGURE 5.20 Spot Checking the Block of Data Using the F2 Shortcut Key

Now that we've tested and checked this formula and are confident that it's giving the correct results based on the start date, we can go back to cell G7 and add in the end date. We want to test whether the current date (2020) falls between the start date (2020) and the end date (2029), so we can use the AND function to test if 2020 is greater than or equal to 2020 and also less than or equal to 2029:

$$=AND(2020>=2020,2020<=2029)$$

Of course, we aren't going to hardcode in the dates, so we'll use the cell references instead.

5. Try out this formula, in a blank cell, and you'll get the result TRUE because both of those statements are indeed true:

$$=AND(G\$6>=\$E7,G\$6<=\$F7)$$

6. Now we can go back to our original formula in cell G7, and replace the **G$6>=$E7** part with the entire AND formula in our existing IF statement to give the nested formula:

$$=IF(AND(G\$6>=\$E7,G\$6<=\$F7),\$D7,0)$$

7. Copy the formula all the way across and down the block of data. Your completed sheet should look like Figure 5.21.

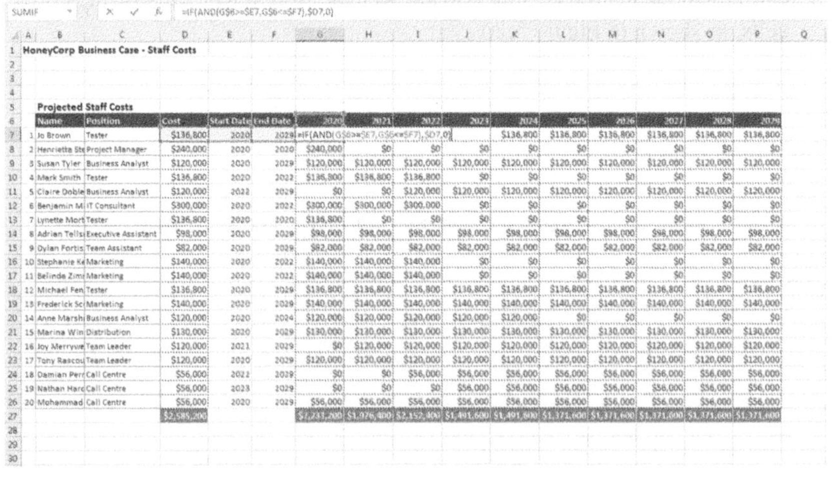

FIGURE 5.21   Completed Nested IF and AND Formula

Auditing a Nested Formula With most functions, we recommend the use of the Insert Function dialog box; however, the Insert Function dialog box does not easily work with nested formulas, and as your formulas get more complex, you need to know the syntax of the formula before attempting to nest it. Because an IF statement is one that is very commonly nested, it is important that you know the IF function syntax.

TIP

If you want to show the Insert Function dialog box on a nested formula, put the cursor next to the function you'd like to show in the dialog box. For example, as shown in Figure 5.22, if you select cell G7 and hit the *fx* button (or use the Shift+F3 shortcut), it will automatically show the IF statement dialog box. However, if you put the cursor with the AND section of the nested formula before pressing the *fx* button, the Insert Function dialog box will show the AND part of the nested formula, as shown in Figure 5.23. This can help when unpicking part of complex nested formulas.

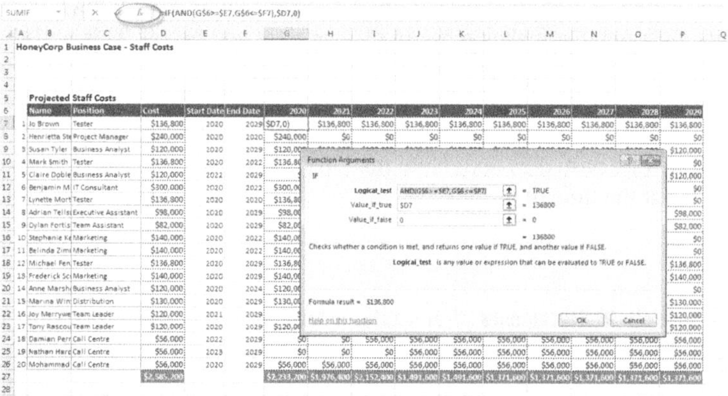

FIGURE 5.22 Showing the IF Insert Function Dialog Box on a Nested Formula

(*continued*)

FIGURE 5.23 Showing the AND Insert Function Dialog Box on a Nested Formula

---

TIP

When trying to take apart nested formulas, you can also highlight a section of the formula that makes sense in its own right and hit F9. This will show you the result of the logic test. For example, in the formula above, you could highlight the section **G$6>=$E7** and then hit F9, giving the result TRUE. Be sure to hit ESCAPE, not ENTER, afterwards; otherwise, the result will be pasted as text. Note that this option is not available in Excel for Mac at the time of writing.

Nesting Multiple IF Statements Let's take a look at another example of a useful nested IF formula. You can try this out for yourself by recreating this sheet or a template can be found, along with the accompanying models to the rest of the screenshots in this book, at www.plumsolutions.com.au/book. In the pricing table shown in Figure 5.24, the price varies depending on how many items are purchased.

If you bought 63 items, you can see that they would be $10.50 each. If you want to create an automatic calculation for this, you'd need to create a nested formula, starting with the following three steps:

1. Start with a basic IF statement. If your volume is less than or equal to five, the price is $15; otherwise, it's $12 (for now). So your formula in cell B8 would be =IF(A8<=B3,C3,C4). With me so far?

	A	B	C	D
1	PRICING TABLE			
2	Min Vol	Max Vol	Price	
3	-	5	$15.00	
4	6	50	$12.00	
5	51	150	$10.50	
6				
7	No Items	Price per item	Total Price	
8	63			
9				

FIGURE 5.24 Volume Pricing Table

2. Once we've got this working, we can make it more complicated. In another cell, say B9, let's do another formula, which will deal with the value if it is greater than five. Create the formula **=IF(A8<=B4,C4,C5)** in cell B9.
3. Once we've got both of these working, you can add them together. Go into the formula in cell B9; highlight and copy the whole formula except for the equal sign using a Control+C shortcut. See Figure 5.25.

4. Now hit Escape (the copied formula will remain on your clipboard), go back to your formula in cell B8, and replace C4 with the formula you have copied onto the clipboard. Do this by highlighting C4 and pressing Control+V.
5. Your entire formula in cell B8 should now be:
   =IF(A8<=B3,C3,IF(A8<=B4,C4,C5)).

	A	B	C	D
1	PRICING TABLE			
2	Min Vol	Max Vol	Price	
3	-	5	$15.00	
4	6	50	$12.00	
5	51	150	$10.50	
6				
7	No Items	Price per item	Total Price	
8	63	$12.00		
9		=IF(A8<=B4,C4,C5)		
10				
11				

FIGURE 5.25 Highlight and Copy IF Statement

B8		▾	⋮	×	✓	*fx*		=IF(A8<=B3,C3,IF(A8<=B4,C4,C5))		

◢	A	B	C	D	E	F	G
1		PRICING TABLE					
2	Min Vol	Max Vol	Price				
3	-	5	$15.00				
4	6	50	$12.00				
5	51	150	$10.50				
6							
7	No Items	Price per item	Total Price				
8	63	$10.50	$662				
9							
10							
11							

FIGURE 5.26   Completed Nested IF Function

6. Multiply your price by the volume in cell C8 so we know the total, using the formula **=B8*A8**.
7. Your sheet should look something like the sheet shown in Figure 5.26.

So, the following rules will apply for the formula in cell B8:

- If cell A8 is less than or equal to 5, the price is $15 each.
- If cell A8 is less than or equal to 50, the price is $12 each.
- If cell A8 is greater than 50, the price is $10.50 each.

Thus, the formula tests cell A1 to see if it is greater than or equal to five. If it is less than five, the formula will stop there and return the first *value if true*. If it is greater than five, however, it is then tested again to see if it is greater than or equal to 50. If it is, it will stop there and return the second *value if true*. If it is greater than five and greater than 50, only then will it return the *value if false*.

IFS Function   An easier way to complete this would be using an IFS function, which was first introduced in Office 365. Rather than breaking it down into several steps, using the IFS function is a much easier way to achieve this result, as it can be done in one step using the Insert Function dialog box. Unlike the nested IF function, where you need to build a separate IF function for each part of the formula, the IFS function allows you to evaluate each section individually within the dialog box:

1. Open up the IFS Insert Function dialog box by searching for it in the Formulas tab, or by typing **=IFS(** and then using the Control+A shortcut.
2. Evaluate the first part of the statement in the first field. We want to test whether the number of items (63) falls within the first tier, so enter **A8<=B3** in the

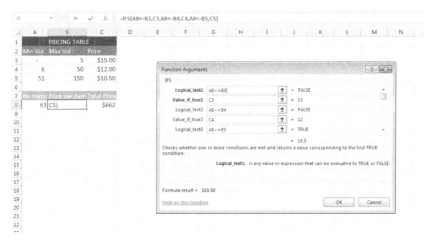

FIGURE 5.27   IFS Insert Function Dialog Box

Logical_test1 field. If this is true, we want the formula to return the value $15 in cell C3, so enter **C3** in the **Value_if_true1**.

3. Follow the same procedure for the second set of fields by entering **A8<=B4** in the **Logical_test2** field and then **C4** in the **Value_if_true2**.

In a nested IF statement, we would then just add a "value if else" here, but with the IFS function, you need to give it a third set of criteria to evaluate.

4. Enter **A8<=B5** in the **Logical_test3** field and then **C5** in the **Value_if_true3** and press OK.

5. The Insert Function dialog box should look like Figure 5.27 and the formula should now be:

$$=IFS(A8<=B3,C3,A8<=B4,C4,A8<=B5,C5)$$

Note that a nested IF statement or IFS function is an appropriate formula to use in this situation. However, if there were **more than three** pricing steps in the table, it is recommended that you use a close match VLOOKUP or LOOKUP function instead, as this is a much simpler function than nesting multiple IF statements. (See the section "Building a Tiering Table" in Chapter 9 for how to do this.) Basically, if you find yourself including more than two or three IF statements in a formula, consider whether the formula should be broken into several steps, or whether an alternative, simpler function should be used instead.

SUMMARY

This chapter introduced the more basic tools and functions that are commonly used in financial modelling, such as basic functions, cell referencing, and named ranges.

We also covered functions such as IF, SUM, AVERAGE, and nesting these, as well as useful shortcuts that will make your model-building faster and more accurate. The fundamental techniques of using cell referencing for best practice, as well as the use of named ranges, are the critical basic knowledge required for financial modellers before moving on to more advanced tools. The Windows and Mac shortcuts named here will also prove invaluable to increasing your speed, productivity, and accuracy as a financial modeller.

CHAPTER 6

Functions for Financial Modelling

In this chapter, we will introduce the most useful functions commonly used in financial modelling. Whilst there are hundreds of functions that can be used in a model, I have attempted to list only the ones you are most likely to come across, and that you will find most useful when building models. Please don't stop here, though! There are many more wonderful Excel functions that you will find useful in your financial modelling and business analysis.

AGGREGATION FUNCTIONS

COUNTIF, SUMIF, COUNTIFS, and SUMIFS are very handy functions to know for modelling and are basic knowledge once you start learning DAX, the formula language for Power Pivot. They add or count ranges of data, and count amongst some of my favourite, most frequently used functions.

COUNTIF

COUNTIF is used to count the cells that match specified criteria. For example, let's say you have sold $6,160 worth of different products on a particular day, as shown in Figure 6.1. You can create this sheet yourself or a template can be found, along with the accompanying models to the rest of the screenshots in this book, at www.plumsolutions.com.au/book.

You'd like to know how many (in terms of number of products) you've sold of each product: books, CDs, and DVDs. Follow these six steps:

1. In cell B18, use the Insert Function dialog box to find the COUNTIF function. (Simply begin typing =**COUNTIF**(and then Control+A, or hit the *fx* symbol next to the formula bar.)
2. Highlight the product names in column A for the range, and the word "Book" in cell A18 for the criteria. **Do not** type in the word "Book", as this is poor

| C14 | ▾ | : | × | ✓ | *fx* | =SUM(C2:C13) |

▲	A	B	C	D	E
1	Product	Customer	Sales $		
2	DVD	Lim	$410		
3	CD	Jenny	$810		
4	Book	Faisal	$220		
5	DVD	Peter	$350		
6	Book	Lim	$530		
7	Book	Jenny	$660		
8	DVD	Faisal	$620		
9	Book	Peter	$560		
10	Book	Lim	$460		
11	CD	Jenny	$950		
12	DVD	Faisal	$310		
13	DVD	Peter	$280		
14	Total		$6,160		
15					
16					
17	Summary	Count #	Sales $		
18	Book				
19	CD				
20	DVD				
21	Total				
22					

FIGURE 6.1　Sales List

modelling practice. It needs to be linked to the input cell so that we can then copy down the formula.

3. Your Insert Function dialog box should look like Figure 6.2.
4. Press OK. The answer is 5. Your formula should look like **=COUNTIF (A2:A13,A18)**.
5. Change your formula to use absolute referencing as follows: **=COUNTIF ($A$2:$A$13,A18)** and copy the formula down the range. You don't want absolute referencing on the criteria, because it needs to change its row references to **CD** and **DVD** as you copy down the formula.

　As a shortcut, highlighting **A2:A13** in the formula bar and pressing F4 will set absolute references **$BA$2:$A$13**. Remember that each time you press F4 it will scroll through the various absolute, relative, or mixed cell referencing options.
6. Copy the formula down, and add a total at the bottom. Your sheet should now look something like Figure 6.3.

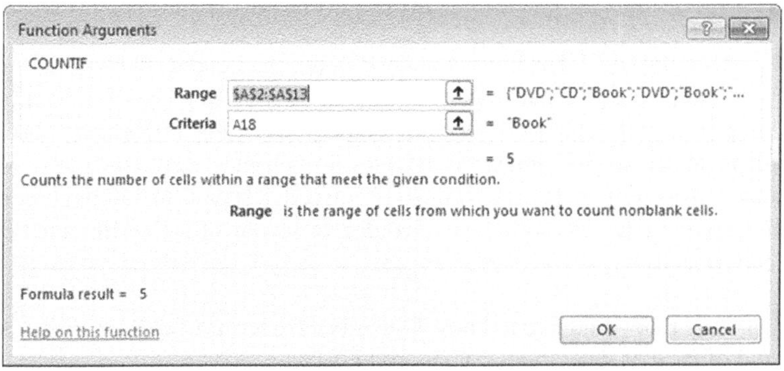

FIGURE 6.2 COUNTIF Insert Function Dialog Box

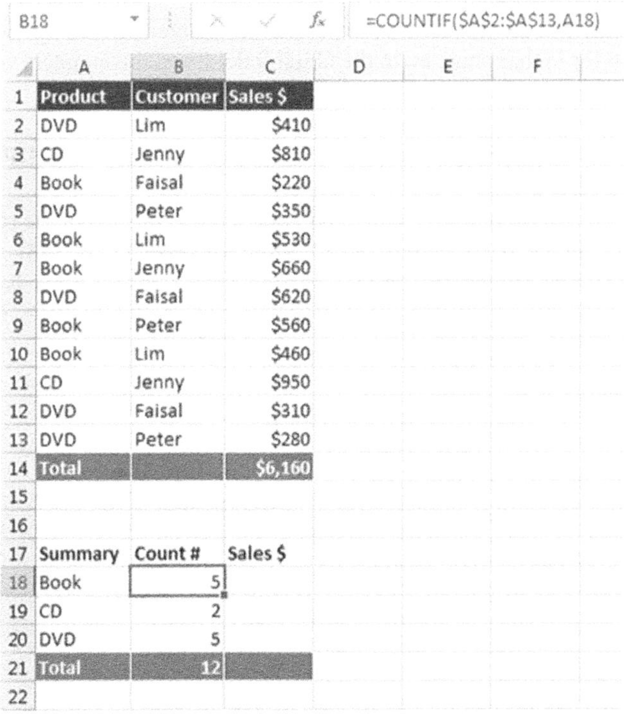

FIGURE 6.3 Completed COUNTIF Function

SUMIF

SUMIF is similar to COUNTIF but it sums rather than counts the values of cells in a range that meet given criteria. SUMIF can be used in place of a PivotTable, and doing so is preferable as it uses less memory and (most importantly) because SUMIF formulas are live links. PivotTables do not update automatically, which can cause errors in models if not refreshed correctly. Therefore, although quicker to build, PivotTables are sometimes avoided in favour of a SUMIF function in financial modelling.

1. Let's say that you'd like to know how much (in terms of dollar value) you've sold of each product: books, CDs, and DVDs.
2. Select cell C18. Find the SUMIF Insert Function dialog box or start typing =SUMIF(. Because there are several fields required for this function, I'd recommend you use the Insert Function dialog box, as it's easier to find your way through the function.
3. The items you are adding together go in the Range field, the criteria you are looking for in that range go in the Criteria field, and the numbers you want to sum together go in the Sum_range field.
4. Your Insert Function dialog box should look like Figure 6.4.
5. Press OK. The answer is 2,430. Your formula should be =SUMIF(A2:A13, A18,C2:C13).
6. Add in the absolute referencing, and copy the formula down the range. Your formula should be =SUMIF($A$2:$A$13,A18,$C$2:$C$13). You don't need absolute referencing on the criteria (A18), because it needs to change its reference as you copy down the formula.
7. Add a total. Your sheet should now look like Figure 6.5.

We've now got a summary report at the bottom, showing us how much we have sold in terms of number and dollar value.

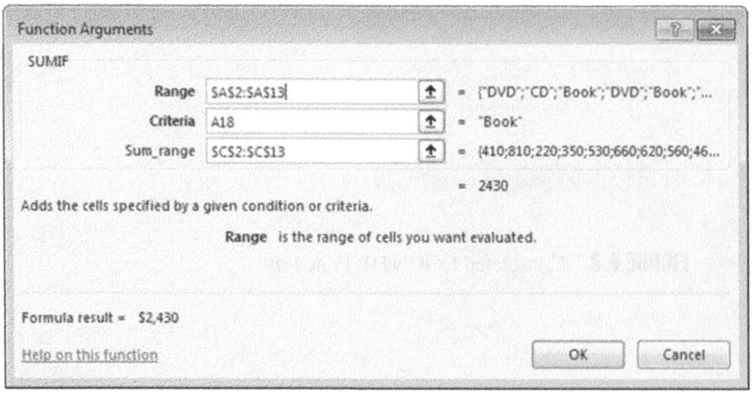

FIGURE 6.4 SUMIF Insert Function Dialog Box

C18	▼	:	×	✓	*fx*	=SUMIF($A$2:$A$13,A18,$C$2:$C$13)		

⊿	A	B	C	D	E	F	G
1	**Product**	**Customer**	**Sales $**				
2	DVD	Lim	$410				
3	CD	Jenny	$810				
4	Book	Faisal	$220				
5	DVD	Peter	$350				
6	Book	Lim	$530				
7	Book	Jenny	$660				
8	DVD	Faisal	$620				
9	Book	Peter	$560				
10	Book	Lim	$460				
11	CD	Jenny	$950				
12	DVD	Faisal	$310				
13	DVD	Peter	$280				
14	**Total**		**$6,160**				
15							
16							
17	Summary	Count #	Sales $				
18	Book	5	$2,430				
19	CD	2	$1,760				
20	DVD	5	$1,970				
21	**Total**	**12**	**$6,160**				
22							

FIGURE 6.5   Completed SUMIF Function

Be careful. If your Range and your Sum_range don't match up, your result will be wrong. For example, **=SUMIF($A$2 : $A$13,A18,$C$1 : $C$13)** will give you an incorrect result without warning! This is a very easy mistake to make, and quite common in financial modelling. You can see in Figure 6.6 that the totals are not the same, because the SUMIF function is picking up the incorrect range. This is the same for COUNTIF functions, but it is not a problem with the SUMIFS, as the formula will return an error and therefore you will notice the error straight away, unlike the SUMIF function.

TIP

We can see that there is an error because the totals in rows 14 and 21 are not matching, but you might like to make this more obvious by adding an error check below the summary in cell C22 to pick up errors such as this. This can be done using a simple minus or equals formula, or see the section "Building Error Checks" in Chapter 4 for greater detail on how to create an error check.

| CELL | ▾ | ⋮ | ✕ | ✓ | fx | =SUMIF($A$2:$A$13,A18,$C$1:$C$13) |

⊿	A	B	C	D	E	F	G
1	**Product**	**Customer**	**Sales $**				
2	DVD	Lim	$410				
3	CD	Jenny	$810				
4	Book	Faisal	$220				
5	DVD	Peter	$350				
6	Book	Lim	$530				
7	Book	Jenny	$660				
8	DVD	Faisal	$620				
9	Book	Peter	$560				
10	Book	Lim	$460				
11	CD	Jenny	$950				
12	DVD	Faisal	$310				
13	DVD	Peter	$280				
14	**Total**		**$6,160**				
15							
16							
17	Summary	Count #	Sales $				
18	Book		5	=SUMIF($A$2:$A$13,A18,$C$1:$C$13)			
19	CD		2	$870			
20	DVD		5	$2,140			
21	**Total**		**12**	**$5,880**			

FIGURE 6.6   Incorrect SUMIF Calculation

Additional Exercise: PivotTable versus SUMIF

1. Create a PivotTable in cell G3 that will give you exactly the same result as the SUMIF function. Your PivotTable should look like this:

Row Labels	Sum of Sales $
DVD	$1,970
CD	$1,760
Book	$2,430
Grand Total	**$6,160**

   See the section "Building a PivotTable" in Chapter 8 for instructions if you don't know how to build a PivotTable.
2. Change one of your values in column C. What happens to the PivotTable? What happens to the SUMIF function?
   You'll notice that the SUMIF formula will change, but the PivotTable does not. This is why the use of PivotTables is not recommended in pure

financial models: because PivotTables do not update automatically. See the section "Using PivotTables in Financial Models" in Chapter 8 for greater detail.

AVERAGEIF

The AVERAGEIF function will average values in the specified range that match specified criteria. This is similar to SUMIF.

1. Let's say that you'd like to know the average in dollar terms of each product sold. Select cell D18. Find the AVERAGEIF Insert Function dialog box or start typing **=AVERAGEIF(**.
2. The items you are interrogating go in the Range field, the criteria you are looking for in that range go in the Criteria field, and the numbers you want to average go in the Average_range field.
3. Press OK. The answer is 486. Your formula should be

$$=AVERAGEIF(A2:A13,A18,C2:C13)$$

4. Use absolute referencing, and copy the formula down the range. Your formula should be

$$=AVERAGEIF(\$A\$2:\$A\$13,A18,\$C\$2:\$C\$13)$$

You don't need absolute referencing on the criteria (A18), because it needs to change its reference as you copy down the column.

COUNTIFS

COUNTIFS (along with similar functions such as SUMIFS and AVERAGEIFS) is a relatively new function that was introduced in later versions of Excel. COUNTIFS applies criteria to cells across multiple ranges and counts the number of times all criteria are met. For instance, COUNTIFS could answer how many of each product had been sold to a particular customer.

1. In row 16, create a filter cell to show which customer we want to show in our summary. So, in cell B16, enter the value **Jenny**. By linking the COUNTIFS function to this cell, we can change it in the future if we want to.
2. In cell B18, use the Insert Function dialog box and find the COUNTIFS function, or simply begin typing **=COUNTIFS(** if you prefer. If you are using the Insert Function dialog box, it should look like Figure 6.7.

   As you can see, we are invited to keep adding more ranges and criteria to the function COUNTIFS, which was not possible in COUNTIF. Use absolute

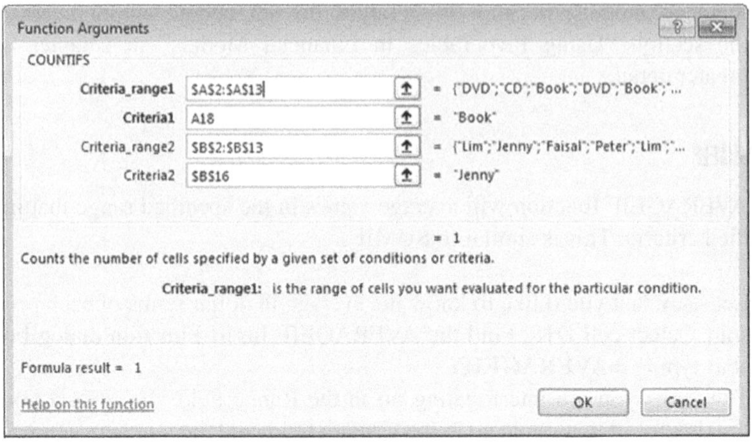

FIGURE 6.7 COUNTIFS Dialog Box

references for all ranges in your formula, with the exception of Criteria1 in cell A18. The reference to the word "Book" will change to "CD" and "DVD" as the formula is copied down.

3. The formula should be

$$=COUNTIFS(\$A\$2:\$A\$13,A18,\$B\$2:\$B\$13,\$B\$16)$$

The result should look like Figure 6.8. The completed version of this exercise can be found, along with the accompanying models to the rest of the screenshots in this book, at www.plumsolutions.com.au/book.

SUMIFS

Like the COUNTIFS function, the SUMIFS function applies criteria to cells across multiple ranges and sums specified columns for which criteria are met. For instance, SUMIF tallied up the value of all products, whereas SUMIFS could add up only those purchased by Jenny.

1. In cell C18, use the Insert Function dialog box and find the SUMIFS function, or simply begin typing =SUMIFS(. Match Criteria_range1 (column A) with a value that appears in the range (the value "Book" in cell A18). Similarly, match Criteria_range2 (column B) with a value that appears in the range (the value "Jenny" in cell B16).

2. The result in cell C18 will be $660 and you can copy it down the range to the result shown in Figure 6.9.

3. The formula should be

$$=SUMIFS(\$C\$2:\$C\$13,\$A\$2:\$A\$13,A18,\$B\$2:\$B\$13,\$B\$16)$$

| B18 | ▼ | : | × | ✓ | *fx* | =COUNTIFS($A$2:$A$13,A18,$B$2:$B$13,$B$16) |

	A	B	C	D	E	F	G	H
1	**Product**	**Customer**	**Price**					
2	DVD	Lim	$410					
3	CD	Jenny	$810					
4	Book	Faisal	$220					
5	DVD	Peter	$350					
6	Book	Lim	$530					
7	Book	Jenny	$660					
8	DVD	Faisal	$620					
9	Book	Peter	$560					
10	Book	Lim	$460					
11	CD	Jenny	$950					
12	DVD	Faisal	$310					
13	DVD	Peter	$280					
14	**Total**		**$6,160**					
15								
16	Filter by:	Jenny						
17	**Summary**	**Count #**						
18	Book	1						
19	CD	2						
20	DVD	0						
21	**Total**	**3**						
22								

FIGURE 6.8 Completed COUNTIFS Function

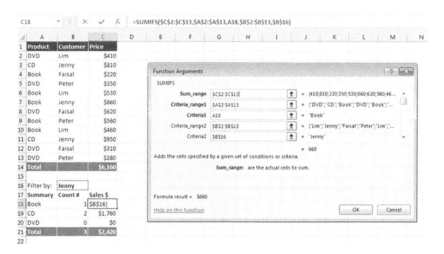

FIGURE 6.9 Completed SUMIFS Function

As you can see, we are able to append one or more ranges and criteria to the function SUMIFS in the form Criteria_range, Criteria which was not possible in SUMIF. When using the SUMIFS function, we can appreciate the value of using the Insert Function dialog box, as it helps to see which criteria match which criteria range.

AVERAGEIFS

AVERAGEIF averages the value of **all** products, whereas we could use AVERAGEIFS in a similar way to average only those products purchased by Jenny.

1. In cell D18, use the Insert Function dialog box and find the AVERAGEIFS function, or simply begin typing =**AVERAGEIFS(**. Enter in the relevant fields to achieve the result in Figure 6.10.

   As with COUNTIFS and SUMIFS, the AVERAGEIFS function also allows you to append one or more additional criteria to it in the form Criteria_range, Criteria.
2. The formula should look like this:

   =**AVERAGEIFS($C$2:$C$13,$A$2:$A$13,A18,$B$2:$B$13,$B$16)**

   As can be expected, the result of this formula will be $660, as there is only one instance of sales that were made to Jenny. Now copy the formula down to cells D19 and D20. D20 returns an error, because Jenny did not buy any DVDs, so we need to use the IFERROR function to suppress this error. Go back to cell D18 and put the IFERROR function around your formula. The formula should look like this:

   =**IFERROR(AVERAGEIFS($C$2:$C$13,$A$2:$A$13,A18,**
   $B$2:$B$13,$B$16),0)

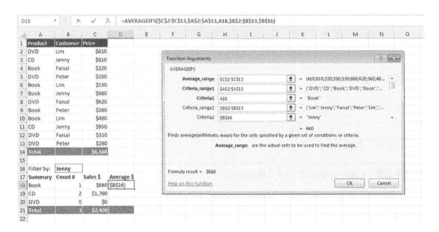

FIGURE 6.10 AVERAGEIFS Insert Function Dialog Box

Then copy the formula down the range. Cell D20 should now show a zero instead of the #DIV/0! error.

TIP

Cell D19 gives us a value of $880, so let's do a sense check to make sure that it is accurate by highlighting both CD sales made to Jenny and looking at the AVERAGE amount showing in the status bar in the bottom left-hand corner, as shown in Figure 6.11.

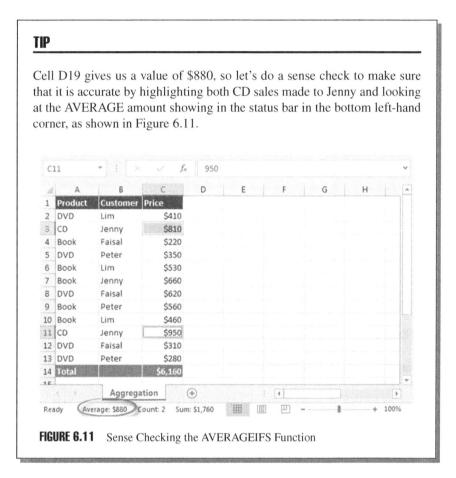

FIGURE 6.11 Sense Checking the AVERAGEIFS Function

To make this table more complete, we need to put a total in cell D21; however, neither the total of the range ($1,540) nor the average of the range ($513) makes sense. In cell B21, we are showing the total number of purchases by Jenny, and then in cell C21, we are showing the total amount of her purchases. Therefore, it makes sense to show the **average** of all purchases by Jenny in cell D21, which is $807. This cannot be done by copying the function down, so we need to create a new AVERAGEIF function, as shown in Figure 6.12. The formula which should look like this:

$$=AVERAGEIFS(\$C\$2:\$C\$13,\$B\$2:\$B\$13,\$B\$16)$$

Now, try changing the word "Jenny" in cell B16 to "Faisal" and watch the numbers change.

D21		▾	:	×	✓	f_x	=AVERAGEIFS($C$2:$C$13,$B$2:$B$13,$B$16)		

◢	A	B	C	D	E	F	G	H
1	Product	Customer	Price					
2	DVD	Lim	$410					
3	CD	Jenny	$810					
4	Book	Faisal	$220					
5	DVD	Peter	$350					
6	Book	Lim	$530					
7	Book	Jenny	$660					
8	DVD	Faisal	$620					
9	Book	Peter	$560					
10	Book	Lim	$460					
11	CD	Jenny	$950					
12	DVD	Faisal	$310					
13	DVD	Peter	$280					
14	Total		$6,160					
15								
16	Filter by:	Jenny						
17	Summary	Count #	Sales $	Average $				
18	Book	1	$660	$660				
19	CD	2	$1,760	$880				
20	DVD	0	$0	$0				
21	Total	3	$2,420	$807				
22								

FIGURE 6.12 Completed Filtered Sales Report

Filtering IFS Functions by a Variable Value Note that instead of filtering to show one customer, we could, for example, show only those products that exceed $50. This is not particularly easy using IFS functions (i.e., SUMIFS, COUNTIFS, and AVERAGEIFS), but it is possible.

Let's remove the word "Jenny" and instead add the minimum $50, and change the label to show that the cell now contains only sales that are greater than $50, as shown in Figure 6.13. Note that we are now showing the filter in column C, because it lines up better with the sales amount, which is also in column C. We can now change the original COUNTIFS function to only aggregate the values greater than $50. It is an idiosyncrasy of all these IFS functions, however, that we cannot easily link when using the greater than (>) or less than (<) symbols. The function will force us to use inverted commas, and enter the filter value directly into the function, rather than linking it to an individual cell on the worksheet. Your formula in cell B18 will look like this:

$$= COUNTIFS(= \$A\$2:\$A\$13,A18,\$C\$2:\$C\$13,">50")$$

This is not very good financial modelling practice, however. Any decent modeller would want to allow the user to change the filter minimum value. We therefore need to use a tricky workaround involving the handy ampersand (&) symbol. We'll

| CELL | ▼ : | × ✓ | *fx* | =SUMIFS($C$2:$C$13,$A$2:$A$13,A18,$C$2:$C$13,">"&$C$16) |

▲	A	B	C	D	E	F	G	H	I
1	**Product**	**Customer**	**Sales $**						
2	DVD	Lim	$410						
3	CD	Jenny	$810						
4	Book	Faisal	$220						
5	DVD	Peter	$350						
6	Book	Lim	$530						
7	Book	Jenny	$660						
8	DVD	Faisal	$620						
9	Book	Peter	$560						
10	Book	Lim	$460						
11	CD	Jenny	$950						
12	DVD	Faisal	$310						
13	DVD	Peter	$280						
14	**Total**		**$6,160**						
15									
16	Filter by Sales Greater than:		$50						
17	Summary	Count #	Sales $						
18	Book		5	=SUMIFS($C$2:$C$13,$A$2:$A$13,A18,$C$2:$C$13,">"&$C$16)					
19	CD		2	$1,760					
20	DVD		5	$1,970					
21	**Total**		**12**	**$6,160**					
22									

FIGURE 6.13   SUMIFS Function with a Minimum Filter

need to replace **">50"** with the phrase **">"&$C$16** instead, and therefore the minimum filter will change according to the value in cell C16. Your formula in cell B18 should now look like this:

$$=COUNTIFS(\$A\$2:\$A\$13,A18,\$C\$2:\$C\$13,">"\&\$C\$16)$$

Copy it down and then try the same technique with the SUMIFS function. The solution for the SUMIFS is shown in Figure 6.13.

Similarly, the AVERAGEIFS function can be completed in the same way and should look like the solution shown in Figure 6.14. As in the last example, the formula to calculate the total for the Average needs to be the average for all Sales greater than $50.

Note that dates can also be used as input criteria for these IFS functions.

LOOKUP FUNCTIONS

LOOKUP functions are very often used in financial modelling and analysis—sometimes a little too often, in my opinion. They are useful to know, but sometimes another function (such as an INDEX/MATCH nested function, as described in the next section) would create a more robust solution.

| CELL | ▼ | : | × | ✓ | fx | =AVERAGEIFS($C$2:$C$13,$A$2:$A$13,A18,$C$2:$C$13,">"&$C$16) | | | | |

	A	B	C	D	E	F	G	H	I	J
1	Product	Customer	Sales $							
2	DVD	Lim	$410							
3	CD	Jenny	$810							
4	Book	Faisal	$220							
5	DVD	Peter	$350							
6	Book	Lim	$530							
7	Book	Jenny	$660							
8	DVD	Faisal	$620							
9	Book	Peter	$560							
10	Book	Lim	$460							
11	CD	Jenny	$950							
12	DVD	Faisal	$310							
13	DVD	Peter	$280							
14	Total		$6,160							
15										
16	Filter by Sales Greater than:		$50							
17	Summary	Count #	Sales $	Average $						
18	Book	5	$2,430	=AVERAGEIFS($C$2:$C$13,$A$2:$A$13,A18,$C$2:$C$13,">"&$C$16)						
19	CD	2	$1,760	$880						
20	DVD	5	$1,970	$394						
21	Total	12	$6,160	$513						
22										

FIGURE 6.14 AVERAGEIFS Function with a Minimum Filter

VLOOKUP

VLOOKUP stands for "Vertical Lookup". It can be used anytime you have a list of data with the key field in the leftmost column, and it is by far the most commonly used form of LOOKUP formula. It's a favourite amongst Excel users, but it's not the most robust of functions as we'll soon see.

Let's say you have a shopping price list like in Figure 6.16. You can create this sheet yourself or a template can be found, along with the accompanying models to the rest of the screenshots in this book, at www.plumsolutions.com.au/book.

In cell C12, we'd like to find out how much it will cost to buy four oranges, using a VLOOKUP.

How to Create a VLOOKUP The following is an 11-step process for creating a VLOOKUP:

1. Find and select the **VLOOKUP** function. Using the Insert Function dialog box is probably going to be the easiest for VLOOKUPs, as there are four parameters it needs.
2. The first parameter is the criteria we are testing, in this case, the word *oranges*, so enter **B12** in the first field.
3. The next parameter is the table, which contains the data you want to reference. This is where it gets tricky. The criteria you are looking for must always be

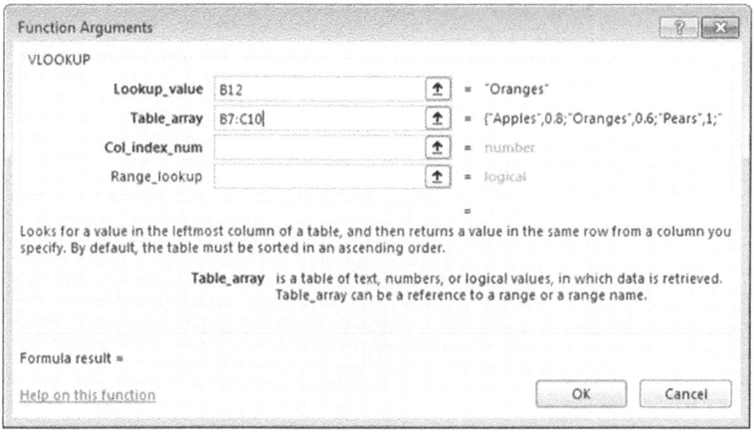

FIGURE 6.15   VLOOKUP Insert Function Dialog Box

in the far left-hand column of the data table you are referencing in the table array. So, in this case, the data we are referencing will be the range **B7:C10**. Figure 6.15 is what your Insert Function dialog box should look like so far.

4. Now, if you were going to copy this formula down the page, you would have to use absolute referencing for the table array, or use a named range. Let's create a named range here.

5. Press Escape to cancel out of the Insert Function dialog box and create a named range for the whole table. Highlight the range **B7:C10** and type over the name box in the top left-hand corner of your screen with the word **FruitList**, and press Enter. We can now use this in the **VLOOKUP**.

Now that we have used a named range, we won't have to worry about absolute referencing in our **VLOOKUP** formula. See Figure 6.16.

6. Go back into the **VLOOKUP** Insert Function dialog box again, re-reference the lookup value to **B12**, and either select the table array in the second field box or simply type in **FruitList**. Make sure you have spelt it the same way as your named range! If you can't remember what you called it, use the F3 shortcut as shown in Figure 6.17.

TIP

When referencing a named range in a formula, you can also use the F3 paste name shortcut to bring up a list of all named ranges in the model, as shown in Figure 6.17.

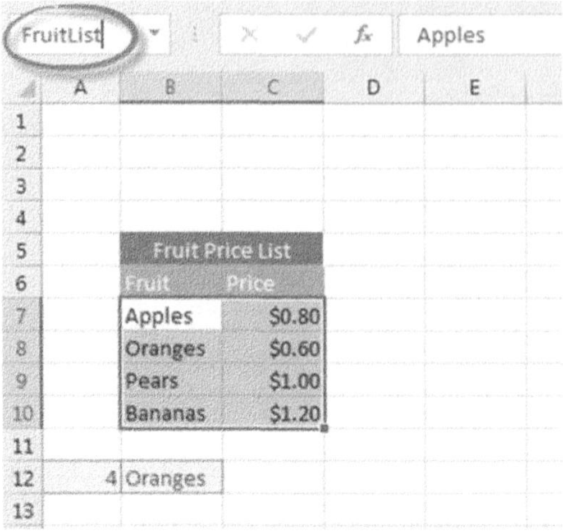

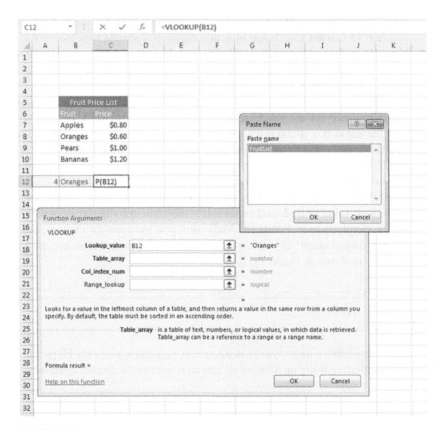

FIGURE 6.16   Creating a Named Range

FIGURE 6.17   Using the F3 Shortcut to Paste Name into a Formula

7. The third field, called **Col_index_num**, tells Excel in which column the value is found. We need to tell the function which column in the table array we want it to return. In this case, we want it to tell us the price. So, counting from the far left-hand side of the table array (starting in column B), we want it to return to the second column. So, we enter a number **Col_index_num** field in the **Col_index_num field**.

8. The optional fourth parameter tells Excel if a close match is okay. If you want an exact match, enter zero; otherwise, leave it blank. You may also enter TRUE or FALSE, but typing a zero or leaving it blank is quicker. Click OK to complete the formula.

NOTE

There are very few instances where you want a close match. (See the section "Building a Tiering Table" in Chapter 9 for an example of using a close match in VLOOKUPs.) In most VLOOKUPs, you want an exact match, so enter a zero in the last field.

---

9. The Insert Function dialog box should look like Figure 6.18 and the formula should now be

=VLOOKUP(B12,FruitList,2,0)

10. Now, try changing the word *oranges* to *apples*. The price should change.

FIGURE 6.18 Completed VLOOKUP Function

11. Last, we need to multiply the price by the number of items we are purchasing. Change your formula to

$$=\text{VLOOKUP(B12,FruitList,2,0)*A12}$$

#N/A Errors in VLOOKUPs   While this example worked out perfectly, when most people use VLOOKUP, that they are usually matching up lists that came from different sources. When lists come from different sources, there can always be subtle differences that make the lists hard to match. This means you will get a #N/A error if the VLOOKUP function cannot find a match. Here are two examples of what can go wrong and how to correct the error.

Example 1. One list has dashes, for example, and the other list does not. The first time that you try the VLOOKUP, you will get #N/A errors. To remove the dashes with a formula, use a find and replace. Replace with nothing (i.e., leave the field blank). Your data will now match and the formula works.

Example 2. One list has a trailing blank space after the entry. This one is subtle because you can't see it with the naked eye, but it is very common. In fact, I've spent many happy hours searching for an invisible space! When you initially enter the formula, you will find all of the answers are #N/A errors. You know for sure that the values are in the list and everything looks okay with the formula.

One easy way to check is to move to the cell with the lookup value. Press F2 to put the cell in edit mode and you can see that the cursor is located one space away from the final letter. This indicates that there is a trailing space in the entry.

One way to solve the problem is to use the TRIM function. Entering =TRIM(D4) as part of your VLOOKUP formula will remove leading spaces and trailing spaces, and will replace any internal double spaces with a single space. In this case, TRIM works perfectly to remove the trailing space. The formula would look something like this:

$$=\text{VLOOKUP(TRIM(B12),FruitList,2,0)*A12}$$

Breaking a VLOOKUP   If you have created a VLOOKUP in a model such as the one above, this should work well—until someone enters or deletes a column in your source data! With a formula such as **=VLOOKUP(B12,FruitList,2, 0)*A12**, it specifically asks for the second column, so it will not work if someone inserts a column within the FruitList range. This is because your required column becomes the third column, but the VLOOKUP is asking for the second.

VLOOKUPs and HLOOKUPs are not very robust formulas—you can see how easy they are to break! For this reason, try some of the alternatives below to make your LOOKUP functions more robust; otherwise, use another function or protect your model so that users cannot insert or delete rows or columns.

Improving VLOOKUPs with MATCH The best way around this is to make the 2 in your VLOOKUP a formula instead of a hardcoded number. One way of doing this is to nest the VLOOKUP with a MATCH function. In the following eight steps, we will create the MATCH formula in a separate cell and then replace the 2 with the MATCH formula.

1. Using the VLOOKUP example above, test the problem by inserting or deleting a column in our sheet. You will see that the value in your VLOOKUP is now incorrect.
2. Now go to another spare cell, say cell **C3**, and create a MATCH formula that will find the word Price in the range **B6:C6** and tell us its position in the range.
3. Your Insert Function dialog box should look like Figure 6.19.
4. By putting a **0** in the Match_type range, you are asking it to return you an exact match instead of a close match.
5. When you hit OK, your formula should be =**MATCH($C$6,$B$6:$C$6,0)** and the result should be 2.
6. Go into the MATCH formula bar, highlight the entire formula (except for the = sign), and press Control+C to copy it. Hit Enter, or Escape. Now, go back to your original VLOOKUP, and replace the 2 in your VLOOKUP formula with this entire MATCH formula by highlighting the 2 within the formula and pasting the MATCH formula over it by pressing Control+V. Hit Enter.
7. Your formula should look like this:

$$=\text{VLOOKUP(B12,FruitList,MATCH(\$C\$6,\$B\$6:\$C\$6, 0),0)*A12}$$

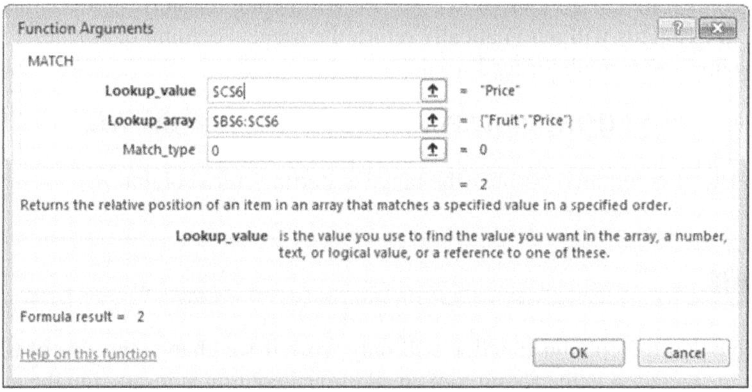

FIGURE 6.19 MATCH Function Dialog Box

8. Test that this works, by inserting or deleting a column. You can now clear the formula in cell C3, as this is no longer necessary.

NOTE

Note that the Insert Function dialog box works most easily when you have a single function in a cell. Now that you have created a nested function (i.e., a function within a function), you cannot simply hit the *fx* button to bring up the dialog box. You can still use the dialog box, but you'll need to click within the formula and put your cursor adjacent to the function that you want to analyse before hitting the *fx* button.

TIP

This technique, whereby we create each function in a separate cell and then nest them together, is by far the easiest method to create nested functions. It becomes confusing and easy to make a mistake if you try to create a nested function all in one go. It's much easier to create a separate function in each cell and then copy and paste them together as shown above.

Another way of making a LOOKUP formula more robust would be to use the COLUMN function for a VLOOKUP or ROW function for an HLOOKUP instead of MATCH. This will automatically return the range's column or row reference. Using this, the formula instead would be

=VLOOKUP(B12,FruitList,COLUMN(C6)-1,0)*A12

(The -1 is required because the range is starting from column B.)

NOTE

Note that the column function will only work if we change the size of the range included in the formula. If an additional column is inserted to the left of the range, the nested COLUMN function returns an incorrect result. For this reason, the MATCH nested function is a superior solution.

HLOOKUP (Horizontal Lookup)

HLOOKUP works in exactly the same way as VLOOKUP, except that the data is arranged horizontally instead of vertically. See Figures 6.20 and 6.21 for examples.

HLOOKUP is subject to exactly the same issues as the VLOOKUP and works in exactly the same way, except for the orientation. If your source data in the range is orientated vertically, use the VLOOKUP, and if it is horizontal, use the HLOOKUP.

LOOKUP Function

The LOOKUP function is much simpler than either the VLOOKUP or the HLOOKUP, and it has the added advantage of being able to have the results

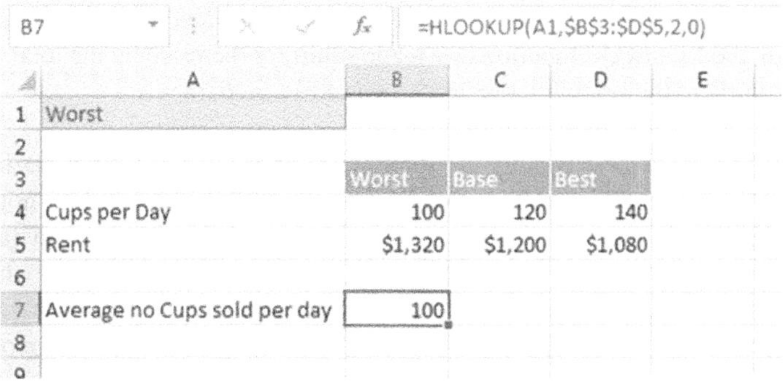

	A	B	C	D	E
1	Worst				
2					
3		Worst	Base	Best	
4	Cups per Day	100	120	140	
5	Rent	$1,320	$1,200	$1,080	
6					
7	Average no Cups sold per day	100			
8					

Formula bar: B7 = HLOOKUP(A1,$B$3:$D$5,2,0)

FIGURE 6.20   Use of the HLOOKUP Function

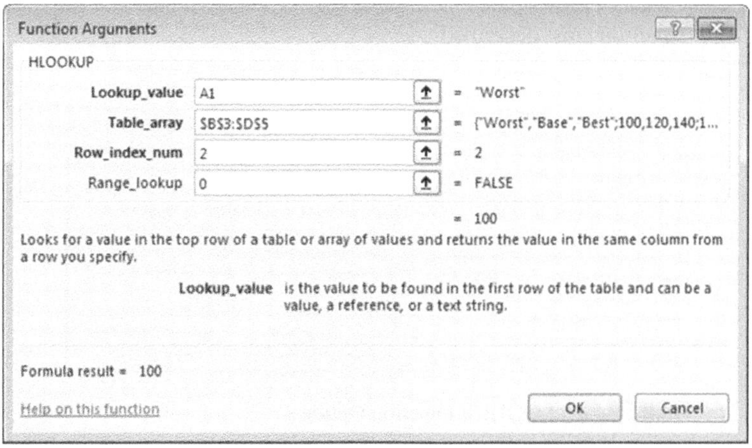

FIGURE 6.21   HLOOKUP Insert Function Dialog Box

column or row either to the left or right of the criteria column or row—a huge advantage. However, the data *must* be sorted in alphabetical order or it won't work. This does limit its usage significantly, and it is for this reason that it is far less popular than the VLOOKUP or HLOOKUP formulas.

It's worth knowing how it works, though, so here's a brief example. Let's say you have a tiered pricing structure, as shown in Figure 6.23. You can create this sheet yourself, or a template can be found along with the accompanying models to the rest of the screenshots in this book at www.plumsolutions.com.au/book.

1. Select LOOKUP from the Insert Function dialog box.
2. There are two types; choose the first option, as shown in Figure 6.22.
3. Similar to an HLOOKUP or VLOOKUP, the criteria being tested go in the first field.
4. The column (or row) containing the criteria goes in the second field, and then the column (or row) containing the result goes in the last field. See Figure 6.23.
5. Copy the LOOKUP function down and multiply the price by the total amount to complete the pricing table, as shown in Figure 6.24.

Note that this works exactly the same whether the data is shown vertically or horizontally. Importantly, unlike a VLOOKUP or HLOOKUP, it does not matter whether the result data is to the left or right, above or below the lookup data.

However, you would use a LOOKUP only for numerical values where the numbers are sorted and you want a close match, not an exact match. You would not use a LOOKUP function for text, as shown in the last fruit shopping list VLOOKUP example, because it will only return a close match, and this is dangerous. This makes the LOOKUP function almost useless in many cases where a LOOKUP is required. The only time a modeller would use a LOOKUP is when he specifically wants a close match. See Table 6.1 for the advantages of the different LOOKUP functions just described.

FIGURE 6.22 LOOKUP Function Option

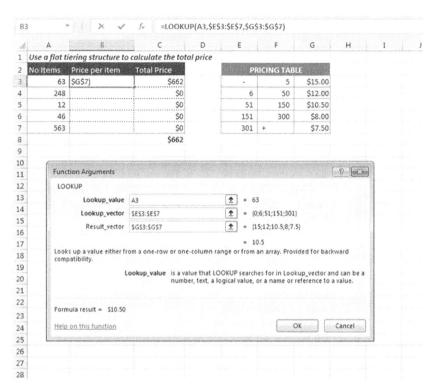

FIGURE 6.23 LOOKUP Insert Function Dialog Box

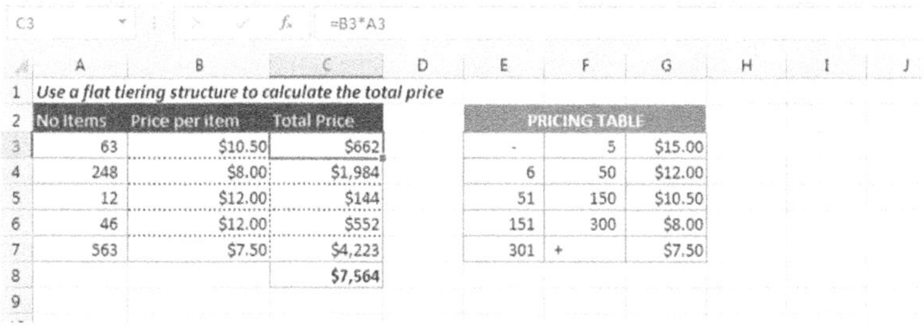

FIGURE 6.24 Completed Pricing Calculation

TABLE 6.1   Advantages and Disadvantages of LOOKUP Functions

Function	Advantages	Disadvantages
VLOOKUP	▪ Data does not need to be sorted alphabetically as long as you use 0 or FALSE in the last field.	▪ The column number is hardcoded, so if a column is inserted, it can mess up the formula. (You can use a MATCH formula to fix this.) ▪ The column containing the results *must* be to the right-hand side of the column containing the lookup criteria.
HLOOKUP	▪ Data does not need to be sorted alphabetically as long as you use 0 or FALSE in the last field.	▪ The row number is hardcoded, so if a row is inserted, it can mess up the formula. (You can use a MATCH formula to fix this.) ▪ The row containing the results *must* be below the row containing the lookup criteria.
LOOKUP	▪ The column/row number is not hardcoded. ▪ It does not matter where the columns or rows are in relation to each other.	▪ Data *must* be sorted or it will give the wrong result.

NESTING INDEX AND MATCH

As described in "Linking to External Files" in Chapter 4, robust formulas, such as a nested formula using a combination of an INDEX and a MATCH, used with named ranges, will make the link a lot less likely to break and cause problems in models.

Using INDEX and MATCH to Create a More Robust Formula

Let's say that you are referencing a table in another file. Your co-worker keeps inserting and deleting rows and columns. The VLOOKUP solution as previously described may work, but with large tables, an INDEX and MATCH formula combination will be more efficient.

Figure 6.25 contains the source data, showing we need to pick up the staff amenities costs for Geelong. You can create this sheet yourself or a template can be found, along with the accompanying models to the rest of the screenshots in this book, at www.plumsolutions.com.au/book.

You could simply reference the cell F5, using the formula =F5, but this will not help you if your file is closed, and someone else changes the referenced table. Let's say your co-worker inserts a column while your model is closed. When you

	A	B	C	D	E	F	G	H	I	J
1	Expense	Campbelltown	Melbourne	Sydney	Parramatta	Geelong	Brisbane	Toowoomba	Perth	
2	Staff Costs	$568,432	$682,118	$511,589	$613,907	$460,430	$552,516	$414,387	$223,954	
3	Superannuation	$51,159	$61,391	$46,043	$55,252	$41,439	$49,726	$37,295	$20,156	
4	Workers Comp	$5,684	$6,821	$5,116	$6,139	$4,604	$5,525	$4,144	$2,240	
5	Staff Amenities	$28,422	$34,106	$25,579	$30,695	$23,021	$27,626	$20,719	$11,198	
6	Consumables	$34,106	$40,927	$30,695	$36,834	$27,626	$33,151	$24,863	$13,437	
7	Recruitment	$17,053	$20,464	$15,348	$18,417	$13,813	$16,575	$12,432	$6,719	
8	Travel	$11,369	$13,642	$10,232	$12,278	$9,209	$11,050	$8,288	$4,479	
9	Total	$716,224	$859,469	$644,602	$773,522	$580,142	$696,170	$522,128	$282,182	
10										

FIGURE 6.25 Sample Data

open your file again, it will still reference F5, but Geelong has moved to column G, so the formula in your model will be wrong!

By using a combination of an INDEX and MATCH formula, we will be able, in 15 steps, to specify the exact coordinates of the required value, even if its position in the table changes.

1. In cell B12, insert the word **Geelong**, and in cell A13, insert the phrase **Staff Amenities**. These cells will become input variables that we will link our formula to.
2. Now let's find the coordinates of the required data. Start by creating a MATCH formula in a spare cell that will find the word Geelong and tell us its position in the range of city names.
3. Your formula should be =**MATCH(B12,A1:I1,0)**, and the result should be 6. Note that you could type the word *Geelong* directly into the formula, but linking it is considered best practice in financial modelling.
4. Now do the same thing for the expense types. In another spare cell, create a MATCH formula that will find the phrase Staff Amenities and tell us its position in the range of expense types.
5. Your formula should be =**MATCH(A13,A1:A9,0)**, and the result should be 5.
6. Now create the INDEX formula that will return the value that you specify. Note that when you use the Insert Function dialog box, it will ask you which argument list you wish to use. Select the first one. See Figure 6.26.

FIGURE 6.26 INDEX Function Options

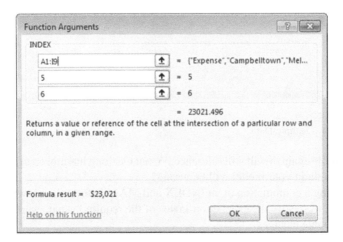

FIGURE 6.27 INDEX Insert Function Dialog Box

7. Once you are in the Insert Function dialog box, enter the array that is the whole range of data, starting from cell A1. Then hardcode in the row number (5 in this case) and the column number (6 in this case). See Figure 6.27.

8. Add the absolute referencing, so your formula should be **=INDEX($A$1: $I$9,5,6)**, and the result should be $23,021.

9. This formula will work fine, as long as no one inserts or deletes rows or columns. We know that hardcoded numbers are not good financial modelling practice and so in order to make it completely robust, we need to replace the 5 and 6 with the results of the MATCH formulas. We are going to turn this into a nested formula, just like we did in the last section, where we nested the VLOOKUP and MATCH functions.

10. Go back into the first MATCH formula bar (the one that returns a 6), highlight the whole thing (except the "=" sign), and press Control+C.

11. Go into the INDEX formula and replace the column reference with this formula. Highlight the 6 and press Control+V.

12. Now do the same for the row reference. Go into the second MATCH formula bar, highlight the whole thing (except the "=" sign), and press Control+C.

13. Go into the INDEX formula and replace the row reference with this formula. Highlight the 5 and press Control+V.

14. Don't forget to add in some absolute referencing. Your formula should now look like this:

=INDEX($A$1:$I$9,MATCH(A13,$A$1:$A$9,0),

MATCH(B12,$B$1:$I$1,0))

15. Test the robustness of your formula by inserting or deleting rows or columns. You can now cut this formula to another file, and it will work in the same way.

NOTE

Remember, if you want to move this formula around, to use the cut and paste functions, not copy and paste. Cutting (Control+X or Command+X) will move all formulas with it. If you cut this formula to another file, you should follow best practice by using named ranges in the formula, particularly where the INDEX function is referencing the data. This way, if the data is added to, the named range will expand accordingly.

In Figure 6.28, we can see that named ranges have been inserted into the original data, and used in the formula, which has been cut and pasted to a separate file. Even if the data file is changed while the report file is closed, the formulas will still remain accurate.

OFFSET FUNCTION

The OFFSET function, in my opinion, is less useful than the other functions we have covered so far, as it can be tricky to build and is complex to audit. However, it can be handy in certain situations, and many financial modellers are fond of including it in their models, therefore you will be likely to come across it and need to know how to decipher it.

OFFSET is used to return the address of a cell or a range of cells through the use of a reference cell and is generally used in order to stagger (or offset) a series of values by a variable amount. For example, if you want to delay a project by a certain number of months, but want the number of months to be variable, the OFFSET function will move the value by the number of months that is specified in the model.

To give a very simple example, let's say, in the data shown in Figure 6.29, that you wanted to pick up the value in cell B3, which is located one column across and two rows down from cell A1.

Using the OFFSET Insert Function dialog box, the reference point given is cell A1, the offset rows are 2, and offset columns are 1, as shown in Figure 6.30.

Don't worry about the height and width for now (this is for when you want the result to be a range, rather than a single cell. For an example of using an OFFSET in a range, see "Dynamic Named Ranges" in Chapter 12.) Your formula will be **=OFFSET(A1,2,1)**, and the result given should be 54.

This is picking up the cell one column to the right, and two rows below the reference cell. If you wanted to pick up a cell above or to the left of the cell, you would have used a negative offset number for the rows and columns (e.g. -2 instead of 2).

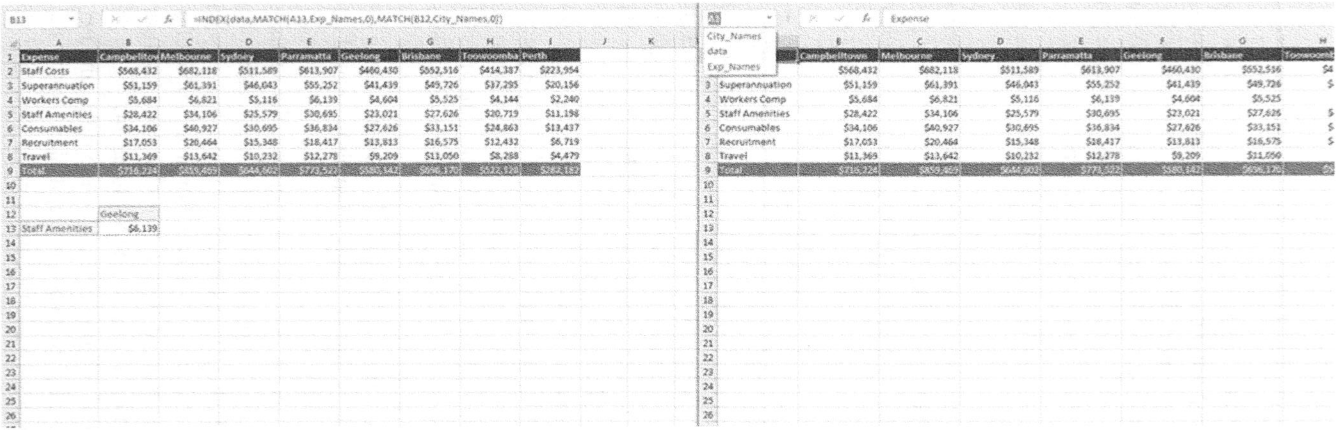

Workbook 1 (cell B13, formula bar: =INDEX(B2:K8,MATCH(A13,Exp_Names,0),MATCH(B12,City_Names,0))

Expense	Campbelltown	Melbourne	Sydney	Parramatta	Geelong	Brisbane	Toowoomba	Perth
Staff Costs	$568,432	$682,118	$511,589	$613,907	$466,430	$652,516	$414,337	$223,954
Superannuation	$51,159	$61,391	$46,043	$55,252	$41,439	$49,726	$37,295	$20,156
Workers Comp	$5,684	$6,821	$5,116	$6,139	$4,604	$5,525	$4,144	$2,240
Staff Amenities	$28,422	$34,106	$25,579	$30,695	$23,021	$27,626	$20,719	$11,198
Consumables	$34,106	$40,927	$30,695	$36,834	$27,626	$33,151	$24,863	$13,437
Recruitment	$17,653	$20,464	$15,348	$18,417	$13,813	$16,575	$12,432	$6,719
Travel	$11,369	$13,642	$10,232	$12,278	$9,209	$11,050	$8,288	$4,479
Total	$716,236	$859,469	$644,602	$773,522	$585,142	$796,170	$522,326	$282,182

	Geelong	
Staff Amenities	$6,139	

Workbook 2 (Name box: City_Names, formula bar: Expense)

Expense	Campbelltown	Melbourne	Sydney	Parramatta	Geelong	Brisbane	Toowoomba
Staff Costs	$568,432	$682,118	$511,589	$613,907	$466,430	$652,516	$4...
Superannuation	$51,159	$61,391	$46,043	$55,252	$41,439	$49,726	$...
Workers Comp	$5,684	$6,821	$5,116	$6,139	$4,604	$5,525	$...
Staff Amenities	$28,422	$34,106	$25,579	$30,695	$23,021	$27,626	$...
Consumables	$34,106	$40,927	$30,695	$36,834	$27,626	$33,151	$...
Recruitment	$17,653	$20,464	$15,348	$18,417	$13,813	$16,575	$...
Travel	$11,369	$13,642	$10,232	$12,278	$9,209	$11,050	$...
Total	$716,236	$859,469	$644,602	$773,522	$585,142	$696,170	$5...

FIGURE 6.28 Completed INDEX Function Using Named Ranges in Separate Workbooks

	A	B	C	D
1	45	36	76	
2	24	75	65	
3	13	54	2	
4	2	33	87	
5				

FIGURE 6.29 Example Data

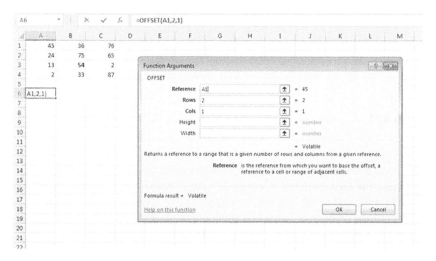

FIGURE 6.30 OFFSET Insert Function Dialog Box

Using an OFFSET to Model Cash Flow

So now that you know how to do an OFFSET function, let's see how it's used in a more practical context. Let's say that you have monthly sales data, but the terms of payment are one month, as shown in Figure 6.31. This means the cash is received one month after the sale is made.

You can create this sheet yourself or a template can be found, along with the accompanying models to the rest of the screenshots in this book, at www .plumsolutions.com.au/book.

Let's create a Cash Receipts line in row 5 using the OFFSET function, which will delay the cash receipts by the number in cell B1. We have indicated that this number can be changed by formatting the cell as an input using the Styles menu.

1. Start in cell C5 and create an OFFSET function that uses cell C4 as a reference point and offsets the number of columns by the number of months in cell B1.

FIGURE 6.31 Calculating a Dynamic Cash Flow Using the OFFSET Function

2. Leave rows blank, as you do not wish to move rows.
3. Make the offset number of columns a negative number, because you wish to return the cell to the left, not the right.
4. Your Insert Function dialog box should look like Figure 6.31, and the formula in cell C5 should be **=OFFSET(C4,,-$B$1)**.
5. Copy this formula across the row.

Nesting OFFSET and COLUMN Formulas

The formula that we have created works when the terms are one month, but if you change the number of months in cell B1 to 2, it will pick up the word Sales in cell A4.

Copy the formula all the way across the row, and B5 returns a #REF! error value, as shown in Figure 6.32. This is a very common problem when using the OFFSET function; we need to edit the formula now to make this model more robust.

One method is to suppress the errors and text. Note that we have three possible value types being returned by this OFFSET:

1. Error (in cell B5)
2. Text (in cell C5)
3. Number (in the rest of the cells in row 5)

FIGURE 6.32 OFFSET Function with Error and Text Values

If we suppress only the error using the IFERROR function, then this will allow the text. We could create a complex nested function that would suppress both the error and the text, like this:

=IF(OR(ISERROR(OFFSET(B4,,-$B$1)),ISTEXT(OFFSET (B4,,-$B$1))),0,OFFSET(B4,,-$B$1))

But a simpler way would be to return the value only in the case of a number (hence, specifying the value we want, not the values we don't want!). Your formula should look like this, as shown in Figure 6.33:

=IF(ISNUMBER(OFFSET(B4,,-$B$1)),OFFSET(B4,,-$B$1),0)

FIGURE 6.33 Completed Dynamic Cash Flow Using a Nested OFFSET Formula

Test the formula by changing the value in cell B1 and check that the result is what you expect. If you are expecting no delay in cash receipts, you can enter a zero in cell B1, and the formula will still work.

TIP

Copy and paste the **OFFSET(B4,,-$B$1)** part of the formula, rather than creating it twice.

Alternatively, you could also nest a COLUMN function to give a similar result. A COLUMN function will return the column reference of the formula. For example, **COLUMN(B3)** returns the value **2**.

We need to add a formula in front of our OFFSET function to say that if the number of months in cell B1 is greater than the column position, it should return a zero. Your formula would look like this:

$$\textbf{=IF(\$B\$1>=COLUMN(B4)-1,0,OFFSET(B4,,-\$B\$1))}$$

See the sheet named "Fig 6.33a" in the supplementary Excel files for this chapter for a working demonstration in Excel.

TIP

Note that cell C1 contains the word *month/s* instead of *month* or *months*. If you insert the formula **=IF(B1=1,"month","months")** into cell C1, the syntax will always be correct no matter what value you insert in cell B1.

REGRESSION ANALYSIS

If you highlight a range of cells in either a column or a row and then drag down or across using the mouse, Excel will use linear regression to forecast what the expected outcome will be. This is fine for a quick piece of analysis, but for a financial model, it's important to show exactly where the numbers came from, so using an auditable function is much better practice.

Using a FORECAST or TREND Function

The FORECAST function in Excel predicts or forecasts data based on historical data, using the linear trend. These functions are a simple way of performing regression analysis in Excel and are useful to include in forecasting models. The TREND function almost always gives the exact same result (but uses the least-squares method instead of the linear trend), so for our purposes, the two can be used interchangeably.

Select the FORECAST (or TREND) function from the Insert Function dialog box.

Basically:

- X is the date or number for which you want the numbers to be forecast.
- Known_ys is the known historical data.
- Known_xs is the known historical dates or numbers.

Let's say, for example, that you have the following historical data available, and you need to provide a forecast for July 2020. You can create this sheet yourself or a template can be found, along with the accompanying models to the rest of the screenshots in this book, at www.plumsolutions.com.au/book.

Date	Sales
Jan-20	650
Feb-20	660
Mar-20	680
Apr-20	670
May-20	700
Jun-20	690
Jul-20	
Aug-20	
Sep-20	
Oct-20	
Nov-20	
Dec-20	

If we were to quickly chart these numbers, we could add a linear trend line to visually see what we expect the forecast to look like. Create the chart by highlighting all the data and then selecting Line Chart from the Insert tab on the ribbon. To create the linear trend line, right-click on the series and select Add Trendline. See Figure 6.34.

We can see from the trajectory of the trend line that, based on historical data, the sales in July 2020 should be somewhere between 700 and 710. The formula tells us the slope, which is what the FORECAST function uses to calculate the projections. See Figure 6.35.

FIGURE 6.34   Inserting a Linear Trend Line

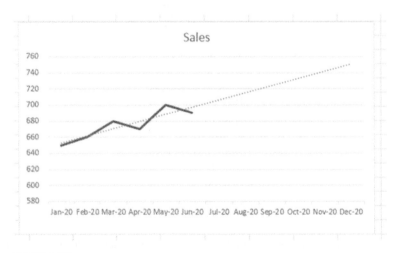

FIGURE 6.35   Linear Trend Line

This is exactly how the FORECAST function calculates forecasts. It looks at the historical relationship between the X-axis and the Y-axis, and projects based on these numbers.

1. To create the FORECAST function, select cell B8.
2. Bring up the **=FORECAST** Insert Function dialog box. The inputs for our formula fields will be:
   - X: A8 (Jul 20) as the date for which we want to forecast.
   - Known_y's: B2:B7 (650 to 690) as the historical data we know already.
   - Known_x's: A2:A7 (Jan 20 to Jun 20) as the corresponding years for the numbers we know already.
3. Your Insert Function dialog box should look something like Figure 6.36.
4. The forecast sales for July 20 is 706, and the line chart that you created earlier will show forecasted values that match the trend line exactly, as shown in Figure 6.37.

TIP

Be sure to use absolute referencing in the second two ranges of your FORE-CAST function. If you don't, then the forecast's original data range will move, making it less accurate over time.

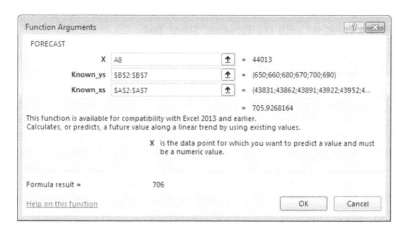

FIGURE 6.36 FORECAST Insert Function Dialog Box

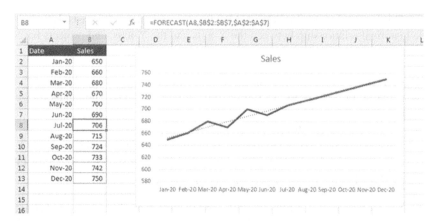

FIGURE 6.37   Completed Line Chart Showing Results of FORECAST

NOTE

If you were in a hurry, you could have simply highlighted the original data and dragged it down, returning the exact same results as the FORECAST or TREND functions. However, this will hardcode the data, making it very difficult to audit, so using a function to forecast your data is much better financial modelling practice.

Creating a Forecast with the Forecast Sheet Tool

A new tool, introduced in Excel 2016, was the Forecast Sheet. By selecting the data and using the tool, it automatically creates the forecast for you, without having to build the functions as described in the previous section.

To try it out, select the historical data or click within the table and, as shown in Figure 6.38, on the Data tab, in the Forecast section, select the Forecast Sheet button. This will bring up the Create Forecast Worksheet dialog box showing a preview of what the chart will look like. Expand the options button in the bottom left-hand corner of the chart, and here you can change some of the options such as the chart type, confidence interval, range, and seasonality.

Press OK, and a new sheet is created with the chart, and new formulas have automatically been created as shown in Figure 6.39.

Note that the FORECAST.ETS function is not available in previous versions of Excel, so you should only use this tool if the model users are on Excel 2016 or later.

FIGURE 6.38   Select the Forecast Sheet Button to Bring Up the Create Forecast Worksheet Dialog Box

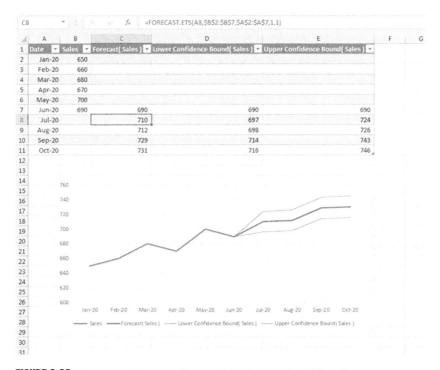

FIGURE 6.39   Completed Forecast Sheet with FORECAST.ETS Function

CHOOSE FUNCTION

The CHOOSE function returns a value from a list of values based on a given position.

For example, let's say you want to pick up the second value in the following list of data in Figure 6.40.

1. Type out the list of days, starting with Sunday.
2. Select cell A9. Go into the Insert Function dialog box and select CHOOSE.
3. Index_num is the value that you want the formula to return. Enter 2 in this field.
4. Enter the values from which you want the formula to choose. Note that you can hardcode these, or use a reference the way that we have done here. See Figure 6.38.
5. Hit OK, and your formula should be

$$=CHOOSE(2,A1,A2,A3,A4,A5,A6,A7)$$

Using a Nested CHOOSE Formula with Dates

Let's say you'd like to be able to enter in any date and have a formula that tells you, in words, the day of the week it is.

1. Go to cell B9 and enter your date. This could be your birth date, or you could create a formula with today's date by typing **=TODAY()**. Every time you

FIGURE 6.40   CHOOSE Insert Function Dialog Box

open the model, it will show the current date. Note that =**NOW**() will show the date and the time.

2. The formula =**WEEKDAY(B9)** will return the day of the week as a number, with Sunday being the first day of the week. Therefore, Sunday=1, Monday=2, and so on.

3. Go back to your previous formula in cell A9, and turn it into a nested formula by replacing the hardcoded 2 with the WEEKDAY formula.

4. Your formula should be:

=**CHOOSE(WEEKDAY(B9),A1,A2,A3,A4,A5,A6,A7)**

Now, each time you open the model, the formula in cell A9 will show the day of the week. See the next section for more date options.

WORKING WITH DATES

Excel treats dates and times as numbers, which means they can be computed mathematically. For example, you can subtract two dates to find the number of days in between. This feature is invaluable in financial modelling, as a very large proportion of financial models are time-series based.

You can add some number of days to a date by using simple formulas. Since Excel stores dates as a number of days, you can change the date by including the date in a formula. For example, to add seven days to 1 Jul 2022 in C3, use =**B3 + 7**, which gives 8 Jul 2022, and hence a weekly cash flow report. See Figure 6.41.

Handy Functions

Many financial models require specific dates or sections of dates for analysis. Excel has a fantastic collection of functions to isolate various parts of dates and calculate special dates like the last day of the month. Given below are some of the more commonly used handy date functions in Excel.

C3			f_x	=B3+7					
◢	A	B	C	D	E	F	G	H	I
1									
2			Weekly Cash Flow Statement						
3	Cash Received	1-Jul-22	8-Jul-22	15-Jul-22	22-Jul-22	29-Jul-22	5-Aug-22	12-Aug-22	
4	Opening Balance	$23,650	$35,899	$47,849	$48,349	$45,849	$35,849	$51,749	
5	Cash Sales	$35,000	$25,000	$18,000	$14,000	$8,000	$30,000	$22,000	
6	Receivables Collected	$2,500	$3,450			$6,000	$2,400	$1,200	
7	Total	$61,150	$64,349	$65,849	$62,349	$59,849	$68,249	$74,949	
8									
9									

FIGURE 6.41 Using a Formula to Calculate Dates

=TODAY(). This function gives today's date, whenever you open the model.

=NOW(). This function gives the exact date *and time*, whenever you open the model.

=EOMONTH. This function gives you the last date of the month, with reference to any date. The snapshot in Figure 6.42 shows how this formula works.

EOMONTH is an extremely useful function because it will always take you to the last day of the month, regardless of how many days it contains. In Figure 6.42, we have a project start date of 6 July 2022 in A2. The last date of the next month is 31 August 2022, which is represented in B2 and can be copied across the row.

The alternative way of doing a variable start date would be to use formula **=A2+30**, and copy it across. But this is not very accurate, and if you have interest calculations running from the dates, for example, the calculations will not be exactly correct.

The other benefit of using the EOMONTH function is that it handles leap years very well. In Figure 6.43, if we have a February start day, and want to show six monthly milestones, you can see that by using the EOMONTH function, it will always give us the last day of the month.

B2			f_x	=EOMONTH(A2,1)			
	A	B	C	D	E	F	G	H
1	Project Start Date	Month 1	Month 2	Month 3	Month 4	Month 5	Month 6	
2	6-Jul-22	31-Aug-22	30-Sep-22	31-Oct-22	30-Nov-22	31-Dec-22	31-Jan-23	
3								
4								
5								
6								

FIGURE 6.42 Using the EOMONTH Function

B3			f_x	=EOMONTH($A$3,B1)			
	A	B	C	D	E	F	G	H
1		6	12	18	24	30	36	
2	Project Start Date	Month Milestone	Month Milestone	Month Milestone	Month Milestone	Month Milestone	Month Milestone	
3	8-Feb-19	31-Aug-19	29-Feb-20	31-Aug-20	28-Feb-21	31-Aug-21	28-Feb-22	
4								
5								
6								
7								
8								

FIGURE 6.43 The EOMONTH Function Calculates a Leap Year Correctly

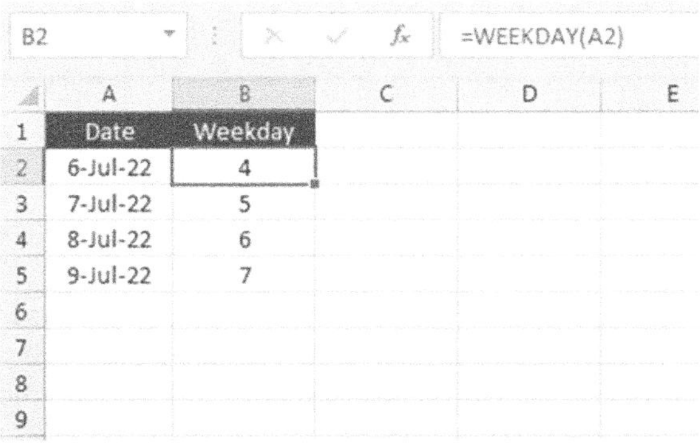

FIGURE 6.44 The WEEKDAY Function Returns the Day of the Week

The year 2020 is a leap year, so cell C3 gives us 29 February 2020, whereas cell E3 gives us 28 February 2021, as 2021 is not a leap year.

While finding the last date of the month is the standard output of the EOMONTH function, with some improvisation you can also get the first day of the month. Since Excel treats dates as numbers, EOMONTH() +1 will give you the first day of the next month if this is required in your model.

=WEEKDAY. This function gives you the day number in the week corresponding to the date specified. In Figure 6.44 you have the dates corresponding to 6 July 2022 through to 9 July 2022. 9 July 2022 returns a 7 because it is the last day of the week, a Saturday.

In your financial model, you may have to make some decisions based on the day of the week, and in such cases, the WEEKDAY function can be a useful filter criterion. For example, trading or stock prices are not shown on the weekends, so you would skip those days for certain calculations.

NOTE

The complete syntax of the WEEKDAY function is **=WEEKDAY(date, return type)**. The return type lets you decide the week cycle for your model. Here are the various options Excel offers you for the return type.

Value	Series of Weekdays
1	Sunday (1) to Saturday (7)
2	Monday (1) to Sunday (7)
3	Monday (0) to Sunday (6)

NOTE
_____

The input to this function must be a valid date in Excel. If the text is not in proper date format, you will get garbled output.

=**YEAR.** This function is used to identify the year in a specified date. If your model needs to use the year in the date for a particular calculation or analysis, this function can help you build the necessary logic. Note that the YEAR function does not help if your fiscal year does not match the calendar year. For example, in Australia, the financial year ends at the end of June, so if you need to return a fiscal year (e.g., 2020/21), you need to create a table showing which dates fall in each financial year, and then use a formula such as a VLOOKUP function to return the value.

=**MONTH.** This is another very similar function that returns the month number in the date.

These functions are particularly useful for summarising and collating raw data. For example, we can use the MONTH function to identify the month, which can then be used as the criteria in a chart, PivotTable, or a SUMIF formula to summarise the raw data into the required format. In Figure 6.45, we have used a MONTH function in column B to automatically pick up the month number of the date. This has then been used as a range in a SUMIF function in column G to aggregate the data, which can then be shown on a column chart. You can create this sheet yourself or a template can be found, along with the accompanying models to the rest of the screenshots in this book, at www.plumsolutions.com.au/book.

NOTE
_____

If using a PivotTable instead of a SUMIF function, as shown in the example in Figure 6.45, the Group feature in PivotTables will automatically aggregate the months.

=**DAY.** This returns the day in the date. As evident, this is very similar to the MONTH and YEAR function. Note that this is different from the WEEKDAY function, which will return the day of the week. DAY will return the day of the month. For example, as shown in Figure 6.46, on 6 July 2022 the DAY function will return a 6, rather than a 4 as shown previously when using the WEEKDAY function in Figure 6.44.

G2 =SUMIF($B$2:$B$28,E2,$C$2:$C$28)

	A	B	C	D	E	F	G
1	Date	Month	Sales			Month	Sales
2	1-Jul-22	7	$1,771		7	July	$12,642
3	8-Jul-22	7	$1,386		8	August	$9,673
4	15-Jul-22	7	$3,954		9	September	$14,645
5	22-Jul-22	7	$3,861		10	October	$11,778
6	29-Jul-22	7	$1,670		11	November	$12,035
7	5-Aug-22	8	$2,959		12	December	$8,997
8	12-Aug-22	8	$3,843				
9	19-Aug-22	8	$1,423				
10	26-Aug-22	8	$1,448				
11	2-Sep-22	9	$3,377				
12	9-Sep-22	9	$3,958				
13	16-Sep-22	9	$3,808				
14	23-Sep-22	9	$2,466				
15	30-Sep-22	9	$1,036				
16	7-Oct-22	10	$3,150				
17	14-Oct-22	10	$1,968				
18	21-Oct-22	10	$2,703				
19	28-Oct-22	10	$3,957				
20	4-Nov-22	11	$3,972				
21	11-Nov-22	11	$2,958				
22	18-Nov-22	11	$1,759				
23	25-Nov-22	11	$3,346				
24	2-Dec-22	12	$1,423				
25	9-Dec-22	12	$2,498				
26	16-Dec-22	12	$1,648				
27	23-Dec-22	12	$2,131				
28	30-Dec-22	12	$1,297				

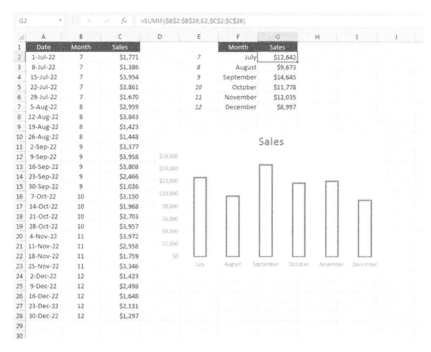

FIGURE 6.45 The MONTH Function Used to Aggregate Data

B2 =DAY(A2)

	A	B
1	Date	Day
2	6-Jul-16	6
3	7-Jul-16	7
4	8-Jul-16	8
5	9-Jul-16	9

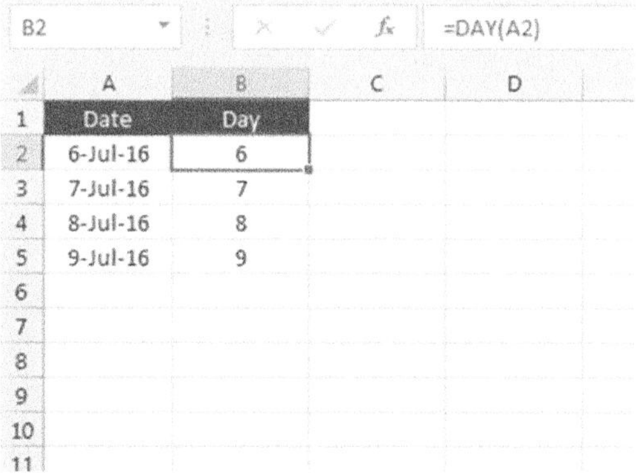

FIGURE 6.46 Using a DAY Function to Return the Calendar Day of the Month

Note that for all three functions MONTH, YEAR, and DAY, the input must be in a valid date format. Without proper input, the desired results cannot be returned.

Date Format Dilemma

Two of the most popular standards used in the world today are the dd/mm/yy (UK) and the mm/dd/yy (US) formats. Depending on the regional relevance of the information, the first two numbers could mean the month or the date. Your financial model must eliminate any such ambiguity, particularly if the model is working across several different regions. It is, therefore, best practice to format dates as 5 June 2021 instead of 5/6/21. This way there is no chance of it being interpreted erroneously as 6 May 2021.

Long and Short Date Formatting

A shortcut exists on the Home tab that allows you to very quickly change the date format on any cell from the Number ribbon, as shown in Figure 6.47.

In the drop-down menu, you should see both the options Short Date and Long Date. (Note that this may differ depending on your regional settings.) The samples for both are shown in the drop-down itself for easy understanding. While you could use any format in your calculations, you can eliminate confusion by sticking to long date format for any information that requires user interaction.

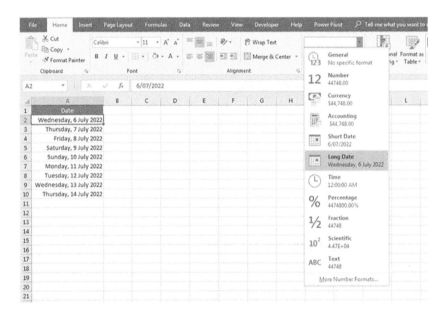

FIGURE 6.47   Shortcut Date Formatting Drop-Down

The short and long dates are not the only formats that Excel provides; you can choose from a much wider range of formats by clicking on the dialog box launcher in the Number ribbon, or by selecting More Number Formats shown at the bottom of the drop-down menu in Figure 6.47.

This brings up the Format Cells dialog box, which you can use to change the way the date appears. In Excel for Mac, the Format Cells dialog box can be found by selecting Format—Cells from the toolbar, or use the shortcut Command+1.

Note that in all versions of Excel, the Format Cells dialog box can be found by right-clicking on the cell and selecting Format Cells.

See the section "Custom Formatting" in Chapter 7 for greater detail on how to create different formats.

FINANCIAL PROJECT EVALUATION FUNCTIONS

Financial functions are designed to save Excel users time when calculating long and complicated formulas such as interest repayments, depreciation, or net present value (NPV). They can be created manually, and if you have studied business or finance at university level, you will have had to create these calculations the long way or using a financial calculator. The predefined function in Excel saves time and makes it much easier to carry out commonly used financial calculations.

There are three financial functions that are commonly used to assess a business case or any series of cash flows: NPV, internal rate of return (IRR), and payback period. There are predefined functions in Excel for calculating NPV and IRR, but there is not one for payback period. For methods on how to calculate a payback period manually, see the section "How to Calculate a Payback Period" in Chapter 9.

Net Present Value

NPV is the value of the expected future cash flows from an investment, expressed in today's dollars. The investor specifies a target rate of return (the cost of capital) for investing capital; it is an opportunity cost concept. Investors have the choice of investing in a project, or putting their funds elsewhere, so they determine the hurdle rate or the amount they want to get back from the project.

The general rule (and the one you would have studied in your university finance textbooks) for considering the investment is: If the NPV is greater than zero, the investment should be accepted; if the NPV is negative, it should be rejected. A positive NPV means the investor can expect to earn a rate of return greater than the required return rate for such an investment. However, from a financial modelling perspective, the decision-making process is much more complicated than a deal or no-deal situation. It really depends on the scenario and sensitivity analysis from the financial model to test whether or not the project should go ahead. Large companies often have policies regarding the standard cost of capital or how long the payback period can be before it is rejected.

What Cost of Capital Should We Use?   How much time is spent calculating the cost of capital really depends on how detailed your modelling is. Many models will simply use a nominated amount and document this as an assumption. This nominated cost of capital could be anything between, say, 6 and 15 percent (although sometimes higher), and it can fluctuate depending on the perceived risk of the project. We may decide to use a very high required rate of return for a risky project, to compensate for the risk taken.

However, instead of simply nominating a cost of capital amount, as we will do in the example in Figure 6.48, you may decide to calculate the weighted average cost of capital (WACC). This calculation takes into account the mixture and rates of debt and equity in the company and is, therefore, a much more accurate way of evaluating the expected rate of return for a project. For greater detail on how to calculate the WACC, see the section "Weighted Average Cost of Capital (WACC)" in Chapter 9.

What is Wrong with the NPV Function?   Note that a key assumption of the NPV function is that the cash flows occur at the end of the period, whereas in reality, they will probably occur unevenly throughout the year, with a large portion of costs spent closer to the beginning of the period. In the example shown below, we have included the initial investment in the first year. If, however, we know that a large initial investment will be made prior to the start of the project, then this should be included in year 0, and added to the NPV calculation like this: **=NPV(B4,B2:F2) + Y0_investment**.

HOW TO CALCULATE THE NPV

With a series of cash flows as shown in Figure 6.48, the NPV is calculated as follows:

1. Select NPV function. At the Rate prompt, link it to the cost of capital, which we will assume is 12 percent.
2. At the Value1 prompt, link the formula to the cells that contain the expected return (i.e., as we are calculating the 5-year NPV, it will be the profit or loss for 2020 to 2024). The formula should be **=NPV (B4,B2:F2)**.
3. The result of your formula should be $127,568.

In this case, the NPV is greater than zero, meaning that the return is greater than the required rate of return of 12 percent stated by the company.

This means that, theoretically, the project should be accepted. However, scenario and sensitivity analysis will help determine how sensitive the model is to changes in inputs and gain a better perspective on whether or not this project should be accepted.

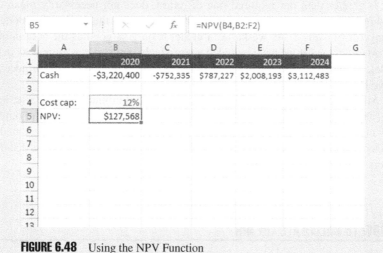

FIGURE 6.48   Using the NPV Function

Internal Rate of Return

IRR equates the present value of the cash inflows and the present value of the cash outflows. The decision rule, in this case, is: If the IRR is greater than or equal to the investor's required rate of return, the investment should be accepted; otherwise, it should be rejected.

Comparing IRR with the Risk Factor   Knowing about the IRR is of little use unless you can make decisions using it. To do that, you must compare the IRR with the risk factor.

There are two possible outcomes when you compare the IRR with risk.

1. The projected returns from the investment are greater than the risk. In other words, the returns from the investment are high enough to justify the risk of the investment. This is a positive recommendation to invest.
2. The projected returns from the investment are less than the risk. In other words, the returns from the investment are not high enough to justify the risk of the investment. This is a negative recommendation, cautioning against investment.

Like NPV, IRR uses all three criteria—returns, risk, and time—in its evaluation, and for this reason, many managers find it an easy, accurate, and dependable tool to use.

Using NPV and IRR to Make Decisions Just because the NPV is positive, and our IRR is greater than our required rate of return, does not necessarily mean that we should go ahead with the project! Blindly accepting the output of a model is a dangerous business. As we know, a model is only as good as the assumptions that go into it, and if we have included aggressively optimistic assumptions in our model, of course, the NPV will look good—but this does not mean the project will do well!

All financial models should be subjected to, at minimum, a base-case, best-case, and worst-case scenario, which are used to evaluate the sensitivity of outputs to changes in inputs. The NPV, IRR, and payback period, which are calculated by the model, should be used as decision-making factors and not the ultimate deciding factors of the fate of the project.

HOW TO CALCULATE THE IRR

Using the same investment assumptions as in the previous example, the rate of return on the initial investment can be calculated as follows:

1. Select the IRR function.
2. At the Values prompt, select or specify the cells that contain the requested information.
3. Leave the Guess prompt blank at this stage. (See the section "The Problem with IRR" for greater detail on when and why you need to include a guess.) In this instance, all the cash flows are positive, so we don't need to enter a guess.
4. Click on the OK button and the yield (IRR) is displayed. The formula should be: **=IRR(B2:F2)**.
5. The result of your formula should be 13.3 percent and look something like Figure 6.49.

In this case, the IRR is higher than the required rate of return of 12 percent, as stated by the company. This means that, theoretically, the project should be accepted.

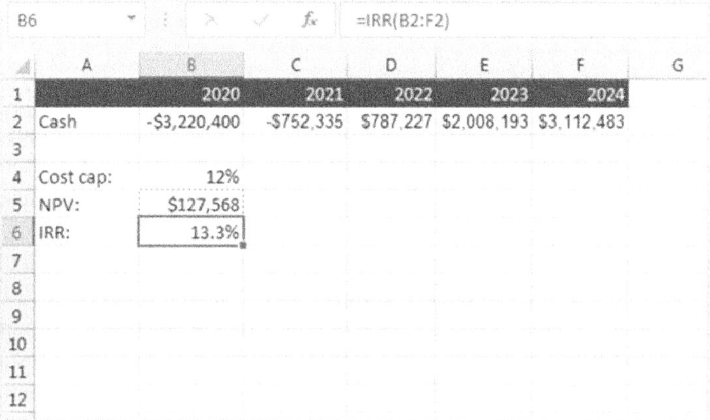

B6 =IRR(B2:F2)

	A	B	C	D	E	F	G
1		2020	2021	2022	2023	2024	
2	Cash	-$3,220,400	-$752,335	$787,227	$2,008,193	$3,112,483	
3							
4	Cost cap:	12%					
5	NPV:	$127,568					
6	IRR:	13.3%					
7							
8							
9							
10							
11							
12							

FIGURE 6.49 Using the IRR Function

The Problem with IRR There are a few issues with the IRR function that the modeller needs to be aware of.

Sometimes the IRR function in Excel can produce multiple results. Every time the cash flows change sign (i.e., from negative to positive or from positive to negative), the formula will create another solution. This is why it is a good idea to insert a guessed amount—especially if the sign of the cash flows is not consistent.

Take the following set of cash flows in Figure 6.50 as an example.

If we use the ordinary IRR function without using the guess [entered as **=IRR(B2:H2)**], we get a result of 13 percent. However, because there are several negative returns in this series of cash flows, there are multiple results. If you enter the following guesses, different IRRs will be returned:

=IRR(B2:H2) gives a result of 13 percent.

=IRR(B2:H2,0) gives a result of 6 percent.

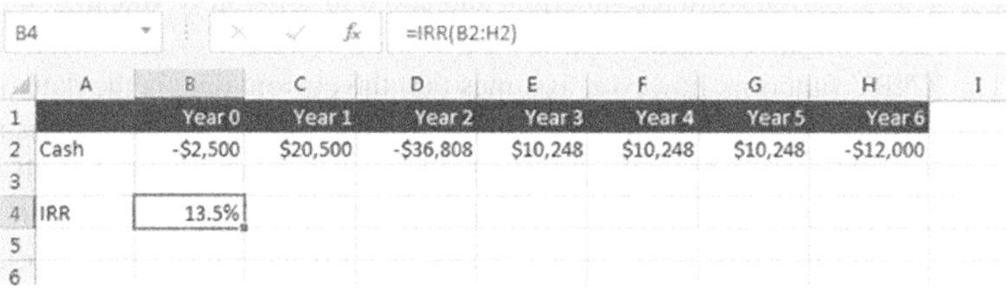

B4 =IRR(B2:H2)

	A	B	C	D	E	F	G	H	I
1		Year 0	Year 1	Year 2	Year 3	Year 4	Year 5	Year 6	
2	Cash	-$2,500	$20,500	-$36,808	$10,248	$10,248	$10,248	-$12,000	
3									
4	IRR	13.5%							
5									
6									

FIGURE 6.50 IRR Calculation with Multiple Results

=IRR(B2:H2,30%) gives a result of 25 percent.

=IRR(B2:H2,400%) gives a result of 481 percent.

Which one is correct? They all are! There are several valid IRRs. Excel goes through an iterative process and comes up with the first solution it finds, which does not necessarily give you the result you want. This is why it's important to use the guess. If the guess is omitted, IRR is assumed to be 10 percent because this is close to a usual rate of return.

Another issue with the IRR is that the way the IRR function calculates in Excel, it assumes that cash generated during the investment period will be reinvested at the rate that has been calculated by the IRR. If the project is generating a lot of cash, the IRR calculation can overstate the financial benefits substantially, which is something that needs to be considered and possibly manually manipulated in the calculations.

We don't normally make any changes to the calculations to account for these problems, but it's important to be aware of these issues when calculating the IRR.

What Difference Does an X Make? XNPV and XIRR   The NPV formula assumes that the values entered into the formula are annual, are in chronological order, and occur at the end of the period.

XNPV and XIRR are relatively new functions introduced for Excel 2007 that offer more flexibility, as you can specify exactly when the payments occur.

XNPV allows you to enter payments that occur at varying intervals, not necessarily in chronological order (although the first payment must still be shown first), and occur at any time. Therefore, it is a much more flexible and useful function. Also, because it does not assume that the payments occur at the end of the period, the XNPV formula will be more accurate.

Be careful when comparing the NPV and XNPV functions, as the NPV assumes the current period (the date we are in right now) is a full year prior to the first cash amount and therefore discounts the first amount back by a full 12 percent (or whatever the nominated discount rate is). If this is not the case, you need to exclude the first period from the function, and add it in separately, like this: **=NPV (B4,B2:F2) + Y0_investment**.

The XNPV function, however, assumes that the current date is the date of the first cash flow, so, in the example shown in Figure 6.51, the current date is assumed to be 1 June 2021. Therefore, the first cash amount is not discounted at all. IRR and XIRR have the same issue. This is quite misleading, as most people naturally assume that the functions, being slight variations on the same formula, work in a similar way, but the way they treat the first cash amount is quite different!

HOW TO CALCULATE THE NPV USING THE XNPV FUNCTION

If you were to be more precise about the actual timings of the expected cash flow, you would get a more accurate NPV calculation using XNPV.

Instead of saying that you expect a net outflow of $3.2 million in 2021, let's be a little more specific about when the outflows actually occur. Let's say you split that into $2 million in June 2021, and the rest at the end of the year. We will also put a date in the middle of the year for subsequent years, which is more likely to accurately reflect what will happen, instead of assuming that payments are made or received at the end of the period, as it does with the NPV calculation.

Figure 6.51 shows the cash flows.

B5		∧ ✓	f_x	=XNPV(B4,B2:G2,B1:G1)			
	A	B	C	D	E	F	G
1		1-Jun-21	31-Dec-21	30-Jun-22	30-Jun-23	30-Jun-24	30-Jun-25
2	Profit / Loss	-$2,000,000	-$1,220,400	-$752,335	$787,227	$2,008,193	$3,112,483
3							
4	Cost cap:	12.00%					
5	XNPV:	$189,779					
6	XIRR:	13.8%					
7							

FIGURE 6.51 XNPV Function

Using the XNPV formula, and assuming that the cost of capital is, say, 12 percent, the formula should be: **=XNPV(B4,B2:G2,B1:G1)**, giving us a result of $189,779.

Similarly, the XIRR can be calculated using the formula **=XIRR (B2:G2,B1:G1)**, giving us a result of 13.8 percent.

LOAN CALCULATIONS

Calculating debt is an important part of many financial models, and understanding the theory behind how loan repayments are calculated will help in financial modelling. The way that interest, principal, and periodic payments are calculated can be complicated, and fortunately for us, Excel has many useful functions that make calculating loans a lot easier. However, you should still have a basic understanding of how loan calculations work.

Loan-Interest Calculation Method

Interest on loans can be calculated using either the simple interest method or the compound interest method. The simple interest method charges the same amount of interest each year, but under the compound interest method, the interest is added to the loan, thereby increasing the loan amount each year. From the moment at which the interest is added to the loan, it charges interest on itself, increasing the interest on a compounding basis. The compound interest method is by far the most commonly used method, and in the examples in this chapter we assume that the interest is compounding.

When evaluating a loan, you may also need to consider the compounding frequency. If the interest is added to the loan on a daily basis, this would actually make the loan interest payments much higher than if it were added monthly or annually. Most loans are normally calculated on a daily basis, and this means the interest rate actually charged is higher.

Note that the PMT function shown further on, if calculated on an annual basis, does not compound the interest. You will need to convert the interest rate from a nominal or effective rate before using it in the calculation.

Nominal and Effective Interest Rates We are used to seeing interest rates expressed as an annual rate (e.g., an interest rate of 12 percent means that we are charged 12 percent per year). However, this is only the nominal rate, and this does not mean that we are charged 1 percent per month. In fact, if the interest is calculated daily, we are charged 12 percent divided by 365, or 0.33 percent on the first day of the loan. This amount is added to the principal, so on day two, we are actually paying interest on the interest from the previous day. I know this sounds trivial, but it can make a big difference to your calculations on a large debt.

TIP

An easy way to work out the effective interest rate is to use the EFFECT function (available since Excel 2007) to calculate the effective rate of 12 percent, compounded daily. Use the formula **=EFFECT(12%,365)**. The answer is 12.75 percent. See the section "Understanding Nominal and Effective (Real) Rates" in Chapter 9 for greater detail on how to use this function, as well as the NOMINAL function.

Loan Repayment According to an Amortisation Schedule

The most common form of calculating loan repayments is to apply an amortisation schedule. Regular repayments of equal value made over the term of the loan are used to pay both the interest charged as well as a portion of the principal amount. With each repayment, an amount equal to the value of the interest charged for the period is applied first to the interest portion, and the remainder of the repayment is then set off against the principal. In this way, the principal decreases after each repayment and the interest calculated for the next period will, therefore, be less, as it is calculated on a smaller principal amount.

To calculate the amount of the equal repayments to be made, the interest rate, the principal amount, and the term of the loan must be known. As interest rates are usually subject to change, the monthly repayment will often have to be revised during the course of the loan.

If you need to calculate the repayments in longhand using the amortisation method, the following formula is used:

$$\text{Repayment} = \left(\frac{\text{Loan amount} \times i(1 + i)^n}{(1 + i)^n - 1} \right)$$

where

i = the interest rate per annum, which must be divided by the number of repayment periods per annum (e.g., 12 if payments are made monthly)

n = the number of repayment periods (e.g., 24 if the loan is for a period of 2 years and repayments are made monthly)

Excel Amortisation Functions   Whilst it's good to know the theory of how the repayments are calculated, fortunately, Excel offers several loan calculation functions that can easily be included in financial models. The following are some of the most common functions available in Excel for loan-related calculations.

PMT. This is the very basic function that calculates the fixed amount you need to pay at regular intervals to repay the loan along with fixed interest. The syntax for PMT is **PMT(rate, number of payments, principal amount, final amount, type)**. In this syntax, the following applies:

Rate. This is the fixed interest rate for the loan period.

Number of repayments. This is the number of instalments within which you want to repay the loan.

Principal amount. Amount of original loan (no interest included).

Final amount. The total amount at the end of all the instalments. This is not a mandatory field and the default value is set to zero.

Type. This determines when the payment needs to be made. The default value is zero, which means at the end of the period; one means at the start of the period.

In Figure 6.52, we have a loan of $1 million repaid over a 10-year period (annually) at 8 percent interest rate. You can create this sheet

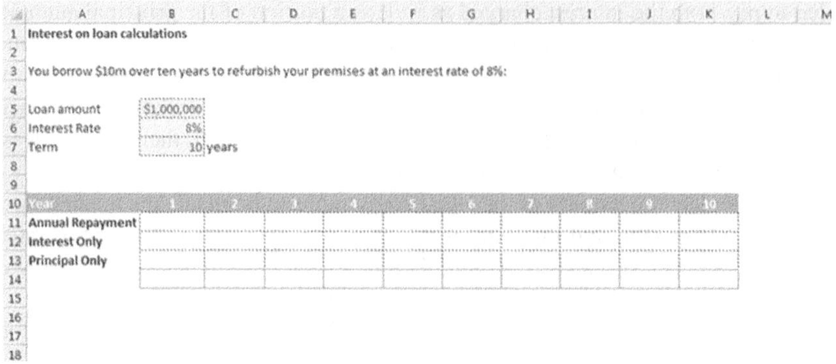

FIGURE 6.52   Loan Template

yourself or a template can be found, along with the accompanying models to the rest of the screenshots in this book, at www.plumsolutions.com .au/book.

In cell B11, the PMT function can calculate the fixed payment amount payable each year, which in this case is $149,029. The Insert Function dialog box should look like Figure 6.53.

IPMT. The IPMT function is complementary to the PMT function. While PMT calculates the entire repayment instalment amount, IPMT gives the interest component of the instalment. Like PMT, this is calculated for a fixed principal and interest rate for a given duration of time. The syntax

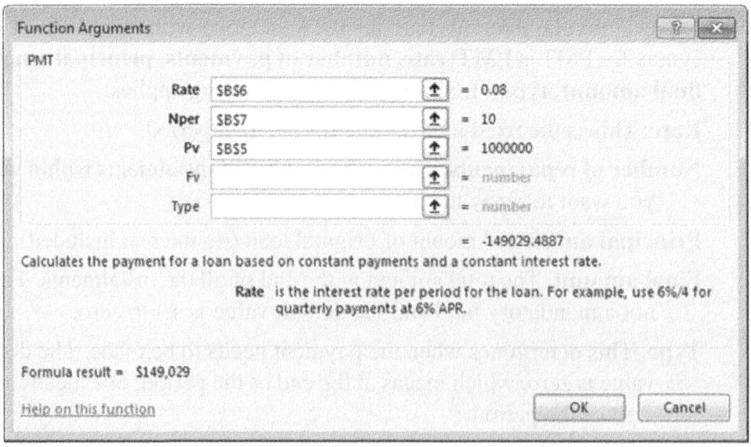

FIGURE 6.53   PMT Insert Function Dialog Box

for IPMT is **IPMT(rate, period, number of payments, principal amount, final amount, type)**, where the following applies:

Rate. This is the fixed interest rate for the loan period.

Period. This is the period for which the interest amount needs to be calculated. For the first period (week, month, year, etc.) this would be 1, and for subsequent periods it will increase as 2, 3, 4, and so on.

Number of repayments. This is the number of instalments within which you want to repay the loan.

Principal amount. Amount of original loan (no interest included).

Final amount. The total amount at the end of all the instalments. This is not a mandatory field and the default value is set to zero.

Type. This determines when the payment needs to be made. The default value is zero, which means at the end of the period; one means at the start of the period.

In Figure 6.54, C10 represents the period that changes in the formula, while all other parameters are fixed references to the loan amount.

PPMT. This is another complementary function to the PMT function. PPMT is similar to IPMT, but it returns the other component of the instalment: principal amount. The syntax for PPMT is **PPMT(rate, period, number of payments, principal amount, final amount, type)**. In this syntax, the following applies:

Rate. This is the fixed interest rate for the loan period.

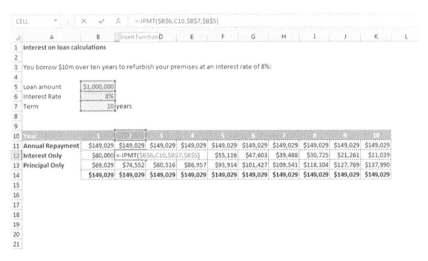

FIGURE 6.54 IPMT Function

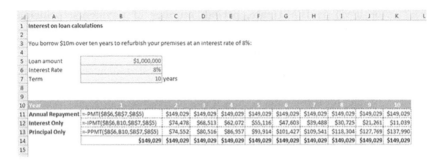

⏃	A	B	C	D	E	F	G	H	I	J	K	L
1	Interest on loan calculations											
2												
3	You borrow $10m over ten years to refurbish your premises at an interest rate of 8%:											
4												
5	Loan amount	$1,000,000										
6	Interest Rate	8%										
7	Term	10 years										
8												
9												
10	Year		1	2	3	4	5	6	7	8	9	10
11	Annual Repayment	=-PMT($B$6,$B$7,$B$5)	$149,029	$149,029	$149,029	$149,029	$149,029	$149,029	$149,029	$149,029	$149,029	$149,029
12	Interest Only	=-IPMT($B$6,B10,$B$7,$B$5)	$74,478	$68,513	$62,072	$55,116	$47,603	$39,488	$30,725	$21,261	$11,039	
13	Principal Only	=-PPMT($B$6,B10,$B$7,$B$5)	$74,552	$80,516	$86,957	$93,914	$101,427	$109,541	$118,304	$127,769	$137,990	
14			$149,029	$149,029	$149,029	$149,029	$149,029	$149,029	$149,029	$149,029	$149,029	$149,029
15												

FIGURE 6.55 Loan with Completed PMT, IPMT, and PPMT Functions

Period. This is the period for which the interest amount needs to be calculated. For the first period (week, month, year, etc.) this would be 1, and for subsequent periods it will increase as 2, 3, 4, and so on.

Number of repayments. This is the number of instalments within which you want to repay the loan.

Principal amount. Amount of original loan (no interest included).

Final amount. The total amount at the end of all the instalments. This is not a mandatory field and the default value is set to zero.

Type. This determines when the payment needs to be made. The default value is zero, which means at the end of the period; one means at the start of the period.

In Figure 6.54, C10 again represents the period that changes in the formula, while all other parameters are fixed references to the loan amount. All three completed functions can be seen in Figure 6.55.

TIP

If you want to verify your calculations, always remember that the sum of IPMT and PPMT must equal PMT. This is a great opportunity to enter an error check!

Why Does the Interest Amount Decrease on a Fixed Interest Rate?

When using an amortisation schedule for loan repayment calculations, the initial interest amounts are high, but with each period the interest amount goes down and

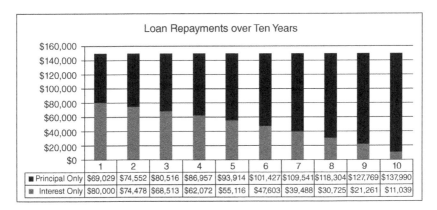

FIGURE 6.56 Principal (PPMT) and Interest (IPMT) Components of Loan Repayments over 10 Years

the principal amount increases. This is reflected in Figure 6.56, which is a stacked column chart based on the results in Figure 6.55.

Looking at the graph, the calculations may initially seem incorrect, since the interest rate is constant but the interest amount is decreasing. This can be better understood by delving into the actual amounts. The original principal amount was $1 million and the interest was calculated on this principal amount as $80,000. The rest of the instalment ($69,029) went towards repaying the principal.

In the second year, the principal amount was reduced by the first instalment ($69,029 went towards the principal). This means that the new principal is $1 million less the first instalment, which is $930,971. Due to the reduced principal amount, the net interest amount is reduced. However, to maintain the constant instalment amount, the principal amount is increased. Extrapolating this calculation, it is evident that as the period number increases, the unpaid principal amount decreases, and so does the interest amount. However, the principal amount being repaid increases to maintain constant repayment instalments.

SUMMARY

In this chapter, we have covered a few of the important aggregation, lookup, referencing, date, and finance functions that, at minimum, are important for a financial modeller to know. As we know, however, there is a lot more to being a good financial modeller than knowing hundreds of different Excel functions! The most challenging part is to know *when* to use these functions in your modelling. When faced with a problem, creating a modelling solution that contains the most appropriate tools and functions is the task faced by the financial modeller. Usually, there are several different possible tools that can be used, and the one that is the most concise, yet easiest to follow, will be the best solution.

CHAPTER 7

Tools for Model Display

L eaving aside the formulas and calculations of a model, in this chapter we will focus on the look and feel of a model. There are many Excel tools that can be used to make the model more attractive and friendly to the user. We'll look at the basic formatting, then more complex custom formatting, conditional formatting, and then form controls, which can be built to help the user interact with the model more easily.

BASIC FORMATTING

Believe it or not, as simple as it may sound, good formatting is an important part of building a financial model. While it's critical of course to get the numbers right, making your model look good is the next logical step. A model that is well formatted will be more readable, user-friendly, and easy to navigate. Additionally, you, the modeller, will find it easier to work with the model if it is clearly formatted.

In the latest version of Excel, all the formatting options for colour, font, and alignment are clearly displayed on the Home tab. A shortcut exists on the Home tab where you can very quickly change the number format on any cell from the Number ribbon, as shown in Figure 7.1.

For detailed instructions on the more basic formatting tools, including changing number formats, percentage and currency formatting, number alignment, cell attributes, and styles, please see the supplementary material at www.plumsolutions .com.au/book, available for download in PDF format.

FIGURE 7.1   Formatting in the Ribbon

CUSTOM FORMATTING

We can go one step further with our formatting to customise the way data is displayed in cells without changing the underlying data. For instance, the function **NOW()** gets the current date and time from your computer and, by default, displays it in the format "dd/mm/yyyy hh:mm" (or according to the date conventions in your computer's Region and Language Options within Control Panel).

We can change the look of this date without disturbing its intrinsic value by formatting it differently. Let's have a look at how we'd do this:

1. Open a blank spreadsheet and type into cell A1 **Report as at**, and into cell B1 type the function =**NOW()** or =**TODAY()**, as shown in Figure 7.2.
2. Size the column widths to match the data, then select cell B1 for formatting.
3. Choose the formatting drop-down in the Home tab on the ribbon. Select More Number Formats at the bottom of the drop-down list that appears.

   In Excel for Mac, from the Format menu, select Cells.

   The dialog box in Figure 7.3 appears, showing how Excel has already customised the cell.

   As can be seen from the dialog box, there are many preset formatting options for numbers, from General to Accounting to Custom. As suggested within the dialog box, we can type our own codes over preset ones if the format we want isn't available.
4. To create a customised format, select Custom from the Category list. Overwrite Excel's choice of "dd/mm/yyyy hh:mm" with just the three characters "mmm" and observe what Excel does with your date. Add a further "m" to make our custom formatting "mmmm" and the result will be, after reflection, obvious.
5. Custom format your current date to the following format: 24 Feb 2017 (your date will be different in content).

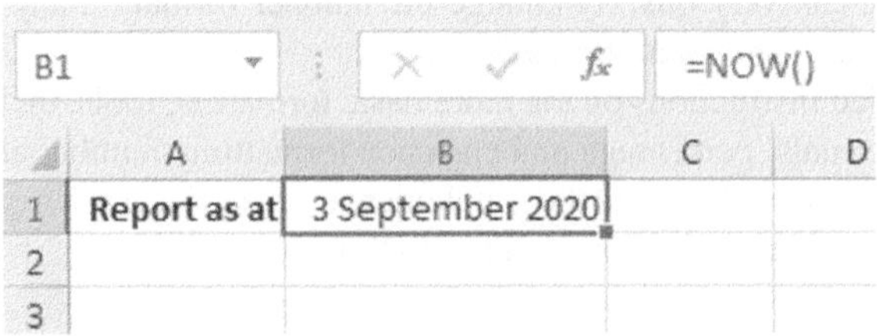

FIGURE 7.2 Showing the Current Date and Time Using the =NOW() Function

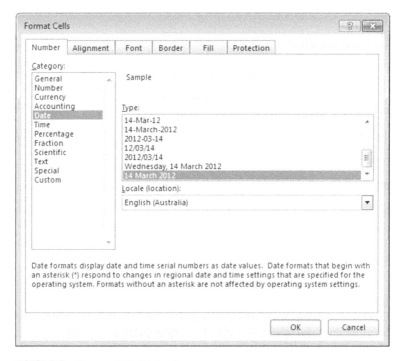

FIGURE 7.3 Format Cells Dialog Box

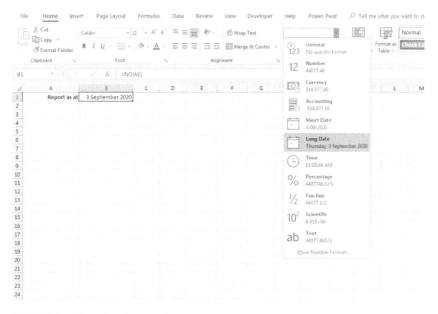

FIGURE 7.4 Changing the Date Format

TIP

In all Windows Excel versions, the shortcut key Control+1 will invoke the formatting dialog box as seen in step 3 above.

The ribbon has an additional shortcut to preset formats in the Number section of the Home tab, as seen in Figure 7.4.

Custom Currency Symbols

As mentioned earlier, changing the look of a cell doesn't affect the underlying data. So far we've played with dates (which are numbers to Excel, even though they're generally displayed as text), but there are plenty of other preset number formats that we can, if necessary, customise in four steps.

1. Go to a blank sheet, and type **582504** into a cell. If you have not defined any formatting on that cell yet, Excel will assign a General format to it.
2. Change the number to currency, preceded by your country's monetary symbol, by using the Currency category in the Format Cells dialog box.
3. Change the currency symbol to that of the Japanese Yen, or some other commonly used currency.
4. Change the currency symbol to that of a currency we've made up—Elbonian Spree (EL).

As you might have suspected, the Elbonian Spree isn't available in the list of symbols. We'll have to build a custom format for it.

Select the Custom category and overwrite Excel's ¥ symbol with EL, as follows: **[$¥-804]#,##0** is changed to **"EL"#,##0**.

Note that EL, as invented by us, is probably unknown to your version of Excel and therefore must be presented as a string (i.e., in quotes). This custom currency symbol will be saved with the workbook and will be available for future use.

Understanding Excel's Number Formats Number formats have four elements:

1. Positive number
2. Negative number
3. Zero
4. Text

Each is separated by a semicolon. None of them is mandatory, but there should be a positive element at least.

Consider the elements in the format **$*#,##0; [Red]$*-#,##0; $*"4";"*"**.

	Positive	**Negative**	**Zero**	**Text**
Format	$*#,##0	[Red]$*#,##0	$*"4"	"*"
Value	1000.00	100.00	0.00	Jack
Representation	$1,000	$100	$	*

Leading zeros of both positive and negative numbers will be suppressed wherever # is specified. Negatives will show the minus symbol after $ and zeros will display. The text Jack will be represented as a single asterisk. The monetary symbol asterisks ($*) indicate that the symbol must be fixed to the left and not follow the number as it shrinks or expands.

You'll note that Excel sometimes uses codes, particularly in currency formats. These are used, for instance, in differentiating between Australian and US dollars—and we know that specifying currency units is critical for financial modelling best practice.

The important thing to remember is that the underlying number doesn't change, no matter how we format it. It retains its decimal places even if we can't see them. Arithmetic can continue to be done on a cell's contents, even if it's invisible.

Useful Formatting Options If you intentionally leave an element blank, it will be rendered invisible. **$#,##0.00;;** will show positives only, all the other elements being deliberately suppressed. The entry **;;** will make everything in the cell invisible (so will changing the font colour to match the background).

To display a number as 000s, while still retaining its full value, custom format it as **$#,##0,** (the format followed by a comma). Millions are represented by **$#,##0,,"m"**. $458,243,555.42 will display as $458m, which, if multiplied by one, will return $458,243,555.42. *If this doesn't work, your digit grouping symbols within Region and Language Options in the Control Panel are not set as commas.*

To physically change a number to rounded thousands, use the ROUND, ROUNDUP, or ROUNDDOWN functions, employing minus digits. **ROUND(458 243,-3)** will change the number to $458,000. The format **$#,##0,** will display $458, which could easily lead to misinterpretation of the numbers, so I recommend the use of the format $#,##0"k" instead.

To make currency negatives by default show in brackets (parentheses), change your negative Currency Format options within Region and Language Options in the Control Panel to default to parentheses.

Custom Formatting in Reporting

Let's say you have a report similar to the one shown in Figure 7.5. You can create this sheet yourself or a template can be found, along with the accompanying

⊿	A	B	C
1	Report as at	3 September 2020	
2			
3	Current Assets		
4	Cash in bank	582504	
5	Accounts receivable	235527	
6	Inventory	150534	
7	Prepaid expenses	43	
8	Other current assets	642015	
9	Total Current Assets	1610623	
10			

FIGURE 7.5 Sample Report

models to the rest of the screenshots in this book, at www.plumsolutions.com.au/book.

We are going to format the numbers in the following two steps so that they look like Figure 7.6 (without changing the underlying data):

1. Highlight the data and, as described above, go to the Custom Formatting dialog box.
2. Add a comma to the end of the format type, as shown in Figure 7.6.

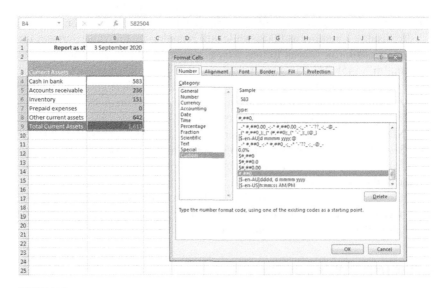

FIGURE 7.6 Custom Formatting Using the Format Cells Dialog Box

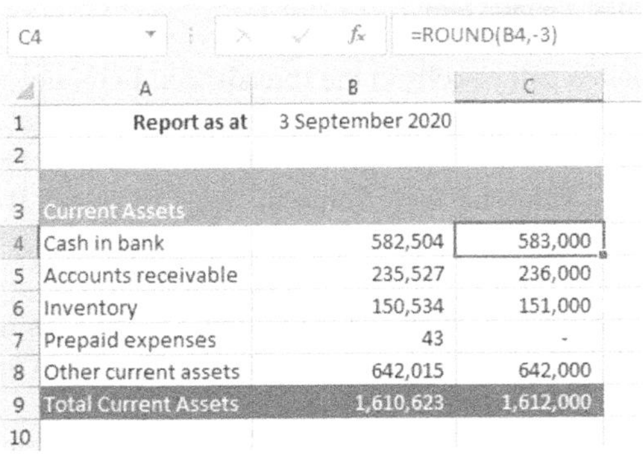

FIGURE 7.7   Using the ROUND Function to Truncate
Values

This will change the look of the numbers without changing the value of the
numbers at all. We can see in the formula bar in Figure 7.6 that the underlying
value of cell B4 is 582504, but because of the custom formatting we have used,
the cell shows the value 583.

Next, add up the visible values of the cells B4:B8 manually like this:
=583+236+151+0+642. You'll see that the total should be $1,612, not $1,611!
Use the **ROUND** function, as shown in Figure 7.7, to round the numbers to the
nearest thousand, such that your report or PowerPoint slide is correct. Change the
formatting back to show the additional zeros if you wish. Your formula should
be **=ROUND(B4,-3)**. Normally, the ROUND function is often used to remove
decimal places, but in this case, it has been used to remove precision in reporting.

CONDITIONAL FORMATTING

Conditional Formatting is a tool that allows you to apply formats to a cell or range
of cells, and have that formatting change, depending on the value of the cell or the
value of a formula. For example, you can have a cell appear bold only when the
value of the cell is greater than 100. When the value of the cell meets the format
condition, the format you select is applied to the cell. If the value of the cell does
not meet the format condition, the cell's default formatting is used.

This is handy for variance analysis on a profit and loss (P&L), for example.
If you want to highlight any instance where a variance is 10 percent higher than
budget or more, the cell will turn red.

Remember that Conditional Formatting is the same as adding one or more
formulas to each cell in which you use it, so applying Conditional Formatting to
a large number of cells may cause performance degradations—use caution when
applying to large ranges.

To Apply Conditional Formatting

1. Select the desired cell or cells in the spreadsheet. Let's say, for example, you wanted to highlight with a red font any cell value that is between 1 and 10.
2. On the Home tab, in the Styles group, select Conditional Formatting. Select Highlight Cells Rule and then Between. Type in 1 and 10, and define the desired font colour. See Figure 7.8.

Add a new rule for each new condition; you can have as many as you like (unlike in the old Excel 2003, where you were limited to three rules).

To Remove Conditional Formatting

On the Home tab, in the Styles group, select Conditional Formatting. Select Manage Rules, and you can delete your chosen rules one by one. Alternatively, you can clear rules from selected cells or from the entire sheet by clicking on Clear Rules.

Data Bars

Data bars are dynamic bar charts that you can apply to any numerical data in Excel. They graphically show the relative size of each value, as shown in Figure 7.9.

FIGURE 7.8   Applying Conditional Formatting

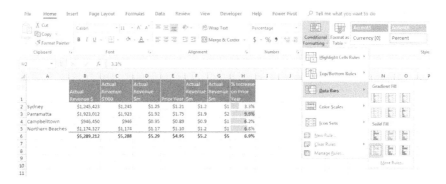

FIGURE 7.9   Applying Data Bars

You can create your own examples or a template can be found, along with the accompanying models to the rest of the screenshots in this book, at www .plumsolutions.com.au/book.

Go to a table of numeric data, and highlight the numbers in the following three steps:

1. On the Home tab, in the Styles group, select Conditional Formatting, and then Data Bars.
2. Choose your desired bar.
3. Practice changing the underlying numbers, and see the bars change.

Icon Sets and Colour Scales

Icon Sets allow you to conditionally display a small icon that represents changes in data. For example, if revenues are down this month compared to last, you may choose to represent this with a red arrow pointing down, or if your cash balance is above a certain threshold, you could use a green checkmark to give the user a quick way to see that everything is okay.

Your options for icons are shown in Figure 7.10, and these are extremely useful in dashboards and other reports.

TIP

While the traffic lights are popular choices for icon sets in dashboards and reporting, the round shapes are not very informative when the report is printed in black and white, nor are they useful for those afflicted by the commonest form of colour blindness. Consider using the up–down arrows, or checkmarks and crosses instead of the traffic lights.

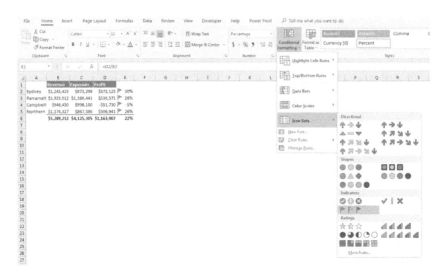

FIGURE 7.10   Accessing Icon Sets

	A	B	C	D	E	F	G	H	I
1		Jan	Feb	Mar	Apr	May	Jun	Jul	
2	Investment 1	0.50	0.44	0.21	0.10	0.18	-0.20	-0.27	
3	Investment 2	0.60	0.33	0.36	0.25	0.08	0.30	0.44	
4	Investment 3	0.20	0.45	0.28	0.27	0.32	0.39	0.44	
5	Investment 4	0.08	0.17	0.21	0.01	0.28	0.31	0.05	
6	Investment 5	0.07	0.08	0.11	0.31	0.35	0.01	0.26	
7	Investment 6	0.02	-0.08	-0.13	-0.25	-0.26	-0.21	-0.27	
8									

FIGURE 7.11   Sample Report without Formatting

Another handy feature of conditional formatting is colour scales. Looking at Figure 7.11, how would you be able to quickly assess what is good, bad, and in between?

By using colour scales, you can assign rules for data in the table and add an extra layer of meaning to the numbers with colour. You can see in Figure 7.12 how data is more useful when the user can quickly spot areas of concern.

Enhancements to Conditional Formatting

More icon options have been added to conditional formatting in recent versions, including triangles, stars, and boxes. You can also more easily hide icons from view, as is evident in Figure 7.13. Editing the rule gives you a variety of options, such as hiding certain icons, or even hiding the numbers and showing the icon only.

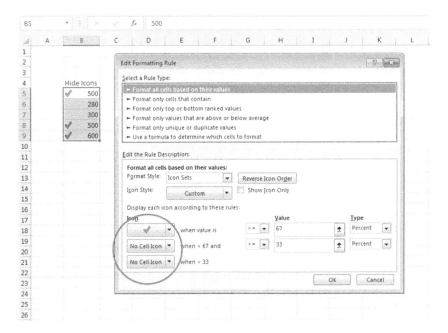

FIGURE 7.12   Sample Report Using Colour Scales

FIGURE 7.13   Edit Formatting Rule to Hide Icons

You can also easily mix and match data bars, colour scales, and icons from different sets. In Figure 7.14 the same range has both data bars and icons.

SPARKLINES

Excel also has a useful micro charting feature termed the "sparkline", which is a great way of displaying data trends in a small space. These lines are not as descriptive as regular graphs and charts, but they are very effective in displaying a quick view about the trends in the data or metrics.

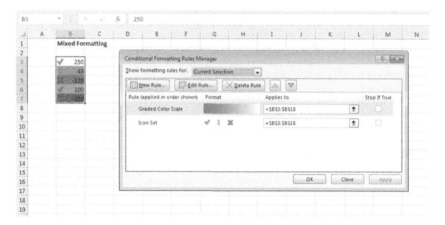

FIGURE 7.14 Applying Multiple Types of Conditional Formatting to the Same Range

HOW TO CREATE A SPARKLINE

1. Select the data series for which the sparkline needs to be created, as shown in Figure 7.15. You can create your own examples or a template can be found, along with the accompanying models to the rest of the screenshots in this book, at www.plumsolutions.com.au/book.

2. Under the Insert tab in the Sparklines group, select Line. The Sparklines group has been highlighted in Figure 7.15.

3. In the Create Sparklines dialog box, the data range is automatically selected, so enter the cell or cell range in which you want the sparklines to be placed and click OK. See Figure 7.16.

4. The sparklines are drawn in the selected cells. See Figure 7.17.
    Note that it is good practice to show a border around the sparkline, to give the line a better perspective if the gridlines are not showing.

FIGURE 7.15 Choosing Sparklines from the Ribbon

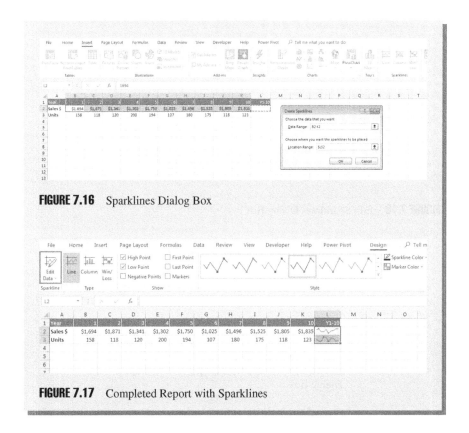

FIGURE 7.16 Sparklines Dialog Box

FIGURE 7.17 Completed Report with Sparklines

Editing Sparklines

The attributes of the sparklines can be modified from options under the Design tab. You can easily change the sparkline from a line to a column or a win/loss chart by selecting the sparklines and clicking on one of the three options in the Type group under the Design tab.

To edit data, select the sparklines and click on Edit Data in the Sparkline ribbon under the Design tab, as shown on the left of Figure 7.17.

This will open the Edit Sparklines dialog box, where you can change the data range, the sparkline location or change to columns as shown in Figure 7.18.

To highlight important data points, such as high point or low point, as has been done in Figure 7.17, select from a series of checkboxes in the Show group, under the Design tab. You can also edit the style of the sparklines by changing the line colours and marker colours.

Note that you can also Merge cells if you don't want to widen the columns or rows but want to make the sparkline bigger. To do this, highlight the cells that you want to merge, and select Merge & Center from the Alignment section on the Home tab.

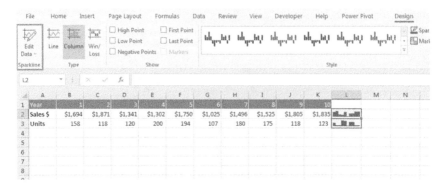

FIGURE 7.18   Edit Sparklines Dialog Box

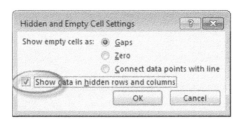

FIGURE 7.19   Hidden and Empty Cell Settings
Dialog Box

Hiding the Sparklines' Data Source   Sparklines are good at showing a lot in a small space and so we often want to hide the underlying source data for the sparkline. However, like charts, if you hide the underlying data, the sparkline also disappears. If you'd like to hide the rows or columns which contain the sparkline data then you'll need to click on the sparkline, go to the Design tab and in the Sparkline section, click on the drop-down below Edit Data and choose Hidden and Empty Cells. When the Hidden and Empty Cell Settings dialog box appears, tick "Show data in hidden rows and columns", as shown in Figure 7.19.

TIP

In the previous example, the column chart could have been chosen instead of the line for a different effect. If you have negative as well as positive numbers, then try the win/loss sparkline. Try out different types of sparklines to see which looks best with your data. Use a combination of sparklines and icons to create more meaningful representations of data points.

Changing Properties for a Group of Sparklines While each sparkline represents a unique series of data, you can edit the properties of a group of sparklines using the group and ungroup features. When the sparklines are grouped, you can edit the properties for the entire group, even if you select just a single line from the group. To separate out the sparklines in the group, select Ungroup in the Group ribbon under the Design tab.

TIP

If you want to create a series of sparklines for a series of data points, you can create it for the first series and just copy and paste, or drag the sparkline to automatically create it for the rest of the series of data.

BULLETPROOFING YOUR MODEL

If your model is publicly available, or if you have a lot of users entering data into it (*especially* if you are not sure of their level of Excel skill), it's a good idea to spend some time protecting it and making sure that all your hard work is not inadvertently corrupted!

Protection

Once you have completed building your model, there are three basic layers of protection you can include:

1. **Protect the file** so that no one can open it without the password.
2. **Protect the structure** of the workbook so that no structural changes can be made (normally used for hiding sheets and restricting access to them).
3. Unlock individual cells on the worksheet and then **protect the sheet** so that only those cells that are unlocked can be changed.

Protecting the structure or worksheets can be done with or without a password. Passwords are case sensitive.

WARNING

Bear in mind that passwords can be hacked reasonably easily. There are programs that can decode a password. (Try typing "crack Excel password" into Google sometime.) If your file contains highly sensitive information, do not rely on passwords in Excel. Password protection is intended to be a deterrent, not a definitive solution.

Protect the File　This is done by changing the options and saving over the existing copy of the file. There are two options with this: protecting the file with a password or recommending read-only access.

Password-protect a file if you don't want anyone to be able to open your file without a password, or make changes without a password. This is done under General Options. You can select Password to Open or Password to Modify.

This is recommended if you are emailing a confidential file and are concerned that it might be intercepted or viewed by the wrong person!

Read-only recommended—instead of using a password to prevent access, you could use the read-only option to deter users from changing your workbooks. This way you prevent inadvertent changes to models.

HOW TO PASSWORD-PROTECT A FILE

1. Click on the File menu in the top left-hand corner of your screen and select Save As.
2. Click on the Tools button and select General Options (Options... in Excel for Mac).
3. Enter the password and save over the file.

HOW TO ENABLE READ-ONLY

1. Follow the instructions as above ("How to Password-Protect a File").
2. Instead of typing a password, check the Read-Only Recommended checkbox.

Protect the Structure　The most common use of protecting the structure is to protect hidden sheets, but it also stops users from adding or deleting sheets, or changing other structural aspects of your model, but not from editing cell contents. If you want to stop users from entering data or changing values in cells, you need to protect the worksheet.

Protecting hidden sheets—if you have a sheet containing sensitive data, you can hide the entire sheet, and then protect the workbook so that the sheet cannot be viewed. This is particularly handy if, for example, you have salary data on a sheet in a budget model and don't want all users to have access to the information.

Protect the Worksheet This is the most commonly used form of protection. If you have created a spreadsheet that you do not want to be altered by the others who might view it, you can protect the sheet. You can either protect the whole sheet, or just certain key cells in the sheet (probably those containing the formulas) so that new data can still be entered onto the sheet.

NOTE

If the sheet has been protected, it is sometimes not possible to adjust column width. This can be very frustrating for the user, so make sure your columns are the correct width!

HOW TO PROTECT A WORKSHEET

1. Go to the sheet you wish to protect.
2. On the Review tab, in the Changes group, select Protect Sheet.
3. This will bring up the Protect Sheet dialog box, in which you can enter a password to prevent users from unprotecting the sheet. You do not have to use a password; you can just leave the Password box empty, and this may be enough of a deterrent to prevent users from modifying your model.
4. Enter a password (if desired) and click OK.
5. If you have entered a password, you will be asked to confirm the password.
6. Type the password again.
7. The whole sheet is now protected. Users will not be able to change the contents of any cell. If you need to change cell contents, you will need to unprotect the sheet.

HOW TO PROTECT HIDDEN SHEETS

1. Put all sensitive information on one sheet.
2. Hide the sheet. Right-click on the sheet tab name and select Hide.

(continued)

3. Now protect the structure of the workbook so that users cannot unhide sheets. On the Review tab, in the Changes group, select Protect Workbook and then Protect Structure and Windows from the drop-down box.

4. If you enter a password, users will need a password in order to view the sheet(s) you have hidden.

Protect Data by Locking Cells   By following the process outlined above to protect the worksheet, you will find that you won't be able to make any changes at all to any cell! If you want to allow entry into certain cells, but leave part of the sheet protected (perhaps the cells containing formulas), you'll need to unlock those cells to be edited first, before protecting the sheet. Make sure you turn off your protection before unlocking cells!

By default, every cell in a sheet has a lock applied to it. It is the lock that is activated when the sheet is protected and stops people from editing cells. You need to unlock those cells that should be changed.

HOW TO UNPROTECT A WORKSHEET

1. Select the tab name of the sheet you wish to unprotect.

2. On the Review tab, in the Changes group, select Unprotect Sheet.

3. If no password was originally used to protect the sheet, then the sheet will automatically be unprotected at this point.

4. If a password has been used, the Unprotect Sheet dialog box will appear. Enter the password and click OK.

HOW TO LOCK OR UNLOCK SPECIFIC CELLS

You will need to have sheet protection turned off before you do this. These instructions are the same in all versions of Excel.

1. Select the cells you wish to change.

2. Right-click and select Format Cells to bring up the Format Cells dialog box.

3. Then select the Protection tab.

4. Turn off Locked if you want users to be able to edit the selected cells once the sheet has been protected.

5. The Hidden option is used to stop users from viewing the formulas of the selected cells in the formula bar (once the sheet has been protected).

6. Click OK. Now when you protect the sheet, cells that are no longer locked will be editable.

CUSTOMISING THE DISPLAY SETTINGS

The following is an example of a model that's been very highly protected, and the display settings have been changed so that it almost does not even look like an Excel file. You can download a copy of this file, called "Repayment Comparison Calculator", from www.plumsolutions.com.au/book and if you would like to unprotect it, use the password **plumsolutions**. You will need to unprotect the sheet as well as the file structure, and how to do this is outlined in this section.

To make your model highly protected, like the model in Figure 7.20, you may choose to change a few settings to make your model look less like an Excel sheet, and more difficult for the user to change.

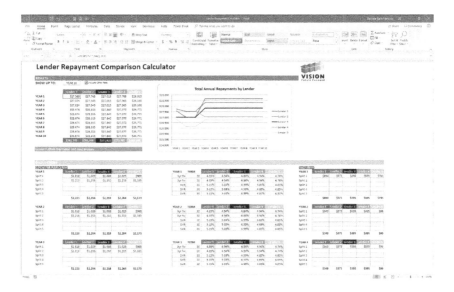

FIGURE 7.20   Model with Customised Display Settings

Useful Display Settings

Display settings can be changed by clicking on the File tab in the top left-hand corner, and then selecting Options. On the Advanced tab, there are a number of useful settings that can be edited to make your model more "bulletproof":

- Hide row and column headings by unselecting Show Row and Column Headers.
- Remove sheet tabs by unselecting the Show Sheet Tabs box.
- Disable the scroll bars by unselecting the Show Vertical and Horizontal Scroll Bars.
- Hide the formula bar by unselecting Show Formula Bar.

In Excel for Mac, these options can be found under Excel, then Preferences and under View, in the Window Options section.

Minimising the Ribbon

Note that minimising the ribbon only changes the view in *your* Excel on your computer; it does not change the model. Hence, if colleagues open up the same model and their Excel settings have the ribbon maximised, they will see the whole ribbon.

To minimise the ribbon, go to the top right-hand corner of your screen and click on the little icon as shown in Figure 7.21; select Auto-hide Ribbon, or Show Tabs from the menu.

TIP

You can also minimise or maximise the ribbon by simply pressing Control+F1 (Option+Command+R in Excel for Mac).

Restrict the Work Area

You can also make the work area of the sheet much smaller so that users cannot enter data in cells you don't intend them to. See Figure 7.22.

FIGURE 7.21   Minimising the Ribbon

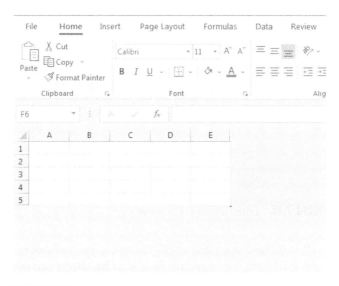

FIGURE 7.22 A Worksheet with Restricted Work Area

To restrict the work area:

1. Highlight the first column you don't want to see (for example, column F) and press Control+Shift+Right Arrow. Now right-click and select Hide.
2. Highlight the first row you don't want to see (for example, row 6) and press Control+Shift+Down Arrow. Now right-click and select Hide.

To unhide, highlight column E and then click-drag the cursor across to where column F would be. Let go of the mouse button, and move the cursor back to column E. Right-click, and then select Unhide. Unhiding the rows works in exactly the same way.

Restricting Incorrect Data Entry with Data Validations

Usually, we are building models for others to use, and they might not have the same level of Excel skill as we do. Users often have a knack for finding strange and wonderful methods of entering data in the wrong format, which can mess up your formulas. They might enter text where the model requires numbers, or spell names in a different way to what the criteria in a VLOOKUP are expecting, for example. If unsure of a number they sometimes write **TBA** (for *to be advised*), or if the value is a range, they might enter **5–10%**. They don't realise that the model must have a numeric value to calculate properly, and so they need to choose between 5 and 10 percent or enter the average of 7.5 percent! Using data validation will allow you to control the data that is typed into your model, and avoid errors.

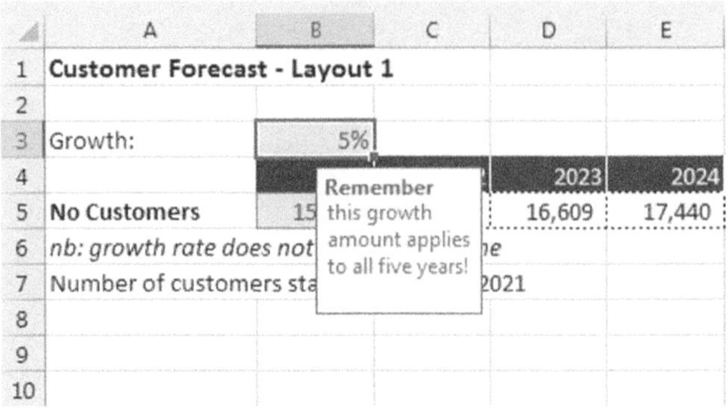

FIGURE 7.23 Data Validation Comment

Every cell will allow any value at all. Therefore, you can enter any type of data, of nearly any length (up to several thousand characters) into any cell. You can use the data validation feature to restrict the values users enter into cells in the model.

Data validations take protection one step further. Instead of restricting *where* data can be entered, they can also restrict *what* can be entered into the cell.

Once users enter a wrong value, they have to either enter the right value or hit the Esc (escape) key to get out of the error message. Hitting Esc will clear the entry in the cell they are trying to enter data into.

There are a couple of handy little tools you can add into the data validation while you are here. You can enter in cell comments on the Input Messages, as shown in Figure 7.23. Some text will pop up to help users or give them important information whenever the cell is selected.

See the section "Methods and Tools of Assumptions Documentation" in Chapter 3 for more information on how to create the data validation comment shown in Figure 7.23.

HOW TO APPLY DATA VALIDATIONS

1. We'd like to restrict a cell's entries so that it will only allow values between 1 and 10.
2. Select your input cell(s) (either select a single cell or highlight a whole range).
3. On the Data tab, from the Data Tools group, click on the Data Validation button.

4. Choose Whole Number under the Allow drop-down.

5. Leave the Between option as it is, and enter the values 1 and 10 under the Minimum and Maximum value fields; click OK.

In the Data Validation dialog box, you can also enter your own, customised error message on the Error Alert tab, as shown in Figure 7.24. This message will be shown if users enter invalid data. Resist the temptation to write something silly (or rude!). Now try entering incorrect data, and your error message will pop up, as shown in Figure 7.25.

Note that you can control how vigilant the data validation restrictions on your model will be. One day your department may have grown and it will suddenly become valid to have more than 500 staff. If you change the options on the Error

FIGURE 7.24 Creating a Customised Error Message

FIGURE 7.25 Customised Popup Error Message

Alert tab to Warning instead of Stop, then the message will alert users and discourage them from entering staff number 501, but it will allow this, if necessary. The error message will then prompt users that the restriction should be changed. The users can choose Yes to allow the entry of 501.

If you change the options on the Error Alert tab to Information instead, users are alerted that they entered an unexpected value, but the message defaults to OK and allows them to keep the value that they entered.

Using Validations to Create a Drop-Down List

Instead of specifying a range, you can be more specific and only allow certain predefined entries. This is how we can create drop-down lists with data validations.

1. First, create a list of valid regions, such as the list below:

   United Kingdom

   Germany

   India

   Australasia

   France

   United States

2. Select the cell that should contain the drop-down list.
3. Bring up the Data Validation box:
   - On the Data tab from the Data Tools group, click on the Data Validation button.
4. In the Allow section, change Any Value to List, as shown in Figure 7.26.
5. In the Source field, enter the range that contains the data you want to appear in the drop-down list. Leave "In-cell dropdown" selected. See Figure 7.27.
6. Any time that the cell is selected, a drop-down arrow will appear and users will be able to select from the list. See Figure 7.28.

If users try to enter data that is not on the list, an error alert will appear. Also, if you change the source data, the drop-down options will also change. Practice this; try changing United Kingdom to Britain. You'll see that Britain now appears on the list instead of United Kingdom.

Be aware, however, that it is possible to paste values over a restricted cell! You may have spent a long time protecting and setting up your worksheet so that users cannot enter incorrect data; however, it is very easy for users to inadvertently (or perhaps deliberately) paste over a data validation without receiving the error message or restrictions that would have appeared had they tried to enter the data directly into the cell.

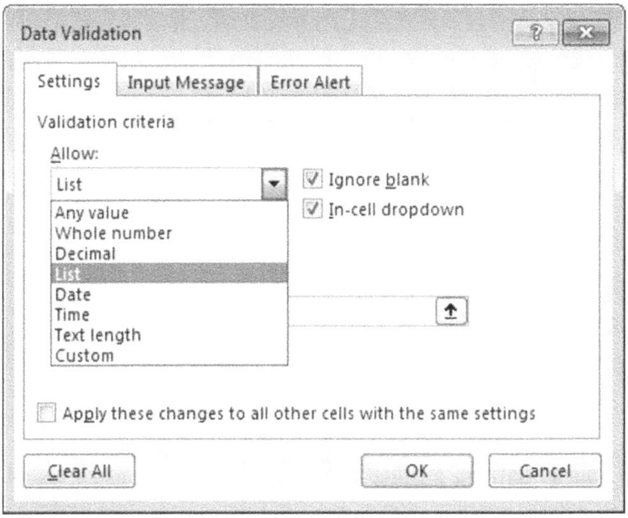

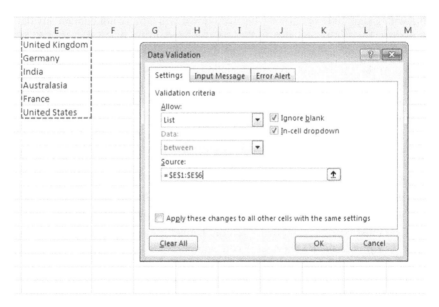

FIGURE 7.26 Creating a Drop-Down List

FIGURE 7.27 Enter the Source Data Range

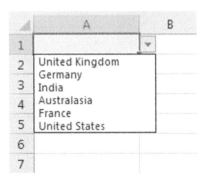

FIGURE 7.28 Completed Drop-Down List

Referencing Source Data on Another Sheet In older versions of Excel, a restriction with data validation drop-downs was that the source data and the drop-down needed to be on the same page. In newer versions of Excel, we can now link directly to source data on other sheets when creating a data validation drop-down box without having to use a named range. However, the file will not be compatible with Excel 2007 or earlier—the drop-down will simply not contain any data in the list. Microsoft says that it did install a patch to fix this in Excel 2007 but when testing this on various clients who were still using 2007, I found that it still did not work. It is therefore recommended to always use named ranges when linking drop-down boxes to source data on another page to ensure compatibility with earlier versions of Excel. Here's how to use a named range in a data validation drop-down box:

1. Highlight the source data list and assign a named range to the list (for example, **countries**). See the section "Named Ranges" in Chapter 5 for instructions on how to do this.
2. When creating the data validation drop-down, in the List box, enter an equal sign followed by the name of the range, as shown in Figure 7.29.

   You must type "=" and then spell the named range correctly for it to work. *Tip*: Use the F3 shortcut if you cannot remember exactly how you spelt the named range.

FORM CONTROLS

Form controls are objects such as drop-down boxes and option buttons that sit over the top of Excel sheets like charts do. They can interact with formulas so that when the option is selected, it changes the formula and can drive the model. They can

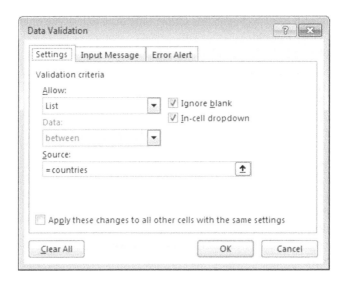

FIGURE 7.29   Creating a Drop-Down List Using a Named Range

be especially useful for scenario selection and assumptions in a financial model, as well as interactive, dynamic dashboards.

Building form controls into a financial model can be time-consuming for the modeller, but they do make the model look very professional and the interface becomes extremely easy to use.

Accessing Form Controls

You will need to have the Developer tab showing in the ribbon. If you cannot see it in the ribbon, you'll need to change your options.

Showing the Developer Tab in the Ribbon

The Developer tab contains several functions that are useful when developing macros and form controls. Take a look at Figure 7.30, which shows the Developer tab in the ribbon. The default installation version of Excel will not have the Developer tab showing in the ribbon, so if you can't see this tab, you'll need to

FIGURE 7.30   The Developer Tab

install it. You will need to change this setting only once unless you reinstall Excel, or move to another machine.

To display the Developer tab in the ribbon:

1. Click on the File menu in the top left-hand corner of your screen.
2. Scroll down to Options at the very bottom and select it.
3. Select Customize Ribbon.
4. In the box to your right, tick the Developer box.

In Excel for Mac:

1. Click Excel in the upper left-hand corner.
2. Click Preferences.
3. Select Ribbon & Toolbar.
4. On the right-hand side, check the Developer box.
5. Click Save.

Checkboxes

Checkboxes are very handy tools that can help users choose their desired options from a list. By building checkboxes into a financial model, the developer allows users to customise the model by adjusting the combinations of inputs for the financial model's assumptions.

HOW TO CREATE CHECKBOXES

1. Go to the Developer tab on the Excel toolbar and click on Insert. See Figure 7.31. If you cannot see the Developer tab, follow the instructions above on how to show the Developer tab in the ribbon.

   Figure 7.32 shows how the Developer tab looks in the ribbon if you are using Excel for Mac.

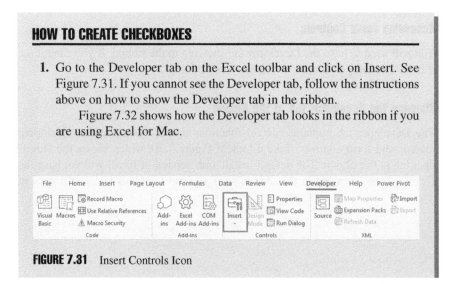

FIGURE 7.31   Insert Controls Icon

FIGURE 7.32 Form Controls in Excel for Mac

2. From the Form Controls menu, select the checkbox as shown in Figure 7.33.

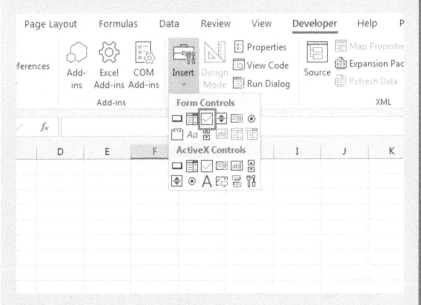

FIGURE 7.33 Inserting the Checkbox

3. Draw the checkbox anywhere in your sheet, and you should see the box with a name Checkbox 1. Subsequent checkbox names will be Checkbox 2, Checkbox 3, and so on. You can move it around, or change the checkbox name to anything you like by holding down the Control key.

(continued)

4. You can now link the checkmark in this box to any cell in your model. To do that you need to open the Format Control associated with the checkbox. Right-click on the checkbox and select Format Control, as shown in Figure 7.34.

   Alternatively, select the checkbox and click Properties on the ribbon under the Developer tab.

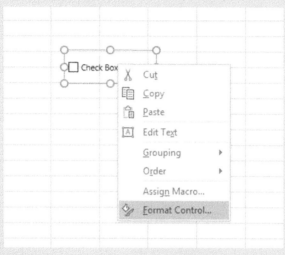

FIGURE 7.34 Selecting Format Control to Assign Checkbox Options

5. In the Format Control dialog, you can select the default value of the checkbox (unchecked, checked, or mixed) and the cell to which you want to link the checkbox status. In Figure 7.35, it is linked to C5. To enhance the look of the checkbox, you can select "3-D shading".

6. The cell to which the status is linked will have a Boolean value of TRUE or FALSE. Because TRUE has a value of 1 and FALSE has a value of 0, we can use this in our calculations as shown in Figure 7.36. See greater detail in "Boolean Logic (Binary Code)" later in this chapter.

7. You can add multiple checkboxes corresponding to the items in the list. Based on the Boolean status, you can design your financial model to pick the respective items, such as the example in Figure 7.36.

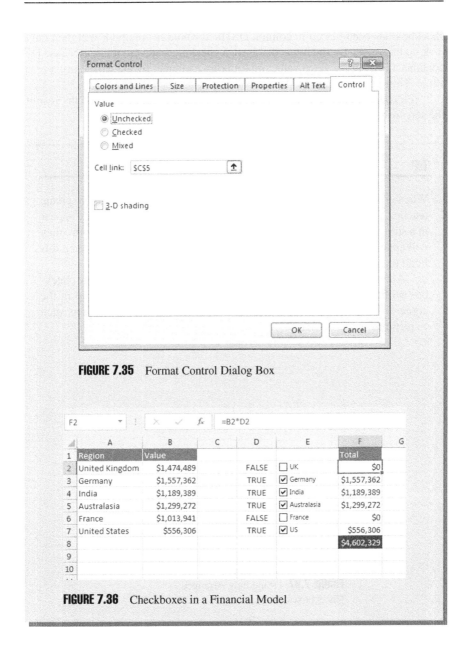

FIGURE 7.35 Format Control Dialog Box

FIGURE 7.36 Checkboxes in a Financial Model

Columns A and B contain the raw data. A group of checkboxes has been created in column E, and the format control output cell that corresponds to each checkbox has been placed in column D. The formula in column F will then only pick up the values for the items that have a checkmark next to them. Because D2 contains a FALSE (or zero) value, multiplying a number by D2 will return a zero value. This technique can easily be applied to charts and dashboards.

You can find this model, along with the accompanying models to the rest of the screenshots in this book, at www.plumsolutions.com.au/book.

TIP

When creating a list of checkboxes, or option buttons, it's easiest to create one in a single cell and then copy that cell multiple times so that they appear in a straight line below each other. If you create each object free-form, they will appear in random locations, as shown in Figure 7.37, and it's then difficult to get them lined up neatly.

Alternatively, you can hold down the ALT key whilst moving the checkbox with the mouse to "snap to grid" and make the object line up in the corner of the cell. This works with all form controls and other objects such as pictures, icons, or charts.

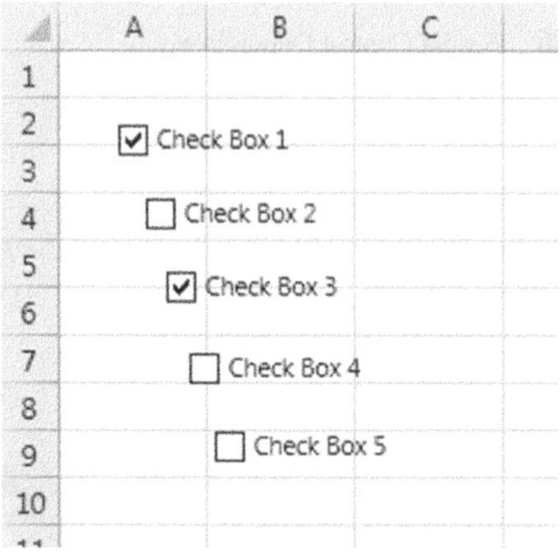

FIGURE 7.37   Randomly Arranged Checkboxes

Option Button   Sometimes users may need to choose one item from a list, which drives the rest of the calculations and analyses. The Option button (sometimes called a Radio button) offers you the ability to create this logic to restrict the number of options users can choose in the financial model.

HOW TO CREATE OPTION BUTTONS

1. Go to the Developer tab on the Excel toolbar and click Insert.

2. From the Form Controls menu select the Option button, as shown in Figure 7.38.

   In Excel for Mac, go to the Developer tab on the Excel toolbar. Select "Option Button", as shown in Figure 7.39.

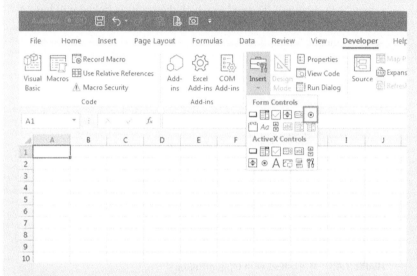

FIGURE 7.38   Inserting the Option Button

FIGURE 7.39   Option Button in Excel for Mac

3. Draw the Options button in front of the item in the list. Like the checkboxes, the Option button default name starts with Option Button 1 and increases by one number with each new button. The name can be changed by holding down the Control key.

(continued)

4. You can edit the properties of the button using Format Control. You can access the Format Control dialog in the same manner as for checkboxes. Right-click and select Format Control, or click Properties in the ribbon under the Developer tab.

5. In the Format Control dialog box, you can select the default value of the Option button (unchecked or checked) and the cell to which you want to link the Option button status. (In the example shown in Figure 7.40, it is linked to E1.) To enhance the look of the Option button you can select "3-D shading". The cell to which the status is linked will have a numerical value of the item in the list. In Figure 7.40, the fifth item was selected, hence $E$1=5$.

F1	▼	:	✕	✓	f_x	=INDEX(B2:B7,E1,1)		

⊿	A	B	C	D	E	F	
1	Region	Value			5	$1,013,941	
2	United Kingdom	$1,474,489			○ UK		
3	Germany	$1,557,362			○ Germany		
4	India	$1,189,389			○ India		
5	Australasia	$1,299,272			○ Australasia		
6	France	$1,013,941			⦿ France		
7	United States	$556,306			○ US		
8							
9							

FIGURE 7.40   Worksheet with Option Button

6. You can add multiple Option buttons corresponding to the items in the list. Based on the item number selected, you can design your financial model to carry out the necessary analysis.

7. Practice adding multiple items to the list and associating Option buttons to each item. As you switch between each item in the list, you can observe the number change in the linked cell.

8. The next step would be to create a formula linked to the output cell. If you want to display the value for the selected option, then use an INDEX or CHOOSE function to return the fifth result from the table, as shown in cell F1 of Figure 7.40.

NOTE

By design, all the Option buttons will always refer to a single cell, unlike checkboxes. If you change the cell link for one Option button, it will automatically update the rest.

Spin Buttons   Spin buttons are useful for controlling what users can enter into the input fields in your financial models. By including a Spin button, users can increase or decrease the number in the increments that you specify. For example, if you set it to increments of 5, and the current value is 400 when users hit the up arrow, it will change to 405, then 410, 415, and so on, and the same with the down arrow.

HOW TO CREATE A SPIN BUTTON

1. Go to the Developer tab on the Excel toolbar and click on Insert.
2. From the Form Controls menu select the Spin button, as shown in Figure 7.41.
   In Excel for Mac, go to the Developer tab on the Excel toolbar. Select "Spinner", which is beside "Option Button" as shown in Figure 7.39.
3. Draw the Spin button next to the input box for the value you want to control. Figure 7.42 shows an example of a completed Spin button that has been incorporated into a model.

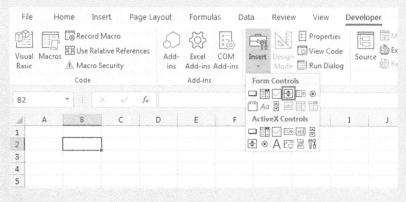

FIGURE 7.41   Inserting the Spinner

(continued)

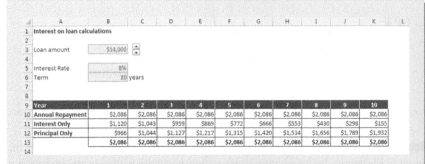

	A	B	C	D	E	F	G	H	I	J	K	L
1	Interest on loan calculations											
2												
3	Loan amount	$14,000										
4												
5	Interest Rate	8%										
6	Term	10	years									
7												
8												
9	Year	1	2	3	4	5	6	7	8	9	10	
10	Annual Repayment	$2,086	$2,086	$2,086	$2,086	$2,086	$2,086	$2,086	$2,086	$2,086	$2,086	
11	Interest Only	$1,120	$1,043	$959	$869	$772	$666	$553	$430	$298	$155	
12	Principal Only	$966	$1,044	$1,127	$1,217	$1,315	$1,420	$1,534	$1,656	$1,789	$1,932	
13		$2,086	$2,086	$2,086	$2,086	$2,086	$2,086	$2,086	$2,086	$2,086	$2,086	
14												

FIGURE 7.42 Completed Spin Button in a Financial Model

4. You can edit the properties of the button using Format Control. You can access the Format Control dialog in the same manner as for a checkbox. Right-click and select Format Control, or click Properties in the ribbon under the Developer tab.

5. Figure 7.43 shows the Format Control dialog box for the Spin button in Figure 7.42. Here you should specify the minimum value for the Spin

FIGURE 7.43 Format Control Dialog Box

button (here it is set to 0), the maximum value (here it is 30,000—which is the highest amount possible), and the incremental change (here it is 1,000). You must also specify the cell in which you want to change the values in the cell link—in this case B3, the loan amount in our model.

6. Practice pressing the arrows up and down and see the values in the model change. You can find this model, along with the accompanying models to the rest of the screenshots in this book, at www.plumsolutions .com.au/book.

NOTE

There are a few annoying limitations with a Spin button. The maximum value cannot be greater than 30,000, and the incremental change cannot be less than one. This means that if you want to use it for percentages, you need to do a workaround, and divide the output cell by 100 to express a percentage driven by a Spin button.

NOTE

Note that the scrollbar works in a very similar way to the Spin button, except that the button is oriented horizontally instead of vertically.

Combo Boxes

Creating a drop-down box is an important tool in many user-friendly models where the modeller wants the user to select from a predefined number of options, making the model easier to use, and also avoiding mistyping and potential errors. The advantage of combo boxes is that you eliminate any ambiguity in user inputs and still keep things simple for users to provide the inputs. See Figure 7.44.

Drop-Down The combo box is an alternative to using the data validation drop-down tool. See the section "Bulletproofing Your Model" earlier in this chapter for instructions on how to create a data validation, in-cell drop-down box. The only advantage of the combo box is that the drop-down arrow is visible whether the cell is selected or not. This is a significant advantage if users are not very Excel savvy.

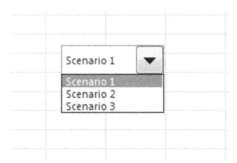

FIGURE 7.44 Completed Combo Box

From the modeller's perspective, however, a combo box takes much longer to build, requiring more cells for the process, and is, therefore, less efficient. For these reasons, most modellers prefer the data validation drop-down tool.

HOW TO CREATE A COMBO BOX

1. Go to the Developer tab on the Excel toolbar and click on Insert.
2. From the Form Controls menu select the combo box as shown in Figure 7.45.
3. Draw the combo box next to the input box for which you want to control input. Figure 7.46 shows an example of the combo box. Note that it does not need to fit neatly into a cell.

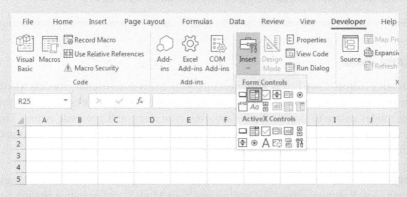

FIGURE 7.45 Inserting the Combo Box

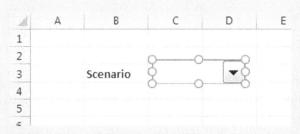

FIGURE 7.46 Drawing the Combo Box

4. To fix the inputs, create an input box with inputs such as shown in Figure 7.47.

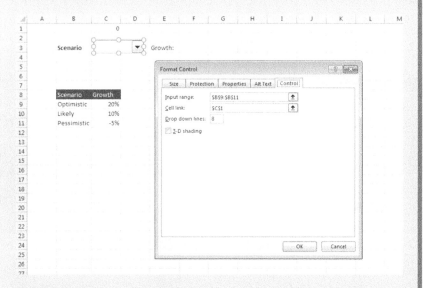

FIGURE 7.47 Scenario Source Data

5. You can now associate these inputs with your combo box using Format Control. You can access the Format Control dialog box in the same manner as for the other form controls. Right-click and select Format Control, or click Properties in the ribbon under the Developer tab.

6. In the Format Control dialog box, give the Input Range (here it is B9 to B11) and the Cell Link (here it is C1). See Figure 7.47.

The output cell will only indicate the item number selected, so C1 will reflect a value of 1 for optimistic, 2 for likely, and 3 for pessimistic.

(continued)

To translate these numbers into meaningful percentages from the chart, you need to link the growth amounts in column C to C1; this can be done using IF, INDEX, or even a CHOOSE function in Excel (and I'm sure you can think of even more options).

7. INDEX is a more elegant way of representing this link than an IF, for example. Use the formula **=INDEX(C9:C11,C1,1)** to create the necessary linkage. See Figure 7.48.

8. Practice changing the combo box, and see the values change.

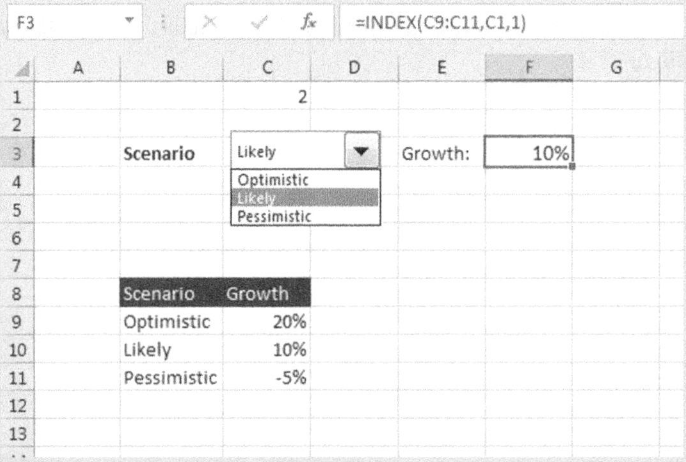

FIGURE 7.48 Using the Combo Box Output in a Formula

TIP

To keep the model tidy, you can change the font colour of cell C1 to white or light grey so that the text is less visible to the user but available for calculation. Alternatively, you can hide the output cell behind the combo box. Move the combo box out of the way, cut and paste the output cell to cell C3, and then move the combo box back over C3 to hide the output cell value. This is the most common method as it stops other users from inadvertently deleting the output cell value.

Boolean Logic (Binary Code)

Most form controls use Boolean logic, which converts everything to one of two values: a one or a zero. For example, if a checkbox is selected, it will return a value in the output cell of TRUE, which equals 1; and if it is left blank, it will be FALSE, which equals zero. We can use the output cell to drive a formula.

In Figure 7.49, the output cell is B5. When the checkbox is checked, it shows the value TRUE, which is equal to one, so this has been incorporated into the model by using the formula **=B7*((B5*B2)+1)**.

If the checkbox is left blank, the output cell would display FALSE, which gives the value zero, and according to the formula, the GST would then not be included in the total. See Figure 7.50.

B8			$\times$ $\checkmark$ f_x	=B7*((B5*B2)+1)		
1 2	A	B	C	D	E	F
1						
2	GST:	10%				
3		☑ Include GST				
4						
5		TRUE				
6						
7	Net Price	$4,000				
8	Gross Price	$4,400				
9						
10						
11						
12						

FIGURE 7.49 Checked Checkboxes Drive Calculation

B8			$\times$ $\checkmark$ f_x	=B7*((B5*B2)+1)	
1 2	A	B	C	D	E
1					
2	GST:	10%			
3		☐ Include GST			
4					
5		FALSE			
6					
7	Net Price	$4,000			
8	Gross Price	$4,000			
9					
10					
11					
12					

FIGURE 7.50 Unselected Checkboxes Drive Calculation

Similar formulas can be created to link to other form controls, such as Option buttons and combo boxes.

Form Controls versus ActiveX Controls

You may have noticed that the Insert button under the Developer tab has two sets of options: form control and ActiveX controls. While both have the same set of functions, they have a slight difference. The ActiveX controls are tailor-made for a Microsoft Office environment and use Microsoft ActiveX to enhance their functionality. If you are absolutely certain that your financial model would be used in the MS Office environment only, then you could possibly add a few additional enhancements to your controls. However, if your users might also be using other environments like Mac OS, the ActiveX controls can cause problems—as Apple's operating system does not, at the time of writing, support Microsoft ActiveX.

Form controls generally provide all the functionality we need for financial models, so it is simpler to stick to them unless you specifically need the advanced functionality of ActiveX. If you want to keep your financial modelling product platform independent, stick to form controls. As far as core functionality is concerned, form controls will offer you all the necessary flexibility required for a smooth user experience.

SUMMARY

Formatting and displaying the data and inputs are important parts of building a financial model. Of course, the accuracy of the model and its calculation are most important, but having a model that looks good and is easy to use certainly adds to the integrity and usability of the model. A model in which the model builder has obviously taken care to use clear colour coding, borders, and correct formatting will be trusted more and given more credibility by the user. Therefore, good modellers should spend a little time (not too much) during the model build to format colours, borders, and styles to make it more accessible.

CHAPTER 8

Tools for Financial Modelling

In this chapter, we'll look at the basic, commonly used tools of hiding and group-ing. We'll then cover some more advanced tools such as array formulas, goal seeking, PivotTables, and macros. Whilst the best financial models are the sim-plest and easiest to understand (and therefore often don't contain these complex tools), it's important that the financial modeller has a grasp on how to use these tools if functionality requires.

HIDING SECTIONS OF A MODEL

Being able to hide sections of a model is a very handy tool, especially when tidy-ing up a model to conceal cells that are necessary for the model to work, but not necessary for the user to see. You can hide rows or columns in the model, or you can hide an entire sheet. If you have information in a model you don't want users to see (for example, unnecessary detail or a calculation that will only serve to distract from the model), you can hide the section of the model that contains the data.

Columns and Rows

It is possible to hide a column or row of data to stop it printing out, or to stop other people from viewing it.

HOW TO HIDE A COLUMN OR ROW

1. Select the column or row by clicking on the heading.
2. Right-click and select Hide.

The column or row will be hidden from view. But if you look at the column or row headings, you can see which column or row is missing.

TIP

If you have hidden column A, or row 1, it can be tricky to unhide it. You'll
need to hold down the mouse and select across the row or column headings
left or upward in order to unhide the column or row. The trick is that you have
to right-click with the mouse in the highlighted row or column, as shown in
Figure 8.1. If you click elsewhere, it won't work.

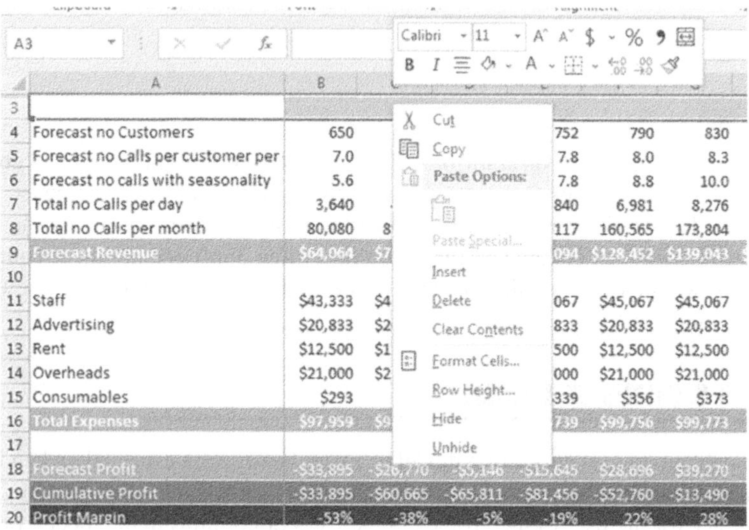

FIGURE 8.1   Unhiding Rows 1 and 2

You can hide multiple columns or rows at the same time. Just select all the
columns or rows at the same time and follow the steps outlined above.

Sheets

Hiding sheets is also very useful. If you have information on a model you do not
want users to see at all (e.g., salary information on budget models), you can hide
the sheet with sensitive information, and then protect the workbook. The hidden
sheets disappear from view, but links are retained as the sheet has not been deleted
from the workbook.

NOTE

Although we can easily hide multiple worksheets at a time by selecting several sheets using the Control key, only one sheet can be unhidden at a time.

HOW TO VIEW (UNHIDE) A COLUMN OR ROW

The difficulty of bringing back a hidden column or row is that you need to select it first. As it is hidden, you cannot see the row or column to click on it. The trick is to select the headings on either side of the hidden column or row. This will select the columns or rows before and after, as well as the hidden column or row itself.

1. Click and drag across the headings to select those before and after the hidden column or row.

2. Right-click and select Unhide, as shown in Figure 8.2.

FIGURE 8.2 Unhiding Rows

TO HIDE OR UNHIDE A SHEET

1. Select the sheet(s) you want to hide or unhide.
2. Right-click on the sheet tab and select Hide/Unhide.

TIP

A way to hide a sheet even more securely is to change the properties of the sheet in the Visual Basic code to Very Hidden. This method is less commonly known and will ensure that only a user experienced with programming will be able to work out how to unhide your sheets.

1. To try this out, right-click on the tab name of your worksheet, and select View Code, as shown in Figure 8.3.
2. This will bring up your Visual Basic Editor. This should look fairly similar no matter which version of Excel you are using.
3. Click on the sheet that you want to hide in the top left, and change the properties of that sheet in the bottom left from Visible to Very Hidden, as shown in Figure 8.4.

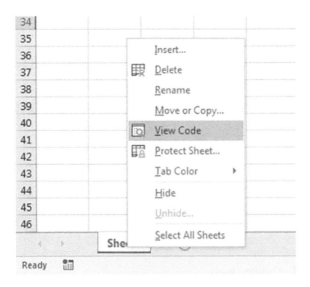

FIGURE 8.3   Viewing the Source Code

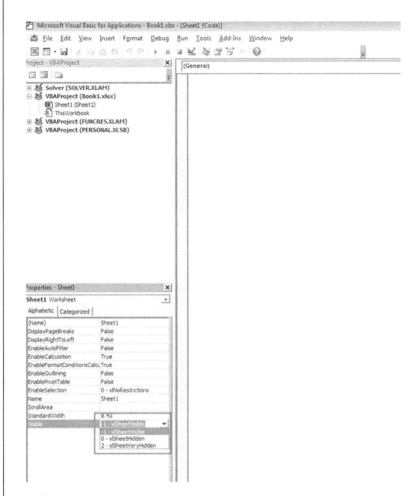

FIGURE 8.4 Changing the Visibility Options in the Visual Basic Editor

By default, all sheets are set to Visible. If you change the properties to Hidden, this will change the sheet so that it is hidden using the ordinary Hide Sheets tool, and it can be unhidden as easily as normal. If it is "Very Hidden" it cannot be seen even when you try to unhide the sheets. The only way to unhide a Very Hidden sheet is to change the properties in the VBA code.

For more information on the Visual Basic Editor using macros, see the section "Macros in Financial Modelling Case Studies" later in this chapter.

Using Protection As just outlined, there are two methods of hiding: either hide rows and columns or hide the worksheet itself. Depending on what is hidden, you might want to use another layer of protection to ensure that the data cannot be viewed. Password protection is a good option in such a case.

See the section "Bulletproofing Your Model" in Chapter 7 for greater detail on how to apply protection to models.

Errors Caused by Hiding

Hidden sheets, rows, and columns may hide complexity from the user and make the model less confusing, but many users don't like using what they perceive to be a black box. It's up to you, the model developer, to decide how much power you will give to model users. If you hide everything and then protect the model so that they can't see how it has been calculated, this makes the model easy to use, but it does not inspire confidence in users. It often depends on who is using the model. If a model is for other modellers to use, they probably won't appreciate being locked out of certain sections of the model, as they'd like to check it for themselves to ensure that it is working properly. If users have limited Excel use, then hiding with protection is appropriate to make sure they don't mess up the formulas or make unauthorised changes.

There are many well-documented cases where hidden rows and columns have been overlooked in financial models and caused significant errors. Barclays Capital was forced to file a legal relief motion relating to its acquisition of Lehman Brothers' US assets after a reformatting error in an Excel spreadsheet resulted in 179 toxic deals being mistakenly included in the purchase agreement.

The spreadsheet contained nearly 1,000 rows with more than 24,000 individual cells and had to be reformatted and converted into a PDF document before being posted on the bankruptcy court's website by the end of the day. A junior associate reformatting the work was unaware that the original Excel document included hidden rows containing contracts that were marked with an **n** to signify they should not be part of the deal. The document was posted on the website, but the hidden cells had become visible when the employee globally resized the rows in the spreadsheet—without the original **n** designations. The error was not spotted until Barclays posted a revised list of contracts, with notice to the affected parties.

This story illustrates why it is highly recommended to use the Grouping Tool when hiding rows and columns in financial models. Google "Excel Horror Stories" and you'll find a long list of the latest horrific Excel error stories. For more tips on how to avoid being part of your own Excel horror story, see the section "Error Avoidance Strategies" in Chapter 4.

GROUPING

Determining whether there are hidden rows or columns on your worksheet can be difficult. Using the grouping tool can make hidden data more obvious and avoid its being overlooked.

HOW TO PROTECT HIDDEN SECTIONS OF A MODEL

If you have hidden rows or columns, apply the protection to the worksheet itself by selecting Protect Sheet from the Review tab.

If you have hidden a sheet, apply protection to the structure of the workbook by selecting Protect Workbook from the Review tab.

Go to the Data tab and select Group/Ungroup from the Outline section. When grouping is applied to a model, it will look like Figure 8.5 when collapsed. You can find this example, along with the accompanying models to the rest of the screenshots in this book, at www.plumsolutions.com.au/book.

The same sheet will look like Figure 8.6 when expanded.

Notice the little 1 and 2 numbers in the top left-hand corner for the rows and the columns. Clicking on these numbers is a very quick and easy way to expand and contract hidden rows and columns. Clicking 1 will contract the data, and 2 will expand it. One consideration when using the grouping tool is that it does make the viewing screen smaller, which might be a problem if space is an issue.

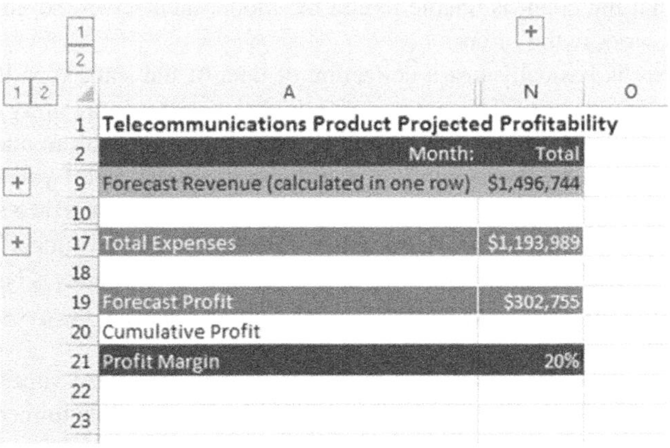

FIGURE 8.5   Collapsed Grouping

	1	2	3	4	5	6	7	8	9	10	11	12	Total
1 Telecommunications Product Projected Profitability													
2 Month	1	2	3	4	5	6	7	8	9	10	11	12	Total
3 Forecast no Customers	650	683	717	752	790	830	871	915	960	1,008	1,059	1,112	
4 Forecast no Calls per customer per day	7.0	7.2	7.5	7.8	8.0	8.3	8.6	8.9	9.2	9.5	9.9	10.2	
5 Forecast no calls with seasonality	5.6	6.5	7.5	7.8	8.8	10.0	10.3	9.8	9.2	9.5	8.9	8.2	
6 Total no Calls per day	3,640	4,450	5,374	5,840	6,981	8,276	8,994	8,960	8,652	9,620	9,409	9,089	
7 Total no Calls per month	80,080	89,005	118,221	105,117	160,565	173,804	197,876	197,122	177,043	192,401	207,001	172,696	1,870,930
8 Forecast Revenue (calculated in detail)	$66,066	$71,204	$94,577	$84,094	$128,452	$139,043	$158,301	$157,697	$141,634	$153,921	$165,601	$138,156	1,496,744
9 Forecast Revenue (calculated in one row)	$66,094	$71,204	$94,577	$84,094	$128,452	$139,043	$158,301	$157,697	$141,634	$153,921	$160,601	$138,156	$1,496,744
11 Expenses													
12 Staff	$43,333	$43,333	$45,067	$45,067	$45,067	$45,067	$45,067	$45,067	$45,067	$45,067	$45,067	$45,067	$537,333
13 Advertising	$20,833	$20,833	$20,833	$20,833	$20,833	$20,833	$20,833	$20,833	$20,833	$20,833	$20,833	$20,833	$250,000
14 Rent	$12,500	$12,500	$12,500	$12,500	$12,500	$12,500	$12,500	$12,500	$12,500	$12,500	$12,500	$12,500	$150,000
15 Overheads	$21,000	$21,000	$21,000	$21,000	$21,000	$21,000	$21,000	$21,000	$21,000	$21,000	$21,000	$21,000	$252,000
16 Consumables	$293	$307	$322	$339	$356	$373	$392	$412	$432	$454	$476	$500	$4,656
17 Total Expenses	$97,959	$97,974	$99,722	$99,739	$99,756	$99,773	$99,792	$99,812	$99,832	$99,854	$99,876	$99,900	$1,193,989
19 Forecast Profit	-$33,895	-$26,770	-$5,146	-$15,645	$28,696	$39,270	$58,509	$57,886	$41,802	$54,067	$65,725	$38,256	$302,755
20 Cumulative Profit	-$33,895	-$60,665	-$65,811	-$81,456	-$52,760	-$13,490	$45,019	$102,905	$144,707	$198,774	$264,499	$302,755	
21 Profit Margin	-53%	-38%	-5%	19%	22%	28%	37%	37%	30%	35%	40%	28%	20%

FIGURE 8.6   Expanded Grouping

ARRAY FORMULAS

Array formulas are an advanced type of Excel calculation. Before we launch into what an array formula is, let me begin by saying that I don't recommend you deliberately include array formulas in your models unless there is no other practical way to achieve the same result. Array formulas can be difficult to understand, especially in older versions of Excel, and hard to edit if you don't know what they are, because you cannot change part of an array. In general, array formulas are very difficult to edit and audit because they add a new layer of complexity that is sometimes unnecessary. Most array formulas I have seen are legacy models built in older versions of Excel or Lotus, long before some of the more efficient functions became available. Other array formulas have been built by consultants who want to ensure that the client is unable to edit the model themselves, so guaranteeing themselves work in the future!

An array is basically just a collection of data of the same type that can be treated as a single entity. These types of formulas treat the entire array as a single input to the formula. The reason that array formulas are difficult to understand is that they don't follow the usual rules of ordinary formulas and if you have never seen an array formula before, they can be difficult to work out. Trace Precedents and Trace Dependents will work on arrays, but don't help very much. Therefore, if you are building a model for others to use, using array formulas is best avoided where possible, because they may have difficulty making the necessary changes to the model.

However, in order to seriously consider yourself an Excel super user, you should know how to build an array formula—or at least be able to recognise and edit one if you come across it—if only to remove it from the model and replace it with a far more auditable and user-friendly formula.

Array formulas are very powerful tools, and there are many reasons why modellers use them. One of the main advantages is security—nobody can accidentally delete part of the array block when using an array formula. Also, because the data can be manipulated as a whole block and used in the formula as a single unit, it's a lot harder to make a mistake when building the formula.

You can identify an array formula because, in Excel 2016 or earlier, it includes curly brackets (like these: {}). Note that Dynamic Arrays have been introduced to Excel 2019/365, which means that the curly brackets are no longer necessary. You can identify an array formula by the spill area, which shows as a fine blue line appearing as a border around the range when it is selected, as shown in Figure 8.8 below.

Data tables are a type of array formula—probably one of the most useful ones—especially for the financial modeller. (See "Using Data Tables for Sensitivity Analysis" in Chapter 11 for how to build a data table.)

Advantages and Disadvantages of Using Array Formulas

The advantages of using array formulas are as follows:

- They ensure consistency, because all formulas in the table are exactly the same.
- A model containing arrays will use less memory and be more efficient.
- Because it's not possible to change a single cell on its own within an array formula, it is unlikely that you or someone else will change your formula accidentally.
- Because array formulas are difficult to understand, it means that those with only basic Excel knowledge are less likely to change (and mess up) your formulas.
- Array formulas do make it possible to perform some calculations that would otherwise be impossible. This is really the only reason you should use an array formula.

The disadvantages of using array formulas are as follows:

- Although array formulas use less memory, if you use too many large arrays in one model it can slow down your calculations.
- You cannot use column references (such as A:A or D:D) in your array formulas. This is not best practice in financial modelling anyway, so no great loss!
- They are difficult to audit for many Excel users and require specialist skills, although this can be considered both an advantage and a disadvantage.

Simple Array Formula Example

1. Create two simple blocks of data (arrays), as shown in Figure 8.7.
2. Now, instead of simply multiplying Quantity by Price, we are going to create an array formula instead. Highlight the block of cells C1:C10 and type/select **=A2:A10*B2:B10** in the formula bar, as shown in Figure 8.7.

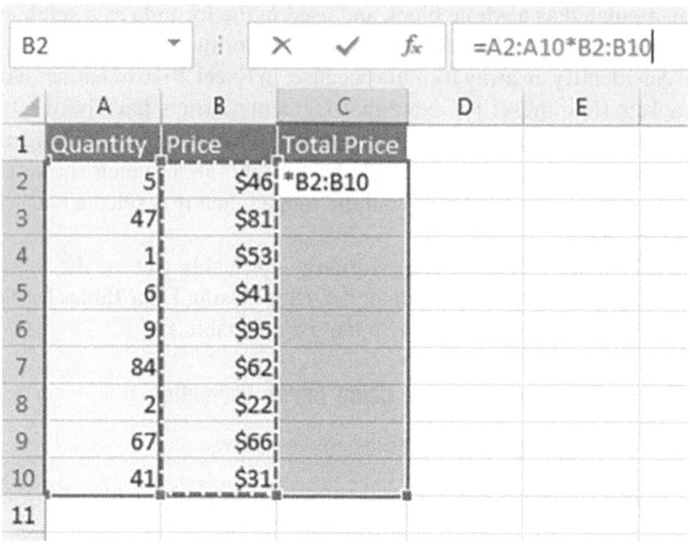

| B2 | ▼ | ⋮ | ✕ ✓ | *fx* | =A2:A10*B2:B10 |

◢	A	B	C	D	E
1	Quantity	Price	Total Price		
2	5	$46	*B2:B10		
3	47	$81			
4	1	$53			
5	6	$41			
6	9	$95			
7	84	$62			
8	2	$22			
9	67	$66			
10	41	$31			
11					

FIGURE 8.7   Entering an Array Formula

3. Now, if you are using Excel 2016 or earlier, hold down the Control and Shift keys while hitting Enter at the same time (Control+Shift+Enter). Excel 2019 users can simply hit Enter.
4. The formula will appear in the whole array block, as shown in Figure 8.8.

Try deleting one of the lower cells in column C. Note that with the exception of cell C2, you now cannot make any changes to the array block by changing an individual cell.

Please also note that array formulas were sometimes referred to as CSE formulas in Excel 2016 or earlier, because you had to press Control+Shift+Enter to enter them.

Array Formula Uses

Financial modellers generally resort to the use of array formulas only when it is not possible to do something any other way. There are many such instances, but some examples of these situations are as follows:

▪ Data tables are a form of array formula that is extremely useful for scenarios and sensitivity analysis in financial modelling. Instead of changing inputs one at a time, an array shows hypothetically what an outcome would be *simultaneously* in a single table.

C2 =A2:A10*B2:B10

	A	B	C	D	E
1	Quantity	Price	Total Price		
2	5	$46	$230		
3	47	$81	$3,807		
4	1	$53	$53		
5	6	$41	$246		
6	9	$95	$855		
7	84	$62	$5,208		
8	2	$22	$44		
9	67	$66	$4,422		
10	41	$31	$1,271		
11					

FIGURE 8.8 Completed Array Formula

- TRANSPOSE allows you to transpose a range of data, either vertically or horizontally, and retain links. We'll take a look at how to use this very handy technique in a moment.
- Using a SUM and a VLOOKUP together as an array formula makes a very concise formula. For example, **=SUM(VLOOKUP(value, list, {2,3,4},0))** will give you a sum of values in rows 2, 3, and 4 instead of having to do **=VLOOKUP(value,list,2,0)+VLOOKUP(value,list,3,0)+VLOOKUP (value,list,4,0)**. Note that if you are using Excel 2016 or earlier, you need to hold down Control, Shift, and Enter for the array version of this formula to work.

Transposing Data Using an Array

One of my favourite uses of an array formula is to create a TRANSPOSE function, which will transpose data, allowing a link to be maintained within the model.

Let's say you have some city and temperature data in a table, as shown in Figure 8.9, but you'd like to transpose the data so that months and cities are

	A	B	C	D	E	F	G	H	I	J	K	L	M	N
1	Average Temperature Degrees Celsius													
2	Cities	Jan	Feb	Mar	Apr	May	Jun	Jul	Aug	Sep	Oct	Nov	Dec	
3	London	6.9	5.5	8	9.8	13.1	16.2	18.9	18.5	16	12.8	8.9	7.1	
4	New York	-1.8	-1.2	3.5	9	14.6	19.5	22.8	22.7	19.1	12.5	6.6	1.2	
5	Sydney	22.1	22.1	21	18.4	15.3	12.9	12	13.2	15.3	17.7	19.5	21.2	
6	Moscow	-10.2	-8.9	-4	4.5	12.2	16.3	18.5	16.6	10.9	4.3	-2	-7.5	
7														
8														

FIGURE 8.9 Temperature Data

	London	New York	Sydney	Moscow
Jan	5.9	-1.8	22.1	-10.2
Feb	5.5	-1.2	22.1	-8.9
Mar	8	3.5	21	-4
Apr	9.8	9	18.4	4.5
May	13.1	14.6	15.3	12.2
Jun	16.2	19.5	12.9	16.3
Jul	18.9	22.8	12	18.5
Aug	18.5	22.7	13.2	16.6
Sep	16	19.1	15.3	10.9
Oct	12.8	12.5	17.7	4.3
Nov	8.9	6.6	19.5	-2
Dec	7.1	1.2	21.2	-7.5

FIGURE 8.10   Transposed Temperature Data

switched around, as shown in Figure 8.10. You can create this sheet yourself, or a template can be found along with the accompanying models to the rest of the screenshots in this book at www.plumsolutions.com.au/book.

Before you start cutting and pasting, try the transpose values tool first:

1. Highlight the original table, and copy it to the clipboard using Control+C.
2. Right-click in the cell that you want the data to appear, and select Paste Special.
3. Check the Transpose box as shown in Figure 8.11, and click OK.

This will paste all the transposed values as hardcoded data in a new table. Using this method creates two separate, independent tables of data.

Using a TRANSPOSE Array Function   You may wish to maintain the original table as the source data and have the second table linked to the first. Instead of linking each cell individually (which is time-consuming and prone to error), you could use a TRANSPOSE Array Function instead.

If you are using Excel 2019/365, select cell A9, type the formula =TRANSPOSE(A2:M6), and press Enter to create a transposed version of this table in range A9:E21. Note that if there is any cell already in the range blocking the spill area, the error #SPILL! will appear. Remove the obstructing cell and the array area will automatically respill.

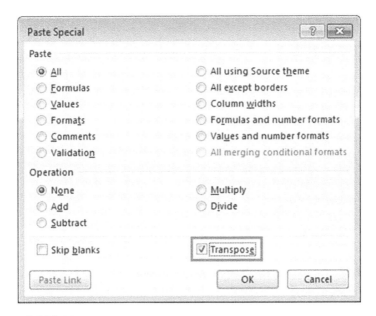

FIGURE 8.11   Paste Special Dialog Box

For users of Excel 2016 or earlier, follow these five steps:

1. Highlight a range with exactly the correct rows and columns for the destination data.

TIP

It's difficult to see exactly how many rows and columns you'll need, so it's easiest to use the Paste Special—Transpose procedure as described above to determine exactly how big the selection range needs to be.

---

2. In the formula bar, type the formula =TRANSPOSE, referencing the original data (i.e., **=TRANSPOSE(B3:M6)**), as shown in Figure 8.12.
3. Now, hold down the Control and Shift keys while hitting Enter at the same time (Control+Shift+Enter).

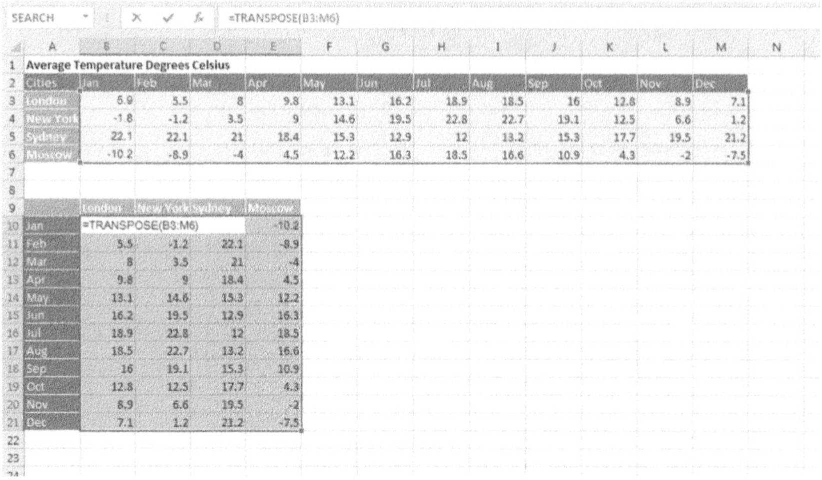

Cities	Jan	Feb	Mar	Apr	May	Jun	Jul	Aug	Sep	Oct	Nov	Dec
London	6.9	5.5	8	9.8	13.1	16.2	18.9	18.5	16	12.8	8.9	7.1
New York	-1.8	-1.2	3.5	9	14.6	19.5	22.8	22.7	19.1	12.5	6.6	1.2
Sydney	22.1	22.1	21	18.4	15.3	12.9	12	13.2	15.3	17.7	19.5	21.2
Moscow	-10.2	-8.9	-4	4.5	12.2	16.3	18.5	16.6	10.9	4.3	-2	-7.5

	London	New York	Sydney	Moscow
Jan	=TRANSPOSE(B3:M6)			-10.2
Feb	5.5	-1.2	22.1	-8.9
Mar	8	3.5	21	-4
Apr	9.8	9	18.4	4.5
May	13.1	14.6	15.3	12.2
Jun	16.2	19.5	12.9	16.3
Jul	18.9	22.8	12	18.5
Aug	18.5	22.7	13.2	16.6
Sep	16	19.1	15.3	10.9
Oct	12.8	12.5	17.7	4.3
Nov	8.9	6.6	19.5	-2
Dec	7.1	1.2	21.2	-7.5

FIGURE 8.12 Creating a TRANSPOSE Array Formula

4. The formula will appear in the whole array block. Note that the curly brackets will appear around the formula: **{=TRANSPOSE(B3:M6)}**. Remember that Control+Shift+Enter is not required for Excel 2019/365, there is no need to select the destination cells first, and the curly brackets will not show.
5. Note that changes you make in the original block of data will be reflected in the second block.

GOAL SEEKING

Goal seek is a very handy and commonly used tool in financial modelling and analysis. Goal seek is used to adjust the value in a specified cell until a formula dependent on that cell reaches the result you specify. In other words, it will change the inputs such that the output is set to the exact amount you want it to be.

In order to run a goal seek, you must have:

- A formula.
- A hardcoded cell that drives that formula.

The formula and its input cell do not need to be on the same sheet or even in the same model. As long as there is a direct link between the two (no matter how many calculations are in between), the goal seek will work.

However, it's important to remember that the input cell must be hardcoded. An input cell that contains a formula will not work.

A common use of goal seek is in break-even analysis. We normally want to know how many units we need to produce to break even (i.e., how many units we need to produce in order to recover our costs). In this instance, we'd change the number of units in the model until the profit amount is set to zero. See "Break-Even Analysis" in Chapter 9 for an example of this.

Here's another example in 10 steps. Let's say you borrow $1 million at an interest rate of 6.5 percent:

1. Use the PMT function to calculate the monthly repayments over 15 years.
2. If you use the PMT Insert Function dialog box, your input should look as shown in Figure 8.13.
3. The result will be **−$8,711**. Put a minus sign in front of it to make it a positive number.
4. Your formula should be **= −PMT(B2/12,B3*12,B1)**.

   See "Loan Calculations" in Chapter 6 for greater detail on how to use PMT and other loan calculation functions.

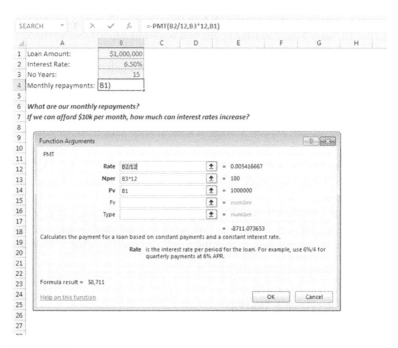

FIGURE 8.13 Loan Repayment Calculation Using PMT Function

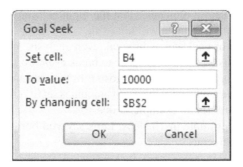

FIGURE 8.14   Goal Seek Dialog Box

Let's say that we can afford for our repayments to go up to, say, $10,000 per month. How much of an increase in interest payments can we afford? Maybe we should fix our rate.

5. On the Data tab, in the Data Tools group, click on What-if Analysis and select Goal Seek from the drop-down list.
6. In the Set Cell box, enter the reference for the cell containing the formula that produces the desired end result (**B4**, in this case) as shown in Figure 8.14.
7. In the To Value box, enter the result you would like to achieve in the Set Cell (type in **10000**).
8. In the By Changing Cell, enter the reference for the cell that Excel is to change (**B2**, the interest rate).
9. This will bring up the Goal Seek Status dialog box containing the result of your seek.
10. Click OK to accept the new values, or Cancel to go back to the original values.

The answer to this problem is that we can afford for interest rates to increase to 8.75 percent. If the bank were to offer us a fixed interest rate of 8 percent, then we should take it!

Whilst this calculation could have been done by trial and error, it's much quicker to use a goal seek. Goal seek will work in huge models and run through a large number of calculations, giving the result you need to achieve your desired outcome.

STRUCTURED REFERENCE TABLES

The Table feature in Excel (not to be confused with PivotTables or Data Tables) is a great tool for organising and analysing large amounts of data. For this reason, like PivotTables, they are not used much in pure financial modelling, but as a very useful tool in reporting and analysis, they are also worth a brief mention.

The two useful features of a Table are:

1. A Table will automatically resize depending on the number of rows. If you have a formula or a PivotTable referencing the Table, additional data will automatically be included in the range.
2. Formulas created within a Table are automatically populated, hence ensuring consistency in formulas for blocks of data—a fundamental point of financial modelling best practice.

Also note that once you start using some of the Modern Excel tools for analysis or reporting, your data *must* be structured into a Table in order to feed into Power Query, Power Pivot, or Power BI, so that's another reason to get familiar with them.

TO CREATE A TABLE

1. Organise your data so that it is arranged in a block, with headings on each column, as shown in Figure 8.15. You can create this sheet yourself, or a template can be found along with the accompanying models to the rest of the screenshots in this book, at www.plumsolutions.com.au/book.
2. Click on any cell within the sheet and select Table from the Insert tab, or use the shortcut Control T.
3. This will bring up the Create Table dialog box, and if your data is arranged correctly with headings on each column, you can leave the checkbox "My table has headers" selected, and press OK.
4. When the table has been created, it will format the table using alternate fill colour. You can easily change the colours from the Table Styles section on the Design tab. Note that the Design tab is called the Table tab in Excel for Mac.
5. You can also change the name of the table in the Table Name box in the far left of the Design tab, as shown in Figure 8.15. This may seem similar to creating a named range, but it's an entirely different feature.
6. Now try typing in an extra heading, such as "GST" in cell E1. You'll see that the table automatically expands to include the additional column. If you add a formula in cell E2, you'll see that the formula is automatically copied down the entire column in the table.

(continued)

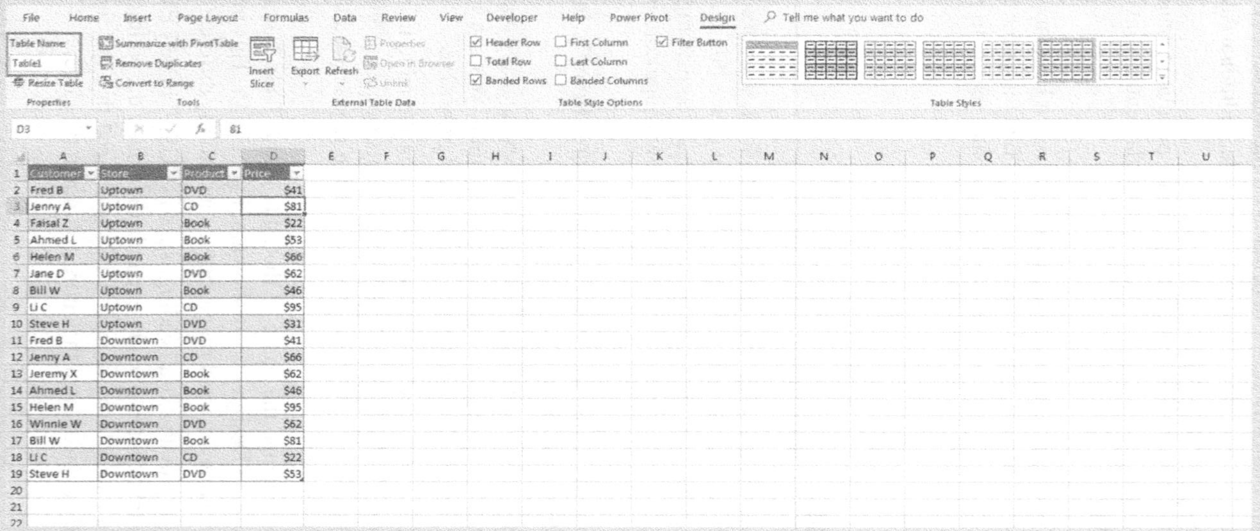
File
Home
Insert
Page Layout
Formulas
Data
Review
View
Developer
Help
Power Pivot
Design
Tell me what you want to do
Table Name:
Table1
Resize Table
Properties
Summarize with PivotTable
Remove Duplicates
Convert to Range
Tools
Insert Slicer
Export
Refresh
External Table Data
Header Row
Total Row
Banded Rows
First Column
Last Column
Banded Columns
Filter Button
Table Style Options
Table Styles
D3
81
Customer
Store
Product
Price
Fred B Uptown DVD $41
Jenny A Uptown CD $81
Faisal Z Uptown Book $22
Ahmed L Uptown Book $53
Helen M Uptown Book $66
Jane D Uptown DVD $62
Bill W Uptown Book $46
Li C Uptown CD $95
Steve H Uptown DVD $31
Fred B Downtown DVD $41
Jenny A Downtown CD $66
Jeremy X Downtown Book $62
Ahmed L Downtown Book $46
Helen M Downtown Book $95
Winnie W Downtown DVD $62
Bill W Downtown Book $81
Li C Downtown CD $22
Steve H Downtown DVD $53

FIGURE 8.15 Creating a Structured Reference Table

If you want your data to stop being a Table and revert to being an ordinary block of data, click on the Table, and on the Design tab; under the Tools section, click on Convert to Range.

TIP

Note that if you have formulas that reference Tables, they will behave a little differently from those which reference ordinary ranges. Take care when copying and pasting formulas, as highlighting and dragging the cell to copy, which ordinarily performs the same action as the Control+C, Control+V copy/paste shortcuts, will copy references in a different way to using shortcuts.

PIVOTTABLES

Excel PivotTables are another very useful and powerful feature of Excel to very quickly summarise, analyse, explore, and present your data. Figure 8.16 shows an example of a PivotTable that has been used to summarise the spend by location and product.

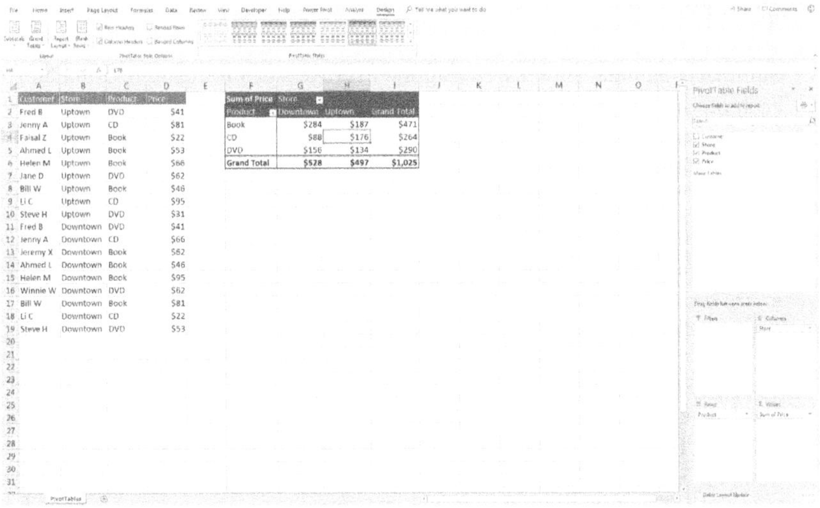

FIGURE 8.16 Source Data and PivotTable

Using PivotTables in Financial Models

Useful as they are, PivotTables are not used very widely in building pure financial models. They are a very popular tool, however, and so it's difficult to be good at using Excel for business and financial modelling (which is the title of this book) without knowing how and in what context to use PivotTables. For this reason, I have provided a brief overview of PivotTables in this chapter.

The reason I don't recommend the use of PivotTables in pure, dynamic financial models is that they are static until refreshed, and this does not fit very well with the methodology of most financial models. As discussed in earlier chapters, the whole point of financial modelling is that you are able to change the inputs, and the outputs change! It's far too easy for a user to change the inputs, and then forget to refresh the PivotTable. This results in using incorrect outputs from the model.

As an alternative, I recommend the use of an alternative live, dynamic formula, such as SUMIF or SUMIFS, in place of a PivotTable when building a classic financial model that depends on inputs being changed. See "Aggregation Functions" in Chapter 6 for how to use the SUMIF and SUMIFS functions.

Whilst it is possible to change the settings so that the PivotTable will automatically refresh whenever the file is opened, there is no guarantee that the user will open and close the file before using the data, and it cannot be relied upon. It's not a bad idea to change the settings to automatically refresh in any case, however. You can do this by right-clicking on a PivotTable, then go to PivotTable Options as shown in Figure 8.17. On the Data tab, select "Refresh data when opening the file".

Common Uses of PivotTables PivotTables are widely used in data analysis, management reporting, and building dashboards. Here are some commonly used examples of PivotTables:

- Summarising data, such as finding the average sales for each region and for each product, from a product sales data table.
- Listing unique values in any column of a table (this can also be done with the remove duplicates functionality).
- Filtering, sorting, and drilling down data in the reports without writing any formulas or macros.
- Transposing data (i.e., moving rows to columns or columns to rows).

Other Things You Should Know About PivotTables

- You can apply any formatting to the PivotTables. Excel has some very good PivotTable formats that can be easily accessed via the Styles on the Design tab.
- You can easily change the PivotTable summary formulas. Right-click on the PivotTable and select the Summarise Data By option from Sum to Count or Average, for example.

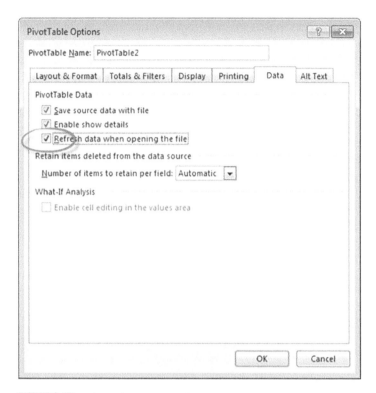

FIGURE 8.17 PivotTable Options Dialog Box

- You can also apply conditional formatting to PivotTables, although you may want to be a bit careful as PivotTables scale in size depending on the data.
- Whenever the original data from which PivotTables are constructed changes, just right-click on the PivotTable and select Refresh Data.
- Recommended PivotTables, as shown in Figure 8.18, is useful as it gives you a preview of what your data will look like in a PivotTable.

TIP

If you want to drill down on a particular summary value, just double-click on it. Excel will create a new sheet with the data corresponding to that pivot report value.

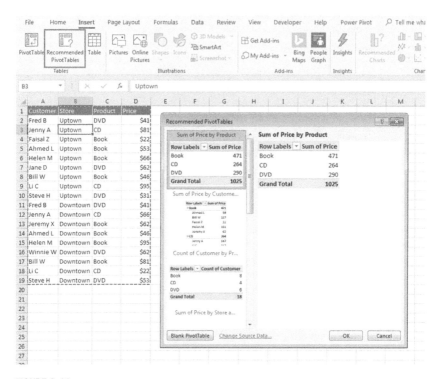

Building a PivotTable

If you need to create a report summarising sales by customer, for example, you can follow these eight instructions:

1. Highlight the entire database, ensuring that the headings are at the top of the range, or just click somewhere in the block of data.

TIP

If you convert your source data to a Structured Reference Table first, before creating the PivotTable, and then use this as the source data, then the range will automatically update when the data expands or contracts.

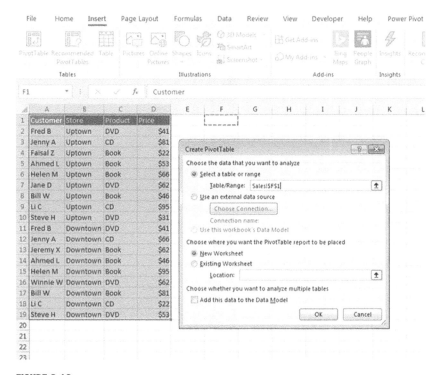

FIGURE 8.19   Creating a PivotTable

2. Select PivotTable from the Insert tab, in the Tables section. See Figure 8.19.
3. By default, it will put your PivotTable on a new page. If you prefer, you can change the options to locate it on the existing or a different page.
4. Press OK. The PivotTable Field List will appear on the right-hand side.
5. If you drag Customers into the Row Labels field and Price into the Values field, it will summarise your data and create a PivotTable report that looks like Figure 8.20.
6. If you now drag the Product field to the Rows field below the Customers field, it will split your report into subcategories.
7. Try slicing and dicing your data in different ways. Swap the customer and product fields, or try moving products from the Rows field to the Column field.
8. The PivotTable can now be quickly formatted using the drop-down styles on the Design tab.

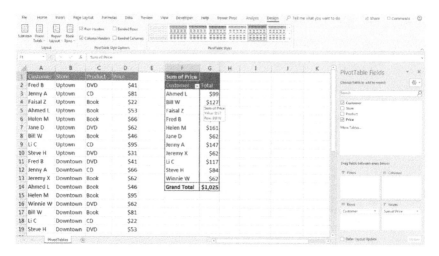

FIGURE 8.20 Completed PivotTable with Field List

	A	B	C	D	E	F	G	H
1								
2								
3	Sum of Annual Fee	Column						
4		+1987	+1988	+1989	+1990	+1991	+1992	+1993 +1
5								
6	Row Labels							
7	Accounts				100			
8	Admin					100	650	
9	Brokerage							
10	Communications							
11	Enterprise					100	650	
12	Finance						650	
13	HR							650
14	Insurance					100		
15	Legal					100		
16	Maintenance					100		
17	Resourcing							1300
18	Sales					100		
19	Support				100			
20	Transport				100			
21	Grand Total				300	600	1950	1950 1

Context menu: Copy, Format Cells..., Refresh, Sort, Filter, Subtotal "Years", Expand/Collapse, Group..., Ungroup..., Move, Remove "Years", Field Settings..., PivotTable Options..., Hide Field List

FIGURE 8.21 Grouping the Dates in a PivotTable

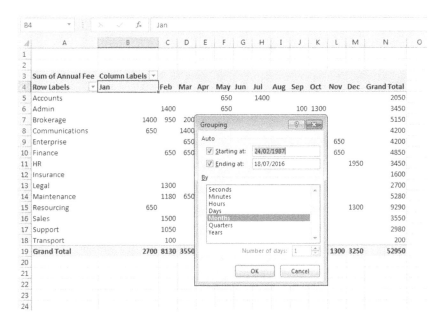

FIGURE 8.22 Grouping by Month

Note that in versions later than Excel 2016, PivotTables automatically group dates in the column or row fields, as shown in Figure 8.21. If you'd prefer to group the dates manually, follow these steps:

1. Click on the first date in the column field, as shown in Figure 8.21, and select Group.
2. Choose Months, Quarters, Years, or however you'd like the dates to be aggregated. In the example shown in Figure 8.22, we have chosen to group by Months, so we can see a forecast of fees by month in this PivotTable.

Filtering and Using Slicers

Using the data from the previous example, we could drag the Product field into the Filters field in order to filter the data by Product, as shown in Figure 8.23.

This filter can be used to show DVDs only, CDs only, or a combination. Note, however, that if we select "Multiple Items" as we have done in Figure 8.24, it ceases to show which items have been selected, which is not very helpful from a reporting perspective. Using a slicer in this instance will make the report more user-friendly.

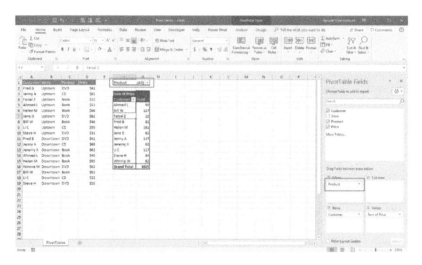

FIGURE 8.23 Filter in a PivotTable

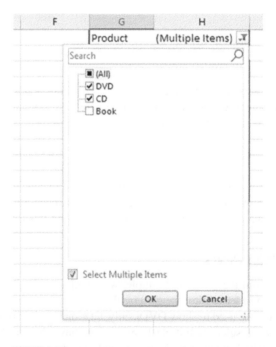

FIGURE 8.24 Selecting Multiple Items in a Filter

TO INSERT A SLICER

1. Remove any filters by clearing (selecting all options) and dragging the filtered field out of the Filter Field List.
2. Click on the PivotTable and select Slicer from the Insert tab on the ribbon, or from the Insert Slicer icon on the Analyze tab.

   If the Slicer icon is greyed out, it could be either because you haven't clicked on the PivotTable, or the file is in Compatibility Mode. Slicers are not supported in old versions of Excel, so make sure the file is saved as a .xlsx file type.

   You can also add a slicer by right-clicking on the field name in the field list to the right of the page.
3. The Insert Slicers dialog box will appear, so select the field by which you would like to slice (or filter) the data. Let's choose Product in this case.
4. It's not good practice to put images, charts, or slicers below or to the right of a PivotTable (because these are designed to expand or contract), so resize your columns E or F and resize the slicer to fit nicely to the left of the PivotTable, as shown in Figure 8.25.
5. Try clicking on one of the buttons to slice the PivotTable. If you want to show multiple items, hold down the Control key, or use the Multi-select icon at the top of the slicer.
6. Use the Clear Filter button at the top right-hand corner of the slicer to restore your PivotTable to full view.

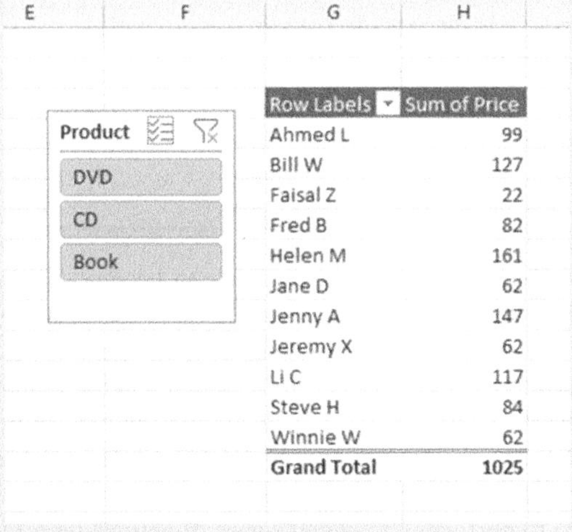

E	F	G	H
		Row Labels ▾	Sum of Price
	Product ⊟ ▽ₓ	Ahmed L	99
		Bill W	127
	DVD	Faisal Z	22
	CD	Fred B	82
	Book	Helen M	161
		Jane D	62
		Jenny A	147
		Jeremy X	62
		Li C	117
		Steve H	84
		Winnie W	62
		Grand Total	**1025**

FIGURE 8.25   Slicer in a PivotTable

TIP

Slicers can now also be applied to Structured Reference Tables.

TIP

If you have a large number of items in your slicer, consider rearranging the slicer to have multiple columns instead of a single row. To do this, click on the slicer and on the Options tab which appears under the Buttons section, increase the number next to Columns as shown in Figure 8.26. Drag the slicer by the handles until it's the correct size to show all the headings.

FIGURE 8.26   Increasing the Number of Columns in a Slicer

MACROS

Many aspiring modellers think that they need to be proficient in macro building in order to become serious financial modellers. Whilst it's not a bad idea to have a working knowledge of macros—and the language they are built in, Visual Basic for Applications (VBA)—it's certainly not critical for a financial modeller to become a super VBA programmer. As discussed in previous sections, the best sort of financial model uses the simplest tools and introducing macros to a financial model brings a whole new level of complexity. It's also useful to note that if you are using a macro to perform a repeated series of actions on a regular basis, you should consider using Power Query instead as that might be a simpler and more robust way of achieving the same result.

Before launching further into the pros and cons of including macros in your financial model, let's have a quick overview of what macros are and how to build them. VBA in Excel is a huge topic in itself, and one I'm not planning on going into too deeply here. Once you start writing macros, it's quite easy to get hooked, as you can do some truly amazing things in Excel, which will bring the functionality of your work to a whole new level. If you develop an interest in the subject, there are lots of books and training courses specifically focused on macros and VBA. Make sure that you buy a book or attend a course on VBA for Excel and its use in finance, as there is a lot of programming done in VBA that is not finance-related.

A macro is a collection of commands performed in a set order. A macro enables you to repeat operations that you would normally do by hand, but it is much faster and, when written correctly, much more reliable. Often, a macro will do in seconds what takes hours or days by hand. It can also perform tasks that are physically impossible manually. If you find you are performing the same commands or actions over and over again, in exactly the same sequence, you can create a macro to record all those actions for you. You can then assign the macro to a button and run it using a single click, or you can even assign the macro to a keyboard command.

Macro Settings

Before we begin creating macros, there are a few settings in Excel you'll need to change:

- Showing the Developer tab in the ribbon is not strictly required to record and run macros, but it contains tools that make it easier to run and edit macros, as well as some handy control tools and buttons.
- Changing the security settings is required, and you *must* change this setting if you want to run macros.

The default installation version of Excel does not have these settings. You will need to change these settings only once, and you will not need to do it again unless you reinstall Excel, or move to another machine.

Showing the Developer Tab in the Ribbon Whilst it is possible to record a macro by clicking on the launch button in the bottom left-hand corner of your screen, as shown in Figure 8.27, the Developer tab contains other functions that are useful when developing macros and other tools, so it's best to install the Developer tab.

If you do not see the Developer tab, click on File—Options—Customize Ribbon. Check the Developer box. Excel for Mac users go to Excel—Preferences—Ribbon & Toolbar and check the Developer box. For more detailed instructions on how to do this, read "Showing the Developer Tab in the Ribbon" under "Form Controls" in Chapter 7.

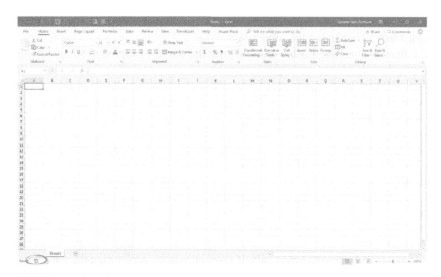

FIGURE 8.27   Macro Launch Button

Setting Macro Security Levels   Macros perform various automated functions that run via executable code. While most macros are useful and harmless, some malicious macro viruses can destroy data or otherwise damage your machine. For this reason, many people decide to disable macros altogether or turn security up so that macros can be run only from documents written by trusted publishers. However, turning up the security may disable legitimate macros, so changing the security level is an individual decision. You may also want to change this setting before you open documents from different sources.

You will need to determine the level of security appropriate for the way that you work. If you only ever run macros that you have written yourself, then Low may be suitable. High will be difficult to work with, as it won't allow you to run macros at all! If you often run macros from a trusted location, you may choose to select the Enable All Macros option.

To change your macro security settings:

1. Click on the File menu in the top left-hand corner of your screen.
2. Scroll down to Options or Excel Options at the very bottom and select it.
3. Select Trust Center and click on Trust Center Settings.
4. Choose the desired level of security.
5. Close the model down, and then reopen it.

In Excel for Mac:

1. Click on the Excel menu at the top left-hand corner of your screen.
2. Click Preferences.

3. Click the Security button, and go to the Macro Security section.
4. Choose the desired level of security.
5. Close the model down, and then reopen it.

Recording and Running a Simple Macro   The best way to get started with macros is to record one.

TO RECORD A MACRO

These are the basic steps to create a simple macro by recording it:

1. In the View tab in the Macros section, click on the arrow under the Macro button, then Record Macro. See Figure 8.28.

    This will launch the Record Macro dialog box and Excel will come up with the suggested name Macro1. You can type over this. Macro names must be one word with no spaces. It is best to give the macro a name that relates to what it does (e.g., Print-CompanyData), rather than a non-descriptive name such as Macro1. Type a name for the macro into the Macro Name box. You can also allocate a shortcut key.

    You are now recording your macro. Every command or action you perform will be added to the macro.

2. Perform all the actions you wish to be included in the macro. For example, print, save, change colour, and insert or delete rows and columns will all be included in the macro if you perform these actions while the macro is recording.

3. When you wish to stop recording the macro, click on the arrow under the Macro button, then Stop Recording.

FIGURE 8.28   Accessing Record Macro from the Ribbon

This macro will save within the Excel file you used when recording the macro. This macro is available whenever you have the file open.

TO RUN THE MACRO

1. In the View tab in the Macros section, click the Macro button. This will bring up the Macro dialog box, containing a list of all the available macros.
2. Click in the list to select the macro you wish to run.
3. Click on the Run button. All the actions you performed in the steps above will repeat themselves.

Practical Exercise Let's try recording a macro that will be useful. Say you want to change the formatting of a cell from 150000 to $150,000—a very commonly performed task. (This macro will save you some time, as it's not possible to change this formatting with a single mouse click or keystroke.) Follow these 12 steps:

1. Type **150000** into cell A1 on a blank worksheet.
2. Begin recording, as shown above. Call the macro **FormatCurrency**. Assign a shortcut key (e.g., Ctrl+m), and click OK. See Figure 8.29.
3. Select cell A1 and change the formatting to $150,000. This can be done through the menu bar, or right-click "Format cells" and change the currency to the desired format.
4. Stop recording.
5. Now we can test to see if the macro worked. Go back to cell A1 and change the formatting to a percentage, for example.

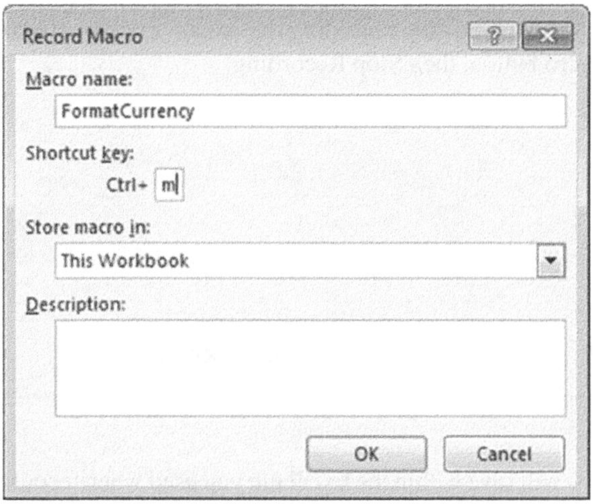

FIGURE 8.29   Naming the Recorded Macro

6. Run the macro as shown above. The formatting of cell A1 will revert to the formatting we specified in the macro. Now we can edit the macro and make changes within the VBA code as follows:

   a. Select the Macros icon from the View or Developer tab on the ribbon. The Macro dialog box contains a list of all the available macros.

   b. Select the macro that you want to edit and press Edit. This will take you into the VBA coding editor, where you can manually edit a macro.

   c. Change things such as sheet names or cell references, rather than re-recording the macro. You can even make the macro run more efficiently by removing the duplication of the **.Select** command.

   d. Change the code, and close down the editor.

7. Try editing your macro. If you haven't been into the VBA editor before, it can seem a bit scary, but don't worry. You can always close down the editor to get back to your Excel model.

8. The VBA editor screen should look something like Figure 8.30.

    The text in green font is purely descriptive. Any text preceded by an apostrophe (') will be ignored by the macro when running. You can delete or replace this with documentation of your own, describing what the macro does.

    Take a look at the code. It contains two steps: it selects cell A1, and formats it as we have specified. This means that every time we run this macro, it will select cell A1 and format it. If we remove the reference to cell A1, it will change the formatting of whatever cell is selected. This is much more useful!

9. Remove the descriptive text and the first line of code. Your code should now be:

    Sub FormatCurrency()

        Selection.NumberFormat=″$#,##0″

    End Sub

10. Close down the VBA editor and return to your model.

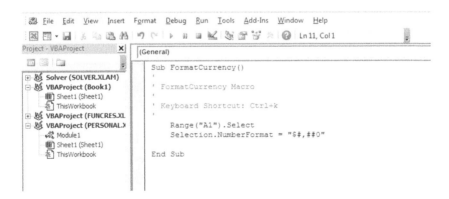

FIGURE 8.30   Viewing the Recorded Macro in the VBA Editor

11. Type some random numbers anywhere in your model—even on a different page.
12. Select the cells and run the macro by using the shortcut. These numbers should change to your desired format.

NOTE

The next time you save this file, it will prompt you to save it as a macro-enabled file type (.xlsm), or you may get the warning message shown in Figure 8.31. If you click Yes on the warning message, this will save it as a macro-free workbook (.xlsx), then all your macros will disappear! As soon as you start creating a macro, save it immediately as a macro-enabled file.

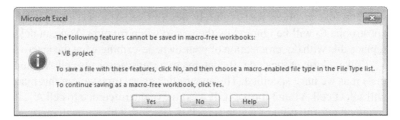

FIGURE 8.31   Macro-Free Workbook Warning

Creating Macro Buttons

You can assign a macro to almost any object or shape on your Excel worksheet, including shapes, buttons, and even combo box drop-downs. The most commonly used object is a rectangular-shaped button. There are two ways of creating these buttons, either as shapes or traditional form buttons.

HOW TO CREATE A SHAPE

1. On the Insert tab, in the Illustrations group, a Drawing Shape can be used as a macro button. The style can be changed to look like a coloured rectangular button.
2. Right-click to add descriptive text (e.g., Press Me or Run Macro).
3. Right-click to assign a macro to the button. Whenever you press this button, the assigned macro will automatically run.

Alternatively, the more traditional macro button can be used.

If you wish to create a traditional form of macro button in later versions of Excel, it's still possible, but it's been hidden very well. You need to have the Developer tab showing before you can create these buttons. See the explanation from earlier in this chapter on how to make the Developer tab show in the ribbon.

HOW TO CREATE A TRADITIONAL FORM BUTTON

1. On the Developer tab, in the Controls group, select the Insert button and select the Form button. In Excel for Mac, on the Developer tab, in the Form Controls group, select the Button button. Yes, I just called it the Button button.
2. Now click and drag over the spreadsheet to create the shape.
3. When you let go of the mouse button, the Assign Macro dialog box will appear. Select the appropriate macro.
4. To change the assigned macro, right-click on the shape and click on Assign Macro.
5. You should add the appropriate text and format the shape with colour, shadow, and so on.

Macros in Financial Modelling Case Studies

There are hundreds of situations where macros can save time and increase accuracy. They might not necessarily be built and saved within financial models, but they could be used in the collection of the data that goes into the model. Here is a small sample of a few of the most common problems in financial modelling that are solved by macros. You can download some of these example models from www.plumsolutions.com.au/book.

- A company is doing a salary comparison between different countries and wants to know how much they would need to pay in Malaysian ringgit (MYR) so that their salary is the same as someone working in Singapore. If a worker in Malaysia earns the equivalent of 100,000 MYR after tax, how much would the company need to pay the worker before tax? The problem is that tax is calculated on pre-tax salary, so our formula gives us a circular reference. We can use a macro with a goal seek to repeatedly set the pre-tax salary to the amount entered by the user.

- Fifty identical budget templates have been created, and you discover a formula needs to be changed. Instead of making the change 50 times, record a macro. It will be much quicker and far less prone to error.
- A nonprofit organisation sets its pricing so that all costs are fully recovered to break even. The costs keep changing though, and the user is a senior account manager who doesn't know how to do a goal seek in Excel. The modeller creates a simple macro using a goal seek so that all the user needs to do is change the costs and press the button to find out how much the pricing needs to change under the new costing.
- A dump of information containing several thousand rows is exported from a database into Excel every day. The data needs to be formatted and manipulated manually to be used in a daily takings report. Automating this with a macro (or with Power Query) can literally save hours of manual data manipulation.
- A reporting model is built using a PivotTable, but when new data is entered, the user sometimes forgets to refresh the PivotTable. The modeller builds a button to refresh the PivotTable every time it's pressed.

Dangers and Pitfalls of Using Macros

Handy as they are, macros should always be used with caution. Quite often formulas or filtering will achieve the desired result, without the need for building a macro. Always try a formula or standard Excel solution before considering the inclusion of a macro in your model.

- Unless ranges are defined properly using relative cell references, macros don't move their references the way that formulas do, and therefore named ranges are recommended when building macros. If any data has moved since the macro was written, the macro will refer to the wrong cell. A badly written macro can copy and paste over data, and you won't know what it has done!
- Visual Basic is a complex programming language and a skill that many people don't have. Therefore, many people are not able to edit or follow what a macro is doing—especially if it hasn't been documented properly.
- Macros are time-consuming to write, and often a much quicker and more transparent solution can be built just as easily with a plain formula.
- Running macros requires security settings to be changed (as shown above), and if your model is used by other people, they may not realise they need to change their settings, causing the model to not work properly.
- Macro-enabled files need to be saved in .xlsm file format. If they are accidentally saved as a .xlsx macro-free workbook, the macros will be removed from the file. If this happens, the macros have been deleted and you'll need to either rewrite the code or copy it back in from a backup copy!

- Unless you will be maintaining the model yourself, most business Excel users have more than enough to do without also trying to learn how to program.
- If you're the one running the macro each time the model needs to be updated, that's fine, but what will happen after you're gone? If the process stops working due to a macro problem, it can hold up monthly procedures significantly.

Basically, there are more things that can go wrong if a financial model contains macros. When it comes to building financial models, consider whether a VBA solution is absolutely necessary before including it in your model. When building a financial model, macros should not be used unless there is no other option to achieve the required result.

SUMMARY

The tools for financial modelling covered in this chapter range from the basic, such as hiding and grouping, to more complex tools such as macros and array formulas. As always, we try to make our models *as simple as possible, and as complex as necessary*. Therefore, if you can create a model using just basic functions and tools, by all means do so.

If, however, you find that your simple solution does not provide your model with the desired functionality, then you may consider including a more complex nested formula, or even possibly a macro. The best sort of financial models are those that are clearly laid out and use very simple and clearly defined tools—not because we don't know how to create complex models, but because they are easier to follow. So, in conclusion, it's very difficult to be a top-notch financial modeller without knowing all the complex tools and functionality in Excel, but that does not mean that you should use these tools in every model. On the contrary, complex tools should be used only when absolutely necessary.

CHAPTER 9

Common Uses of Tools in Financial Modelling

Now that we know how to use many of the useful tools, functions, and features of Excel, let's take a look at actually using these tools to solve common problems, calculations, and situations encountered in financial models.

ESCALATION METHODS FOR MODELLING

There are several different ways of applying a growth, indexation, or escalation method over a period of time to a principal amount. We often need to be able to include escalation in our models for the purpose of forecasting sales growth year-over-year, for example, or increasing costs by an inflation amount. Calculating a growth amount might seem straightforward initially, but there are several different methods that can be used, and when applying growth rates in a model you need to be clear about which method you are using.

Whilst we can use functions to calculate future values based on set or varying growth rates, we'll first calculate them manually so that we understand the mechanics of the calculations, and then use the functions.

Using Absolute (Fixed) Growth Rate

Here we have compound growth over five years at a fixed interest rate. The capital grows each year by 5 percent. At the simplest level, our formula is **base amount* (1+growth)** The reason we are adding 1 (effectively 100 percent) to the growth rate (5 percent) is that we want the capital sum returned along with the accrued interest. Multiplying an amount by (1+growth) is a very common calculation technique when building financial models.

◢	A	B	C	D	E	F	G	
1	**Comparison of Escalation Methods**							
2								
3	Option 1a:	Absolute (fixed) Growth rate, compounding						
4	Growth:	5.0%						
5		Actual			Forecast			
6		2021	2022	2023	2024	2025	2026	
7	Sales	$5,015						
8								

FIGURE 9.1   Fixed, Compounding Exercise

Exercise: Fixed and Compounding   You can create this example yourself in the following five steps, or you can find this template, along with the accompanying models to the rest of the screenshots in this book, at www.plumsolutions.com.au/book.

1. Create the exercise as shown in Figure 9.1. The rate is fixed in a single cell (B4). Therefore, we need an absolute reference, namely $B$4. So, after the first year (in 2021), create the formula in cell C7: **=B7*(1+$B$4)**.
2. Copy the formula in C7 to cells D7 through G7.
3. This method grows the amount at a fixed rate, which compounds each year.
     With most models, we normally want to show the amount that is forecast in each year, but if you want a shortcut formula that will show, in a single cell, how much we'll have at a fixed 5 percent growth after five years, we can use the Future Value (FV) function. Let's verify the amount you calculated for the year 2026 by using this function.
4. Somewhere in a cell to the right of this table, enter Excel's FV function. Either type **=FV(** into the cell and follow the prompts, or select FV from the Insert Function dialog box. Because there are no periodic payments being made, we need to include the yearly rate, the period in years, and the present value (PV).
5. Prefix the function with a minus symbol to get a positive result. Your formula should be **=-FV($B$4,5,0,B7)**, and the totals using both methods should be the same. Your sheet should look something like Figure 9.2.

Exercise: Fixed and Non-compounding   Another variation on this escalation method is to still use a fixed growth rate, but not compound it. To do this, we will use an escalation index across the top. This may be more practical in some model designs but bear in mind that it yields different results. See Figure 9.3.

1. In row 10, create your escalation index row using the formula **=B10+$B$11** in cell C10, and copying across.
2. Escalate in cell C14 by using the formula **=$B$14*C10**, and copying across.

| C7 | | | ✕ | ✓ | fx | =B7*(1+$B$4) | | | | |

▲	A	B	C	D	E	F	G	H	I	J
1	Comparison of Escalation Methods									
2										
3	Option 1a:	Absolute (fixed) Growth rate, compounding							USING A FUNCTION	
4	Growth:	5.0%								
5		Actual			Forecast				FV function	
6		2021	2022	2023	2024	2025	2026		=-FV($B$4,5,0,B7)	
7	Sales	$5,015	$5,266	$5,529	$5,805	$6,096	$6,401			$6,401
8										
9										
10										

FIGURE 9.2   Completed Fixed, Compounding Exercise

9	Option 1b:	Fixed growth rate, non-compounding					
10	Growth:	100%	105%	110%	115%	120%	125%
11		5.0%					
12		Actual			Forecast		
13	Sales	2021	2022	2023	2024	2025	2026
14		$5,015	=$B$14*C10		$5,767	$6,018	$6,269
15	What's the difference between Option 1a and Option 1b? Why are the answers different?						

FIGURE 9.3   Fixed, Non-compounding Exercise

This formula gives you a lower result in Year 5 than the exercise examining fixed and compounding interest because it is not compounding on the previous year. It simply adds a flat $5,015 × 5 percent each year, instead of adding the growth rate to the increased total.

Using Relative (Varying) Growth Rates

The next example returns the future value of an initial principal after applying a series of interest rates. While the rate was fixed in the example above, here it fluctuates from year to year. This is considered to be a superior model design, as it allows for fluctuation of growth rates. Even if the growth rate does not change from year to year, by building the model in this way, we are allowing for changes in the future. By using the aforementioned design with a single growth rate, we are restricted to having only a rate that does not change.

We'll no longer use absolute references for the interest rate but will allow both it and the value to change from year to year as we copy the formula across D22 through to G22. Cell C22's formula is **base amount*(1+growth)**, as previously, but this time the growth does not have an absolute reference applied to it. The formula is **=B22*(1+B19)**.

Exercise: Relative and Compounding

1. Complete cell C22 in the exercise workbook as described above, then copy the formula to the right.

Let's try a shortcut function to get directly to the results without going through the annual calculations.

2. To the right of the results, enter Excel's FVSCHEDULE function to verify the figure for 2026.
3. Use the function FVSCHEDULE in your exercise spreadsheet.

Your sheet should look something like Figure 9.4.

Exercise: Relative and Non-compounding   In this next example, we are using another escalation index across the top. See Figure 9.5.

1. In row 25, create your escalation index row by using the formula $= B25 + B26$ in cell C25, and copying across.
2. Escalate in cell C29 by using the formula $=\$B\$29*C25$, and copying across.

This formula gives you a lower result in Year 5 than the fixed and compounding example, because it is not compounding on the previous year.

17								
18	Option 2a: Relative (varying) Growth rate, compounding							
19	Growth:	5.0%	5.5%	5.1%	5.3%	4.8%		
20		Actual		Forecast				FVSCHEDULE function
21		2021	2022	2023	2024	2025	2026	=FVSCHEDULE(B22,B19:F19)
22	Sales	$5,015	=B22*(1+B19)		$5,839	$6,148	$6,443	$6,443
23								
24								

FIGURE 9.4   Relative, Compounding Exercise and FVSCHEDULE Function

C29		▼	:	✕	✓	f_x	=$B$29*C25	
◢	A	B	C	D	E	F	G	H
24	Option 2b: Relative (varying) Growth rate, non-compounding							
25		100.0%	105.0%	110.5%	115.6%	120.9%	125.7%	
26	Growth:	5.0%	5.5%	5.1%	5.3%	4.8%		
27		Actual		Forecast				
28		2021	2022	2023	2024	2025	2026	
29	Sales	$5,015	$5,266	$5,542	$5,797	$6,063	$6,304	
30								

FIGURE 9.5   Relative, Non-compounding Exercise

Using Exponential Operations on an Absolute (Fixed) Growth Rate

This exercise is similar to the first one, except that we will include the use of the caret symbol (^) to perform exponential (to the power of) operations. For instance, $3 \times 3 \times 3 = 27$. So does 3^3 and, in Excel's equivalent, 3^3.

Exercise: Complex Escalation   Figure 9.6 shows compound growth over a period at a fixed 5 percent per annum interest rate.

Our formula will allow for start and end dates to the period, in the form

$$\text{Base amount}*((100\% + \text{growth})^{\hat{}}(\text{End year-Start year}))$$

Excel will perform the exponential operation before the multiplication, so the encompassing set of parentheses is not essential. The formula in C37 is therefore

$$=\$B\$37*((1+\$B\$4)^{\hat{}}(C36-\$B\$36))$$

Note that instead of using **End year-Start year**, you may also insert a helper row at the top to link to instead, which makes a slightly less complex formula. The next exercise shows how this can be done.

1. Complete the formula for cell C37 and copy it across to achieve the results in the diagram below.
2. The formula **=FV(B34,G36-B36,0,B37)** will verify the answer for the year 2026, as shown in cell I37 of Figure 9.6.

Practical Usage of Exponential Growth Rates

You will notice that we achieved the same result ($6,401) under the fixed, compounding exercise as we did under the relative and compounding exercise, but with a far less complex formula. Using exponential growth rates is useful when you need to compound the growth rate, but want each cell to operate independently.

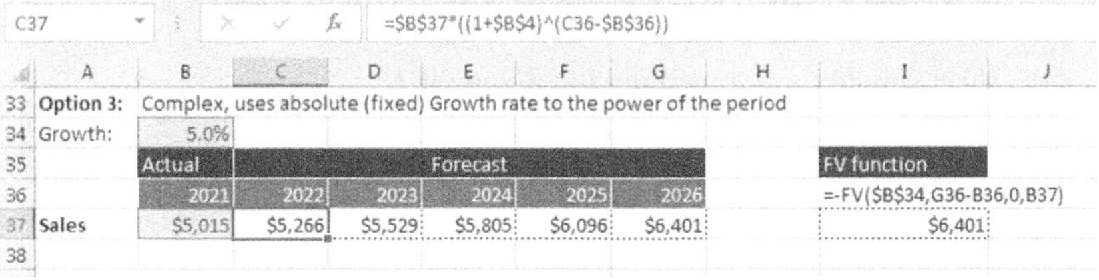

C37			f_x	=$B$37*((1+$B$4)^(C36-$B$36))						
	A	B	C	D	E	F	G	H	I	J
33	Option 3:	Complex, uses absolute (fixed) Growth rate to the power of the period								
34	Growth:	5.0%								
35		Actual			Forecast				FV function	
36		2021	2022	2023	2024	2025	2026		=-FV($B$34,G36-B36,0,B37)	
37	Sales	$5,015	$5,266	$5,529	$5,805	$6,096	$6,401		$6,401	
38										

FIGURE 9.6   Complex Escalation

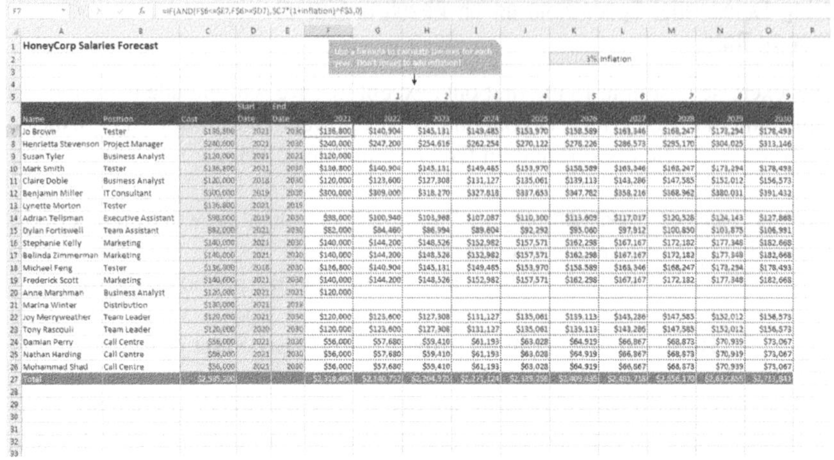

FIGURE 9.7   Completed Staff Calculation Using Exponential Growth Rates

If, for example, you have start dates and end dates that need to be included in a formula as well as compounding escalation, you will need to use exponential growth rates. In Figure 9.7, we will create a formula to evaluate the start date and end date, only inserting the cost in the relevant years and then compounding the inflation.

This will require the IF and AND functions to be used in combination to establish whether the column heading year falls within an employee's start and end dates.

For instance, in English terms we will be checking that **IF(AND(2021> =Employee Start Date,2021<=Employee End Date))** is true before writing inflation-escalated costs into the appropriate cell of column F. Otherwise we will write a zero.

Use the term in years (row 5) to exponentially escalate the costs (in column C). For instance, if the year 2021 (F6) meets the IF test, F7 will equate to **Cost*(1+inflation)^0**, which leaves it, in this case, unchanged.

Your formula should be

$$\text{=IF(AND(F\$6<=\$E7,F\$6>=\$D7),\$C7*(1+inflation)^F\$5,0)}$$

and the sheet should look something like Figure 9.7.

UNDERSTANDING NOMINAL AND EFFECTIVE (REAL) RATES

From a financial modelling perspective, there are two interesting aspects of nominal and effective rates that we should be aware of.

1. **Escalation calculations.** We need to consider whether an escalation, growth rate, or indexation amount includes the effect of inflation (i.e., whether it is real or effective) and what this actually means in real terms.

2. **Loan calculations.** When comparing and calculating interest rates, the frequency of compounding can make a difference to the amount of interest actually paid. This can be calculated in Excel using the EFFECT and NOMINAL functions.

When including escalation or growth rates in a financial model, we sometimes need to consider whether the growth percentage is expressed as a nominal or real rate. Normally we express the growth percentage as a nominal rate, meaning that we don't take into consideration the effect of inflation or other factors that would impact the value of that rate. The real or effective rate will include the effect of other factors, such as inflation, to give you the real or adjusted value.

For example, if you earn a $100,000 salary, and after a year of working for the company your boss unexpectedly gives you a raise of 10 percent, you might think you're going to have an extra $10,000 in your pocket, right? Well, not exactly. Theoretically, in the 12 months since you began working for the company, your cost of living has increased and eroded the purchasing power of your salary. Therefore, if we assume that the consumer price index (CPI), or rate of inflation, is 3 percent, then your $100,000 is not buying you as much now as it did when you first started the job. To calculate the effective salary increase that you received, you'd need to deduct the inflation from the raise. Your nominal increase was 10 percent, but the real or effective raise was only 7 percent.

Normally, when modelling escalation amounts, we use the nominal rate and we know, when considering the calculations, that it does not take into account the purchasing power in the future. For example, in the exercise described in the previous section, we indexed the sales revenue at 5 percent, as shown below. It goes without saying that this 5 percent is a nominal amount. We know that the $6,401 received in Year 5 is not *really* $6,401 in today's terms, because inflation will have eroded its purchasing power. See Figure 9.2.

If we want to compare an investment in today's terms, we need to use the effective rate and to calculate this, we simply deduct the inflation amount—let's say 3 percent—from the growth rate, and hence our effective growth rate is 2 percent. As always, we need to be very explicit about the rates we have used. Note that expressing amounts in effective terms is not commonly used in financial models and, unless stated otherwise, the user would assume that a rate is nominal. Therefore, if you choose to use an effective rate, make sure that you state it clearly as an assumption, as shown in Figure 9.8.

Adjusting Loan Rates with NOMINAL and EFFECT Functions

Calculating effective growth rates as outlined above is quite simple, and we certainly don't need a dedicated Excel function for this. There is another use for the nominal and effective concept in finance, and the calculation is far more complex.

C7	▾	:	×	✓	ƒₓ	=B7*(1+$B$4)			

◢	A	B	C	D	E	F	G	H
1	**Comparison of Escalation Methods**							
2								
3	Option 1a:	Absolute (fixed) Growth rate, compounding						
4	Effective Growth Rate: ¹	2.0%						
5		Actual			Forecast			
6		2021	2022	2023	2024	2025	2026	
7	Sales (effective $)	$5,015	$5,115	$5,218	$5,322	$5,428	$5,537	
8	1. Nominal growth rate of 5% less 3% inflation = 2% effective growth rate							
9								

FIGURE 9.8   Assumption Documentation in Growth Calculations

Nominal and real rates affect mortgage calculations, too. As discussed in "Loan Calculations" in Chapter 6, due to the effect of compounding, we actually pay a higher interest rate than is expressed in the nominal rate when quoted by the lender. Most loans are calculated and compounded daily, and therefore every single day we pay interest on the interest that was charged on the previous day.

The nominal rate is basically the simple interest rate for the complete period of the mortgage (i.e., the rate you are quoted when you take out the loan). The effective rate takes into account the compounding and will, therefore, be higher, depending on how frequently the loan is compounded.

The nominal and effective rates in Excel are related as follows:

$$\text{Effective interest rate} = \left(1 + \frac{\text{Nominal interest rate}}{N}\right)^N - 1$$

where N is equal to the number of compounding intervals in the year.

As usual, Excel has made these calculations simple for us by offering two important predefined functions to convert nominal to effective rates, and effective to nominal. These are NOMINAL and EFFECT.

=**NOMINAL( ).** This function returns the annual nominal interest based on the effective rate and compounding intervals in the year. The syntax for this command is **NOMINAL(Effective_Rate, Compounding_Period)**, where:

- **Effective_Rate** is the effective interest rate for the year.
- **Compounding_Period** is the total number of compounding intervals in the year.

=**EFFECT( ).** This function returns the effective interest based on the annual nominal rate and compounding intervals in the year. The syntax for this command is **EFFECT(Nominal_Rate, Compounding_Period)**, where:

- **Nominal_Rate** is the annual nominal interest rate for the year.
- **Compounding_Period** is the total number of compounding intervals in the year.

The next exercise shows how the effective rate can be calculated from the nominal rate.

Exercise: Comparing Two Nominal and Effective Interest Rate Offers Let's say you need to borrow some money, and you're offered two different interest rates from competing lenders.

1. Lender A is offering a nominal rate of 7.9 percent, compounded daily.
2. Lender B is advertising an effective rate of 8.2 percent, compounded monthly.

Which is the best deal? Here are four steps to arrive at the answer:

1. Set up the inputs side by side, so that you can compare the effective rate, as shown in Figure 9.9.
2. Calculate the effective rate of Offer A using the EFFECT function.
3. Your formula in cell B4 should be **=EFFECT(B2,B3)**.

    The effective rate of Offer A is 8.2219 percent, which means that Offer B is, in fact, a lower effective rate.

    Let's calculate the nominal rate of Offer B, for interest's sake.
4. Your formula in cell C2 should be **=NOMINAL(C4,C3)**.

    Let's see what effect the number of compounding periods has on the rate. If Lender A had compounded monthly instead of daily, would that have made a difference to the effective rate? It certainly would! Change the number of periods in cell B3 from 365 to 12, and we will see that this drops the effective rate to just slightly lower than that of Offer B. See Figure 9.10.

Although only a very simple calculation, this is a good example of how, by following financial modelling best practice and linking the formulas to the hard-coded input variables, we can easily perform sensitivity analysis on our numbers by changing the calculation assumptions.

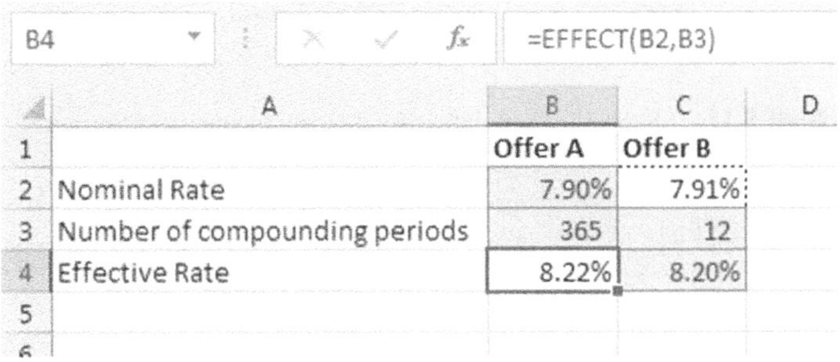

B4			f_x	=EFFECT(B2,B3)		
	A			B	C	D
1				Offer A	Offer B	
2	Nominal Rate			7.90%	7.91%	
3	Number of compounding periods			365	12	
4	Effective Rate			8.22%	8.20%	
5						
6						

FIGURE 9.9 Comparison of Interest Rates

C2				f_x	=NOMINAL(C4,C3)	

	A	B	C	D
1		Offer A	Offer B	
2	Nominal Rate	7.90%	7.91%	
3	Number of compounding periods	12	12	
4	Effective Rate	8.19%	8.20%	
5				
6				

FIGURE 9.10 Comparison of Rates with Changed Compounding Periods

CALCULATING A CUMULATIVE SUM (RUNNING TOTALS)

As always, we try to follow best practice when building financial models, and one of the important points of best practice is to ensure that formulas are as consistent as possible. Calculating a cumulative sum, or running totals, is common in financial modelling, and this is one such situation where ensuring consistent formulas can be tricky.

We need to calculate the cumulative number of customers in order to calculate the revenue, and Figure 9.11 shows one solution to the problem. It will achieve a correct total, but it necessitates using different formulas in adjacent cells.

Sometimes this is the only solution (without creating an overly complicated formula) and, if necessary, you may simply need to resign yourself to the fact that consistent formulas are not possible. There is, however, a simple solution. Using the formula =SUM($B$3:B3) and then copying it across will achieve the same result with consistent formulas, as shown in Figure 9.12.

	A	B	C	D
1				
2		2021	2022	2023
3	Expected Customer Acquisition	29700	29968	30234
4	Gross Cumulative Customers at YE	=B3	=C3+B4	=D3+C4
5				
6				

FIGURE 9.11 Method 1: Cumulative Total Using Inconsistent Formulas

	A	B	C	D	E
1					
2		2021	2022	2023	20
3	Expected Customer Acquisition	29,700	29,968	30,234	30,49
4	Gross Cumulative Customers at YE	29,700	59,668	=SUM($B$3:D3)	
5					
6					

FIGURE 9.12 Method 2: Cumulative Totals Using a Consistent Formula

> **TIP**
>
> Although my preference is method 2 because of the consistency of the formulas, using this method with a large number of cells can slow down Excel's calculation. If calculation speed is an issue, you may consider using method 1 instead.

HOW TO CALCULATE A PAYBACK PERIOD

There is no dedicated formula in Excel (yet) for calculating a payback period. However, there are a couple of different ways of doing it manually. Demonstrated below are two methods, but this is by no means an exhaustive list. The first method is very simple, but not very accurate, and the second is quite long-winded, but more precise. You can find this template, along with the accompanying models to the rest of the screenshots in this book, at www.plumsolutions.com.au/book.

Simple Payback Calculation

In a business case summary, as shown in Figures 9.13 and 9.14, we can see that the payback period (the point at which the sum of our cash flows becomes positive) is between three and four years—at 2024. We can easily estimate this by highlighting the cash totals for each year and looking at the sum amount at the bottom right-hand corner of the page, as shown in Figure 9.13. However, we would like to create a cell that automatically calculates the payback year so that as inputs change

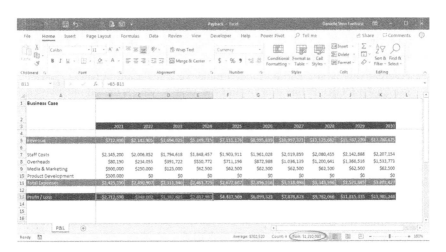

FIGURE 9.13   Manually Calculating the Payback Year

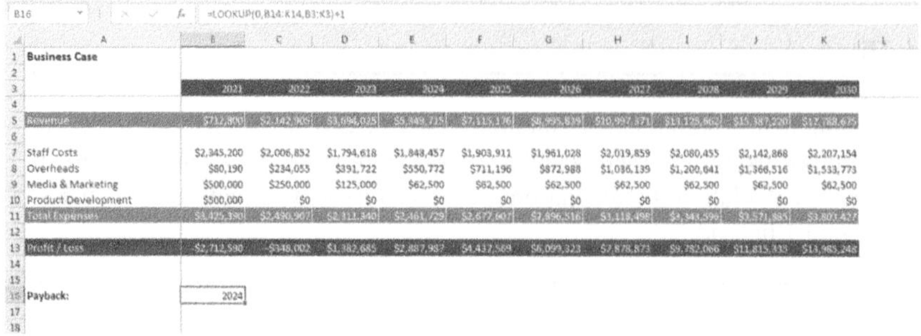

FIGURE 9.14 Completed Simple Payback Calculation

due to scenario and sensitivity analysis, the payback year will always be shown in the model, based on the cash flow amounts.

1. In row 14, create a formula that calculates the cumulative amount of cash. See "Calculating a Cumulative Sum" above for how to do this. Your formula should be **=SUM($B$13:B13)**.
2. In cell B16, insert a formula that will return the year in which the cumulative cash amount becomes positive. Remember that we want to look along the row and find the moment at which it becomes zero or greater. Your formula should be something like this: **=LOOKUP(0,B14:K14,B3:K3)**. For greater detail on how to use LOOKUP versus VLOOKUP or HLOOKUP, see "LOOKUP Functions" in Chapter 6.
3. Note that this formula is looking for a close match, which means that it will look along row 14 until it finds zero, and it will return the value before it passes zero. In this case, it will find the value under −1,677,907, as this is the last value before zero.
4. This will give you the value 2023, but we actually want 2024, so simply add **+1** to the end of the formula. Your formula should be **=LOOKUP (0,B14:K14,B3:K3)+1**.
5. Alternatively, you could add the cumulative calculation in row 2, and then use an HLOOKUP function to find the year at which the cumulative cash flow becomes positive. In this case, your formula in cell B16 would be **=HLOOKUP(0,B2:K3,2,TRUE)+1**. Having the cash flow showing above the years looks a little odd, so you'd probably hide it. I prefer the LOOKUP solution for this reason.

Note that this method is only a sample of several different tools and functions that could be used to calculate the payback period. For example, you could use a nested IF function instead, and an INDEX/MATCH combination. See Figure 9.14 for what your completed version could look like.

As the numbers for your business case change, so will your payback year. The result is only a rough estimate. For a more specific (albeit theoretical) payback date, we can use a more complex calculation, as shown in the following.

More Complex Payback Calculation

If you want to see exactly the year and month at which—theoretically—your project turns a profit, there is a more complex method. This way is also quite straightforward, but a little more time-consuming.

1. On a new sheet, in column C, type in **1 Month 2 Months...1 Year and 1 Month**, and so on, up to 10 years or so.
2. In column A, insert the years that correspond to the months. In this case, the first year is 2021, so enter 2021 in cell A2. Copy this down, and change it to 2022 after 12 months. This can most easily be done by entering the formula **A2+1** into cell A14 and copying it right down to the bottom.
3. We are going to use column A as the criteria to pick up the cash in each year. In column B, enter a formula that will reference the profit and loss (P&L) page, and return the cash for that year, which should be divided by 12 to show the cash for each month. Your formula in cell B2 should be **=HLOOKUP (A2,P&L!$B$3:$K$13,11,0)/12**. This is (theoretically) how much cash the project has cost after one month of operation. We are assuming, in this formula, that the sheet containing your cash flow is called P&L.
4. Then make this a cumulative amount in column B, by changing the formula in Month 2 so that it adds to the previous total. Your formula in cell B2 should be **=HLOOKUP(A3,P&L!$B$3:$K$13,11,0)/12+B2**. Copy this down the column.

Your sheet should look something like Figure 9.15.

Unfortunately, the cumulative SUM calculation that was performed in the last exercise will not work in this instance, so we need to create an inconsistent formula. If this really bothers you, you could add a row and put a zero in cell B2 instead, so that the formulas are consistent.

5. Continue this calculation right down the page until you reach Year 7 or 8, or as far as you want your payback calculations to work. Remember that if you're doing sensitivity and scenario analysis on this later, you don't want the formula to return an error if the calculations can't handle a larger value, so always go down a little bit further than you think you'll need.
6. You can now perform a close-match VLOOKUP or LOOKUP, which will return the year and month at which the return becomes positive. This is the payback period.
7. Enter the formula **=VLOOKUP(0,Payback!B1:C200,2,TRUE)** in the payback period cell on the P&L sheet. This will return the exact month and year

	B3	▼	:	×	✓	*fx*	=HLOOKUP(A3,'P&L'!$B$3:$K$13,11,0)/12+B2			

◢	A	B	C	D	E	F
1	Year	Cumulative Cash	Payback			
2	2021	-$226,049	1 month			
3	2021	-$452,098	2 months			
4	2021	-$678,148	3 months			
5	2021	-$904,197	4 months			
6	2021	-$1,130,246	5 months			
7	2021	-$1,356,295	6 months			
8	2021	-$1,582,344	7 months			
9	2021	-$1,808,393	8 months			
10	2021	-$2,034,443	9 months			
11	2021	-$2,260,492	10 months			
12	2021	-$2,486,541	11 months			
13	2021	-$2,712,590	12 months			
14	2022	-$2,741,590	1 Year and 1 month			
15	2022	-$2,770,590	1 Year and 2 month			
16	2022	-$2,799,590	1 Year and 3 month			
17	2022	-$2,828,591	1 Year and 4 month			
18	2022	-$2,857,591	1 Year and 5 month			
19	2022	-$2,886,591	1 Year and 6 month			
20	2022	-$2,915,591	1 Year and 7 month			
21	2022	-$2,944,591	1 Year and 8 month			
22	2022	-$2,973,591	1 Year and 9 month			
23	2022	-$3,002,591	1 Year and 10 month			

FIGURE 9.15   Payback Period Workings

that the project will hypothetically become profitable. See Figure 9.16. Of course, the close-match VLOOKUP will return the value preceding the value which is greater than zero. You may deem this to be close enough, or else move the months and years down by one row.

TIP

There is some debate as to whether the payback period should be discounted or not. I generally do not discount payback periods (as shown in this example), but whether or not it has been discounted needs to be stated clearly in your assumptions.

WEIGHTED AVERAGE COST OF CAPITAL (WACC)

Before investing in a project or new venture, we need to evaluate whether the expected returns justify the risks. Many financial models are built for the purpose

B15	▾ ⋮ × ✓ *fx*	=LOOKUP(0,Payback!$B$2:$B$121,Payback!$C$2:$C$121)		

⊿	A	B	C	D	E	F
1	**Business Case**					
2						
3		2021	2022	2023	2024	
4						
5	Revenue	$712,800	$2,142,905	$3,694,025	$5,349,715	$7,11
6						
7	Staff Costs	$2,345,200	$2,006,852	$1,794,618	$1,848,457	$1,90
8	Overheads	$80,190	$234,055	$391,722	$550,772	$71
9	Media & Marketing	$500,000	$250,000	$125,000	$62,500	$6
10	Product Development	$500,000	$0	$0	$0	
11	Total Expenses	$3,425,390	$2,490,907	$2,311,340	$2,461,729	$2,67
12						
13	Profit / Loss	-$2,712,590	-$348,002	$1,382,685	$2,887,987	$4,43
14						
15	Payback:	3 Years and 6 months				
16						
17						

FIGURE 9.16   Completed Payback Calculation

of new project evaluation, and the most commonly used tools that we use for evaluating the expected returns are NPV (net present value), IRR (internal rate of return), and payback period. How to calculate these measures is discussed in detail in "Financial Project Evaluation Functions" in Chapter 6.

However, in order to calculate the NPV, we need to know our cost of capital or our required rate of return for the project. You may also hear the cost of capital referred to as the discount rate or hurdle rate. The cost of capital is basically the opportunity cost of the funds invested, or, in other words, the rate of return that investors would expect to receive if they invested the money somewhere else, rather than in this particular project. In effect, by investing in the business, the investor is willing to forego the returns from other avenues. Therefore, cost of capital is the minimum required return for a project—the returns need to be greater than the cost of capital for the project to be accepted.

The importance of WACC is that it becomes a baseline to determine suitable investments for the success of the business. WACC is typically represented as a percentage, so any investment decisions taken by the company must aim to deliver returns greater than the WACC to make them worthwhile. For example, if the WACC of a company is 15 percent, then most of the investments that the company makes must be with the goal of generating returns greater than 15 percent. WACC is not just calculated for the entire company or business. It can also be calculated for individual projects to determine if it is worthwhile for the company to pursue the project.

Company capital is sourced from many avenues and is targeted for various areas of business growth and sustenance. Typically, the two major sources of capital are debt and equity. Both these tools are distinctly different, have different costs, and hence need to be considered differently in our calculations. As a result, not all capital carries the same weight, which is why we sometimes need to calculate the WACC in order to work out how much our capital is worth. Sometimes, when calculating the NPV of a project, a modeller may simply use a nominated cost of capital (we used a rate of 12 percent in the section "Net Present Value" in Chapter 6), but to evaluate a project more accurately, we can calculate which WACC will give us the exact cost of capital for that company. Note that the WACC will be completely different for each company, depending on its individual mix of equity and debt.

How to Calculate the WACC

The WACC is the average return on capital weighted proportionally based on category. Typically, a company sources its capital from stocks (common and preferred), bonds, and long-term debts. Each category of capital is invested in different avenues to help the business sustain and grow. WACC represents the average cost of capital, with proportional contributions from the various sources.

WACC can be calculated using the given formula:

$$\text{WACC} = \left(\frac{\text{Debt}}{\text{Debt} + \text{Equity}} \times \text{Cost of Debt} \right) \times (1 - \text{Tax Rate})$$
$$+ \left(\frac{\text{Equity}}{\text{Debt} + \text{Equity}} \right) \times \text{Cost of Equity}$$

where:

Debt = total capital raised from debts.

Equity = total capital raised from equity. Note that if the company has common and preferred shares, then the two need to be weighted and factored accordingly.

Cost of debt = the cost of raising the debt. If taken as bank loans, then it is the interest that needs to be paid to the banks.

Cost of equity = the return that the shareholders or investors expect from their holding in the company. Common ways of calculating this are the capital asset pricing model (CAPM) or Gordon's growth model.

Tax rate = the prevalent corporate tax rate.

Exercise: Calculating the WACC in Excel While the formula looks very complex, once the concepts are clear, WACC can be calculated relatively easily in Excel. Let's do an exercise where we need to manually calculate the WACC.

Let's say you have the following inputs:

- Debt is $6,023,000, for which you are paying 8.5 percent.
- Equity is $4,421,000, for which you expect a return of 15 percent.
- Tax is 30 percent.

1. Set up your sheet as shown in Figure 9.17.
2. In row 4, calculate the cost of debt and equity before tax.
3. Your formula in cell B4 should be =B2*B3. Copy it across to cell C4.
4. In row 6, remove the tax from the debt amount.
5. Your formula in cell B6 should be = B4*(1 – B5). Copy it across to cell C6. Although there is no tax applicable to the equity amount, we'll still copy the formula across to maintain consistency of formulas (hence following best practice).
6. Add together the value of debt and equity in cell D2, and cost after tax in cell D6.
7. Now calculate the WACC, which will be the cost after tax of debt and equity as a proportion of the total.
8. Your formula in cell D7 should be =D6/D2, and your worksheet should look something like Figure 9.18.

Hence, the weighted average cost of capital for this company is 9.78 percent. This means that when this company is evaluating new opportunities, the minimum required rate of return would be 9.78 percent, as this is what its capital is currently costing it. When calculating the NPV for a new project, this would be the input for the discount rate in the NPV function. Theoretically, the NPV at this discount rate must be greater than zero, and the IRR of a series of cash flows needs to be higher than this amount in order for a project to be accepted.

◢	A	B	C	D
1		Debt	Equity	Total
2	Value	$6,023,000	$4,421,000	
3	Cost %	8.50%	15.0%	
4	Cost before tax			
5	Tax Rate	30.00%		
6	Cost after tax			
7	WACC			
8				

FIGURE 9.17 WACC Calculation Layout

D7	▾	⋮	✕	✓	*fₓ*	=D6/D2	

◢	A	B	C	D	E
1		Debt	Equity	Total	
2	Value	$6,023,000	$4,421,000	$10,444,000	
3	Cost %	8.50%	15.0%		
4	Cost before tax	$511,955	$663,150		
5	Tax Rate	30.00%			
6	Cost after tax	$358,369	$663,150	$1,021,519	
7	WACC			9.78%	
8					

FIGURE 9.18 WACC Completed Calculation

BUILDING A TIERING TABLE

Calculating an amount based on tiering tables is a pretty complex formula, and is commonly used in pricing models. There are two types of tiering tables (also called volume breaks, block, or stepped pricing). The simplest version calculates the entire amount at the tier. The more complex table, like the tax tiers, is progressive such that the first number of units is calculated at the first tier and the next number of units at the next tier, and so forth.

For example, in a tax table where an income of $8,000 would be taxed at zero for the first $6,000 and then the next $2,000 is taxed at 15 percent, you would only pay $300 (15 percent of $2,000), not 15 percent on the whole amount.

Flat Tiering Structure

Let's say, for example, you have the pricing structure shown in the pricing table in Figure 9.19. If the customer purchases 5 items, each item costs $15, but if the order is for between 6 and 50 items, they are priced at $12 each, and so on.

We'd like to calculate how much a customer would be charged at different volumes.

A horribly long and complicated IF statement will do the trick:

=IF(A3<F3,G3,IF(A3<F4,G4,IF(A3<F5,G5,IF(A3<F6,G6,G7)))))

Alternatively, an IFS statement is somewhat easier to build, but not much easier to follow:

=IFS(A3<F3,G3,A3<F4,G4,A3<F5,G5,A3<F6,G6,A3>E7,G7)

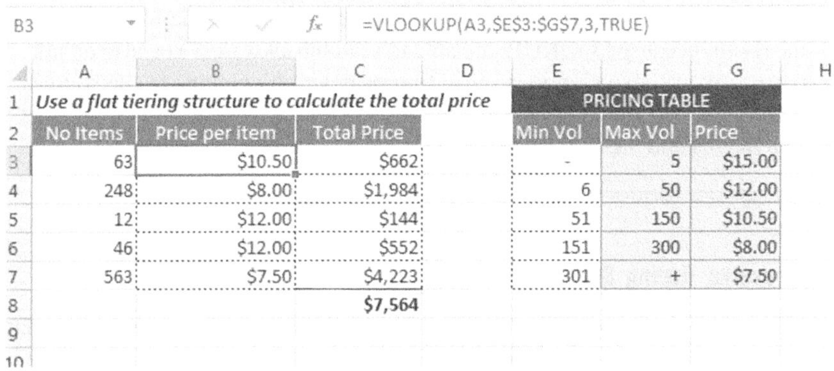

B3		▾	⋮	✗	✓	*fx*	=VLOOKUP(A3,$E$3:$G$7,3,TRUE)		

⊿	A	B	C	D	E	F	G	H
1	*Use a flat tiering structure to calculate the total price*				PRICING TABLE			
2	No Items	Price per item	Total Price		Min Vol	Max Vol	Price	
3	63	$10.50	$662		-	5	$15.00	
4	248	$8.00	$1,984		6	50	$12.00	
5	12	$12.00	$144		51	150	$10.50	
6	46	$12.00	$552		151	300	$8.00	
7	563	$7.50	$4,223		301	+	$7.50	
8			$7,564					
9								
10								

FIGURE 9.19   Completed Flat-Tiered Pricing Calculation

For an example of how to build these formulas, refer to the section "Nesting Multiple IF Statements" in Chapter 5, but there is a much simpler way to build a tiering table using a close-match VLOOKUP or LOOKUP.

1. In cell B3, calculate the per unit price using a close-match VLOOKUP. Your formula should be =**VLOOKUP(A3,$E$3:$G$7,3,TRUE)**.

NOTE

Note that we could also omit the last field: =**VLOOKUP(A3,$E$3:$G$7,3)**. Both will return a close match, not an exact match, but I prefer to include the TRUE because it shows that we are deliberately creating a close-match VLOOKUP and we haven't simply forgotten to put something in the last field.

---

2. Multiply the unit price by the number of units and add them up. Your total should be $7,564, and your sheet should look something like Figure 9.19.

TIP

Because we need a close match, not an exact match, we could have used the LOOKUP function instead: =**LOOKUP(A3,$E$3:$E$7,$G$3:$G$7)**.

(continued)

This has the added advantage of not needing the criteria to the left of the result, because LOOKUPs are able to search backwards. You also do not have to worry about someone inserting or deleting columns in the source data range and messing up the formula. For greater detail on how to use LOOKUPs and VLOOKUPs, see "LOOKUP Functions" in Chapter 6.

Progressive Tiering Structure

If the tiering calculation is not as straightforward as that in Figure 9.19, we may need to calculate under a progressive tiered structure. A good example of this is the way that the Australian tax calculations work, as shown in Figure 9.20. This formula calculation is not for the faint-hearted, so unless you specifically need to calculate a progressive tiering table, feel free to skip this section. You can find this template, along with the accompanying models to the rest of the screenshots in this book, at www.plumsolutions.com.au/book.

The first person's salary is $123,120, which means that this person is in the $80,000 to $180,000 tax bracket. However, we can't do a flat tiering calculation on this because the first $18,200 is tax-free, the next bracket is only taxed at a rate of 19 percent, and so on. The formula in column I takes care of the calculations below the threshold. Note that the tiers begin with one cent (e.g., $18,200.01).

You'll need to split your calculation into several parts, as shown in the diagram. First, work out the lowest tier, and then calculate the difference between the

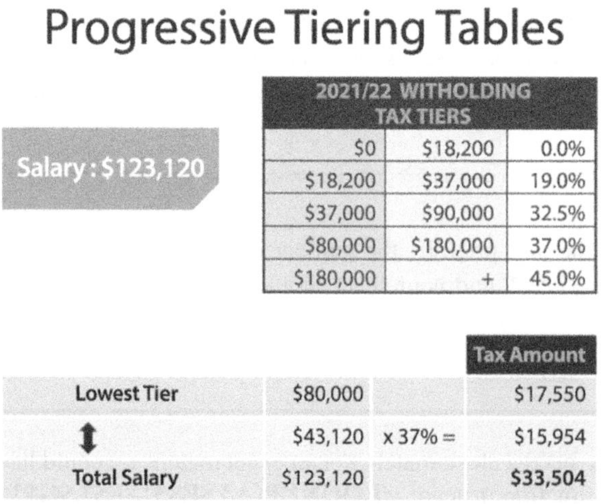

Progressive Tiering Tables

FIGURE 9.20 Tiered Personal Australian Tax Calculation Example

salary and the tier (in this case $80,000). Then the remainder should be calculated at the marginal tax rate.

> **TIP**
>
> This calculation will be easier if you calculate these in separate cells, and then combine them at the end—just like we have done with previous examples of nested functions (e.g., INDEX/MATCH or VLOOKUP/COLUMN).

1. Start by using a close-match VLOOKUP to pick up column I (the amount payable up to the threshold). Your formula should be **=VLOOKUP(C2, $F$2:$I$6,4)**.
2. Next, we need to work out the amount of the total salary that is above the lowest tier (in this example, $123,130 − $80,000 = $43,130). To do this, we'll do another close-match VLOOKUP returning the first column and subtract this from the salary amount. In a separate cell, your formula should be **=C2-VLOOKUP(C2,$F$2:$F$6,1)**. Your answer should be $43,130.
3. Next, we need to find out how much to multiply the $43,130 by (i.e., the highest tax tier). To do this, create a VLOOKUP returning the third column. Your formula should be **=VLOOKUP(C2,$F$2:$H$6,3)**. Your answer should be 37 percent.
4. Now, put all three formulas together:

   =VLOOKUP(C2,$F$2:$I$6,4)+(C2-VLOOKUP(C2,$F$2:$F$6,1))

   *VLOOKUP(C2,$F$2:$H$6,3)

The good news is that if you've used cell referencing correctly, you can simply copy the formula down. See Figure 9.21.

	D2	▾	✓	*fx*	=VLOOKUP(C2,$F$2:$I$6,4)+(C2-VLOOKUP(C2,$F$2:$F$6,1))*VLOOKUP(C2,$F$2:$H$6,3)				
	A	B		C	D	E	F	G	H	I
1	Staff	Position		Salary	Withholding Tax		2021/22 WITHOLDING TAX TIERS			
2	Staff 1	Account Manager		$123,130	$36,755		$0	$18,200	0.0%	
3	Staff 2	Business Development Manager		$196,560	$65,249		$18,200	$37,000	19.0%	-
4	Staff 3	Office Administrator		$80,262	$20,894		$37,000	$90,000	32.5%	3,572
5	Staff 4	Team Assistant		$47,574	$7,008		$80,000	$180,000	37.0%	20,797
6	Staff 5	Executive Assistant		$58,934	$10,701		$180,000	+	45.0%	57,797
7	Staff 6	Accounts Payable		$34,580	$3,112					
8	Staff 7	Accounts Receivable		$38,220	$3,968					
9	Staff 8	Financial Controller		$98,280	$27,561					
10	Staff 9	Project Manager		$159,762	$50,309					
11	Staff 10	Business Analyst		$74,555	$15,777					

FIGURE 9.21 Completed Progressive Tiered Calculation

MODELLING DEPRECIATION METHODS

How we treat capital expenditure, its effect on cash flow, and the subsequent depreciation is an important part of financial modelling—especially if your model includes a P&L statement, cash flow, and balance sheet. Capital expenditure is calculated and recorded in several different places:

1. In the cash flow in the period in which it was purchased.
2. On the balance sheet as a fixed asset.
3. On the P&L statement as depreciation over the useful life of the asset.

In this section, we will focus on translating a purchase of a fixed asset into a depreciation charge to be shown on the P&L.

Why Depreciate?

The definition of a fixed asset is an asset that is used in production, or that supports business activities in some other way. Common examples are machinery, vehicles, and equipment such as computer hardware. Fixed assets, by definition, have an expected useful life of more than 12 months, and the cost of these assets must, therefore, be written off as an expense over the period in which they are used. Depreciation is the charge calculated to write off these assets over their expected useful lives.

In the examples that follow, in Year 1 we purchase a piece of machinery for $200,000 that has a useful life of five years (i.e., it will be generating income for the next five years), as shown in Table 9.1.

Instead of expensing the whole cost in Year 1, we should spread the cost of it over the five years, as this is a much more accurate method of showing the profitability in each year.

TABLE 9.1 Depreciation for a $200,000 Piece of Machinery

	Year 1	Year 2	Year 3	Year 4	Year 5
Sales	$150,000	$160,000	$170,000	$180,000	$190,000
Machinery	($200,000)				
Net Income	($50,000)	$160,000	$170,000	$180,000	$190,000
	Year 1	Year 2	Year 3	Year 4	Year 5
Sales	$150,000	$160,000	$170,000	$180,000	$190,000
Machinery Depreciation	($40,000)	($40,000)	($40,000)	($40,000)	($40,000)
Net Income	$110,000	$120,000	$130,000	$140,000	$150,000

Adjusting depreciation is an attractive way for companies to increase expenses and lower taxable earnings, and for this reason, the regulatory legislation around which method of depreciation can be used is strictly monitored by the tax office. Bear in mind that finance and accounting rules differ between countries. Financial modellers do not need to be accountants, but they do need to ensure that accounting, tax, and finance rules are applied correctly if the calculation method is material to the model.

Depreciation Methods

In the example above, we have used the most common form of depreciation, which is the straight-line method. Under this method, the cost is equally spread over the number of years it is in use. However, there are several more complex depreciation methods also in use. It can be calculated either by using both a fixed rate and a fixed depreciable base value, or by varying one or both of these variables. For this reason, the depreciation charge each year as calculated by the different methods will not be the same. Figure 9.22 illustrates the charges each year.

The exercise below will show step by step how to calculate depreciation using the different methods, and by doing this, we'll see how very different each of the methods is. This is not an exhaustive list of depreciation methods; rather it's an overview of the most common forms of depreciation calculations used in financial modelling.

Straight-Line Method (=SLN Function)   Straight-line depreciation (also called prime cost method) is the simplest and most used technique that calculates depreciation at a fixed rate over the expected useful life of an asset. We estimate the residual value (salvage or scrap value) of the asset at the end of its useful life and will expense a portion of the original cost in equal increments over that

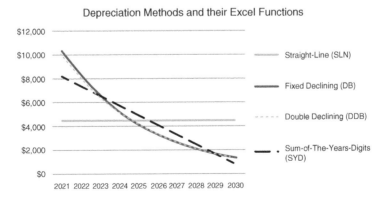

FIGURE 9.22   Comparison of Different Depreciation Methods

period. The salvage value is an estimate of the value of the asset at the time it will be sold or disposed of, but often it is zero. If the asset is expected to have a salvage value at the end of its useful life, we need to take the salvage cost away from the base before depreciating it. The formula for calculating depreciation is, therefore:

$$(Cost + Salvage)/Expected\ useful\ life$$

For example, we purchase an asset for $50,000, its useful life is 10 years, and we think we can sell it for $5,000 at the end of its useful life. We'd simply calculate the amount to be depreciated, which is the cost of the asset minus the residual value **($50,000-$5,000=$45,000)** and divide it by 10, so the depreciation amount on the P&L would be $4,500 per year for 10 years.

It's pretty easy to work this method of depreciation by using this sort of formula: **=(50000-5000)/10**, or you could use the SLN formula: **=SLN(50000, 5000,10)**, which will deliver the same result.

Calculating depreciation using the straight-line method is by far the most common method of calculating depreciation in financial modelling.

In order to demonstrate the comparison of the different methods, let's take a look at Figure 9.23, which shows an asset that has a purchase price of $50,000, a salvage value of $5,000, and a useful life of 10 years.

To prepare a depreciation schedule for this asset in Excel using the straight-line method, the following steps are followed:

1. Using an SLN formula, calculate the depreciation per year in row 11 columns B to K.
2. Your formula in B11 should be **=SLN($B$5,$B$6,$B$7)**. This formula requires cost value, salvage value, and life in years.
3. Once the absolute value signs have been added, the formula in B11 can be copied across into columns C to K. Using the straight-line method, the depreciation charge for each year is the same.

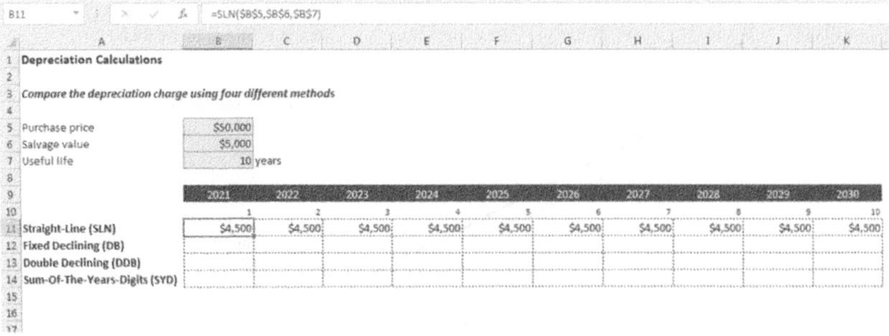

FIGURE 9.23 Asset Depreciation Example

4. The amount in each year should be $4,500. After completing the table, check that the total is equal to the cost less salvage value.

NOTE

Unlike the other depreciation method functions, the SLN function does not stop when it has fully depreciated the asset. If you continue to copy row 11 across to cell K11, you will notice that it continues to apply depreciation, even though the asset has been fully depreciated. If you have assets being fully depreciated during the life of the model, this will need to be calculated manually if using the straight-line method. See "Calculating Depreciation at the End of Useful Life" later in this chapter for how to calculate depreciation on assets that have been fully depreciated.

Declining Balance Value Methods

These methods are also called the reducing balance, diminishing value, or accelerated methods. You could argue that assets are more useful when they are new, and therefore depreciate more quickly in the first few years of acquisition. Therefore, some companies use depreciation methods that provide for a higher depreciation charge in the first year of an asset's life and gradually decrease charges in subsequent years. These are called accelerated depreciation methods.

Fixed Declining Balance Method (=DB Function) The fixed declining balance method calculates depreciation at a fixed rate. This rate is calculated by the formula

$$1 - ((Salvage/Cost)^{\wedge}(1/Life))$$

but it's much easier using the **=DB** Excel function. The depreciation charge for each period is not the same, as the depreciation rate for a period is applied to the net book value at the beginning of that period, and not to the original cost. With this method, the starting net book value is the cost price, so depreciation is applied to cost and not the value of cost less salvage. This is because using this method, the net book value can never reach zero.

Instead of treating each year the same, the fixed declining method depreciates more quickly in early years and more slowly in later years. The book value of the asset at the beginning of the period is multiplied by a fixed rate (e.g., in Year 1, 10 percent of $45,000 is $4,500 of depreciation). In Year 2, the same 10 percent is multiplied by the remaining $40,500 of book value, which then gives a depreciation value of $4,050.

The most difficult part in the fixed declining method is to figure out the correct percentage to use for each year, which is done with a rather complicated algebraic formula. If you use the predefined DB function in Excel, however, you don't need to be concerned with the calculations. Bear in mind, however, that when Excel calculates the rate, it rounds to three decimal places, and this does cause the calculation to be off by a few dollars at the end of the useful life.

Therefore, unlike the straight-line method, you pretty much have to use the Excel formula. Using the example above, your fixed declining formula for Year 1 would look like this: **=DB(50000,5000,10,1)**.

Applied to the example above, to prepare a depreciation schedule for a particular asset in Excel using the fixed declining balance method, the following steps are followed:

1. Using a DB formula, calculate the depreciation per year in row 12, columns B to K.
2. Your formula in B12 should be **=DB($B$5,$B$6,$B$7,B10)**. This formula requires cost value, salvage value, life in years, and period for which depreciation is being calculated.
3. Note that the additional requirement of a specified period is a result of the depreciation calculated each year being unique to that particular year or period. For this formula to return an accurate result, both life and period must be entered using the same unit (e.g., years).
4. Once the absolute value signs have been added, the formula in B12 can be copied into columns C to K.
5. If you create a total in L12, this will not be exactly equal to cost less salvage, as was the case for the straight-line method. This is a result of the fixed declining balance method producing a hyperbolic function and not a linear function and, therefore, never allowing the net book value to be zero.
6. Once the table has been completed, check that the total calculated in L12 is not more than cost less salvage. If this is the case, a manual adjustment to the last period's depreciation charge will be required.

Your worksheet should look something like Figure 9.24.

Double Declining Balance Method (=DDB Function) The double declining balance method also calculates depreciation at a fixed rate. This rate per annum is calculated as

$$(2 \times (100/\text{Expected useful life}))\%$$

Again, the Excel function (=**DDB**) makes this calculation a lot easier. As with the fixed declining balance method, the depreciation charge for each period is not the same. This is a result of the depreciation rate being applied to the net book value at the beginning of each period, and not to the original cost. Here, too, the starting net book value is the cost price and not cost less salvage. This method is

B11			f_x	=SLN($B$5,$B$6,$B$7)								
	A	B	C	D	E	F	G	H	I	J	K	L
1	Depreciation Calculations											
2												
3	Compare the depreciation charge using four different methods											
4												
5	Purchase price	$50,000										
6	Salvage value	$5,000										
7	Useful life	10	years									
8												
9		2021	2022	2023	2024	2025	2026	2027	2028	2029	2030	
10		1	2	3	4	5	6	7	8	9	10	
11	Straight-Line (SLN)	$4,500	$4,500	$4,500	$4,500	$4,500	$4,500	$4,500	$4,500	$4,500	$4,500	
12	Fixed Declining (DB)	$10,300	$3,178	$6,493	$5,156	$4,094	$3,250	$2,581	$2,049	$1,627	$1,292	
13	Double Declining (DDB)											
14	Sum-Of-The-Years-Digits (SYD)											
15												
16												

FIGURE 9.24   Calculating Fixed Declining Depreciation

quite similar to the fixed declining method shown above, except that the first year's depreciation uses double the percentage of the straight-line method. For each additional year of the asset's life, the opening book value is multiplied by the same percentage. When the amount calculated by the double declining method is less than what it would have been using the straight-line method, then the straight-line method is used.

In the example above, using the double declining balance method, the depreciation rate would be 20 percent in the first year instead of 10 percent using the straight-line method. This amount then reduces until it is less than $5,000, and then it switches to the straight-line method.

Using the DDB function, the formula would look like this:

$$= DDB(50000,5000,10,1)$$

To prepare a depreciation schedule for a particular asset on Excel using the double declining balance method, the following steps are followed:

1. Using a DDB formula, calculate the depreciation per year in row 13, columns B to K.
2. Your formula in B13 should be **=DDB($B$5,$B$6,$B$7,B10)**. This formula requires cost value, salvage value, life in years, and period for which depreciation is being calculated.
3. Once the absolute value signs have been added, the formula in B13 can be copied into columns C to K.
4. Once again, the total in L13 will not be exactly equal to cost less salvage, as was the case for the straight-line method. This is a result of the double declining balance method also producing a hyperbolic and not a linear function.
5. Once the table has been completed, check that the total calculated in L13 is not more than cost less salvage. If it is, a manual adjustment to the last period's depreciation charge will be required.

Your worksheet should look something like Figure 9.25.

	A	B	C	D	E	F	G	H	I	J	K
1	Depreciation Calculations										
2											
3	Compare the depreciation charge using four different methods										
4											
5	Purchase price	$50,000									
6	Salvage value	$5,000									
7	Useful life	10 years									
8											
9		2021	2022	2023	2024	2025	2026	2027	2028	2029	2030
10		1	2	3	4	5	6	7	8	9	10
11	Straight-Line (SLN)	$4,500	$4,500	$4,500	$4,500	$4,500	$4,500	$4,500	$4,500	$4,500	$4,500
12	Fixed Declining (DB)	$10,300	$8,178	$6,493	$5,156	$4,094	$3,250	$2,581	$2,049	$1,627	$1,292
13	Double Declining (DDB)	$10,000	$8,000	$6,400	$5,120	$4,096	$3,277	$2,621	$2,097	$1,678	$1,342
14	Sum-Of-The-Years-Digits (SYD)										
15											
16											
17											

FIGURE 9.25   Calculating Double Declining Depreciation

Sum of the Years' Digits Method (=SYD Function)   Unlike the previous three methods of calculating depreciation, the SYD method calculates depreciation at varying rates for each period. As with the straight-line method, however, it uses a constant depreciable base, being cost less salvage value. The sum of the years' digits is calculated as

$$(n(n + 1))/2$$

where n is equal to the useful life in years.

Depreciation for each period is then calculated as

$$(\text{Cost} - \text{Salvage}) \times (\text{Useful life} - \text{Number of previous periods})/$$

$$\text{Sum of the years' digits}$$

The sum of the years' digits is a depreciation method that results in a more accelerated write-off than the straight-line method, but less than the declining balance method. Under this method, annual depreciation is determined by multiplying the depreciable cost by a schedule of fractions.

Use the Excel formula =SYD(50000,5000,10,1). To prepare a depreciation schedule for a particular asset on Excel using the sum of the years' digits method, the following steps are followed:

1. Using an SYD formula, calculate the depreciation per year in row 14, columns B to K.
2. Your formula in B14 should be =SYD($B$5,$B$6,$B$7,B10). As with the previous two methods, this formula requires cost value, salvage value, life in years, and period for which depreciation is being calculated.
3. Once again, the additional requirement of a specified period is a result of the depreciation calculated each year being unique to that particular year or period. Unlike with the two previous methods, however, the difference in yearly depreciation charges is a result of a change in rate and not a change in the depreciable base.

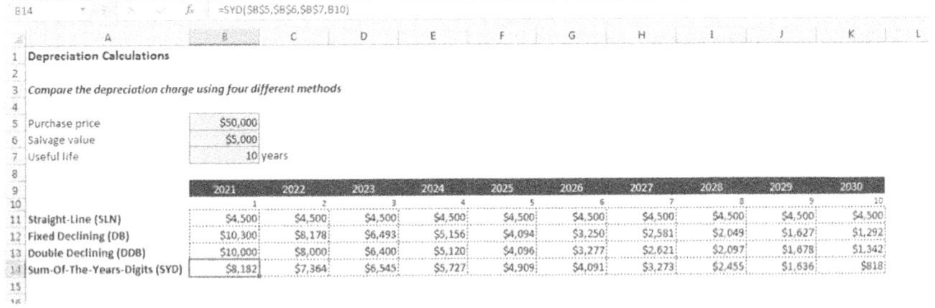

FIGURE 9.26 Calculating Sum of the Years' Digits Depreciation

4. Once the absolute value signs have been added, the formula in B14 can be copied into columns C to K.
5. Check that the total in L14 is, as with the straight-line method, exactly equal to cost less salvage value. Despite using varying rates, this method also produces a linear function.

Your worksheet should look something like Figure 9.26.

Of course, there are many other methods of depreciation, most of which also have an Excel function, to make what would otherwise be an extremely complicated calculation much easier. Don't completely rely on the function, however! As always, sense-check the results and double-check the timing of the purchase date and the period at which the asset is deemed to be fully depreciated.

Calculating Depreciation at the End of Useful Life

When building a model to depreciate assets using the straight-line method, whether calculating it longhand or using the SLN function, it is possible to continue to calculate depreciation on an asset that has already been fully depreciated past its useful life. This results in an ever-increasing negative net book value, which is impossible and can be the cause of an error in the model.

In order to prevent depreciation from being calculated once the asset has reached the end of its useful life, the Excel depreciation formula needs to be amended.

Let's say you have a list of capital items in a database, as shown in Figure 9.27. You can find this blank template, along with the completed version and other accompanying models to the rest of the screenshots in this book, at www .plumsolutions.com.au/book.

The first item on the capital expenditure register is for some IT equipment that was purchased in June 2018. The useful life is three years, which means that it will be fully depreciated in June 2021, and therefore if we create a forecast model for 2021, we need to ensure that the depreciation does not continue past the end of its useful life, and we need to create a formula to do this.

	A	B	C	D	E	F	G	H	I	J	K	L	M	N
G4			f_x	=IF(AND(G$2>=$F4,G$2>=$B4),SLN($D4,$E4,$C4)/12,0)										
1	CAPITAL EXPENDITURE DATABASE													
2	Calculate the depreciation using the straight-line method.						Jan-21	Feb-21	Mar-21	Apr-21	May-21	Jun-21	Jul-21	Aug-21
3	Spend Item	Spend Date	Useful Life	Cost	Salvage Value	End of Useful Life								
4	IT equipment	30-Jun-18	3	$15,000	$2,000	29-Jun-21	$361	$361	$361	$361	$361	$361	$0	$0
5	Bathroom remedial works	31-Mar-18	10	$40,000	$5,000	28-Mar-28	$292	$292	$292	$292	$292	$292	$292	$292
6	Nursecall and communications	31-Jan-21	40	$400,000		21-Jan-61	$0	$833	$833	$833	$833	$833	$833	$833
7	External painting	30-Sep-18	10			27-Sep-28	$0	$0	$0	$0	$0	$0	$0	$0
8	Repair internal elements	31-Dec-18	5	$71,000	$5,000	30-Dec-23	$1,100	$1,100	$1,100	$1,100	$1,100	$1,100	$1,100	$1,100
9	Services, plumbing, electrical etc	31-Dec-17	5			30-Dec-22	$0	$0	$0	$0	$0	$0	$0	$0
10	Fire systems and equipment	31-Mar-18	5	$15,000		30-Mar-23	$250	$250	$250	$250	$250	$250	$250	$250
11	Internal flooring	30-Jun-18	10			27-Jun-28	$0	$0	$0	$0	$0	$0	$0	$0
12	Air conditioning	30-Sep-18	10	$40,000	$5,000	27-Sep-28	$292	$292	$292	$292	$292	$292	$292	$292
13	Carpark, grounds etc	31-Dec-18	15	$15,000	$2,000	27-Dec-33	$72	$72	$72	$72	$72	$72	$72	$72
14	Plant & equipment	31-Dec-17	15			27-Dec-32	$0	$0	$0	$0	$0	$0	$0	$0
15	Building, structural and roofing	31-Mar-20	40	$71,000	$5,000	21-Mar-60	$138	$138	$138	$138	$138	$138	$138	$138
16	Bathroom remedial works	30-Jun-18	10			27-Jun-28	$0	$0	$0	$0	$0	$0	$0	$0
17	Nursecall and communications	30-Sep-18	5	$15,000		29-Sep-23	$250	$250	$250	$250	$250	$250	$250	$250

FIGURE 9.27   Completed Depreciation Calculation on Fixed Assets

This will be a rather long formula, but we'll use a simple building block methodology where we create a simple formula, test it, and check it before adding to it. We then test and check it again, before adding to it. In this way, we minimise errors by making sure the formula syntax is correct.

Begin by calculating the depreciation for January 2021 for the asset in cell G4, using the straight-line depreciation method. Remember it's for a month, not a year. Your formula should look like this:

$$=SLN(\$D4,\$E4,\$C4)/12$$

Test this by copying across and down the page to make sure that the cell referencing is correct.

1. Once we've got this right, we need to consider the spend date. In some instances, the spend date for the item has not yet elapsed, so we need to evaluate whether this date has passed or not, and only allow the depreciation to show if the date has passed. We can achieve this by inserting an IF statement around the SLN function like this: **=IF(G\$2>=\$B4,SLN(\$D4,\$E4,\$C4)/ 12,0)**. Test this by copying across and down the page to make sure that the cell referencing is correct.

2. Now we need to consider the end of useful life date. We could do this all in one formula, but it will make our calculations easier to follow if we insert this as a date within the model. In cell F4, calculate the date at which the item will be fully depreciated. We can do this using the formula **=B4+(C4*365)**. However, note that it gives you a value of 29th June 2021, because 2020 is a leap year. You can get around this by using the EOMONTH or DATE functions or by using 365.25 instead of 365—or you can simply leave it as it is (it won't make a lot of difference to our calculations). Copy the formula down column F.

3. Next, we need to add in the end of useful life date to our formula in cell G4. The best way to do this is by nesting an AND function with the IF.

Your formula should look like this: **=IF(AND(G\$2<=\$F4,G\$2>=\$B4), SLN(\$D4,\$E4,\$C4)/12,0)**.

4. Copy the formula across and down, and test to see if it is working correctly. The depreciation of the IT equipment should stop in July 2021.

Your worksheet should look something like Figure 9.27.

BREAK-EVEN ANALYSIS

Including break-even analysis in a financial model is very useful for budgeting purposes and especially for any business that is starting or expanding its operations. Break-even analysis is a very effective tool to determine profitability and give you a snapshot of the sales volume target that is required to start making a profit. For a new startup venture, this analysis is very effective in projecting sales targets. For established companies that are looking to launch new products and services, this analysis is invaluable in developing the pricing strategy.

There are several different ways to carry out the break-even analysis, depending on the perspective you want to look at. If you keep your pricing fixed, you can determine the units you need to produce and sell to break even (zero profit and zero loss). On the other hand, if your market position allows you to change the pricing, then you can determine the optimal pricing strategy to make your department or business break even within the stipulated target sales.

Let's take an in-depth look at some of the different methods of calculations for break-even analysis. It is also very helpful to show break-even points graphically, so we will also include some line charts when calculating the break-even points in our model in this section.

Calculating the Break-Even Point

The break-even point is dependent on the total cost of production, the price of units, and the number of units. In its most simplified form, the break-even point is achieved when:

$$\text{Total cost of production} = \text{Price} \times \text{Number of units}$$

The cost of production is never completely fixed. There is a variable component to it, which is related to the total units produced. This component includes everything from the price of raw materials to labour costs and additional overheads. Thus, the total cost of production is the sum of the fixed costs and the variable costs:

$$\text{Total cost of production} = \text{Fixed costs} + \text{Variable costs}$$

By varying the total number of units and/or the selling price of each unit, you can calculate the break-even point for your business. Figure 9.28 shows an

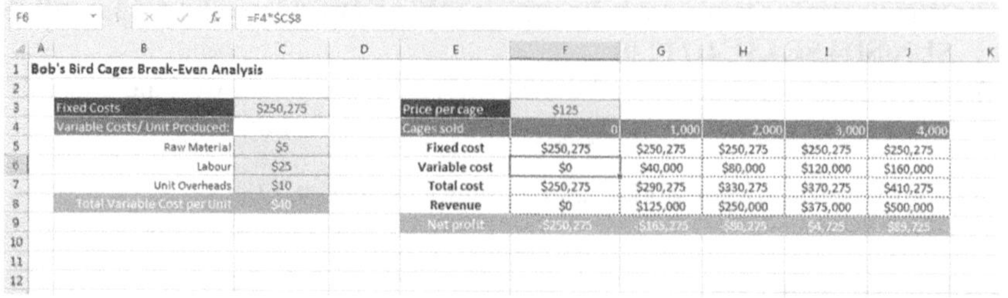

FIGURE 9.28   Break-Even Calculations

example of the example of the profitability of the product at different volumes: 0, 1000, 2000, 3000 and 4000 units of sales. We can see how the variable costs change, while the fixed costs do not.

Example Using Excel   Let's look at an example of how to calculate the break-even point for a new product. Let's say you want to start producing custom-made bird cages. You have determined that your fixed and variable costs for the first year are as follows:

- Fixed costs $250,275 (this includes rent, machinery, electricity, etc.).
- Raw materials of $5 per cage.
- Labour of $25 per cage.
- Overhead of $10 per cage.

Using the layout in Figure 9.28, calculate the net profit at each level of production. Ensure you use consistent formulas. At what level of production does the business begin to make a profit? The answer follows in the numbered list.

1. Fixed costs will remain at $250,275 regardless of the production level. The formula in cell F5 should be =$C$3. Copy it across.
2. Variable costs will fluctuate depending on the volume produced. The formula in cell F6 should be =F4*$C$8. Copy it across.
3. Add together the fixed and variable costs in row 7.
4. Calculate the total revenue in row 8. The formula in cell F8 should be =F4*$F$3. Copy it across.
5. Now calculate the net profit at the various production volumes in row 9.
6. The formula in cell F9 should be =F8-F7. Copy it across.

Your worksheet should look something like Figure 9.28. The completed version of this exercise can be found, along with the accompanying models to the rest of the screenshots in this book, at www.plumsolutions.com.au/book.

We can see that somewhere between 2,000 and 3,000 cages is when the revenue begins to cover our costs.

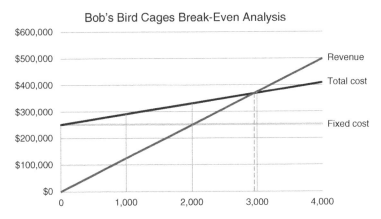

FIGURE 9.29   Chart Showing Break-Even Point

Charting the Break-Even Point

It is also interesting to look at the numbers graphically, and we can create a line chart that shows the point at which the revenue from the business becomes greater than the cost. See Figure 9.29.

For detailed instructions on how to create this chart, see the supplementary material available at www.plumsolutions.com.au/book.

We can see that the break-even point is roughly just under 3,000 units by looking at the chart, but this can be a pretty laborious task when done manually, and it is also not very accurate. We can calculate it exactly, however, using two methods in Excel:

1. A formula calculation.
2. A goal seek.

Calculating Break-Even Using a Formula   Using a formula is the fastest way of calculating the break-even point. It can be calculated using the following formula:

$$\frac{\text{Fixed costs}}{\text{Price} - \text{Variable costs}}$$

Price minus variable costs gives you the gross profit or contribution of each unit. We can then divide the fixed costs by the contribution to see how many units need to be sold to cover the fixed costs. See Figure 9.30.

In our model, we can calculate the break-even point by using this formula:

$$2,944.41 = \frac{\$250,275}{\$125 - \$40}$$

The Excel formula in our model to calculate this is =**C5/(C11-C10)**.

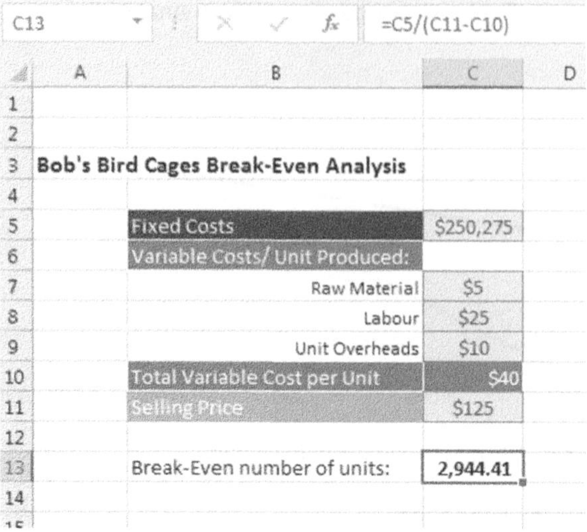

FIGURE 9.30　Break-Even Number of Units Using a Formula

Break-Even Analysis Using Goal Seek

Another way to perform break-even analysis is to use the goal seek tool. For a refresher on how to use this tool, refer to the "Goal Seeking" section in Chapter 8. While this method takes a little longer to set up and run than using a formula as described above, it is more flexible and allows more options for changing inputs.

Using our Bob's Bird Cages example, we need to set up the sheet as a simple P&L calculation, as shown in Figure 9.31.

The number of cages produced is the unknown variable, and we have entered a value of 2,500 in cell C11 as a placeholder in the meantime (which we can see generates a loss). This is the variable that will change when we perform the goal seek. Remember that to perform a goal seek we need a formula and a hardcoded number that drives that formula. The formula will be the profit/loss amount in cell C16, and the hardcoded number is the number of cages in cell C11. Make sure that all of the formulas in cells C13 to C16 contain formulas; otherwise, the goal seek won't work.

So, to perform break-even analysis, we need to set the net profit/loss value to zero by changing the number of cages produced. See Figure 9.31.

When you click OK, Excel calculates the exact break-even point and edits the cell value accordingly, as shown in Figure 9.32.

We can see that we end up with a value of 2944.41176470588. You might like to round it to the nearest unit, which will show a small profit or loss, which might be confusing. Alternatively, change the formatting so that the decimal places don't show.

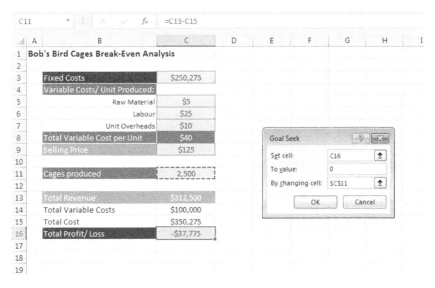

FIGURE 9.31 Using Goal Seek to Calculate Break-Even Point

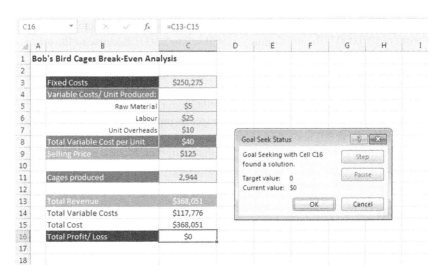

FIGURE 9.32 Completed Break-Even Goal Seek

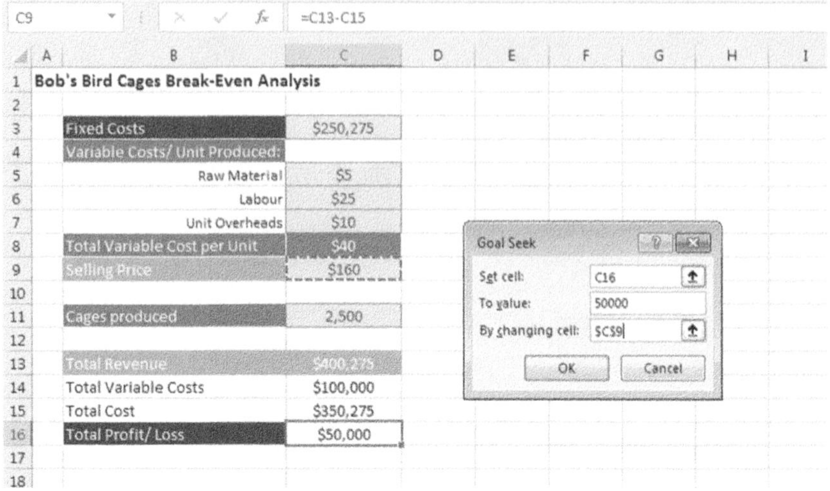

FIGURE 9.33   Break-Even Goal Seek with Changed Inputs

If you have the power to manipulate the unit pricing, then you can change the price points to reach break even at the sale of a fixed number of units, and even set profit targets using the goal seek function. Let's say you don't think you can sell more than 2,500 units. What would you need to set your price to in order to make a profit of $50,000 if the maximum you will sell is 2,500? Because of the way we have set up this model, this is relatively easy to calculate. See Figure 9.33.

If we want to make a profit of $50,000, we'd need to sell 2,500 cages at $160 each.

Whilst the goal seek method takes a little longer to run and set up, it's a great way to run different scenarios and test changes in inputs when performing break-even analysis. If this is something you want to run repeatedly, consider setting up a macro button to run the goal seek. (See the section on Macros in Chapter 8 for more information on how to do this.)

SUMMARY

In the first part of this book, we covered the tools, functions, and techniques financial modellers need to know. In this chapter, we focused on the use of these tools in a financial modelling context. If you are pursuing a career as a financial modeller, you will almost certainly have to calculate escalation at some point, and it is quite likely that you will find yourself needing to use tiering tables, calculate depreciation, or perform break-even analysis.

CHAPTER 10

Model Review

If you are lucky, you will get to build your own model from scratch, but most often you will be handed someone else's model to validate, modify, and make your own. One of the toughest tasks for any financial modeller is trying to use, understand, audit, or validate an existing model. While it may seem like a simple enough task, where the hard work is already done, the real challenge will be to understand how the model was designed.

Excel is such a flexible tool, and there are so many different ways to achieve the same end, that trying to understand the way a model has been built is like trying to get inside another modeller's mind! Give three different modellers a problem, and you'll undoubtedly have three different model designs, as each modeller will approach the model design in a different way and almost certainly using different formulas.

REBUILDING AN INHERITED MODEL

Obviously, the best place to start when trying to understand a model is to talk to the original designer if that is at all possible. There is no one who understands a financial model better than the modeller who designed it in the first place. However, the original modeller is often unavailable, and we therefore need to design the model in such a way that it can speak for itself.

If financial modelling best practice has been used, understanding a financial model in Excel should be a fairly straightforward task. However, many inherited models have not been built by professional modellers but rather cobbled together by different areas of a business to achieve a (usually short-term) outcome. These kinds of inherited models can be a real nightmare to unravel, and often it's simply easier to start from scratch. If this is not practical, there are some tricks and techniques in Excel that can help you to take apart someone else's model. By using these techniques, you can make the task of rebuilding an inherited model more achievable. We will explore some of these techniques in this section.

Removing Redundant Assumptions and Source Data in a Model

Common problems modellers encounter when rebuilding an inherited model are redundant assumptions and sources in the data model. This can happen when modellers need to use source information that is already in the spreadsheet and recreate it without realising that they are entering a duplicate set of assumptions or data. Often, as a model evolves, parts of the model calculations are deleted, but the assumptions that fed into those calculations remain, despite no longer being needed.

The easiest way to see if any formulas are linking to an input cell is to use the trace dependents formula auditing tool. This tool will allow you to trace forwards and backwards throughout the model. One technique you can use to remove redundant cells is to colour code all the input assumption and calculation cells, then go to the model outputs and trace back the formulas. As each input assumption is validated, change the colour of the input cells back to their original colour. At the end of the process, if any cells are still coloured, you will know that they are redundant and can be deleted.

If you think a section of the model is not being used, check it using the trace dependents formula auditing tool as described in this chapter before deleting it. Be aware that there are a few tools and formulas—such as INDIRECT and OFFSET—that can sometimes rely on a cell but do not show up in the formula auditing tool. For this reason, make sure you save before deleting and check the output of the model for #REF! or other errors before continuing. If the deletion has caused a problem, you can simply undo or close without saving to revert to the version of the file prior to deletion.

TIP

It's best to delete entire rows or columns instead of just clearing cells when removing sections of a model in this way. Deleting the cell will show an error and flag the issue if it had been linking to a formula, whereas clearing cells will simply change the value to zero, which will not necessarily return an error. This can cause undetected errors to remain in the model.

Formula Auditing

One of the most effective ways to start understanding a financial model—especially one that you did not build yourself—is to look at the formulas and identify the precedents and dependents. This will give you an idea of the logic used by the previous builder of the model. Usually, the best place to start in this technique is the final output. Take a look at each output and trace back the predecessors until you eventually find out what calculations, source data, and assumptions have been used by the original designer.

If you have a formula and you want to know which cells it uses, an easy way to do this is to use formula auditing. You can access these features in Excel from the Formula Auditing ribbon under the Formulas tab, as shown in Figure 10.1.

Tracing Precedents　To trace the precedents, select the cell you want to audit and click on Trace Precedents in the Formula Auditing ribbon. See Figure 10.1.

The trace precedents feature allows you to see all the other cells whose values are used in the formula in the present cell. It is possible to understand the calculation just by observing the cell formula too, but the arrows make it easier to locate the cells, which reduces the chances of errors in auditing the model. See Figure 10.2.

FIGURE 10.1　Trace Precedents in Formula Auditing Icons in the Ribbon

F4			f_x	=IF(AND(F$3<=$E4,F$3>=$D4),$C4*(1+inflation)^F$2,0)		
	A	B	C	D	E	F	G
1	**HoneyCorp Salaries Forecast**						
2							
3	Name	Position	Cost	Start Date	End Date	2021	202
4	Jo Brown	Tester	$136,800	2021	2030	$136,800	$140,90
5	Henrietta Stevenson	Project Manager	$240,000	2021	2030	$240,000	$247,20(
6	Susan Tyler	Business Analyst	$120,000	2021	2021	$120,000	
7	Mark Smith	Tester	$136,800	2021	2030	$136,800	$140,90
8	Claire Doble	Business Analyst	$120,000	2018	2030	$120,000	$123,60(
9	Benjamin Miller	IT Consultant	$300,000	2019	2030	$300,000	$309,00(
10	Lynette Morton	Tester	$136,800	2021	2019		

FIGURE 10.2　Using Trace Precedents on a Formula

NOTE

Double-clicking on the blue arrows will take you to the preceding cells. If you double-click again, it will bring you back to the original cell. Also note that if the preceding cells are on another page, the blue arrow will show a dotted line. To go to the precedent cell, simply double-click on the dotted line, and it will bring up a list of all the off-sheet references of that cell. Double-click on the reference to go to that cell.

Tracing Dependents Just like precedents, you can also trace the dependents to a particular cell. These are all the cells that use the value in the current cell for the calculations.

Select the Trace Dependents button, which is located directly beneath the Trace Precedents in the Formula Auditing ribbon under the Formulas tab. This is particularly useful if you are considering deleting a cell and want to know what this will affect.

TIP

Click on the Trace Precedents button again to trace the precedents of the precedent cells. This is invaluable in auditing complex models.

While arrows are great visual aids to understand formulas, sometimes they can become a distraction, especially if there are too many of them. You can clear all the arrows by clicking on the Remove Arrows button below the Trace Dependents button. This is also important if you plan to print the spreadsheet. If you don't remove the arrows before printing, they will show up in the printed document.

NOTE

There are some formulas upon which the Formula Auditor will not work very well, such as array formulas, data tables, and the INDIRECT formula. These are visible using the Dependency Auditor tool, which can be purchased separately from Microsoft.

TIP

You can also jump to precedent cells by using these shortcuts:

- Control+[(open square bracket) to jump to and highlight precedent cells.
- Control+] (close square bracket) to jump to and highlight dependent cells.
- Press Control+G or F5 and then enter to return to the previous cell.

These actions can also be performed in Excel for Mac by using the same shortcut keys.

Error-Checking Tools

There are times when we unintentionally introduce errors in the financial model. This could be because we did not comprehend the logic completely or because we mistyped the formula. Excel provides an error-checking function that helps identify the problem. This is extremely useful when your incorrect formula is syntactically correct. Excel indicates the anomalies in the model with a green triangle in the top left corner of the cell.

To understand the nature of the error, select the cell and click on the drop-down menu. There are many categories of such errors, but inconsistent formulas is one of the most common errors, as is omitting adjacent cells, as shown in Figure 10.3.

You can change the kind of error checking you want to perform on your model by selecting Error Checking Options, as shown in Figure 10.4. This will display the screen where you can control the kinds of checks you want to be performed.

You can also access the Excel Options dialog box by selecting the File tab or Microsoft Office button, then Options or Excel Options. In Excel for Mac, access Excel Options by clicking Excel, then Preferences, then Error Checking.

You can review all the errors in the financial model using the error-checking feature in Excel, as shown in Figure 10.5.

Error checking offers two options:

Error checking. Used to check formulas in error.

Trace error. Used to trace the source of the error in the final result. To use this feature, select the cell with the error (usually shown as #ERR?, #NAME?, etc.) and click on Error Checking—Trace Error. Excel will trace back the source of the error with a red arrow, as shown in Figure 10.6.

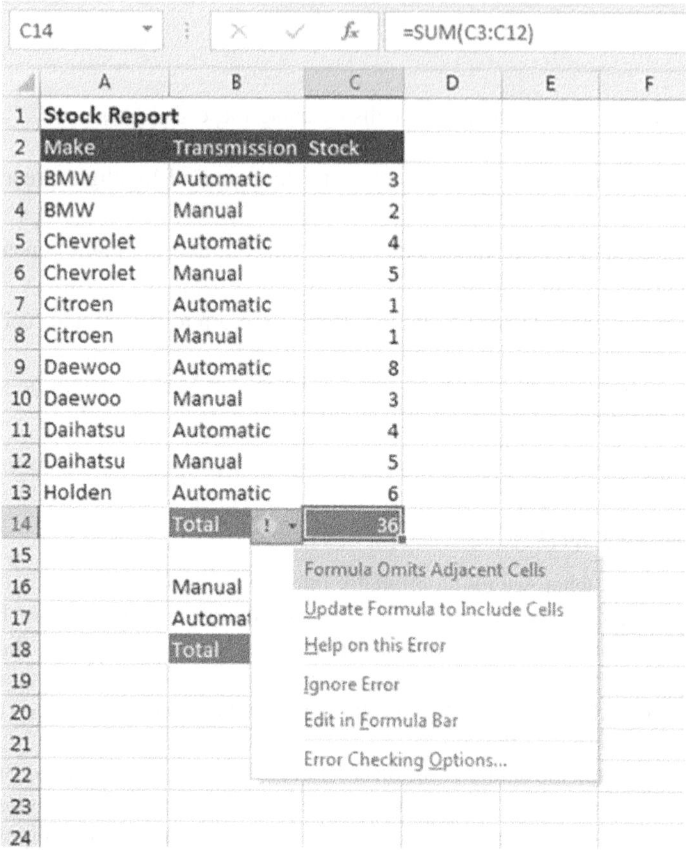

FIGURE 10.3   Error-Checking Tools Showing Error in Sum Formula

Evaluating Formula Tool Sometimes it is difficult to decipher a complex nested formula just by looking at precedents and dependent relations. It is easier to actually evaluate it step by step to understand how it works. Excel facilitates this with the use of the Evaluate Formula feature.

To evaluate a formula in any cell, select the cell and click on Evaluate Formula in the Formula Auditing ribbon under the Formulas tab.

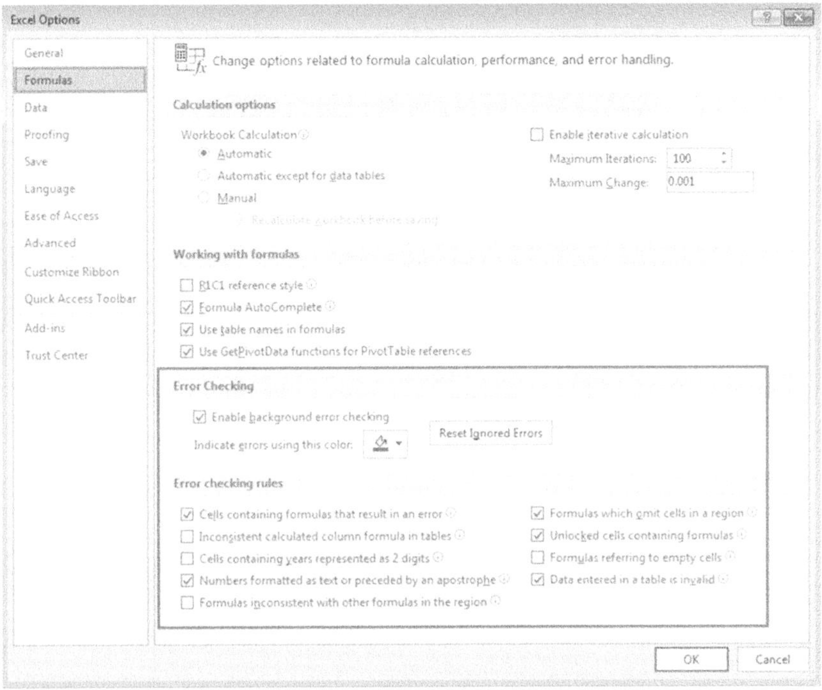

FIGURE 10.4 Editing Error-Checking Options

FIGURE 10.5 Error-Checking Feature

This will display an Evaluate Formula dialog that will show you the complete formula in the cell. Keep clicking on the Evaluate button to see how Excel calculates the value step by step. See Figure 10.7.

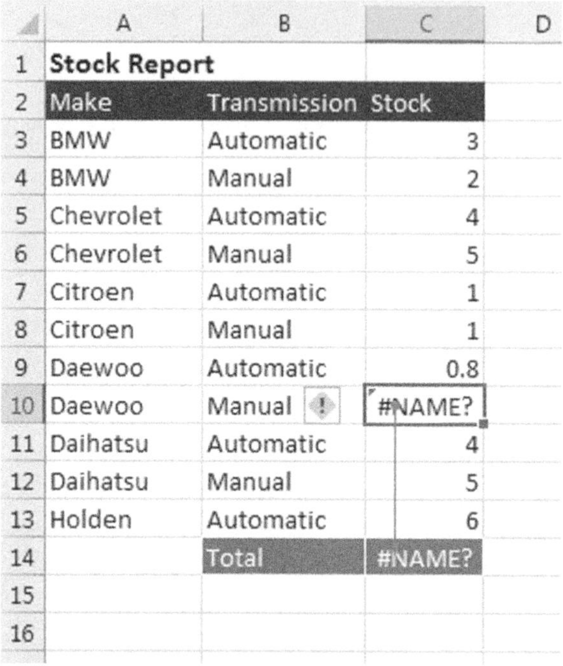

◢	A	B	C	D
1	**Stock Report**			
2	Make	Transmission	Stock	
3	BMW	Automatic	3	
4	BMW	Manual	2	
5	Chevrolet	Automatic	4	
6	Chevrolet	Manual	5	
7	Citroen	Automatic	1	
8	Citroen	Manual	1	
9	Daewoo	Automatic	0.8	
10	Daewoo	Manual ⚠	#NAME?	
11	Daihatsu	Automatic	4	
12	Daihatsu	Manual	5	
13	Holden	Automatic	6	
14		Total	#NAME?	
15				
16				

FIGURE 10.6   Tracing the Error Source

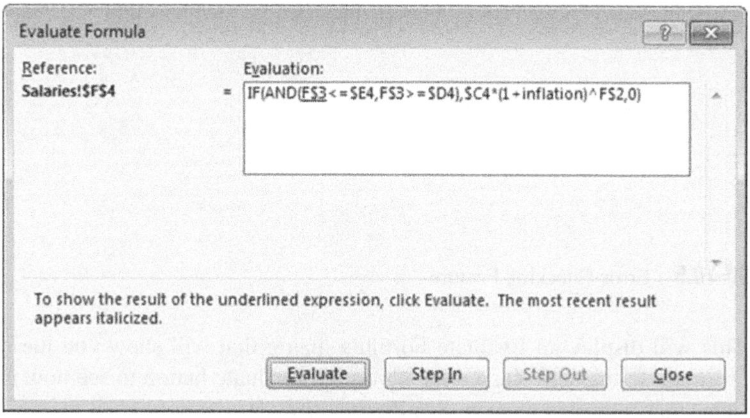

Evaluate Formula

Reference:
Salaries!$F$4

Evaluation:
= IF(AND(F$3<=$E4,F$3>=$D4),$C4*(1+inflation)^F$2,0)

To show the result of the underlined expression, click Evaluate. The most recent result appears italicized.

[Evaluate] [Step In] [Step Out] [Close]

FIGURE 10.7   Evaluate Formula Dialog Box

Once you have looked up the source of the parameter, you can click Step Out to continue the evaluation.

TIP

You can also evaluate a partial formula manually by selecting each expression and pressing F9. You must select an entire section of the formula that makes sense in its own right; for example, in the horribly long and complex formula **=MAX(0,MIN(SUM(B$2:B2),SUM(B$2:B3)))+MIN(0,MAX (SUM(B$2:B2),SUM(B$2:B3)))** shown in Figure 10.8, we can select this portion of the formula: **SUM(B$2:B2)**.

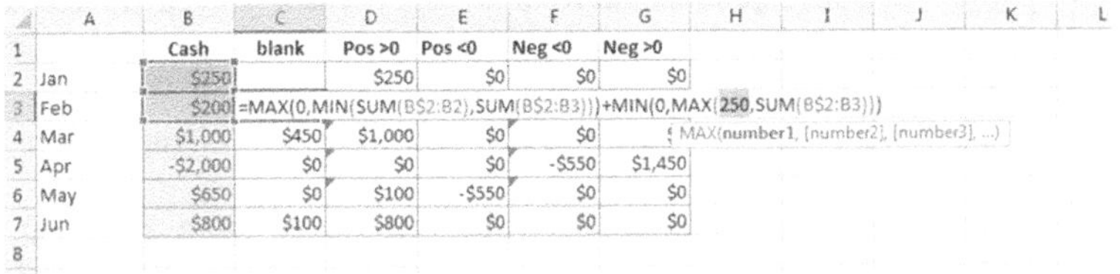

FIGURE 10.8 Viewing the Value of Part of the Formula

By then pressing F9, the formula will display the result of that expression, which in this case is 250. See Figure 10.8.

If you then hit the Enter key, it will paste that value into the formula (usually not what we want to do), but if you hit Escape, it will return to normal. This is a handy little trick that is sometimes easier and less complicated than using the Evaluate Formula tool. For greater detail on why you would want to break up a formula in this way, see "How Long Should a Formula Be?" in Chapter 4.

Viewing All the Formulas If you want to look at all the formulas and not the evaluated value, you can use the Show Formulas option in Excel. This is also a very effective tool to understand the general logic in the model and can sometimes make anomalies more evident.

This can also be done using the CTRL+` shortcut key. Note that ' is usually located below the Esc key at the top left of the keyboard, and should not be confused with the CTRL+' shortcut used to edit cells. See Figure 10.9.

Direct Editing By default, Excel allows users to edit formulas directly in a cell when they double-click that cell. However, while auditing any inherited spreadsheet, this may not be a good idea, as we could inadvertently mess up the formulas that are already in the cell. Excel allows users to disable direct editing, which protects the cells to a degree, but it still allows users to view the formula. It is quite

FIGURE 10.9　Show Formulas Option in the Ribbon

different from protection, which does not let you do anything at all in the cell, and is much easier to turn off and on than protection.

Using this tool is also quite useful for auditing, because you can double-click on the cell to trace back, and ensure that you understand the assumptions made by the original modeller and take care that you are not making any inadvertent changes to the formulas in the cell. You can still make any changes necessary directly in the formula bar.

You can disable Direct Editing from the File menu. Click Options, then Advanced, and select "Allow editing directly in cells". See Figure 10.10. In Excel for Mac, select Preferences from the Excel menu, and then Edit.

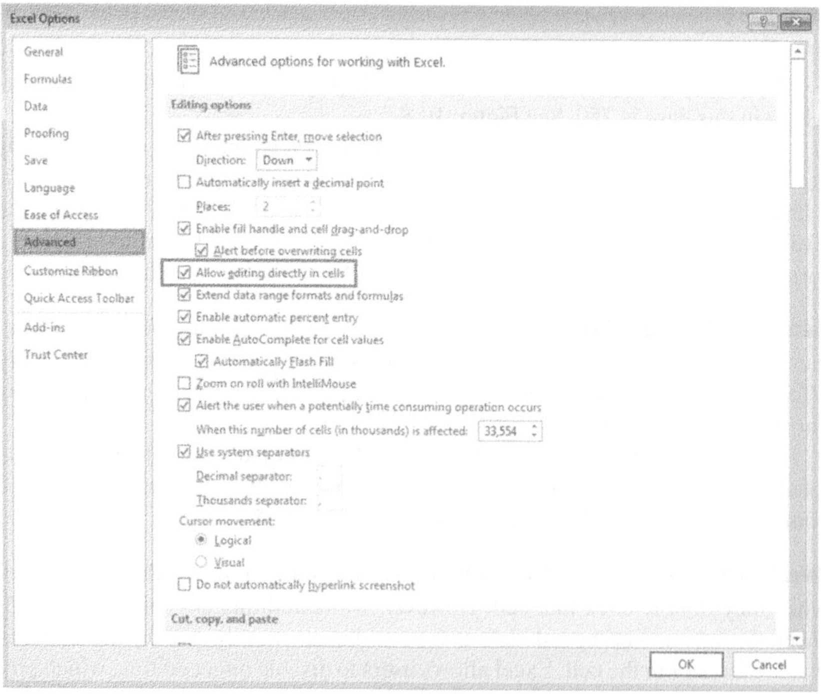

FIGURE 10.10　Disabling Direct Editing in Cells

⊿	A	B	C	D	E	F	G
1	HoneyCorp Salaries Forecast						
2							*1*
3	Name	Position	Cost	Start Date	End Date	2021	2022
4	Jo Brown	Tester	$136,800	2021	2030	$136,800	$140,904
5	Henrietta Stevenson	Project Manager	$240,000	2021	2030	$240,000	$247,200
6	Susan Tyler	Business Analyst	$120,000	2021	2021	$120,000	
7	Mark Smith	Tester	$136,800	2021	2030	$136,800	$140,904
8	Claire Doble	Business Analyst	$120,000	2018	2030	$120,000	$123,600

FIGURE 10.11   Double-Clicking with Direct Editing Disabled

Once this box has been unselected, now when you double-click on the cell it will highlight all the cells used as parameters in the formula, but not let you edit the cell directly. Figure 10.11 shows what happens if you double-click on cell F4 when direct editing has been disabled.

Inspecting the Workbook

Excel also has an often-overlooked tool called Inspect Workbook, which is useful for finding out more information about a model or hidden feature that you would not otherwise easily find—particularly one that has been inherited from someone else. It can help find potentially problematic features that would otherwise be very difficult to find, such as embedded documents, invisible content, and hidden rows and columns.

To use Inspect Workbook, open the file, then press File and on the Info tab, click on the Check for Issues button as shown in Figure 10.12. Inspect Workbook is not yet available in Excel for Mac.

The text under Inspect Workbook will tell you immediately the potential issues you should know about. Then, under the Check for Issues button, there are three options to choose from: Inspect Document, Check Accessibility, and Check Compatibility.

Note that whilst the Inspect Workbook feature is great for *identifying* problem-causing features of a model, it doesn't help with resolving them. It provides a summary of all the items the tool has found, and gives you the option to remove these immediately from the workbook—which is not a good idea. Instead of simply stripping a whole lot of features and the accompanying data from your model, you should take the time to understand what each of the features is, think about why they might have been included in the model, and whether they belong in the model or should be removed.

For example, the Inspect Document tool might reveal that there are hidden sheets in the model and it gives you the option to delete them immediately without looking at them. These hidden sheets might well contain important information and your formulas quite possibly will link to cells in those hidden sheets and so, accepting the recommendations of the document inspector will very likely cause more problems than it solves.

FIGURE 10.12   Accessing Inspect Workbook

IMPROVING MODEL PERFORMANCE

One of the problems that we often have to deal with in inherited files is that of slow, unwieldy, and inefficient models. If the model has not been built efficiently and calculates slowly, there are a number of checks you can perform to improve the model's performance. Most of the time, the performance problems are due to the size of the model. Let's explore some ways of reducing the file size, and hence speed up the model's performance.

Reducing File Size

By far the quickest and most effective way of reducing file size will be to check your file type. Although the .xlsx file type has been around since Excel 2007, models often still end up saved as .xls files. This can sometimes happen when data is extracted from other systems, it defaults to a .xls file type, and the modeller inadvertently uses this as a basis for his model. Because the .xlsx is a much more compact file type, this can make a *huge* difference to your file size.

HOW TO CHANGE FILE TYPE

If you see "Compatibility Mode" at the top of the page next to the file name, then this means your file saved in .xls format. To change it to .xlsx format, go to File, Save as, and save the file again, but this time change the "Save as Type" to Excel Workbook, instead of Excel 97–2003 Workbook, as shown in Figure 10.13.

If you're still having problems with file size, here are some other things you can try:

- Remove any unnecessary formatting or formulas. Ensure colours and other formatting apply only to the necessary range, not an entire row or column. More importantly, go to the outer edges of your workspace and delete all (apparently empty) rows and columns from there to the end of the Excel sheet. There may be formatting in places you are unaware of.

- Hitting Control+End will take you to the last cell in the working range, so that will give you some idea of how large the calculation area of the sheet is.

- Make sure formulas reference only the range they need (i.e., not selecting the entire row or column).

- PivotTables are quite heavy on memory so try saving them as values, if you can live without the functionality. Make sure that if you have multiple live PivotTables in a model, you copy the same PivotTable, rather than creating an entirely new one, as two separate tables will double the memory use.

- Remove external links to other files (use Edit Links to check if there are any external links, and then Break Links to paste them as values).

- If you must have external links, then have the source file open while working with the file, as this can make the model work faster.

- Functions such as INDEX, CHOOSE, and OFFSET are generally considered to use less memory than LOOKUP and SUMIF.

- Consider using array formulas, as these can use less memory.

(continued)

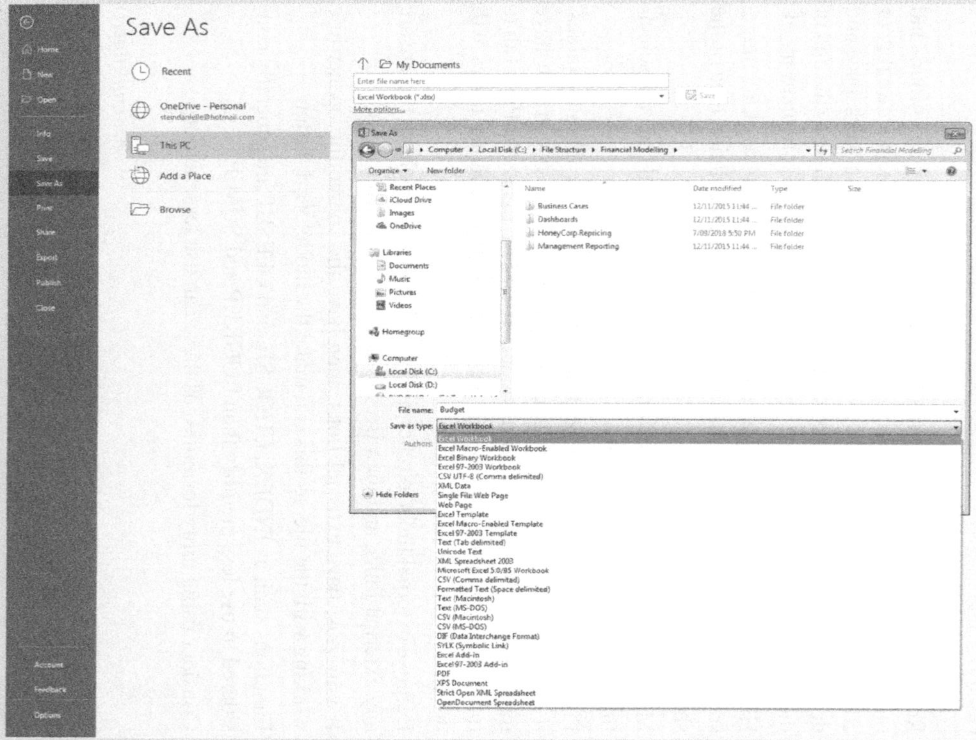

FIGURE 10.13 Save File in .xlsx Excel Workbook Format

- For clarity and better organisation, making charts in a separate sheet is advised over placing them in the same sheet as their data. However, they do take up more memory this way. If you have a lot of charts in your workbook, this could make a difference.
- If all else fails, turn the calculation onto manual, then hit F9 only when you need to recalculate. To turn calculation to manual or back to automatic, select Options from the File menu and under the Formulas tab in the Calculation options, select either Automatic or Manual.
- A last resort method is to leave one cell at the top of the column with the live link and paste all the other cells as values. Copy the cell down and recalculate when you need to refresh. Certainly not a preferred option, but one method you might consider if you are really desperate!

Improving Excel Memory and File Performance

If you have tried the tips suggested above and still have sluggish Excel models, it might not just be the file size that is slowing things down. Often, it's the memory being used and when things get really bad, you might even get a "Not enough memory" or "Not enough system resources to display completely" error message. When you get this frustrating message, the only solution is to close Excel and restart it, so let's look at some ways to improve the performance of your Excel models. Typically, you might consider upgrading your RAM or switching from a laptop to a desktop to counteract these problems, but these are unlikely to help as it's quite possibly the way that Excel is being used that is holding you back—not your machine.

Understanding Excel Memory Allocation If you get a memory error message, check the task manager for memory utilisation. If you have a RAM of more than 4GB you'll know that your computer has ample memory—although Excel is complaining about none being available. The reason for this is that Excel has its own memory manager and memory limits, regardless of the memory capacity of your machine. In fact, all 32-bit Excel is designed to use a maximum of 2GB memory. So, while your computer may have 4GB or even 8GB RAM, Excel can only use 2GB of that. If it reaches this limit, you get the error messages. *This is why upgrading your computer's memory probably won't help!* The 64-bit version of Excel has boosted this memory limit exponentially. Hence, 64-bit Excel versions can use the entire system memory, giving you much better performance, but read the section "32-Bit versus 64-Bit Microsoft Excel" in Chapter 1 before you jump straight in and upgrade.

Countering Memory Exhaustion Problems   Now that you know why you have these limitations, we'll see how to minimise their occurrence. Check the section above on "Reducing File Size", and here are some more tips to reduce the working memory used by your Excel file.

When you are building a model in Excel, there are a few ways of working that are not only good practice, they will also reduce the chances of encountering memory problems in your model.

- **Plan your Excel solution designs properly.** If you insert a new column in the spreadsheet, it forces Excel to recalculate all the formulas affected by that insertion. Depending on the number of impacted formulas and their complexity, you could run out of memory. A better-planned design ensures you can avoid such changes.
- **Work from left to right.** Excel starts calculating from the top left-hand corner, then continues across and down the sheet. This means that input values should be to the left and above the formulas that are referencing them.
- **Avoid creating formulas referencing the entire columns or rows.** Some Excel users create a formula using $D or $AA to reference the entire column, to simplify calculations. While it was fine with older Excel versions, the new versions have over a million rows per column—so entire row or column references cause Excel to calculate the formula a million times, and work much harder than it needs to.
- **Keep things neat.** Try to keep things in one single workbook, as external links can slow things down, as well as cause errors. Keeping input cells and their formulas on one page will also reduce memory, but from a financial modelling best practice perspective it's a good idea to split inputs and assumptions from their calculations.
- **Check your used range.** Sometimes Excel "remembers" a used range, even though you have deleted the reference, and this can increase the file size and memory usage. To check this on each sheet, press Control+End. This will take you to the last used cell of the workbook, and if it's far beyond what you need, then delete the rows and columns that are not being used. This can greatly reduce the file size.
- **Open every large Excel file on a separate "instance"** (i.e., open up a new session of Excel for each workbook). The memory limitation in Excel is for every instance and not for the entire application. Opening every file in a separate instance gives you dedicated 2GB memory rather than shared. Ideally, you'd only have one file open at a time, but if you're running a large process, you might like to keep working in Excel on another file whilst waiting for the large file to finish its process.
- **Use smart fill carefully.** Besides memory restrictions, Excel also imposes a maximum source cell limit of 32,760 cells for smart filling. If you are planning to use the smart fill feature, you should look at just using the last two or three

rows or columns and drag rather than select all the content from the first row. This will help control the number of source cells and ensure you do not reach this limit.

- **Check for unwanted shapes.** If you are adding pictures from websites into the spreadsheet, you could end up importing a lot of shapes that are not clearly visible but are eating into your memory. You need to open the selection panel (from the Home ribbon, Find & Select—Selection Panel) and remove all the shapes that you do not want.
- **Check add-ins and ensure they are updated.** Typically, the updated versions of third-party add-ins are more efficient and can help improve Excel performance greatly.

AUDITING A FINANCIAL MODEL

Any model used to support the output required for decision-making purposes should be checked and tested at some level by an independent party (whether internal or external to the organisation) for both logic and accuracy before it is handed over to the end user. Reviewing, checking, and auditing a model are important parts of the model-building process. As discussed in the section on financial modelling best practice, checking should be done by the modeller during the model-building process. However, once the model is complete, or near completion, it should be reviewed by another party not involved in the model build.

How detailed the audit needs to be will depend on the importance of the financial model to the organisation using it. Whether it's a simple pricing model or a multi-million-dollar merger, at least some level of checking and testing appropriate to the model needs to take place in order to identify and eliminate spreadsheet error and to ensure that the calculations, assumptions, and logic within the model are correct. Below are listed a few different levels of testing and audit that may be appropriate for a model.

- **Informal check.** In many models, this process could be an informal check by a colleague before passing it on to senior staff.
- **Quality assurance (QA) procedure.** For larger projects, such as the one outlined in "Steps to Building a Model" in Chapter 2, particularly if a team is involved, it is an important final step in the build process prior to handing over the model. This would be a more formal QA procedure carried out and documented by the modelling team and is also usually conducted internally.
- **Formal model audit.** When a high-profile transaction, such as an acquisition or high-stakes project finance, is planned, an external auditing specialist will be engaged to conduct an independent audit of the financial model. These audit procedures are often a requirement of banks, lenders, and investors as part of the due diligence process to satisfy themselves that the projections and results of the financial model are reliable and accurate.

The type of audit that needs to take place will depend on the size, scope, and importance of the financial model you have been working on. Unless you work for a model audit firm, you are unlikely to be involved in an external model audit, so let's take a look at how to go about the internal checks you are most likely to be involved with.

Informal Check

Let's face it; the majority of financial models built will only get an informal check from colleagues. Depending on how much time they have available, they could spend anything from an hour to several weeks testing your model. Below are some techniques that can be used to test the integrity of the model on an informal basis.

- The traditional method of auditing is affectionately known as the "tick and bash method", whereby the model checker goes through the model cell by cell to check for consistency and logic. This is not a particularly effective method of checking, as it is highly likely that the tester will very quickly become bored with this tedious task and miss anomalies. It is also a task commonly given to junior staff who often do not have the practical modelling experience to know common errors.
- A more effective, but more costly, method is to commission the development of a parallel model to support the primary model. This can be done by providing an independent modeller with the input page to a model and the output layout required, without the numbers. The modeller is then required to build a high-level parallel model (minus the bells and whistles, of course). This can then be compared to the results produced by the primary model and confirm that the primary model is working correctly. This is a rather time-consuming exercise, but one of the most effective ways of checking model accuracy.
- Ditch the spreadsheet and use a calculator! Print out the results of the model and see if you can roughly achieve the same results offline.
- Another effective method of testing a model is to use scenarios, sensitivity analysis, and stress testing. Change the inputs to something unexpected and see what happens. If you change the price of all your products to zero, does your revenue become zero also? It should, and if it does not then the tester needs to understand why. See "Scenarios and Sensitivity Analysis in a Business Case" in Chapter 11 for greater detail on how to perform sensitivity and stress tests.
- Create lots and lots of charts. Create metrics and plot as many inputs and outputs on the same charts as you have time for. Calculate the revenue per customer and chart it against market share in a line/column combination chart on two separate axes. (See "Charting with Two Different Axes and Chart Types" in Chapter 12 for how to do this.) Make sure that you understand every single trend and movement in the charts, as these can flush out anomalies in the model that may not have been visible previously.

QA Procedure

Working on a QA procedure is the most labour-intensive type of audit most modellers are likely to be involved with. Below are some detailed instructions on how to go about a financial model QA procedure. The QA of a model involves two main tasks:

1. **Logic checking,** which aims to test whether the logic underpinning the model is reflected accurately in the model. These tests check that the model does what it is supposed to do. This form of QA should be carried out once the model is completed and before it is used to generate outputs and the check should be repeated once more if significant changes have been made to the model structure later in the process.
2. **Data checking,** to ensure that the correct input data is used and has been entered into the model accurately. This type of QA may be more appropriately undertaken closer to finalisation of the report, when final decisions have been made on parameters that should be used in the model.

QA Logic Testing

Step 1: Scope of the QA Work   Before you begin, the scope of the QA needs to be established. The person undertaking the QA should clarify what parts of the model need a QA and, in particular, whether there are any parts that need special attention. For example, certain calculations may be crucial to the model and the model developer may want assurance that the logic of the formulas used is appropriate. In some cases, the model developer may seek feedback on possible improvements to the model, so as to enhance transparency, clarity, or some other aspect.

It is important to ensure that all supporting documentation is available to undertake the QA process. The model developer and/or the project team should provide all the documentation and source data in either hardcopy or softcopy.

Step 2: QA Checks of Calculations and Logic   Logic checks are carried out in order to:

- Check that cell referencing in a formula is consistent and correct.
- Ensure that formulas are mathematically correct.
- Confirm that the formulas used are suitable.
- Ensure consistency within the model in relation to the use of inputs, such as:
  - Nominal or real values.
  - Units (e.g., $'000,000 or $'000; kL or ML).
  - Timing assumptions, where applicable.
  - Labelling, which should be clear.

To check the logic of a model, quality assurers must first understand the output the model is required to produce and determine if the calculations correctly produce that output. Some of the tasks required in undertaking a logic check are therefore the same as those that would be done in the model-building process.

To check the calculations and logic, the following five steps should be followed:

1. Understand the purpose and limits of the model. This includes ascertaining what the model is supposed to do, what questions the model is supposed to answer, how the model tries to answer the questions, what the limitations of the model are, and what the model cannot do. This will most certainly require discussions with the project team and model developer.
2. Stress test the model as a whole by entering a wide range of inputs and checking that the outputs are logical. This includes testing values at the extremes to ensure the model processes the input as expected, especially where validation and protection are used. While testing a wide range of combinations of input variables may identify some hidden bugs in the calculations, using 0 or 1 is a good way to highlight obvious errors, as the outputs should be simple. For example, a unit price of zero should generate a revenue of zero, and if it does not, you'll need to investigate why not!

   Another way of testing this is to use historical figures as input and test whether the model can replicate actual results. For example, key outputs such as profit, growth rate, and other financial ratios that are calculated by the model can be compared to known historical results.

   Yet another way is to check the sensitivity of outputs (dependent variables) to changes in inputs (independent variables). This involves checking that the direction and magnitude of the change are in accordance with how you logically expect the outputs to behave.
3. Establish which cells contain formulas. This can be done using audit software such as Spreadsheet Detective (an add-in available for purchase), which allows easy identification of which cells are fully hardcoded, which contain formulas, and whether formulas are consistent across rows and columns.
4. Check both the logic and the reference accuracy of each identified formula. This is usually done by tracing the outputs back to the inputs to ensure that calculations produce accurate and logical output. See the "Formula Auditing" section earlier in this chapter for details on how to use the Trace Precedents tool.

   To assist with the logic and calculation checks, you may choose to write down the formulas in Excel notation using cell names and also in plain English by substituting the cell names in the formula with the actual variable names. For example:

Excel notation: **J25=J6*J9**

Plain English: Total variable cost = Variable cost per unit × Number of units

Logic: Number of units drives total variable cost

This is a simple and effective method to check and document the logic of the formula used by the model developer and pick up any cell-referencing errors. Sometimes a formula can be quite long, especially if Excel nested functions are used. Writing it out and breaking it down into its components makes it easier to thoroughly check each component (e.g., ensuring that they are referenced correctly, consistent in years, units, etc.). Another third-party tool called Dependency Auditor can help with this auditing by providing the Excel notation.

5. Check that the calculations have been suitably applied. For example, an indexation formula may be correct, but may not be suitable where it is applied if, for example, the underlying data is already inflated.

Step 3: QA Checks of the Model's Structural Layout and Documentation Apart from its underlying calculations and logic, each model's structural layout, appearance, and documentation should be checked.

Checking the structural layout of each sheet and workbook involves reviewing these to make sure that they are simple, transparent, and easily navigable. Elements to look out for are:

- Logical sequencing of the components in the model.
- Whether calculations are spread out all over the model or if they follow neatly down and across in a logical fashion. (Note that in larger models, not everything will follow neatly!)
- Whether hardcoding is only on the input sheet.

Checking the model's appearance and documentation involves checking the spelling and formatting, as well as that the documentation and notations in the model are clear, easily understood, and accurately reflect what is in the model.

Step 4: Document Your QA Work The QA procedure needs to be documented. The quality assurer should note all issues (minor and major), bring these to the attention of the model developer, and record the actions taken to remedy any problems.

At the start of the process, quality assurers should make a copy of the model to be audited and insert a new worksheet called QA Log (see the template in the Appendix at the end of this chapter).

All issues should be documented in the QA Log sheet. The quality assurer may also wish to insert comments near the actual cells in the model where issues have been found, as this can be useful for the model developer when locating and fixing the problems identified.

Step 5: Report Your Findings Once the QA work has been completed, any issues should be discussed with the model developer. Alternatively, issues can be progressively discussed and addressed as they arise.

Normally, the model developer will be able to advise whether an identified issue must be corrected, or whether it is intentional and should be left as is. All decisions and reasons should be recorded in the QA Log. Agreed changes should be checked again to ensure that they have been made correctly. This should also be recorded in the log.

Some changes may be very minor. Common sense should be exercised as to which changes can be left to the model developer to change without further final checking.

Input Testing

While logic checks focus on the calculations, structure, and layout of the model, input checks focus on the data entered into a model that is already built. Checks of input will usually involve:

- Matching input values to source documents to ensure that data has been entered accurately.
- Checking that inputs, especially assumptions, are consistent with the original output specifications.
- Checking that units are consistently applied, spelling and naming are consistent throughout the model, and the documentation of inputs and assumptions is clear.

As with a logic check, documenting the QA work and reporting the findings is required when conducting a QA of data inputs.

QA of Model Inputs The aim of checking input data in a model that will be used to produce a report is to ensure that the model and its output are accurate. The following are things to look out for:

- Check the inputs back to the source data for accuracy of data entry. This includes checking the actual numbers and also the units. For example, a common error is that the source data may be in $'000,000, while the model is set up in $'000.
- Check that the inputs used are consistent with those approved by the users of the report to be produced. Where possible, cross-reference the input data back to the minutes of meetings held to determine the required output.
- Check that the naming and explanations for the inputs are clear and easily understood.
- Check that the units are applied correctly and consistently throughout the model.
- Check for spelling and grammatical errors.

SUMMARY

While reviewing, auditing, or taking apart other people's models is certainly not the most fun (or sexy) part of financial models, chances are you'll need to be involved in the process at some stage. Even if you are fortunate enough to be charged only with the model build, it's critical that a good financial modeller understand the model review and audit process, and build the model in such a way as to make the audit process easier for the reviewer.

APPENDIX: QA LOG

The following is a sample QA Log template.

Name of Model_Name of Modeller_Name(s) of QA Staff [File Names and File Path Location]

Purpose of model
1.
2.
3.

Have the following items been checked in the QA?
Yes/No/NA – Are timing assumptions consistent throughout the model?
Yes/No/NA – Are calculations consistent and clearly marked?
Yes/No/NA – Have units been provided for all values and clearly marked?
Yes/No/NA – Have adequate error checks been built into the model?
Yes/No/NA – Other ...

Specific areas of the model that the model developer/project team want assurance on:

QA staff notes:

Details of issues found in the QA that need to be discussed with the model developer/project team:

| Item Number | Date Issue Identified | File Tab/ Sheet | Cell Reference | Issue Description | Responses by Team | | Date Issue | |
					Comments	Model Developer	Action Taken	Resolved
1								
2								
3								
4								
5								
6								

CHAPTER 11

Stress Testing, Scenarios, and Sensitivity Analysis in Financial Modelling

Any good financial model will usually contain scenario and sensitivity analysis functionality, at least to some degree. Scenarios are an important part of financial modelling, and the reason we have left this to near the end of the book is that it is usually a task performed at the end of the model-building process. If the model has been properly designed using best practice, it is not difficult to add, edit, and change scenarios in the model.

Scenarios and sensitivity analysis are great ways to insulate your model from risk. What would be the absolute worst that could happen? If everything that can go wrong does go wrong, will my business/project/venture still be okay? There are usually effects and interactions between multiple variables that may change in the model.

Scenarios can assist with decision analysis. They are laid out in advance so that decision-makers can see the expected impact of each course of action. How close to reality these scenarios are really depends on the accuracy of the assumptions implicit in the model—but that's another story! (See "Document Your Assumptions" in Chapter 3.)

Scenario analysis is a very important part of financial modelling—in fact, in some cases, being able to perform a scenario analysis is almost the whole point of building a financial model in the first place! Many of the principles of best practice in financial modelling discussed in earlier sections were to ensure that the model is set up in such a way that scenarios can easily be included in our model.

There are several different technical methods of creating scenarios and sensitivities in financial models, which we will discuss, but all scenarios involve changing input variables to see the impact of the change on the model outputs.

By following good practice when building the model in the first place—particularly when it comes to linking to the source, and only entering data once—creating scenarios and sensitivities in the model is quite simple. (See Chapter 3, "Best Practice Principles of Modelling".) With a well-built model that has all inputs linked to outputs, it is relatively easy to change inputs and watch the outputs change.

Building scenarios is a task normally best left to the end of the model-building process, because we need to get the model design and layout finalised and make sure the model is working correctly before we can change the input assumptions by adding scenarios. As with many complex model functions, perform a simple task first, then test it, check it, and make sure it is correct, before adding more complexity, such as scenarios.

WHAT ARE THE DIFFERENCES BETWEEN SCENARIO, SENSITIVITY, AND WHAT-IF ANALYSES?

Scenario analysis, sensitivity analysis, and what-if analysis are really only slight variations of the same thing.

A sensitivity analysis, otherwise known as a what-if analysis, in financial modelling refers to the process of tweaking one key input or driver in a financial model and seeing how sensitive the model is to the change in that variable. Scenarios, on the other hand, involve listing a whole series of inputs and changing the value of each input for each scenario. For example, a worst-case scenario could include interest rates increasing, the number of new customers being less than expected, or unfavourable exchange rates.

Scenarios should really focus on the area or assumption around which we have the least certainty. For example, let's say we are analysing the costs of reducing carbon emissions:

Scenario	Fossil Fuel Prices	Non-fossil Fuel Technology Costs
Best Case	10%	+10%
Likely Case	–	–
Worst Case	+10%	10%

In this very simple example, you could model the prices that you think are most likely and then tweak each of these up or down.

It is possible to create many more than three scenarios in a financial model. I'm often asked how many scenarios should be in a model, and it really depends on the amount of time and the degree of detail and certainty that are required for the model. Three scenarios, as shown in this example, should be a minimum. It's possible to have 20, 30, or even 50 scenarios modelled, but it does become rather unwieldy and confusing so unless you really need them, I'd probably recommend sticking to around a dozen scenarios.

Scenarios and Sensitivity Analysis in a Business Case

In a volatile economic environment, creating a business case for a new project or product that contains financial projections is an extremely difficult task. Looking at historical data and extrapolating the numbers to create future projections simply doesn't cut it any more. Creating a business case is imperative for companies to plan for the future, attract investor funding, and gain approval for projects, although most of the time there is so much uncertainty involved that financial projections are way off the mark. How do we create a financial model for a business case that is not complete guesswork?

Thorough stress testing, along with scenario and sensitivity analysis, will provide a business case that has the rigour and robustness to cope with various fluctuations in economic inputs. At an absolute minimum, any business case financial model should have a best, base, and worst-case scenario. The scenario analysis may include answers to the following questions, as well as others specific to the industry. Obviously, particular attention should be paid to the downside!

- What is our break-even number of customers?
- What happens if we lose our biggest expected customer? What if we gain another customer?
- What if we lose a supplier? Will this impact costs?
- What if interest rates increase or decrease?
- What if we lose a key staff member?
- It's unlikely, but what if all of the above negative outcomes eventuate?

Of course, if you count on the worst-case scenario, you'll probably end up doing nothing, and you definitely won't get any funding or approval! However, by creating a well-built, robust financial model, we can know exactly what the possible outcomes are so that we can show we are prepared for the best or worst eventualities.

Stress Testing a Financial Model versus a Business

Following the global financial crisis, there was quite a lot of discussion on the importance of stress testing businesses, and I need to point out that this is quite different from stress testing a financial model. Stress testing a business involves putting the business's financial forecasts through scenario modelling. Stress testing a financial model is more about testing the technical inner workings of the model (i.e., varying the inputs to see how much the outputs change).

Strategies to stress test a model include:

- Set inputs to zero and check that the outputs respond as you would expect. For example, by setting the price to zero, you would expect revenue to also be zero.
- Double your units sold. Does your revenue double?
- If you are indexing costs, try setting the indexation percentage to zero and see if the costs remain flat.

Stress testing your financial model by way of scenario and sensitivity analysis will help you be prepared for varying outcomes as a result of fluctuating external factors. Once you have completed your financial model, you should stress test the workings of the model to ensure that it is robust and accurate.

OVERVIEW OF SCENARIO ANALYSIS TOOLS AND METHODS

Many people will create a financial model and save it as a base case. Then they change all the numbers and save it as a worst case. Then they change all the numbers again and save it as a best case. Whilst this method will work, it's not a very efficient way of performing scenario analysis. If a subsequent change needs to be made to the model, it will need to be made several times, and there is a high possibility that an error will be made between the different versions.

Let's take a look at the technical methods available in Excel for creating scenarios and sensitivities, which will provide a much better way of building models. Essentially, there are three ways:

1. Manual drop-downs
   (a) In-cell drop-downs (using data validation)
   (b) Object drop-downs (using combo boxes)
2. Scenario Manager
3. Data Tables

Manual Drop-Downs

Creating scenario analysis using manual drop-down boxes means that you can only view one scenario at a time.

In-Cell Drop-Downs (Using Data Validation) In an in-cell drop-down, the value sits within the cell of data validation drop-down box. See Figure 11.1.

In this case, the modeller has limited the valid entries to this cell to one of three options: Best Case, Base Case, or Worst Case. This is the easiest and most commonly used type of drop-down box.

FIGURE 11.1   Data Validation
Drop-Down Box

See "Bulletproofing Your Model" in Chapter 7 for how to create a data validation drop-down box, and "Comparing Scenario Methods" later in this chapter for a practical exercise on how to use them in scenario analysis.

Object Drop-Downs (Using Combo Boxes)   There is very little difference from the user perspective with a combo box drop-down, but it's built very differently. See Figure 11.2.

This type of box is an object that sits on top of the sheet, rather than within the cell itself. If you look very closely, you can see that the box is sitting across several cells instead of within a single cell. This type of box is a little more difficult to build, but is easier for the user, as the drop-down arrow appears all the time, rather than only when the cell is selected.

See "Form Controls" in Chapter 7 for how to create a combo box drop-down, and "Comparing Scenario Methods" later in this chapter for a practical exercise on how to use them in scenario analysis.

Scenario Manager

Scenario Manager is an Excel tool in which you can create multiple scenarios. Once it is set up, the user can select a scenario, and input cells will change

FIGURE 11.2   Combo Box Drop-Down

automatically. Scenario Manager is fairly limited and is not particularly helpful in large and complex models. It is therefore not a very widely used tool for scenarios in financial modelling. See Figure 11.3.

Scenario Manager is a tool that has been grouped together with Goal Seek and Data Tables in the What-if Analysis section of the Data tab. Being grouped with other tools that are so useful would lead the aspiring modeller to believe that Scenario Manager is also a critical tool to know. However, despite its useful-sounding name and the good company it keeps, Scenario Manager is quite limited in its functionality and is not particularly helpful in large and complex financial models. It is therefore not commonly used by expert financial modellers; however, for the sake of completeness, we will cover it very briefly in this chapter.

Let's take a very simple example of a person creating her personal budget for next year. Let's assume that she does not know what her mortgage payments will be, due to the changing rate of interest, or how much her travel railcard will cost.

You can define different scenarios and then switch between them to do what-if analysis to see if she will end up in debt or be able to afford a holiday. Scenarios work best on complex spreadsheets where there is a large knock-on effect from changes in the variable data.

FIGURE 11.3 Scenario Manager Dialog Box

Scenarios are created and managed using the Scenario Manager in the following 13 steps:

1. Create and format the spreadsheet as shown in Figure 11.4. You can leave the input variable cells in B6 and B8 empty.
2. On the Data tab, in the Data Tools section, click on the What-if analysis icon, and select Scenario Manager from the drop-down list.
3. This will bring up the Scenario Manager dialog box.
4. Click on the Add button to create a new scenario.
5. This will bring up the Add Scenario dialog box.
6. Enter a name for the first scenario into the Scenario Name box (i.e., Base Case).
7. Enter the cell references for the variable cells into the Changing Cells box. Use absolute references and separate each reference with a comma (if there is more than one), but don't use spaces. You can actually hold down the Control key and click on each cell in the spreadsheet to insert the references into the box. Click OK.
8. This will bring up the Scenario Values dialog box.
9. Enter the variables' values for this scenario (i.e., Base Case). For example, $15,000 for mortgage and $2,000 for travel. Click OK.

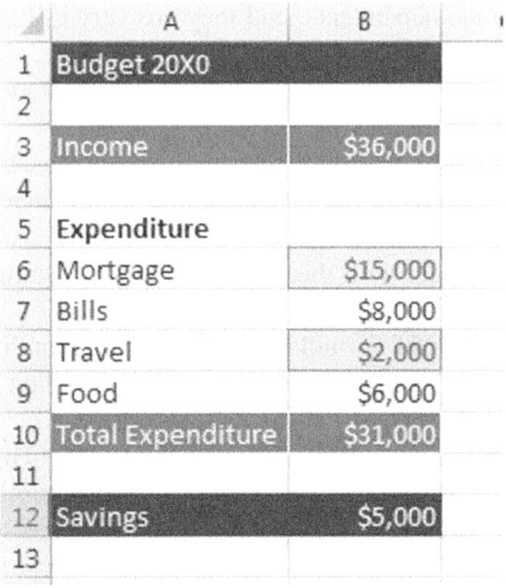

	A	B
1	Budget 20X0	
2		
3	Income	$36,000
4		
5	Expenditure	
6	Mortgage	$15,000
7	Bills	$8,000
8	Travel	$2,000
9	Food	$6,000
10	Total Expenditure	$31,000
11		
12	Savings	$5,000
13		

FIGURE 11.4 Scenario Manager Example

10. This will take you back to the Scenario Manager dialog box.
11. Follow the previous steps again to create each scenario (i.e., Worst Case: $20,000 for mortgage and $3,000 for travel; Best Case: $10,000 for mortgage and $1,500 for travel).
12. When you have created all the scenarios, you can use the Scenario Manager to view each scenario.
13. Scenarios are sheet-specific, meaning they only exist in the sheet where you created them.

As we can see, Scenario Manager is a rudimentary tool, which simply changes hardcoded numbers. It's not very easy to see, display, or print the different options unless we go into the Scenario Manager tool. Using the summary tool creates a summary report of the scenarios created, but they are not dynamic or interactive and are therefore of little use as a modelling tool. The biggest downfall of Scenario Manager is that the user cannot see the results on the sheet unless she actually goes in to view the scenarios.

Using Data Tables for Sensitivity Analysis

Data tables are one of the more advanced and complex financial modelling tools. They can be used for scenarios and sensitivity analysis, but they are not as commonly used as drop-down scenarios, mostly because users don't know much about them. Because data tables use array formulas, they are unlike most other formulas in that you cannot trace dependents, and they are very difficult to follow unless you are familiar with them.

Note that a modeller who is not familiar with data tables will be unable to edit the table, or make any changes.

Let's create an interest rate calculator upon which we can test the sensitivity of monthly repayments to changes in interest rates and loan terms.

1. First, set up the model with the hardcoded input assumptions, as shown in Figure 11.5.
2. In cell B12, use a PMT formula to calculate the monthly repayments. See "Loan Calculations" in Chapter 6 for more information on how to use this function.
3. Your formula should be **=-PMT(B8/12,12*B10,B6)**. The function returns a negative value because this is an expense. For our purposes, change it to a positive value by preceding the function with the minus symbol.

One-Variable Data Table   The data table presents a body of data derived from a function. The rows and columns of the table are drawn from one or two of the inputs

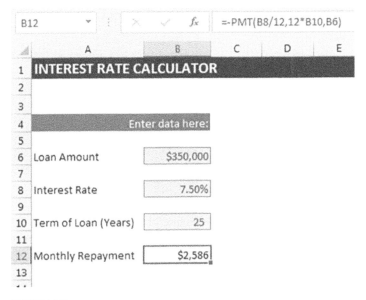

FIGURE 11.5 Loan Calculation Layout

or variables fed to the function. In this case, the data comes from the results of the PMT function, using the interest rate variable (cell B8).

1. We will decide what the column elements will be by entering them in cells E7 to E12. For this exercise, use 6.00 to 8.50 percent in increments of half a percent, as shown in Figure 11.6.
2. Merge cells D7 to D12 and change the orientation under the Alignment tab under Format Cells if you wish to have the interest rate title oriented vertically, as shown in cell D6 of Figure 11.6.
3. Enter in cell F6 the formula **=B12**, which is the cell containing the PMT function. The table, when created, will use the PMT function to populate the table according to the values in the input column (this will become clearer once the table is populated).
4. Highlight cells E6:F12 as shown in Figure 11.6. You must highlight all the cells for it to work. Select What-if Analysis from the Data tab. Choose Data Table from the options that appear.
5. The Data Table dialog box will appear. Because we are only doing a one-variable data table, we only need to enter data for one of the interest rate or term variables, but which one depends on whether our input variable is arranged in a row or a column. Because it is in a column, we should use the Column input cell field. Link this field to the input field for the interest rate (cell B8).

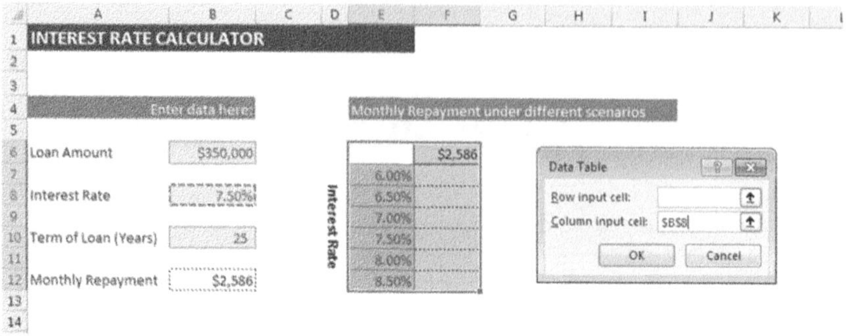

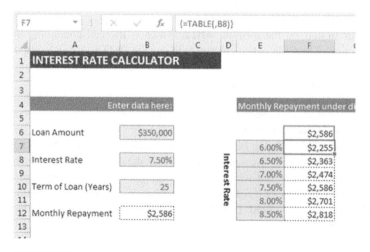

FIGURE 11.6 One-Variable Data Table

6. Your dialog box should look like Figure 11.6.
7. Click OK, and your data table will populate. Note that the formula in the cells will have curly brackets around it, denoting that it is an array formula: {=TABLE(,B8)}. You will not be able to edit the cells.
8. Your sheet should look something like Figure 11.7.

Two-Variable Data Table

1. Now, let's change this to a two-variable data table. Clear cells F7:F12. You will need to highlight and clear them all at once, as you cannot change or delete part of a data table.
2. With a two-variable table, the output cell needs to be at the top left of the table, at the intersection of the row and column variables. Therefore, cut and paste cell F6 to cell E6.

FIGURE 11.7 Completed One-Variable Data Table

3. In cells F6:I6, enter the number of years you wish to test in your data table. For this exercise, enter the values 20, 25, 30, and 35 across the table. Change the formatting as necessary. We now have the makings of a table with the term across the top row and the interest rate down the left-hand column, as shown in Figure 11.8.
4. Now highlight the table area cells E6:I12 as shown. You must highlight all the cells for it to work.
5. Select Data Table from the drop-down list under the What-if Analysis icon in the Data Tools section on the Data tab.
6. Your row input cell will be the entry field for the values shown in the row (the term in years), and the column input cell will be the entry field for the values shown in the column (the interest rate). Your dialog box should look like Figure 11.8.
7. Your table should now look like Figure 11.9.
8. You might wish to change the font in cell E6 to white; while it is required for the data table to work, it does not add any value visually (and is simply confusing).

FIGURE 11.8 Two-Variable Data Table

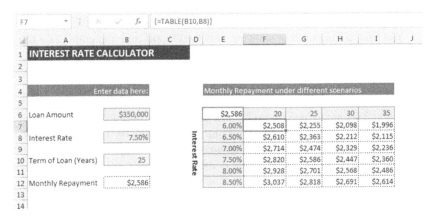

FIGURE 11.9 Completed Two-Variable Data Table

TIP

Data tables look great when you apply colour scales as shown in Figure 11.10, as you can visually see the incremental change to the data. For more information on how to use colour scales, see "Conditional Formatting" in Chapter 7.

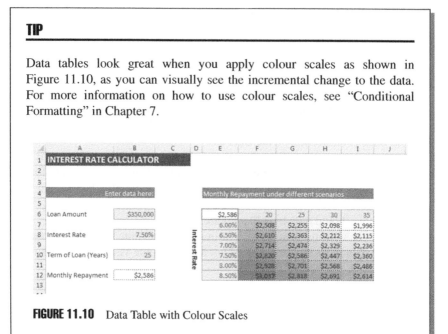

FIGURE 11.10 Data Table with Colour Scales

Limitations of Data Tables We can see from the example above that data tables are a great way to look at multiple scenarios or sensitivity analyses one at a time. Instead of manually changing the interest rate or the term of the loan, we can display at a glance the impact of these changes.

However, data tables have a few limitations that make them inappropriate for some scenarios or sensitivity analysis situations. These three limitations are:

1. The inputs and outputs need to be on the same page.
2. You have a limitation of showing only two inputs and one output at a time. This is not a restriction with other forms of scenario analysis.
3. Formula auditing (trace precedents and trace dependents) doesn't work very well in data tables.

Data tables are extremely useful when, as in the example shown above, you want to see the incremental change of one or two inputs on a single output. For example, how much does my profit margin change if I change my price from $450 to $460, $470, $480, $490, or $500? A data table would not be an appropriate solution if the output of your financial model were a full set of financial statements, for example. In this situation, a drop-down scenario would be most appropriate.

ADVANCED CONDITIONAL FORMATTING

A data table is a good opportunity to use conditional formatting with a formula. We can use advanced conditional formatting to enhance a two-variable data table, making it more visually interesting and interactive for the user.

Our final result will look similar to Figure 11.11, using the term of the loan and the interest rate as the two variables to drive the conditional formatting. You can find the completed version as shown in Figure 11.11 at www.plumsolutions .com.au/book. If you change the interest rate in cell B8 from 7.5 to 7 percent, the row currently being highlighted will change from row 10 to row 9. Similarly, if the term of the loan is changed in cell B10 from 25 to 30, the column currently being highlighted will change from column G to column H. In this way, we can see at a glance which inputs have been selected currently in the model.

For a review of the basics, see "Conditional Formatting" in Chapter 7. As you know, conditional formatting allows you to apply formats to a cell or range of cells and have that formatting change depend on the value of the cell (or the value of a formula).

In this particular example, we want the interest rate and term to intersect at the appropriate repayment instalment. As the variables to the PMT function are changed, the intersection point will move to spotlight the repayment amount.

⁄	A	B	C	D	E	F	G	H	I	J
1	INTEREST RATE CALCULATOR									
2										
3										
4		Enter data here:				Monthly Repayment under different scenarios				
5										
6	Loan Amount	$350,000			$2,586	20	25	30	35	
7					6.00%	$2,508	$2,255	$2,098	$1,996	
8	Interest Rate	7.50%			6.50%	$2,610	$2,363	$2,212	$2,115	
9					7.00%	$2,714	$2,474	$2,329	$2,236	
10	Term of Loan (Years)	25			7.50%	$2,820	$2,586	$2,447	$2,360	
11					8.00%	$2,928	$2,701	$2,568	$2,486	
12	Monthly Repayment	$2,586			8.50%	$3,037	$2,818	$2,691	$2,614	
13										
14										

FIGURE 11.11 Completed Data Table Using Advanced Conditional Formatting

One way we can accomplish this is to apply conditional formatting by means of a formula to each row within the table and, likewise, to each column. For instance, in Figure 11.12, we can stipulate that if cell E10 is equal to the interest rate (B8), then Excel must colour row 10 within the table.

This would require 10 formulas if we were to cover each of the six interest rates and each of the four terms. However, we can accomplish the exercise with two formulas only: the first locks either the rows or columns with absolute references; the second allows other elements of the cell address to float across the row or up and down the column by using relative references. This exercise illustrates how this is done.

1. Select the entire table (cells E6 to I12). Choose Conditional Formatting on the Styles section of the Home tab. Select New Rule from the drop-down list, and then "Use a formula to determine which cells to format".
2. Note that E in Figure 11.13 is an absolute reference to hold us in column E, but that the row number (presently 6) is free to roam down within the column.
3. Format the cell as required using the Format button.
4. Repeat the exercise to format the terms. In this case, the formula will reverse the relative and absolute references like this: E$6, locking in row 6. The rules should look like Figure 11.14.
5. To modify the conditional formatting, highlight the relevant cells (in this case the entire data table). Choose Manage Cells ... from the Conditional Formatting menu.

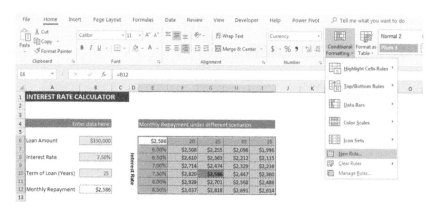

FIGURE 11.12   Highlighting Selected Interest Scenario Using Conditional Formatting

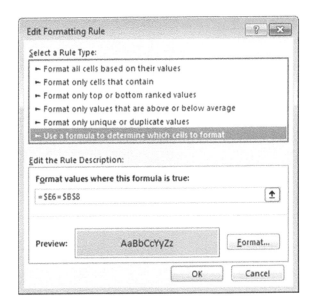

FIGURE 11.13 Conditional Formatting Rule Dialog Box

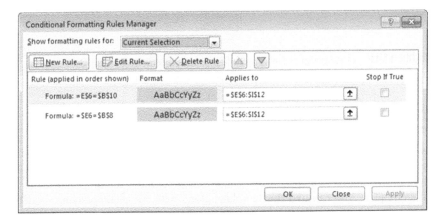

FIGURE 11.14 Conditional Formatting Rule Manager Dialog Box

Alternatively, we can highlight just the single cell where the inputs for the two variables intersect using an ordinary Conditional Formatting Rule, as shown in Figure 11.15.

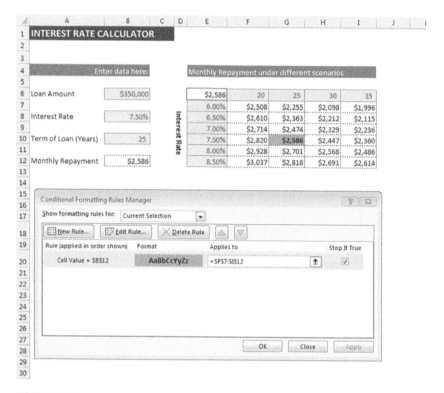

FIGURE 11.15 Conditional Formatting Rule Showing Intersection of Inputs

COMPARING SCENARIO METHODS

Let's create a very simple property development feasibility model to demonstrate the difference between the methods of scenario analysis. You are considering purchasing an empty block upon which you are considering developing a residential villa complex. You can find this template, along with the accompanying models to the rest of the screenshots in this book, at www.plumsolutions.com.au/book.

The assumptions are:

- The land will cost $4.3 million to purchase.
- Council contribution fees will be $750,000.
- The properties that we develop will be 5,000 square metres in total.
- Building costs will be $1,500 per square metre.
- We will sell the properties for $3,000 per square metre.
- Sales commission to the estate agent will be 2.5 percent of the sale price.

To create the working model, follow these eight steps:

1. Lay out the model, and enter the assumptions as shown in Figure 11.16.

   These assumptions are all input variables, so these should be formatted as inputs with blue font and beige background.

2. Calculate the income from selling the properties in cell C11 by multiplying the sale price per square metre by the total number of square metres. Your formula should be =D8*C8.

3. Similarly, calculate the building costs in cell C14 by multiplying the building cost per square metre by the total number of square metres. Your formula should be =B8*D8.

4. Calculate the sales commission by multiplying the income by the sales commission. Your formula should be =C11*E8.

5. Add the expenses in cell C17.

6. Calculate the net profit in cell C19 by deducting the expenses from the profit.

7. Calculate the profit margin in cell C20 by showing the profit as a percentage of the revenue. Your formula in cell C20 should be =C19/C11.

8. The calculations in your model should look something like those in Figure 11.16 so far.

C11		$\times$ $\checkmark$ f_x	=D8*C8			
	A	B	C	D	E	F
1	Scenario:					
2						
3		Building cost per sq mtr	Sale Price per sq mtr	Total no sq mtrs	Sales commission	
4						
5						
6						
7						
8	Assumptions	$1,500	$3,000	5,000	2.50%	
9						
10	Profitability of Land Development					
11	Income - Sale of Properties		$15,000,000			
12	Expenses					
13	Land Costs		$4,300,000			
14	Building Costs		$7,500,000			
15	Council Contributions		$750,000			
16	Sales Commission		$375,000			
17	Total Expenses		$12,925,000			
18						
19	Net Profit		$2,075,000			
20	Profit Margin		14%			
21						
22						

FIGURE 11.16   Model Layout for Drop-Down Scenario Method

We have now completed the workings of the model and are ready to add some scenarios. Note that this is a very simple one-page model, which we will use to demonstrate how to build scenarios. Your model can be a lot more complex than this, containing many more pages and calculations, but the methodology for creating a scenario will be exactly the same.

Manual Sensitivity Analysis

The two input variables that we think are the most likely to change are the building cost and the sale price per square metre. Note that because of the way we have built this model, with these assumptions hardcoded and all the calculations linking to these inputs, we can quite easily change these inputs manually and this will affect the output of the model. We can see that if the building costs were to decrease from $1,500 to $1,200 per square metre, this would increase the profit margin to 24 percent. Additionally, if the sale price were to increase from $3,000 to $3,300 per square metre, this would increase the profit margin further to 31 percent.

You can see that we can also manually change the sales commission and the total number of square metres in the development, although we have determined that these are unlikely to change.

Creating Built-In Scenarios Using a Data Validation Drop-Down Tweaking these input variables manually is a form of sensitivity or what-if analysis, but it's difficult to control and not very auditable. It's much better practice to build some predefined scenarios into the model, and allow the user to switch between the scenarios using a drop-down box.

Let's build some scenarios using this 10-step method:

1. In cells A4 to A6, enter Best Case, Base Case, and Worst Case.
2. Enter in hardcoded assumptions, as shown in Figure 11.17.
3. At the very top of the model in cell B1, create a data validation drop-down box that the user can select from to choose the scenario they'd like to see. For instructions on how to do this, see "Using Validations to Create a Drop-Down List" in Chapter 7.
4. The data validation should be linked to the source cells, as shown in Figure 11.18. The drop-down box should then look like Figure 11.19.
5. Now we need to change the input assumptions in cells B8 and C8 from hardcoded inputs to formulas that will change depending on the scenario that has been selected from the drop-down box.
6. There are several different functions that we can use to achieve this; an IF statement, a VLOOKUP, or a SUMIF will all return a similar result. If you choose a SUMIF, the formula in cell B8 should look like this:

$$=SUMIF(\$A\$4:\$A\$6,\$B\$1,B4:B6)$$

	A	B	C	D	E
1	Scenario:				
2					
3		Building cost per sq mtr	Sale Price per sq mtr	Total no sq mtrs	Sales commission
4	Best Case	$1,250	$3,300		
5	Base Case	$1,500	$3,000		
6	Worst Case	$1,750	$2,700		
7					

FIGURE 11.17 Model Scenario Inputs

FIGURE 11.18 Data Validation Drop-Down List Dialog Box

	A	B	C	D
1	Scenario:	Best Case		
2		Best Case		
		Base Case		
		Worst Case	le Price per	Total n
3		per sq mtr	sq mtr	mtrs
4	Best Case	$1,250	$3,300	
5	Base Case	$1,500	$3,000	
6	Worst Case	$1,750	$2,700	
7				

FIGURE 11.19 Data Validation Drop-Down List

7. If you've got the cell referencing correct, you can simply copy the formula across to cell C8 without changing the formula.
8. Change the cell and font colour of cells B8 and C8 to denote that they now contain formulas instead of hardcoded values.

| B8 | ▾ | : | × | ✓ | *fx* | =SUMIF($A$4:$A$6,$B$1,B4:B6) | | |

▲	A	B	C	D	E	F
1	Scenario:	Best Case				
2						
3		Building cost per sq mtr	Sale Price per sq mtr	Total no sq mtrs	Sales commission	
4	Best Case	$1,250	$3,300			
5	Base Case	$1,500	$3,000			
6	Worst Case	$1,750	$2,700			
7						
8	Assumptions	$1,250	$3,300	5,000	2.50%	
9						
10	Profitability of Land Development					
11	Income - Sale of Properties		$16,500,000			
12	Expenses					
13	Land Costs		$4,300,000			
14	Building Costs		$6,250,000			
15	Council Contributions		$750,000			
16	Sales Commission		$412,500			
17	Total Expenses		$11,712,500			
18						
19	Net Profit		$4,787,500			
20	Profit Margin		29%			
21						

FIGURE 11.20   Completed Data Validation Drop-Down Box Model with Scenario Formulas

9. Your completed sheet should now look something like Figure 11.20.
10. Practice changing the scenario drop-down in cell B1, and watch the numbers change. Under the best case, you'll be making a 29 percent profit, and in the worst case, you'll have a loss of 5 percent.

Creating Scenarios Using a Combo Box Drop-Down   Now that we've got our scenarios working, let's take a look at what we could achieve using a combo box drop-down instead. To review how to create a combo box, refer to the "Form Controls" section in Chapter 7.

If you are using the template provided, choose the next tab across, called "Combo Drop-Down". If you are creating this model from scratch, then leave the scenario model we've just created intact, and make a copy of the sheet by right-clicking on the sheet tab at the bottom. Select Move or Copy and then select Create a Copy and click OK.

1. If you have copied the sheet, then remove the data validation drop-down we created in cell B1. The easiest way to do this is to copy a blank cell and paste it over cell B1. This will mess up your calculations, but don't worry; we'll fix them later.

2. Now create a combo box drop-down in the same area. For instructions on how to do this, see the "Combo Boxes" section in Chapter 7.
3. Right-click on the combo box and select Format Control. On the Control tab, under Input Range, select the words Best Case, Base Case, and Worst Case in cells A4 to A6.
4. Also choose a cell link, which is where you want the output cell from the drop-down box to be. We often choose the cell behind the combo box, in this case, cell B1, as this will be hidden behind the drop-down, and unlikely to be accidentally deleted. You may need to move the combo box out of the way temporarily (select the combo box whilst holding down the Control key to do this).
5. Your Format Control dialog box should look like Figure 11.21.
6. Click OK. Click away from the combo box, and then select it again. Practice changing the options from the drop-down, and you'll notice the number in cell B1 changing. See Figure 11.22.
7. What we need to do now is to change the formula in cells B8 and C8, which are driving the calculations in the model. The SUMIF (or IF, VLOOKUP, or whatever you used) function we created earlier will not work because cell B1 no longer contains the name of the scenario. This now needs a formula that will select the first option if it contains a 1, the second option if it contains a 2, and so on.
8. Again, there are several functions we can use to achieve this, a CHOOSE or an INDEX to name two. If you use a CHOOSE function, your formula in cell

FIGURE 11.21 Combo Box Format Control Dialog Box

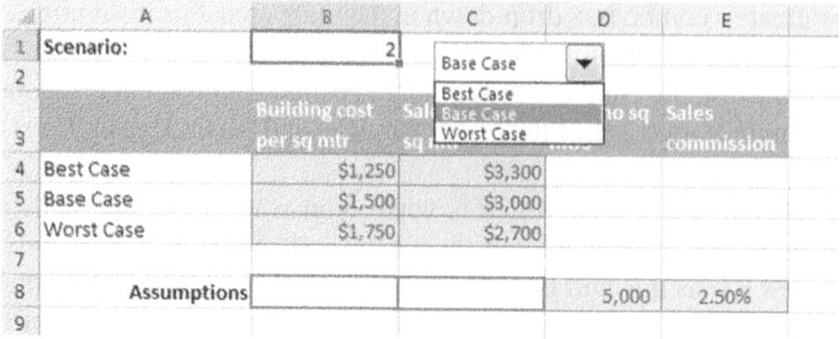

FIGURE 11.22 Model with Combo Box Drop-Down

B8 will be **=CHOOSE($B$1,B4,B5,B6)**. If you use absolute referencing, you can copy this across to cell C8.

9. Practice changing the drop-down box and make sure it works properly. Your model should now work in exactly the same way as it did earlier, except that we are now using a combo box instead of a data validation drop-down.
10. Hold down the Control key, and move the combo box so that it covers the cell link output number in cell B1.
11. Your sheet should now look something like Figure 11.23.

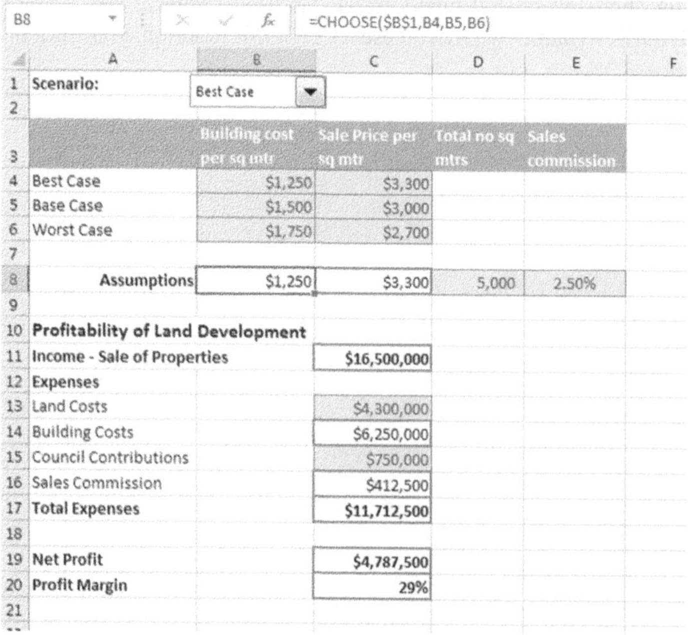

FIGURE 11.23 Completed Combo Box Model

What's the Difference Between a Data Validation and Combo Box Drop-Down?

From the user perspective, the data validation and the combo box drop-down should be almost indistinguishable from each other. They both work in the same way: the user selects from a drop-down list, and the model will change. However, there are a few key differences from the model developer's perspective:

- The combo box takes longer to build, as it requires inputs and outputs.
- As we can see in the previous example, the formulas we use to link to it are quite different.
- The combo box can easily be embedded in a chart.
- We can assign macros to a combo box so that unbeknownst to the user, a macro is launched as soon as an option is selected from the drop-down.
- The source data that appears in the combo box must be oriented vertically, not horizontally. This is an important point when designing the model. If you plan to use a combo box for scenario analysis, make sure that the input assumptions are listed vertically. Sources for data validation drop-down boxes can be oriented either horizontally or vertically.

As shown in Figure 11.24, combo boxes will not work if the source data is oriented horizontally instead of vertically.

Creating Scenarios Using a Two-Variable Data Table

Let's take a look to see if we could achieve the same result on our property development feasibility model using a data table method of scenario analysis instead of a drop-down box.

	A	B	C	D	E	F	G
1	Scenario:		▼				
2		Optimistic					
3		Optimistic	Likely		Pessimistic		
4	Customers per paraplanner:	30	30		30		
5	% Growth	10%	10%		10%		
6	Cost per paraplanner:	$50,000	$50,000		$50,000		
7							
8		Year 1	Year 2	Year 3	Year 4	Year 5	
9	Forecast customers	120	132	145	160	176	
10	Paraplanners	4.00	5.00	5.00	6.00	6.00	
11	Excess Capacity	-	18	5	20	4	
12	Paraplanner Cost	$200,000	$250,000	$250,000	$300,000	$300,000	
13	Cost to serve each customer	$1,667	$1,894	$1,722	$1,878	$1,708	
14							

FIGURE 11.24 Combo Box Drop-Down with Horizontally Oriented Source Data

If you are using the template provided, choose the next tab across, called "Data Table". If you are creating this model from scratch, then leave the scenario model we've just created intact, and make a copy of the sheet by right-clicking on the sheet tab at the bottom. Select Move or Copy, then select Create a Copy and click OK.

Instead of creating base, best, and worst-case scenarios from which users need to select the scenario that they want to display, we are instead going to create a single matrix in six steps, where users can see simultaneously the results of different inputs. If you've copied the sheet, then you'll need to change the design of the model to look like Figure 11.25 in order to create this scenario analysis using a data table instead.

1. To create the titles for the data table inputs, use Merge Cells, and then for the vertically oriented title, wrap text, and right-hand click. Select Format Cells and on the Alignment tab change the orientation. To show the title on the right-hand side of the cell instead of the centre, choose Right text alignment instead of Center under the Text Alignment area.
2. Once we have the layout right, then link cell B2 to profit margin in cell C20, as this is the output we want to show in the data table.

	A	B	C	D	E	F
1				Sale Price / sqm		
2			$3,300	$3,000	$2,700	
3	Building cost / sqm	$1,250				
4		$1,500				
5		$1,750				
6						
7		Building cost per sq mtr	Sale Price per sq mtr	Total no sq mtrs	Sales commission	
8	Assumptions	$1,250	$3,000	5,000	2.50%	
9						
10	Profitability of Land Development					
11	Income - Sale of Properties					
12	Expenses					
13	Land Costs		$4,300,000			
14	Building Costs					
15	Council Contributions		$750,000			
16	Sales Commission					
17	Total Expenses					
18						
19	Net Profit					
20	Profit Margin					
21						

FIGURE 11.25   Model Layout for Data Validation Scenario Method

3. Now create a two-variable data table by selecting the input assumption for sale price for row and building cost for column. For details on how to create a data table, see "Using Data Tables for Sensitivity Analysis" earlier in this chapter.
4. Highlight the entire data table, and go to the Data Table tool under the Data tab, in the What-if Analysis section.
5. The Data Table dialog box will look like Figure 11.26.
6. When completed, the data table will look like Figure 11.27.

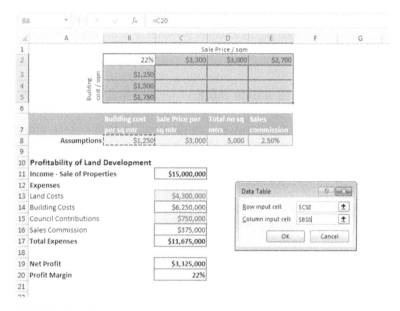

FIGURE 11.26 Creating a Two-Variable Data Table

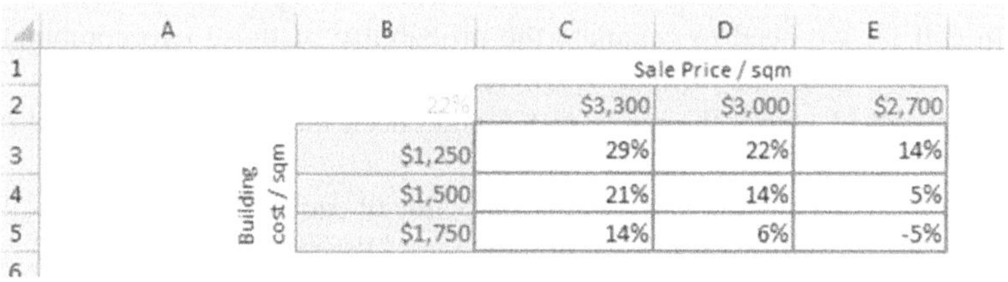

FIGURE 11.27 Completed Data Table

This gives us exactly the same results as the drop-down box options, but instead of having to flick through the drop-downs, the user can see at a glance all the results of the different scenarios simultaneously.

In this situation, the data table is an appropriate option for displaying the sensitivity of our profit margin to changes in inputs (because the inputs and outputs are all on one page, and we are only interested in a single output). We do lose some detail by using the data table method, as we cannot see, for example, the building cost amount under each different scenario, only the final outcome.

This feasibility model shows clearly the difference between three of the scenario methods. We have chosen not to use Scenario Manager because, even though it is perfectly possible for this model, it is not a particularly useful tool. In this example, the data validation drop-down, combo box drop-down, and data table scenario analysis methods are all suitable. However, it really depends on the size, layout, and required output of the model as to which method is best to use.

ADDING PROBABILITY TO A DATA TABLE

After completing the last exercise, we can see from the results of our sensitivity analysis—as shown in the completed data table in Figure 11.27—that the expected profit margin from our financial model will be anywhere between a profit of 29 percent and a loss of 5 percent. In order to actually help the decision-making process, a good financial modeller will try to narrow down the possible outcomes. One way of doing this is to apply some probability to each outcome and then calculate the probability-weighted predicted outcome.

Let's assume that the base case is the most likely, and assign a probability of 50 percent to that outcome under each variable. We then need to assign probabilities to the worst and best cases as well.

1. Complete the data table again, this time showing the net profit, instead of the profit margin.
2. In cells I2:K2 and H3:H5, enter the probabilities as shown in Figure 11.28, and make sure that the probabilities you enter add up to 100 percent.
3. In cell I3, we need to calculate the probability of those two combinations occurring. Enter the formula =$H3*I$2.
4. Copy cell I3 across the range I3:K5 and check that all nine cells add up to 100 percent, as shown in cell L6.
5. Next, we can calculate the exact dollar value of each combination. In cell O3, enter the formula =I3*C3 and copy it across the range O3:Q5.
6. We can now calculate the probability-weighted predicted outcome in cell R6 with the formula =SUM(O3:Q5).
7. The result should be $1,886,250, as shown in Figure 11.28.

FIGURE 11.28   Completed Probability-Weighted Predicted Outcome

SUMMARY

In this chapter, we have covered the different tools that are available in Excel for scenarios and sensitivity analysis. Depending on the inputs and outputs for the scenarios, different tools are most appropriate.

As discussed, the drop-down method is the most popular, as that allows for many different scenario inputs as well as outputs. Scenario Manager is not a particularly useful tool, and data tables are most useful for sensitivity analysis where there are a maximum of two input variables, and only one output that needs to be shown. Whilst there are several different scenario tools available, the methodology and logic behind creating the scenarios remain the same.

CHAPTER 12

Presenting Model Output

Once a model has been built, you then need to display its results clearly and concisely to get your message across, via a written report or oral presentation. The output and presentation of the results are just as important as the rest of the model-building process, because there is no point in having a fantastically built model that none of the decision-makers knows about or is able to interpret. This final stage of the model-building process is sometimes not given much focus by modellers, particularly those whose skills are often more analytical than visual.

PREPARING AN ORAL PRESENTATION FOR MODEL RESULTS

Many analysts and modellers would agree that public speaking is not their favourite part of the job and whilst it might be fun to imagine your senior management in their underwear, it might be more helpful to be prepared and follow these basic tips.

As the person who knows the model best, financial modellers are often requested to communicate the results of the financial model as a formal presentation to the board or senior management. Understandably, many detail-oriented analysts often find that it is quite a challenge to distil their 20MB financial model that has taken weeks to build into a 10-minute presentation.

Although most senior management may not be interested in seeing the model itself, they might like to see live and changing scenarios. If the model is built correctly, you'll be able to make a single change to the input assumptions and the audience will be able to see the effects of these changing scenarios in real time. Make sure that you test all possible inputs in advance—nothing looks less professional than a #REF! error during a live sensitivity analysis.

Not all presentations require you to use PowerPoint, and it's not always appropriate, but in this kind of environment, where it is necessary to convey lots of information, having the summary tables or charts on a slide behind you while you are speaking will be helpful. It can also help to take the focus off you if you are a little nervous.

Follow these basic rules of presentations:

- Only display one key message per slide. Don't crowd it or try to convey too much at once.
- Give them a more detailed report to look through, but what you show on the screen should be a very concise summary of this report.
- Make sure the font is big enough and clear on a data projector. Test it in advance if you can—sometimes colours look great on a monitor, but washed out when projected on the wall.
- If you are showing the model itself on the screen, increase the zoom in Excel so that your audience can see the numbers. Test this in advance, and remember you'll only be able to show a small portion of the screen in this way.
- Use charts and graphics to display your message. Generally, the output from a model will be numerical, and charts are a great way of showing this. Research also shows that audience attention and retention of information increases significantly when graphics are used instead of pure text in presentations.

Most importantly, be prepared for questions regarding the output, inputs, assumptions, or workings of the model. Make sure that you can defend the assumptions that have been made or the way something has been calculated. If you are not comfortable with some of the assumptions, say so up front. The model output is only as good as the assumptions that have gone into it, so you need to make sure that the audience accepts the key assumptions before they will accept the model results.

If you have the opportunity, spend some time with the key audience members in advance and walk them through the assumptions and methodology of the model. They might have some questions or comments that you have not anticipated, and it will give you a chance to make changes or prepare your answers to likely questions in advance.

Summarising and Displaying Model Results

If you have a 10-minute slot during which you need to convey the high-level output of the model, you probably need about four slides. If we have put together a business case for a new product, for example, outputs for a typical financial model may include:

1. A summary of projected cash flows or profitability. You won't be able to fit more than about 5 years onto a PowerPoint slide, so if you need to show 20 years, just show Years 1, 5, 10, 15, and 20, for example.

2. Key assumptions. Use your judgement here to choose which assumptions are important. Select the ones that either impact the model the most, or that you are most certain of.

3. Scenarios analysis. You'll probably be able to fit only four to five scenarios on a slide comfortably, so choose wisely. At a minimum, display best-case, base-case, and worst-case scenarios. See "Scenarios and Sensitivity Analysis in a Business Case" in Chapter 11 for greater detail on how to create these.

4. Results of sensitivity testing. Show the results of tweaking a single assumption. For example, if we were to get our customer take-up amount wrong by 1 percent, this will cause a $500,000 change to the NPV—and this is something the audience most certainly needs to be aware of.

If you have longer than 10 minutes, you might be able to show the model itself, if the presentation is more of a workshop than a formal presentation. In either case, you should be able to give each person a hardcopy summary report of the first few pages of the model with more detailed numbers than you have been able to include in the PowerPoint presentation. If the model has been well written, each page will form the backup data and source information for the model and can be printed or distributed if the recipient of the summary results requests further information.

PREPARING A GRAPHIC OR WRITTEN PRESENTATION FOR MODEL RESULTS

Charts are a way to present a series of data in a visual presentation so that patterns of information can be identified. Charts can be a powerful tool for the end user if they are built correctly and help simplify and summarise data.

A common mistake many analysts make is to try to put as much information as possible into one chart in an attempt to make it look impressive. In reality, the chart just looks cluttered and fails to get the message across. Remember that charts are for the purpose of visually presenting information that is easier to digest than the raw data. When creating a chart, balance the amount of information presented along with the formatting. It may be more useful to create two charts, dividing up the information, rather than putting it all on one chart. Consider Figure 12.1.

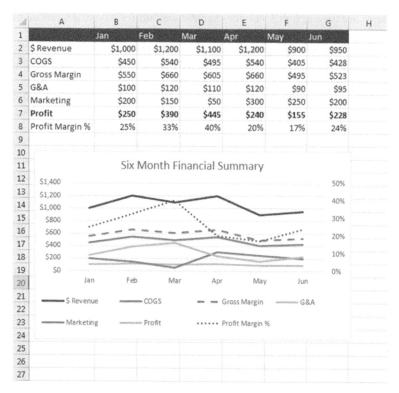

⊿	A	B	C	D	E	F	G	H
1		Jan	Feb	Mar	Apr	May	Jun	
2	$ Revenue	$1,000	$1,200	$1,100	$1,200	$900	$950	
3	COGS	$450	$540	$495	$540	$405	$428	
4	Gross Margin	$550	$660	$605	$660	$495	$523	
5	G&A	$100	$120	$110	$120	$90	$95	
6	Marketing	$200	$150	$50	$300	$250	$200	
7	Profit	$250	$390	$445	$240	$155	$228	
8	Profit Margin %	25%	33%	40%	20%	17%	24%	

FIGURE 12.1   Line Chart with Multiple Series

Is this chart useful? There is so much data presented that the chart has no real value. Also, the type of chart isn't necessarily the best choice. Consider instead Figure 12.2.

With the same set of data, we have created a different chart that gives us much more intelligence, using less of the data. In Figure 12.2, a viewer can see at a glance the trend in revenues and profitability. It also shows the composition of marketing and G&A (general and administrative) expenses month to month. Note that using a stacked bar chart allows the user to see the total expenses, including Cost of Goods Sold (COGS). Compare this to the original line chart, and you can see it is almost impossible to compare the expenses in the line chart, as there is so much interference.

By breaking up the data into two chart types on two separate axes, and limiting the information presented, we have gone from useless and confusing to informative and interesting.

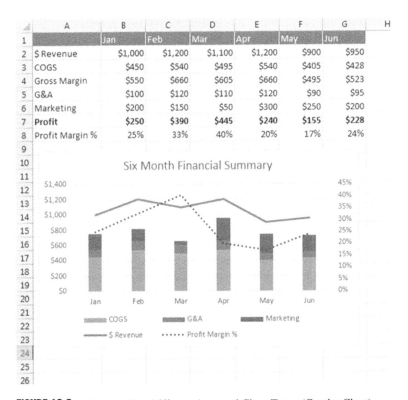

	A	B	C	D	E	F	G	H
1		Jan	Feb	Mar	Apr	May	Jun	
2	$ Revenue	$1,000	$1,200	$1,100	$1,200	$900	$950	
3	COGS	$450	$540	$495	$540	$405	$428	
4	Gross Margin	$550	$660	$605	$660	$495	$523	
5	G&A	$100	$120	$110	$120	$90	$95	
6	Marketing	$200	$150	$50	$300	$250	$200	
7	Profit	$250	$390	$445	$240	$155	$228	
8	Profit Margin %	25%	33%	40%	20%	17%	24%	

FIGURE 12.2   Chart on Two Different Axes and Chart Types (Combo Chart)

Additional Tips for Charting

Use the following tips to really make your charts have an impact:

- Reduce clutter by representing less data, using fewer words in the legend, and avoiding unnecessary labels.
- Use gridlines sparingly. Let the relative ups and downs of the chart speak for themselves.
- Limit the number of bars to seven in a bar chart; limit the number of lines to three in a line chart.
- Use standard imagery instead of special artwork; it's too distracting (i.e., a stack of coins to represent an expense rather than a standard bar).
- Choose your x- and y-axis ranges so that space is utilised effectively.
- If you have fewer than 12 periods for a time-series chart, consider using a bar chart instead of a line chart.

- Avoid the use of 3D charts. Remember: *Keep things simple!*
- Be cautious of excessive use of colours and shading.
- If the data has no natural order, sort the data from largest to smallest.

NOTE

If you are not keen on creating a fully fledged chart to represent data, you can use the sparkline features. To learn more, refer to "Sparklines" in Chapter 7.

CHART TYPES

Before looking at how to build charts from a technical perspective, let's first look at which chart to use. The most common types of charts are line and bar charts, but there are many other charting options Excel has to offer, and which chart types will display the data in the best, most visual way really depends on the available data and the message you are trying to convey.

Choosing a Chart Type

The first step in creating a useful chart is to choose the correct type of chart. Bar charts, pie charts, line charts, areas, scatter plots, donuts, radars, and bubbles are all options. Which one makes the most sense? Note that when displaying the information outputs of a typical financial model, line and bar charts are the predominant types of charts used, but this is not always the case. It's quite a skill to choose the most appropriate chart to display the output information in the best possible way.

Sometimes it's a matter of trial and error. The best way to choose a chart is to try several different charts to get a sense of which one is the best. Fortunately, it's very easy to flick between different chart types in Excel.

Summary of Common Charts and Applications

Table 12.1 is a brief summary of different chart types and their uses for displaying data graphically. The next section describes in detail what each of these charts does and what sort of data it best displays.

Take a look at the sales data and the chart options in Figure 12.3. Which chart type would best represent the sales data to show a regional comparison? We need to create a chart to visually display to our readers the output of our analysis, which is to compare the departments to each other. Which would be the best fit to get our message across?

TABLE 12.1 What Type of Chart Best Fits Your Data?

Chart Type	Suitable for ...	Application in Financial Models
Line	Trend and functional relations; useful for spotting trends	Very useful for time series
Pie	Single series of positive percentages or ratios	Useful, but often overused
Column	Data point (Y) variation over a short range of values (X). Suitable for comparison of data points	Very useful for comparison
Bar	Same as column charts	Very useful
Radar	Displaying multivariate information for statistical analysis	Rarely used
3D	Showing data three-dimensionally instead of two-dimensionally (e.g., cone chart)	Not recommended
Area	Similar to the line chart; represents variation of data points relative to each other	Sometimes used
Donut	Stacking multiple pie charts	Rarely used
Bubble	Enhancing scatter plots with additional variable	Sometimes used

Line charts and area charts are best for showing the connection between the data points, usually in time series, which is not the case, so they are not particularly useful in this situation.

The column or bar chart is best for comparing this kind of information, as we can easily see which area is the highest and which is the lowest. The pie chart shows the proportion and looks visually pleasing, but it is not as good for showing comparisons between the data points.

Detailed Chart Types

Figure 12.3 shows six different chart types that are readily available in Excel. Some of these charting options are better choices than others, so let's go into each of these chart types in a little more detail.

1. **Line charts.** These are lines joining data points to display the information. Line charts are most appropriate for indicating trends. Like column charts, the simplicity of these charts makes them a favourite in displaying data. While column and line charts can be used interchangeably, line charts are best used for trending information and columns are better to study absolute data metrics.

   We can see in Figure 12.3 that a line chart is not the most appropriate method of displaying these different costs, as it insinuates that there is some connection between the data points.

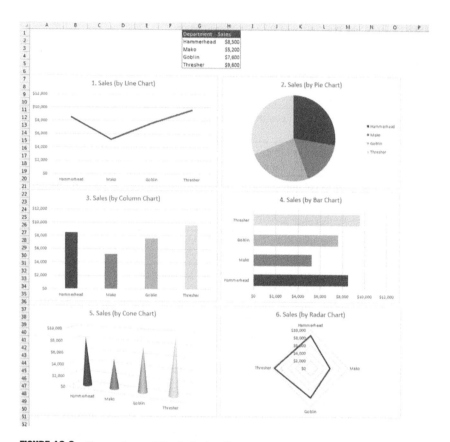

FIGURE 12.3   Comparison of Single Series Chart Types

There are also stacked line and 100 percent stacked line chart options in Excel, as there are with column charts. Sometimes line charts convey information in a more meaningful manner when the data points are marked. Excel offers the line chart with marker options for this purpose.

For detailed instructions on how to build a basic line chart, see the supplementary materials available at www.plumsolutions.com.au/book.

2. **Pie charts.** Pie charts have variable size sectors indicating the percentage of each variable in the overall picture. Pie charts are great for displaying ratios or percentage information, such as market share or penetration. They are very popular, particularly among graphic designers, but are notoriously poor for displaying information. In Figure 12.3, the pie chart is visually appealing, but it conveys very little information and makes it difficult to compare which department has the highest expense.

3. **Column charts.** Column charts are one of the most commonly used charts available in Excel, and they are a staple of presenting unrelated data points graphically. The height of the columns indicates the value or the parameter on the y-axis, while the width indicates the value along the x-axis. Column charts are a very effective method of displaying a message instantly, due to the simple format in which they represent the information. We can see in Figure 12.3 that the column chart is the most accurate way of displaying the sales data in this situation—this one is the best choice for the message we are trying to get across with our data.

4. **Bar charts.** Bar charts are transposed column charts. They represent the same information as column charts from a different perspective. Most times the choice between column and bar charts will depend on how you want to represent the information depending on the space constraints of the display area. Most commonly, bar charts are used to represent time or future projections along the x-axis. See Figure 12.3.

5. **3D charts.** Excel also offers 3D versions of these column charts as bar, cylinder, and cone charts. Whilst 3D bar and cylinder charts are easy to comprehend, understanding cone charts can get complicated, so they are not very commonly used to display data. In general, 3D charts do not convey any more information than 2D charts, so usually a 2D chart is a simpler and clearer way of displaying information. Figure 12.3 shows an example of a 3D chart with a cone shape, which is an extremely poor way of comparing the four sales figures because the pointy tip of the cone is much more difficult to compare to other results than a flat column.

NOTE

The cone chart type feature was an "improvement" added to Excel 2007. They have now (very sensibly!) taken it off the charting options menu, and it is now a column shape instead of a standard chart type. I think it's highly unlikely that anyone will miss it, but you can still find it under Format Data Series > Series Options > Column Shape.

6. **Radar charts.** Radar charts plot the points on a circular axis rather than an x- and y-axis. Hence, the data points are indicated by their relative distances from the centre. They are easy enough to build, but can be confusing and are not particularly good at displaying quantitative information and, therefore, are not commonly used. See Figure 12.3.

Another Example with More Data

Figure 12.3 showed a one-series situation where we had only four numbers to plot. What if we need to show more data on our chart with multiple series? Figure 12.4 shows expenses that have been split into three types: Staff Costs, Admin, and IT. Let's look at a few ways we can display this data in a chart.

Excel offers multiple variations in column, bar, and line charts, such as the seven listed below. Some of them are very effective in conveying the message, while others may look good but distract from your main point.

1. **Clustered column charts.** These are multiple series of basic column charts arranged next to each other. Instead of creating multiple charts for similar information, it may sometimes be better to use the clustered charts instead.

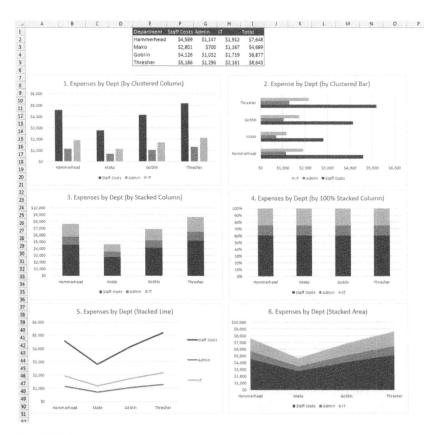

FIGURE 12.4   Comparison of Multi-series Chart Types

However, you must ensure that columns are not too congested, as that would defeat the purpose. A clustered column chart is a good option for Figure 12.4, as there are only three departments and three expense types. It provides a good comparison between the numbers without appearing too cluttered.

2. **Clustered bar charts.** This is also a good way to display the data, although we often reserve the x-axis for time series, so a clustered column is probably a more commonly used solution, and therefore may be more easily understood by the reader.

3. **Stacked column charts.** These are a variation on a basic column chart, with multiple variables stacked on top of each other. They are particularly good for showing proportionate totals. For example, in Figure 12.4, not only can we see how the regions compare to each other, but how much each department contributes to the costs in total. It does, however, make the comparison between IT costs more difficult, for example, so this is where the intention of your message becomes important. If your focus is on total costs, I would choose a stacked column, but if you'd like to compare each of the data points, then a clustered column would be more appropriate.

   Note that including a data table will add more detail to the stacked column chart, and help the reader to compare the values in the upper stacks. See "Handy Charting Hints" later in this chapter for instructions on how to add a data table.

4. **100 percent stacked column charts.** As the name suggests, these are column charts that stack on a percentage basis. They are most appropriate for use in comparing data where we are comparing percentages and ratios rather than an absolute number. When using 100 percent stacked column charts, make sure that the labels clearly show that it is displaying percentages rather than absolute numbers. In Figure 12.4, the percentages are very similar, so not a particularly helpful way of displaying the data in this case!

5. **Stacked line charts.** As with the single series described above, the stacked line is not a helpful way of displaying the data in Figure 12.4.

6. **Area charts.** Area charts are similar to line charts but have a shaded area below. Like line charts, they are good for displaying data that is connected. These can be stacked or not stacked, similar to column charts. Figure 12.4 shows a stacked area chart—again, not a particularly effective way of displaying four different regions with no connection between them.

7. **Donut charts.** Visually, donut charts are pie charts with a hole in the centre. While it may not seem like a big difference at first, this gap in the donut hole allows several series to be stacked in the same chart, which may or may not be a good idea. Pie charts can be used to represent a single series of values; multiple series require a separate chart for each series. This can be overcome with donut charts, where multiple series can be stacked centrally.

However, interpreting donut charts can become cumbersome if there's too much data. If you want to use this chart, you need to plan it properly and make it as intuitive as possible. Consider Figure 12.5. We want to show the Australian population and see if there is any correlation to land area. This donut chart is interesting but quite difficult to interpret.

Combination Charts   Sometimes using the same chart type to represent different data metrics is not very effective. In such cases, using a combination of chart types can be a very powerful solution. One of the most popular representations is the combination of column and line charts. Such combinations can convey a lot of information without cluttering the chart. These are particularly useful in dashboard reporting and other instances where you want to display as much information as possible in a small amount of space.

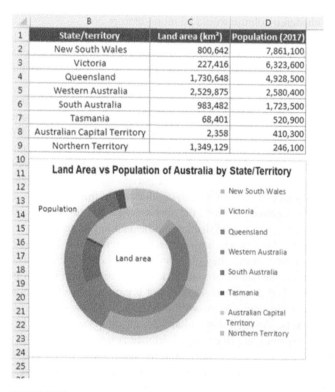

	B	C	D
1	State/territory	Land area (km²)	Population (2017)
2	New South Wales	800,642	7,861,100
3	Victoria	227,416	6,323,600
4	Queensland	1,730,648	4,928,500
5	Western Australia	2,529,875	2,580,400
6	South Australia	983,482	1,723,500
7	Tasmania	68,401	520,900
8	Australian Capital Territory	2,358	410,300
9	Northern Territory	1,349,129	246,100

FIGURE 12.5   Donut Chart

Quite often we might want to show two different measures, such as number of units and profit, on the same chart. For instructions on how to do this, see "Charting with Two Different Axes and Chart Types" later in this chapter.

Consider Figure 12.6, which also displays the population versus the land area. Whilst not as visually appealing as the donut chart, it is somewhat easier to interpret, and we can see that there is very little correlation between population and land area.

Map Charts An even better way of displaying this data would be to show it on a filled map. Using exactly the same data, we can show it visually on a map as shown in Figure 12.7. It's not necessary to add the land area to this map to show our message, as the area is shown in the chart. Population density is shown by the darker colours, which works in a similar way to the colour scales in conditional formatting.

	B	C	D
1	State/territory	Land area (km²)	Population (2017)
2	New South Wales	800,642	7,861,100
3	Victoria	227,416	6,323,600
4	Queensland	1,730,648	4,928,500
5	Western Australia	2,529,875	2,580,400
6	South Australia	983,482	1,723,500
7	Tasmania	68,401	520,900
8	Australian Capital Territory	2,358	410,300
9	Northern Territory	1,349,129	246,100

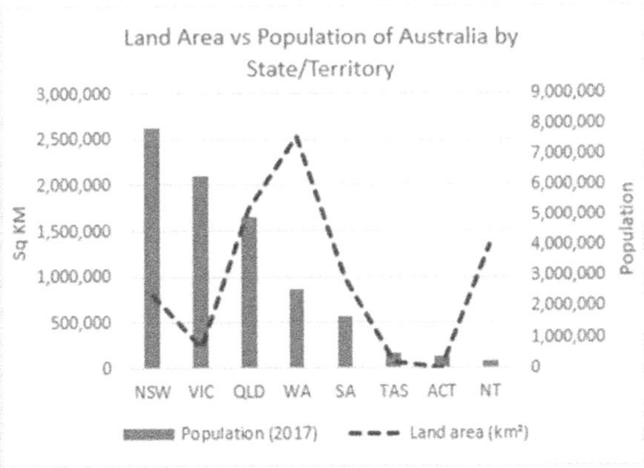

FIGURE 12.6 Combination Chart

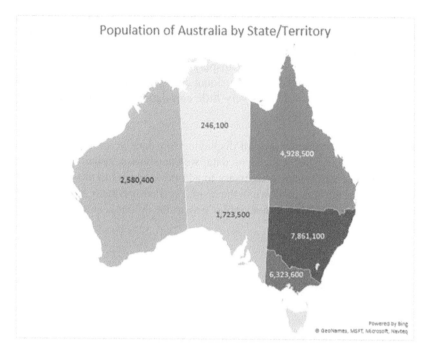

FIGURE 12.7 Map Chart

TIP

One thing to note is that when you first create the map chart, it uses Bing location data, so you'll need to have an internet connection, and be clear in your data labelling of the locations. Try using postcodes or zipcodes, or adding the country if the map chart cannot find the correct location. If you're still having difficulty, consider switching to Power BI desktop to run your map charts, as this enables you to set the data properties to the country, state, or region.

Bubble Chart Bubble charts are another type of chart to consider if you need to show multiple dimensions, and the data is not location-specific. Bubble charts are an enhancement to scatter charts and can compare three characteristics: not only plotting the x- and y-axis, but also reflecting the bubble size for each category.

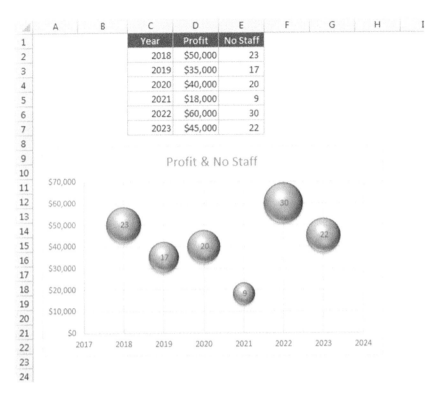

FIGURE 12.8   Bubble Chart

Detailed instructions can be found later in this chapter for how to build a bubble chart. See Figure 12.8.

WORKING WITH CHARTS

The following outlines some of the most commonly used features of charting. Note that in later versions of Excel, a lot of the options that used to appear in the ribbon in earlier versions have now been moved to the chart itself. The Layout tab is no longer in the ribbon, and most of these options have been moved to the chart. You'll notice that when you click on the chart, several new icons appear on the right, as shown in Figure 12.9. These three options are:

1. The plus sign will add chart elements, such as titles and labels to the chart.
2. The paintbrush will help you to change the colours and styles of the chart.
3. The filter is a quick way to change the data, series, or names.

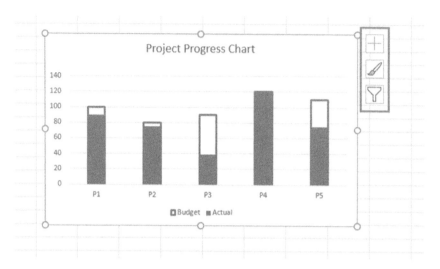

FIGURE 12.9   Editing from the Chart

All the features in these options can also be accessed by right-clicking the chart or via the Chart Design tab, which will appear in the ribbon once the chart has been clicked upon. This is the same in Excel for Mac, however, this is the only way to make these changes on a Mac because, in the current version, the three options do not appear to the right of the chart when you click on it. Chart changes on a Mac can be made through the Adding Chart Elements on the Chart Design tab in the ribbon, as shown in Figure 12.10.

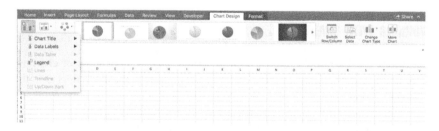

FIGURE 12.10   Adding Chart Elements in Excel for Mac

Changing the Type of Chart

Displaying data graphically is usually an iterative process, and if you create a chart based on your model data and it doesn't look quite right, it is relatively quick and easy to change the chart type displayed.

To change the chart type, display the Change Chart Type dialog box by right-clicking on the chart area and selecting Change Chart Type from the drop-down menu that appears.

Choose the chart you'd like to display and click OK. Note that you can also change the chart type through the Design tab on the ribbon.

Changing the Source Data

You can also quite easily change the source data for your chart while retaining the original chart type.

In Figure 12.11, the pie chart is based on sales data per region (B2 through to B5). To depict expenses per region (E2 through to E5), you would need to change the source data.

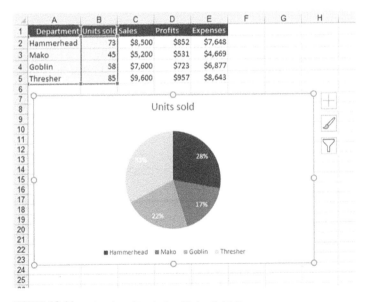

FIGURE 12.11   Pie Chart Depicting Units Sold Data

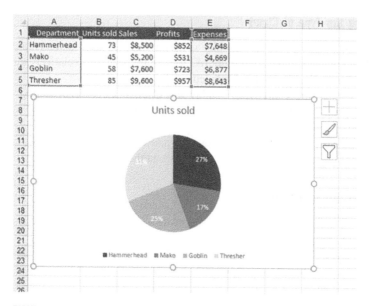

FIGURE 12.12   Changing the Data Source to Depict Expenses

The easiest way to change the source data is to simply click on the chart until the source data is highlighted. We can see in Figure 12.11 that the source data is in columns A and B. Now, just hover the mouse on the blue line to the right of column B, and drag it across to column E as shown in Figure 12.12. This works in any kind of chart where you can see the source data on the same page.

TIP

There is another similar quick trick for adding a series to a chart. Let's say you've got a single series showing on a chart, as shown in Figure 12.13. If you wanted to add Expenses as a new series, simply copy the source data in column E, select the chart, and paste the data straight in using Control+V. Another series will automatically appear in the chart, as shown in Figure 12.14.

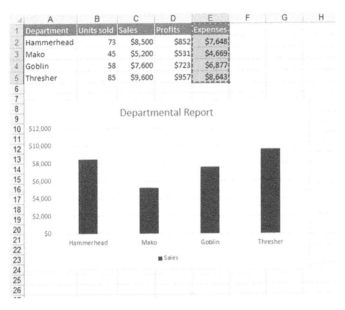

FIGURE 12.13   Single-Series Column Chart

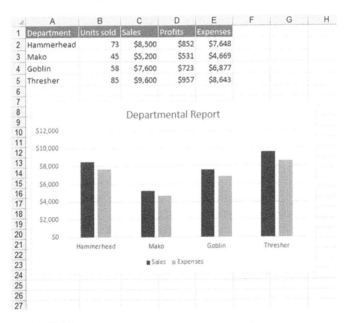

FIGURE 12.14   Double-Series Clustered Column Chart

If the data is not on the same page, or if the change is more complex, then this quick tip may not work and so you'll need to do it the long way, with the seven steps that follow.

1. Right-click on the chart area and click Select Data from the menu that appears.
2. The Select Data Source dialog box will be displayed.
3. The field called Chart Data Range at the top of the dialog box shows the range of cells used in the data source for the chart.
4. Click on the series name (**Units sold**, in this case) and click Edit.
5. Select the new data range from the sheet with your mouse.

TIP

Make sure that you delete all of the original data from the series or it will mess up your graph. See Figure 12.15. This is a rather annoying habit of Excel charting; unless you highlight the existing range and then reselect the new data, it will automatically add it to the range with a plus (+) sign.

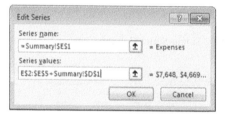

FIGURE 12.15 Edit Series Dialog Box with Incorrect Series Values Data

---

6. When you have completed your data selection, the new data range reference will appear in the Edit Data Source dialog box. Click OK.
7. The chart will change to reflect the new data.

If you want to change the title of the chart to something more interesting than Expenses, simply click on the title, and type over it.

Remember that if you change the underlying data in the model, the chart will change as well. You'd hope so, as that's really the *point* of financial modelling.

Saving a Chart as a Template

If you've spent a lot of time getting the axes, colours, and formats the way you want them, you can save this chart as a template to use again and again.

To save the chart template:

1. Once you are happy with the way the chart looks, right-click on the chart and select Save as Template.
2. Save it in your desired location.

To use the chart template on a new or existing chart:

1. Select a data range and on the Insert tab on the ribbon, click Recommended Charts, which is located at the lower right of the Charts button group to create a new chart, or right-click on an existing chart and select Change Chart Type.
2. On the All Charts tab, press Templates to show your saved templates.
3. Select the template you'd like to use. See Figure 12.16.

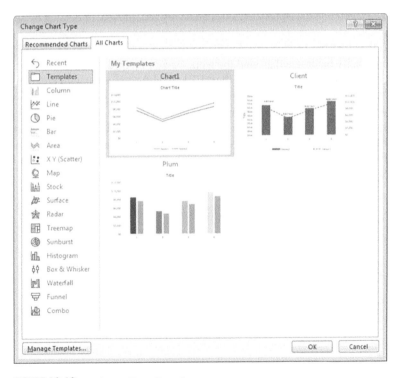

FIGURE 12.16   Using a Chart Template

TIP

Right-click on the template in the Change Chart Type dialog box and click on Set as Default Chart so that each time you create a chart, it will default to your template. This is particularly useful when using the F11 shortcut to create a chart.

HANDY CHARTING HINTS

Here are some handy charting hints:

- The formatting on most of the areas of the chart can be changed by double-clicking on the area you wish to change. You can play with this to make your graph look more attractive.
- The legend on the right-hand side can be resized, moved, or deleted by selecting it.
- If the chart has been inserted in the worksheet, rather than on its own page, it can easily be dragged around the worksheet or resized.
- Align charts by holding down the ALT key whilst you drag with the mouse to "snap to grid" and make the chart line up in the corner of the cell. This works with form controls, buttons, and other images inserted onto the sheet.
- If you hide data in your source sheet, this will not show on the chart. Test this by hiding one of the columns on the Financials sheet and check that the month has disappeared on the chart. You can change the options under Select Data Source so that it displays hidden cells. See Figure 12.17.

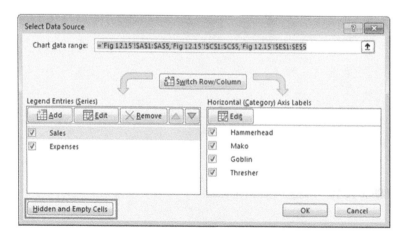

FIGURE 12.17   Changing the Hidden and Empty Cells Option

- The chart can be changed to a different type of chart (e.g., a bar chart or a pie chart) by right-clicking and selecting Change Chart Type.
- Including a data table (not to be confused with a sensitivity analysis data table we covered in Chapter 11) that shows actual values below the chart is a great way to display the information visually while still providing detailed data.

To add the data table, click on the chart to make the Design tab appear and on the Design tab click on the drop-down under Add Chart Element on the far left-hand side. Select Data Table as shown on the left in Figure 12.18, and choose from with or without Legend Keys. Unless you are using Excel for Mac, you can also click on the chart, select the Chart Elements icon (the + symbol), and select the Data Table option, also shown on the right of Figure 12.18.

- Charts can be pasted directly into Microsoft Word or PowerPoint. Note that if you simply copy and paste, the links to the underlying data in Excel will be maintained. This is fine, if you want to be able to edit the Excel data and have the chart update. Normally, when you've copied and pasted a chart into Word or PowerPoint, you have finished it and don't want the chart to change at all. Therefore, it needs to be pasted as a picture. Copy the chart and then Paste Special, pasting the chart into the destination document as a picture to make sure that the chart does not change.

TIP

To create a chart very quickly on a new sheet, highlight the data and use the F11 shortcut. This automatically creates a column chart, but you can change the default settings to a template as described above.

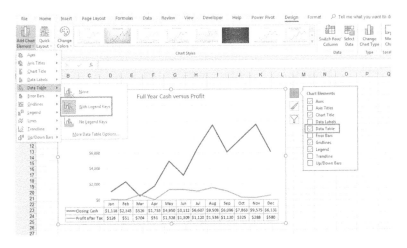

FIGURE 12.18 Line Chart with Data Table

DYNAMIC NAMED RANGES

A common problem in creating charts for modelling is that the size of the source data can change, and cause errors. The problem with specifying a range is that if someone adds data to the right or below the table, it will not be included in the range, and therefore will not show in the chart. Look at the problem shown in Figure 12.19. We have some data used to create a chart. The user has now entered some additional data in row 8, but this has not been included in the chart, because it was created using the static range A1:B7. You can find these templates, along with the accompanying models to the rest of the screenshots in the book, at www .plumsolutions.com.au/book.

There are two ways of making your chart more dynamic:

1. **Structured reference table.** By far the easiest way is to turn the data into a table, and then use the table reference to create the chart. Any additional data appended to the table will automatically be included in the chart. For more information on how to create tables, see the section "Structured Reference Tables" in Chapter 8.
2. **Dynamic named range.** It's not always practical to turn your data into a structured reference table, and therefore we need to make the named range change size depend on the amount of data in the range, which will, in turn, affect the data included in the chart.

Let's explore how to create a dynamic named range and include it in a formula or chart. Be warned, it's not for the fainthearted! Before we start, you should be familiar with the concept of named ranges from Chapter 5, and the OFFSET function from Chapter 6.

Let's start by defining an ordinary named range called Exp_data by highlighting the data in the range and typing the name in the Name box in the top left-hand corner. Now, if a user wants to add data to this table (e.g., another expense item in row 8, or another city in column J), this new data will not be included in the range.

	A	B	C	D	E	F	G	H	I	J	K
1	Expenses	Campbelltown	Melbourne	Sydney	Parramatta	Geelong	Brisbane	Toowoomba		Perth	Canberra
2	Superannuation	$51,139	$61,391	$46,043	$55,252	$41,439	$49,726	$37,295	$20,156	$27,079	
3	Workers Comp	$5,684	$6,821	$5,116	$6,139	$4,604	$5,525	$4,144	$2,240	$3,009	
4	Staff Amenities	$28,422	$34,106	$25,579	$30,695	$23,021	$27,626	$20,719	$11,198	$15,044	
5	Consumables	$34,106	$40,927	$30,695	$36,834	$27,626	$33,151	$24,863	$13,437	$18,053	
6	Recruitment	$17,053	$20,464	$15,348	$18,417	$13,813	$16,575	$12,432	$6,719	$9,026	
7	Travel	$11,369	$13,642	$10,232	$12,278	$9,209	$11,050	$8,288	$4,479	$6,018	
8	Telephone	$8,716	$10,459	$7,844	$9,413	$7,060	$8,472	$6,354	$3,434	$4,613	
9											
10											
11		Total Expenses									
12		=SUM(B2:I7)									
13											

FIGURE 12.19 New Data Not Included in Formula

To make this named range dynamic, first we need to work out how big the range is. We'll do this using a COUNTA formula in row 1 and column A. This counts the number of cells that are not blank. We can include this in the OFFSET, but use the result of the COUNTA function to specify the number of rows and columns in the range.

Note that the data needs to be a block, with no blank rows or columns, as this could throw the formula off by a row or column, and there needs to be a value in cell A1.

Go to the Name Manager, and edit the named range you have just created. However, instead of putting the absolute range of A1:I8 in the Refers To box, enter the formula

=OFFSET(Data!A\$1,0,0,COUNTA(Data!\$A\$1:\$A\$5000),

COUNTA(Data!\$A\$1:\$Z\$1))

Note that it's important to include the absolute references in the range. This is telling the named range to start at A1 and go as far up and down as there is data (within the range A1:Z5000). We are using the height and width sections of the OFFSET function in this case.

See Figure 12.20. You can now refer to this named range in formulas and charts, knowing that additional data will always be captured within the range.

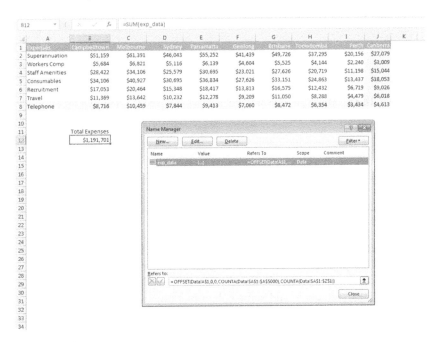

FIGURE 12.20   New Data Included in Named Range, and Formula

NOTE

Be careful not to put anything extra in row 1 or column A, such as the title "Total Expenses", because that will then be included in the COUNTA formula and make the range larger by one row or column. See Figure 12.21, where the title has been put in column A, instead of cell B11 as it is in Figure 12.20.

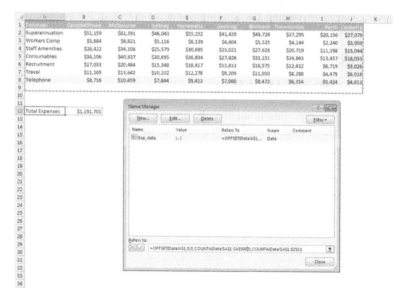

FIGURE 12.21 Having a Title in Column A Will Expand the Named Range by One Row

NOTE

For the formula in the named range, we could instead use the function **=OFFSET(A1,0,0,COUNTA(A:A),COUNTA(1:1))**, but it is not normally good practice to use entire column or row references in formulas because they use a lot more memory. Because we have limited our range to A1:Z5000, we could add some colour markings so that the user knows when he or she has exceeded the range limits.

Using a Dynamic Range Name in a Chart

Dynamic named ranges are helpful when you are creating a chart with a variable number of values. For example, let's say you are creating a chart based on a financial model that contains a variable number of tenants. We know that users are unlikely to need to model more than 5 or 10 tenants in the model, but we've made the model flexible so that users can enter up to 25 tenants, just in case they need that many. If we set up the chart allowing for 25 tenants, it would look perfectly ridiculous. See Figure 12.22.

The chart looks much better if we include only the tenants that actually have data in the chart. See Figure 12.23.

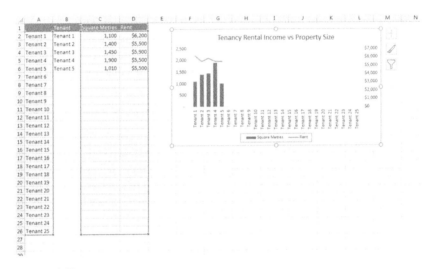

FIGURE 12.22 Chart with Variable Number of Tenants

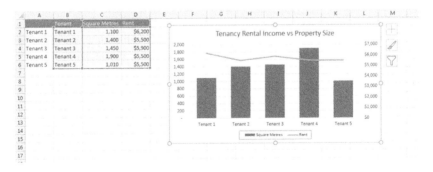

FIGURE 12.23 Chart with Fixed Number of Tenants

However, using an ordinary chart, we'd need users to go into the source data and change the chart range manually, which would be time-consuming and error-prone. The alternative is to create dynamic named ranges in the source data, and then refer to the named ranges when creating the chart. This way the range (and therefore the labels picked up in the chart) will automatically expand and contract, depending on whether the cells contain data or not. Unused tenancy cells will remain blank and will not be included in the chart. See the following four steps.

NOTE

When using dynamic named ranges in a chart, each series must have its own named range and therefore each range must be one-dimensional (i.e., only contain data in a single row or column). You therefore need to create a range for the labels and then a separate range for each series that appears on the chart.

Referring to a multi-dimensional range like the one shown in the first example in Figure 12.20 in a chart will not work. To create a chart using this data, you would need to create a separate named range for each series, for example, one for Superannuation, one for Workers Comp, and so on, which somewhat defeats the purpose of having a dynamic named range.

1. To make this chart dynamic, create three dynamic named ranges, one for each series, as shown in Figure 12.24.
2. Next, create the chart normally and then go into the Select Data Source dialog box by right-clicking on the chart and click on Select Data.
3. Go into each of the two series "Square Metres" and "Rent" and edit the data source. Replace the series values with the dynamic named range, such as "Sqm_data", as shown in Figure 12.25. Note that unlike other named range references, you must leave the sheet reference intact. If you can't remember the name, try using the F3 shortcut.
4. Edit the "Horizontal" Axis Labels in the Data Source to refer to the dynamic named range you have created for the tenant names.

Test the data by adding or deleting tenants, and make sure the chart changes accordingly.

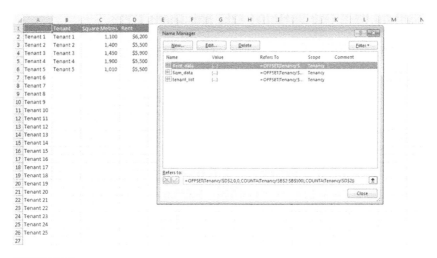

FIGURE 12.24 Create Three Dynamic Named Ranges, One for Each Series in the Chart

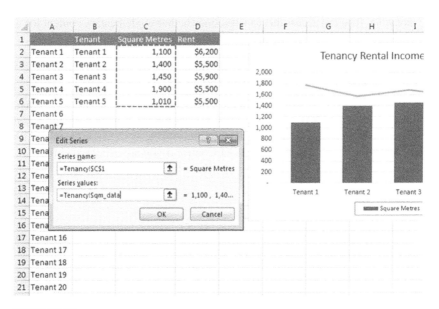

FIGURE 12.25 Referring to the Named Range in the Chart Series

CHARTING WITH TWO DIFFERENT AXES AND CHART TYPES

One of the best ways of analysing the output of your model is to plot two different variables on the same chart so that we can understand trends and look for correlations in the data. Sometimes the only way to spot a trend or an anomaly in the model is to look at it graphically. For example, how does our overall revenue compare to headcount? Surely as revenue increases so should headcount, and if it doesn't we need to understand why. What if we compare regions and their number of units sold and profit? Surely the regions with the highest number of units sold should be the most profitable. This may not necessarily be the case, and there's no better way to analyse this than with a chart plotting both pieces of information on two separate axes. Let's take a look at some data, and plot the number of units sold and the profits using two different chart types on two axes.

TIP

Note that the Combo Chart was added as a standard chart type in Excel 2013. If you are using a previous version of Excel, the following instructions will not work. You can access these instructions in the supplementary content for this chapter, which can be found at www.plumsolutions.com.au/book.

If we have the data shown in Figure 12.26, we can create a chart to compare units sold and profits. The easiest way to select the ranges is to highlight the data in columns A, B, and D by holding down the Control key, as shown in Figure 12.26. Hold down the Command key instead of Control if you are using Excel for Mac.

	A	B	C	D	E	F
1	Department	Units sold	Sales	Profits	Expenses	
2	Hammerhead	73	$8,500	$852	$7,648	
3	Mako	45	$5,200	$531	$4,669	
4	Goblin	58	$7,600	$723	$6,877	
5	Thresher	85	$9,600	$957	$8,643	
6						
7						

FIGURE 12.26 Selecting Non-consecutive Ranges by Holding Down the Control Key

Creating a Combo Chart

1. Select Recommended Charts from the Insert tab on the ribbon. The Insert Chart dialog box will appear.
2. Select the All Charts tab, and select Combo, which can be found at the bottom of the dialog box, as shown in Figure 12.27.

Alternatively, you can select the Combo icon directly from the ribbon in the Charts section of the Insert tab.

3. Click on Secondary Axis for one Series Name, which will move it to the other axis, and press OK.
4. Insert a title and an axis label from the Chart Elements option, which appears when you click on the chart.
5. Your completed chart should look like Figure 12.28.

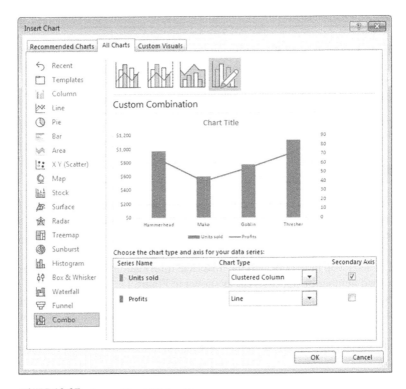

FIGURE 12.27 Insert Chart Dialog Box

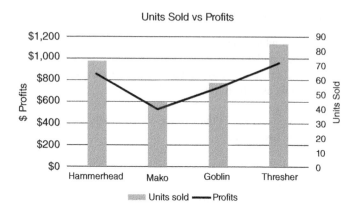

FIGURE 12.28　Completed Combo Chart

TIP

These charts can be a little confusing if you try to put too much in, so keep it simple by sticking to only two series. Make sure that the axes are formatted correctly if currency symbols are appropriate. Leave the legend, which will make it clearer which section of the chart refers to which series.

BUBBLE CHARTS

Bubble charts are a variation of other types of graphs, combining elements from column and scatter charts. They give the user a way to compare values based on the relative size of the bubble, as well as the location within the chart. They are most useful when there are three data points to display.

Let's say you have collected the historical information about your company's profits and number of staff by year as shown in Figure 12.29.

Since you have three data points, it is difficult to represent this as a 2D graph. Consider the following example of how the data could be charted as shown in Figure 12.29. It can be difficult to compare the relativity of the profits and number of staff. Essentially, having all of the information in this format loses the intended purpose.

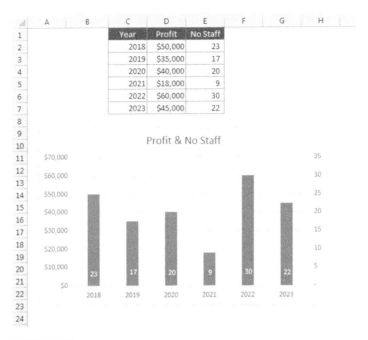

FIGURE 12.29 Data Shown in a Two-Dimensional Chart

In this situation, we can consider using a bubble chart. The same data presented in a bubble chart tells a different story. You are able to compare the profits and staff by using the vertical rise of each bubble (profit) and its corresponding y-axis value, along with comparing the staff numbers by looking at the size of the bubbles.

Creating a bubble chart is a bit more involved than a standard bar chart, but the few extra steps are worthwhile. See the following 12 steps.

1. Open up a blank worksheet and start by entering the data, as shown in Figure 12.29.
2. The columns are reflected on the bubble chart, as shown:
   a. The first column contains the values for the horizontal x-axis and it must contain numerical data—text such as Area A, Area B, and so on will not show up on the x-axis.
   b. The second column contains the values for the vertical y-axis.
   c. The third column will be shown as the size of the bubble.

3. The first trick with a bubble chart is that all data needs to be formatted as Number; otherwise, it will not be properly displayed. Change the formatting to ensure the data has been formatted as a number.

4. We can now create a bubble chart from this data. The easiest way to do this is to highlight the whole range C2:E7 and create the chart. It is important to remember NOT to include the headers—another trick with bubble charts. Doing so will cause errors.

5. Select either the 2D or 3D bubble chart from the X Y (Scatter) in the Charts section on the Insert tab, and the basic bubble chart will appear automatically. See Figure 12.30.

6. The chart should now look something like Figure 12.30 (although the colours and background might look a little different, depending on which version of Excel you are using).

7. If the series legend appears, select and delete it.

8. Add the title "Profit & No Staff".

9. Right-click on the bubbles to select them all, then choose Add Data Labels, or add them via the Chart Elements option.

10. The default will be the profit amounts. To change this, right-click again on the bubbles, and choose Format Data Labels.

11. Under Label Options, unselect Y Value, select Bubble Size, and also select Center under label position as shown in Figure 12.31.

12. To bold the data labels, you can highlight them first, then press Control+B.

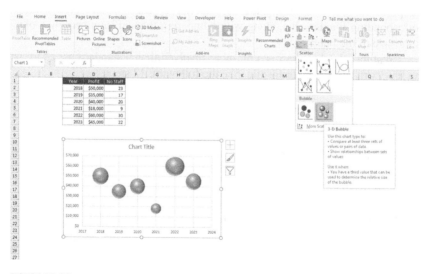

FIGURE 12.30 Inserting the Bubble Chart

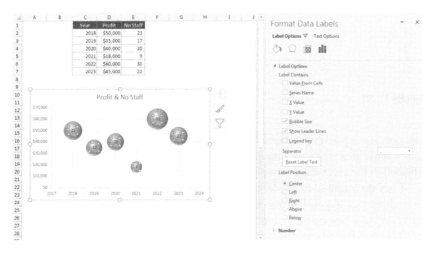

FIGURE 12.31 Changing the Labels

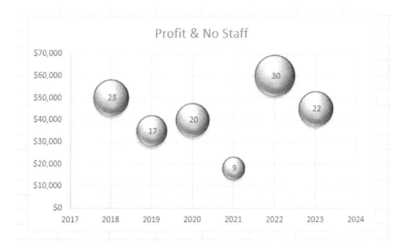

FIGURE 12.32 Completed Bubble Chart

Your bubble chart should look something like Figure 12.32.

CREATING A DYNAMIC CHART

When creating charts in financial models or reports, we should still follow best practice and try to make our models as flexible and dynamic as we can. As discussed in Chapter 3, "Best-Practice Principles of Modelling", we should always

| P3 | | | | *fx* | =SUMIF($R$2:$M$2,$P$2,$B3:$M3) | | | | | | | | | | | | | |

	A	B	C	D	E	F	G	H	I	J	K	L	M	N	O	P	Q	R
1	Average Temperature Degrees Celsius														Temperature Comparison for Apr and May			
2	Cities	Jan	Feb	Mar	Apr	May	Jun	Jul	Aug	Sep	Oct	Nov	Dec		Cities	Apr	May	
3	London	8.9	5.5	8	9.8	13.1	16.2	18.9	18.5	16	12.8	8.9	7.1		London	9.8	13.1	
4	New York	-1.8	-1.2	3.5	9	14.6	19.5	22.8	22.7	19.1	12.5	6.6	1.2		New York	9.0	14.6	
5	Sydney	22.1	22.1	21	18.4	15.3	12.9	12	13.2	15.3	17.7	19.5	21.2		Sydney	18.4	15.3	
6	Moscow	-10.2	-8.9	-4	4.5	12.2	16.3	18.5	16.6	10.9	4.3	-2	-7.5		Moscow	4.5	12.2	
7																		

FIGURE 12.33   Creating the "Active Range"

link as much as possible in our models, and this goes for charts as well. It therefore makes sense that when we change one of the inputs in our model, this should be reflected in the chart data, as well as the titles and labels.

Let's do a simple example with 13 steps to see how we can make our charts more dynamic. If you had the temperature data as shown in Figure 12.33, we could create a comparison chart whereby the user could compare the temperature between months in different cities. You can find this template, along with the accompanying models to the rest of the screenshots in this book, at www .plumsolutions.com.au/book.

1. Create drop-down boxes in cells P2 and Q2 from which the users can select the months they wish to compare. See "Using Validations to Create a Drop-Down List" in Chapter 7 for how to do this.
2. Link the cities in column O.
3. In columns P and Q, create formulas that will become the "active range" for our chart and automatically pick up the months selected in the drop-downs. There are several formulas that could be used here, but I have chosen one of my favourites, the SUMIF function in this instance. If you choose the SUMIF, your formula in cell P3 should look like this: =SUMIF($B$2: $M$2, P$2, $B3:$M3).
4. Copy it across and down the whole of the range P3:Q6.
5. Try changing the months, and check that it is picking up the correct temperatures for each city. Your model should look something like Figure 12.33 so far.
6. Next, create a clustered column chart from the active range. It should look something like Figure 12.34.
7. Try changing the drop-down boxes, and you'll notice that the data will change.
8. Add a data table by checking the Data Table checkbox on the Chart Elements option on the chart, or by selecting Data Table from the Add Chart Elements on the Design tab in the ribbon.
9. Remove the legend and change the colours if you wish.
10. Now we want to create a title for this chart, but we'd like to make it very obvious what is contained in the chart, so we'd like to include the months selected by the user in the chart title as well. In cell O1, create some linked text that we will use for our chart title. For a recap on how to combine text

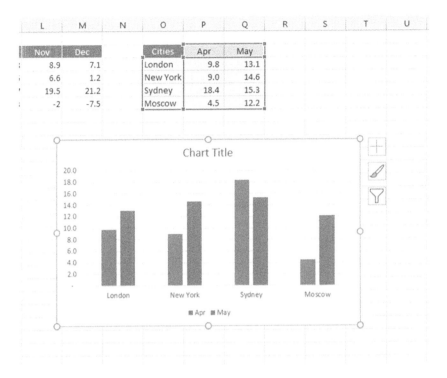

FIGURE 12.34 Creating a Chart Based on the Active Range

and cells together, see the section "Linked Dynamic Text Assumptions Documentation" in Chapter 3.

11. Your formula in cell O1 should look something like this: **="Temperature Comparison for "&P2&" and "&Q2"**.

12. Insert a chart title if one is not already showing, and click on the title in the chart. Now, go to the formula bar, press "=", and click on cell O1. The text in cell O1 will now appear on the chart, as shown in Figure 12.35.

13. Try changing the months in cells P2 and Q2, and watch the chart change.

Additional Exercise

Try creating some additional commentary in a cell in your sheet, such as the maximum temperature for the selected period. Your formula would be

="The maximum temperature for the period is "&MAX(P3:Q6)

Add a text box into the chart, by clicking on the Text Box icon in the Text group on the Insert tab in the ribbon, and then link that text box to the single

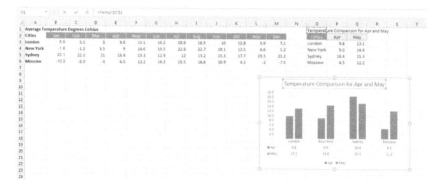

FIGURE 12.35   Completed Dynamic Chart

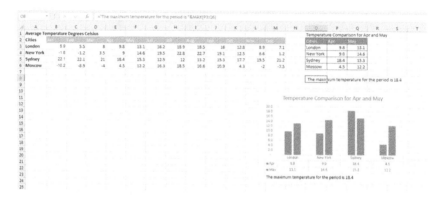

FIGURE 12.36   Completed Dynamic Chart with Linked Text Box

cell in the same way as you linked the chart title above. Your chart should look
something like Figure 12.36.

TIP

Similar text containing a date can also be created in a single cell, and
then linked to a title or text box in a chart. If you would like the current
date to always show on the chart, use the **=TODAY()** function in your
formula, and format it using the TEXT function so that it shows the date in
your preferred format. In the section "Linked Dynamic Text Assumptions
Documentation" in Chapter 3, we used the TEXT function to format
commentary as a percentage, but it can also be used for dates.

> Use the formula **="Report for" & TEXT(TODAY( ), "mmm yy")**, and each time you open the first file it will give you a title that includes the current month, such as: "Report for Oct 20", assuming the current month was October 2020.

WATERFALL CHARTS

Waterfall charts, also called bridge or stepped charts, have become popular in recent years, particularly when displaying the output of a financial model. A waterfall chart displays very effectively the incremental impact of each period of time or unit. It is a type of bar chart where the value of the second bar generally begins where the first one finished. To illustrate, a waterfall chart might look something like Figure 12.37.

Despite their popularity, waterfall charts were only relatively recently added as a standard chart type in Excel, and to create one in a version prior to Excel 2016 can get very complicated. Please refer to the supplementary content for this chapter, which can be found at www.plumsolutions.com.au/book, for detailed instructions on how to create a waterfall chart in previous versions of Excel using the "dummy stack" and the up/down bars method.

Let's say you have a forecast for cash inflows and outflows for the next six months (see the data list that follows).

Month	Cash
Jan	$250
Feb	$200
Mar	$1,000
Apr	−$500
May	$650
Jun	$800

You could forecast it as a cumulative bar chart. See Figure 12.38. But we'd like to see the incremental contribution of each month individually, which will add a new dimension to the analysis.

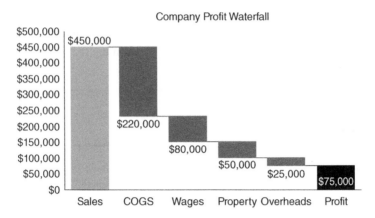

FIGURE 12.37   Completed Company Profit Waterfall

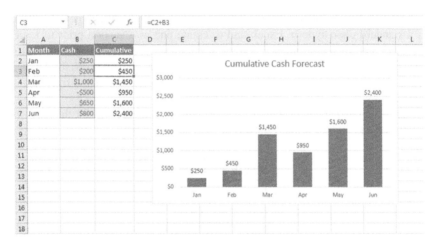

FIGURE 12.38   Cumulative Bar Chart

Contrary to popular belief, you don't need fancy software to build a basic waterfall chart. They are really not that difficult to build in Excel and are achieved with a few little tricks, as shown in the following list of four steps.

1. Open a blank worksheet and start by entering the dates and your cash amount in columns A and B, as shown.
2. Highlight all the data and select the Waterfall Chart icon from the Charts section of the Insert tab on the ribbon; the chart will appear as shown in Figure 12.39.
3. The legend does not add much to the chart, so you can remove it by clicking on it and pressing delete.
4. Change the chart title by clicking on it and typing over the words "Chart Title".

FIGURE 12.39   Creating a Waterfall Chart

If you'd like to show the total amount on the waterfall chart, add it by follow-ing these further four steps:

5. Add the total in row 8 by adding the formula **=SUM(B2:B7)** to cell B8.
6. Add this to the chart by clicking on the chart, and resizing the source data by dragging the range down one cell as shown in Figure 12.40. Alternatively, you can change the source data range of the chart by right-clicking on the chart, choosing Select Data, and manually changing the chart data range.
7. You'll notice that the Total amount appears as a separate column at the end, added to the previous columns, which is incorrect. To show this as a total, simply right-click on the Total column (making sure to select only that column and not the entire series), and select Set as Total, as shown in Figure 12.41.
8. This will change the last column to show only the total and your completed waterfall chart should look something like Figure 12.42.

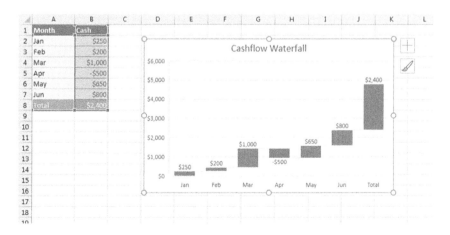

FIGURE 12.40   Editing the Source Data Range of the Waterfall Chart

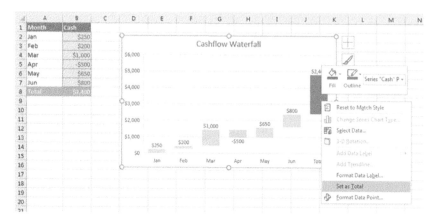

FIGURE 12.41 Setting the Total Column

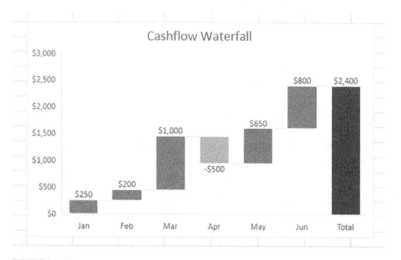

FIGURE 12.42 Completed Waterfall Chart

There are then a few optional changes you can make:

- Change the colours of the columns if desired; three different colours are recommended—one for the positive values, one for the negative values, and one for the total.
- If you remove the gridlines by selecting them with the mouse and pressing delete, the connected lines between the columns will show more clearly.
- If you wish to remove the connector lines, right-click on the lines and select Format Data Series. In the Series Options which appear on the right-hand side, untick the "Show connector lines" box.

SUMMARY

Presenting the completed model is a part of the model-building process that is typically not done well by most financial modellers. The majority of the focus has been on the building, structure, design, and layout, and on getting accurate calculations and results.

When senior managers or clients commission a financial model to be built, they are less interested in the structure or calculations of the model than they are in the output and the results of scenario analysis and sensitivity testing. Quite often the modeller does not consider how to best present and communicate these results to senior managers or clients.

It's important that at the end of the model-building process, the modeller spends some time thinking about what the viewer of the model needs to see, whether it is a report, a chart, or a table, and how best to communicate both verbally and visually the methodology, assumptions, and results of the model in the clearest and most informative way.

About the Author

Danielle Stein Fairhurst is the principal of Plum Solutions, a Sydney-based financial modelling consultancy. With her talent for analytical modelling and professional approach, Danielle helps her clients create meaningful financial models for business analysis. She has worked in a number of industry sectors, including telecom, information systems, manufacturing, and financial services, with solutions such as business cases, pricing models, and management reports. She is regularly engaged as a speaker, facilitator, and consultant around Australia and globally. She holds an MBA from Macquarie Graduate School of Management and has taught management accounting at Sydney University. She is a judge for the Financial Modelling Innovation Awards and is a Certified Financial Modeller and approved training provider with the Financial Modelling Institute (FMI). Danielle lives in Sydney with her husband and two children. She travels widely and enjoys the challenge of balancing a healthy family lifestyle with her passion for financial modelling.

About the Website

Welcome to the website to accompany *Using Excel for Business Analysis: A Guide to Financial Modelling Fundamentals, Third Edition* by Danielle Stein Fairhurst, located at www.wiley.com/go/steinfairhurst.

The content of the website consists of several documents that supplement the information in the book, including additional instructions, materials, downloads, and models. Each chapter (except Chapter 1) has its own Excel file(s), which contain a soft copy of the many screenshots shown throughout the book and their applicable page numbers. Using these files, you'll be able to recreate many of the modelling situations, tools, and functions described in the book. Several Excel model exercises and sample models have also been included. These accompanying files have been made freely available by the author, but they might not make sense without the book.

For updated model templates and additional supplementary downloads, please check the author's website, www.plumsolutions.com.au/book. Please also visit www.plumsolutions.com.au/elearning if you would like to register for the author's online courses that correspond to the book.

The supplementary content available on the website includes:

DOWNLOADABLE RESOURCES

These downloadable PDFs contain additional explanations and content we didn't have room for in the book:

- How to create a break-even chart (Chapter 9).
- Excel versions (Chapter 5) contains an overview of the history and key differences among the versions of Excel in use and how they impact model building.
- Online resources (Chapter 1) includes a list of websites, blogs, and tutorials for Excel and financial modelling.
- Shortcuts (Chapter 5) is a printable three-page cheat sheet of the most useful shortcuts for financial modelling in Excel.
- QA log template (Chapter 10, Appendix 10.1) is a sample template that can be used during the model QA process.
- Creating a waterfall chart in previous versions of Excel

Models

These fully functioning models have been referred to in the book:

- Model assessment checklist (Chapter 3).
- Lender repayment calculator (Chapter 7).
- Scenario comparison (including both *exercise* and *completed* versions) (Chapter 11).

Technical Exercise Files

These files contain the examples from the screenshots exactly as they appear in the book. You can use them to work through the examples and follow the instructions in the book to master each tool and technique.

Chapter 3

- Assumptions documentation methods

Chapter 4

- Internal and external links
- Circular references

Chapter 5

- Cell referencing
- Named ranges
- Nesting logical functions; IF and AND

Chapter 6

- Aggregation functions
- LOOKUP functions
- Nesting INDEX and MATCH
- OFFSET Function
- Regression analysis
- Date functions
- Investment return functions; NPV, IRR
- Loan calculations; PMT, IPMT & PPMT

Chapter 7

- Conditional formatting
- Sparklines
- Protection
- Form controls

Chapter 8

- Array formulas
- Dynamic arrays
- Goal seeking
- Structured Reference Tables
- PivotTables
- Macros

Chapter 9

- Growth and Escalation formulas
- Nominal and effective rates
- Calculating a cumulative sum (running totals)
- Payback periods
- Weighted average cost of capital (WACC)
- Tiering (volume break) tables
- Depreciation
- Break-Even analysis

Chapter 11

- Scenarios using drop-down boxes
- Sensitivities with data tables

Chapter 12

- Combo charts
- Map charts
- Bubble charts
- Using Dynamic named ranges in charts
- Dynamic charts
- Waterfall charts

Index

Printed and bound by CPI Group (UK) Ltd, Croydon, CR0 4YY

23/04/2025

14660947-0002